UMBRIA:
THE GREEN HEART OF ITALY

UMBRIA: THE GREEN HEART OF ITALY

Tim Jepson

First published 1989

British Library Cataloguing in Publication Data

Jepson, Tim
Umbria: the green heart of Italy.
1. Italy. Umbria — Visitors' guides
I. Title
914.5'6504928

ISBN 1-85336-069-4

Equation is part of the Thorsons Publishing Group Limited, Wellingborough, Northamptonshire, NN8 2RQ, England

Typeset by Harper Phototypesetters Limited, Northampton, England
Printed in Great Britain by Butler & Tanner, Frome, Somerset

10 9 8 7 6 5 4 3 2 1

CONTENTS

PREFACE

While every effort has been made to ensure the accuracy of information, much will quickly and inevitably go out of date. I would very much welcome any comments, corrections or criticisms readers might want to make. Please write to me c/o of the publishers. All contributions will be acknowledged in subsequent editions.

Many thanks for help and encouragement to Nicola, Rossella and Marella Caracciolo, Cally Flood, Emma Parkinson, Victoria Bean, Neil Bibby, Robert and Kim Barclay, James Hypher, Graham Truscott, Patrick Clare, Jane Lambert, Dave and Christine Stansfield, Fiona Norden, Mark Ellingham at the 'Rough Guides' and all at the Italian State Tourist Office.

Special thanks to James Darell and David Leffman.

Photographs by James Darell (JD). Additional pictures by David Leffman (DL) and by kind permission of the Italian State Tourist Office (ISTO).

Cover and title page photographs by James Darell.

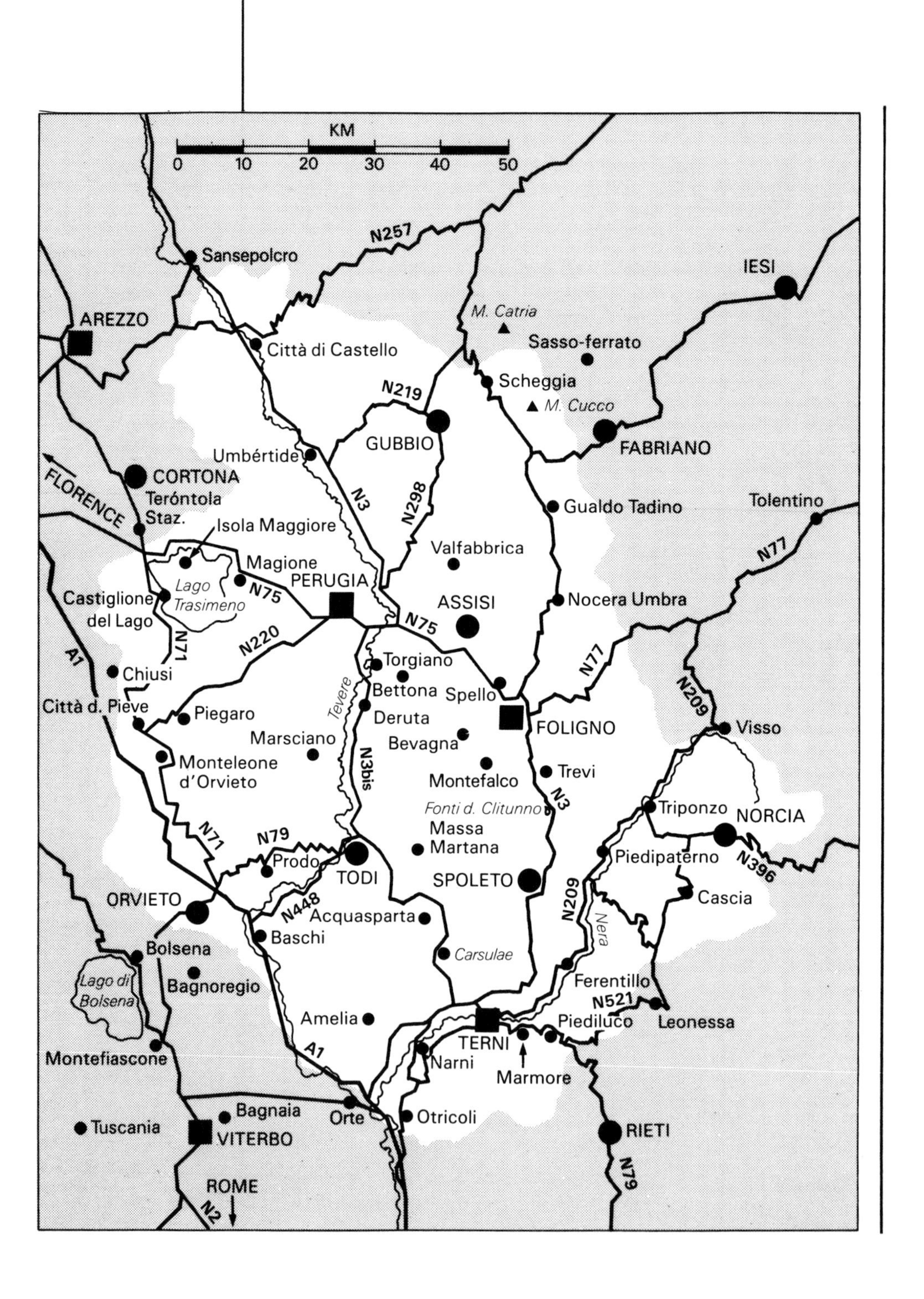
KM
0
10
20
30
40
50
Sansepolcro
N257
IESI
AREZZO
M. Catria
Sasso-ferrato
Città di Castello
Scheggia
N219
M. Cucco
GUBBIO
FABRIANO
Umbértide
CORTONA
FLORENCE
Teróntola Staz.
N3
N298
Gualdo Tadino
Tolentino
Isola Maggiore
Valfabbrica
N77
Magione
Lago Trasimeno
PERUGIA
Castiglione del Lago
N75
ASSISI
Nocera Umbra
N71
N220
N75
A1
Torgiano
N77
N209
Chiusi
Bettona
Spello
Città d. Pieve
Piegaro
Tevere
Deruta
FOLIGNO
Visso
Marsciano
Bevagna
Monteleone d'Orvieto
N3bis
Montefalco
Trevi
Fonti d. Clitunno
N3
Triponzo
NORCIA
N71
N79
Massa Martana
Prodo
TODI
Piedipaterno
N396
SPOLETO
ORVIETO
N448
Cascia
Acquasparta
N209
Nera
Baschi
Bolsena
Carsulae
Bagnoregio
Lago di Bolsena
Ferentillo
N521
Leonessa
Amelia
Piediluco
TERNI
A1
Montefiascone
Narni
Marmore
Bagnaia
Orte
Otricoli
Tuscania
VITERBO
RIETI
N79
ROME
N2

GENERAL INFORMATION

*U*mbria clearly cannot be taken in isolation from the rest of Italy. Yet it is not within the scope of this book to provide a background briefing for the whole country. In some instances, therefore, the information given is specific and regional; in others it tries to anticipate the more general hiccups you might encounter *en route*. Hopefully the balance between the two is about right.

It is also an obvious failing of guide-books to be outdated even before they are in print — opening hours alter, galleries close, paintings are removed for restoration, and so forth. This problem is particularly acute in Italy, where all things bureaucratic are infamously flexible and liable to change. So, while every effort has been made to provide up-to-date information (and, as far as Umbria goes, comprehensive information) there will inevitably be occasions when all is not as it should be. Wherever possible try to double-check details with tourist offices.

Climate and when to go

*T*his, of course, is largely a matter of common sense. Suffice it to say that the tourist season runs from April to the end of October, and grows longer every year. Some places are much busier than others. Assisi, for example, suffers the burden of year-round pilgrimages, and is doubly hectic over the Easter period. Similarly Spoleto's summer festival means that the town is impossibly full unless you have booked or planned well in advance. (Though obviously there would be no problem with a one-day flying visit.) Certain well-known spots, such as Orvieto and Perugia, are likely to be crowded whenever you visit. Out-of-the-way villages, however, of which there are hundreds, will always be gloriously empty.

Bear in mind that the Italians, like the French, take their holidays *en masse* in August, with dire consequences for all concerned. They depart punctually, lemming-like, on the first Saturday of the month, and return in one vast, tanned traffic jam on the last. Most, however, choose to make for the sea, so Umbria escapes the worst of the rush. None the less, it is a busy period, with the added drawback that shop- and restaurant-owners take their holidays at the same time as everyone else.

As to the temperature, the kindest times are spring (March–April) and early autumn (September–October). Umbria is as stifling as the rest of Italy in midsummer; if anything, it is slightly hotter than elsewhere because of its distance from sea-breezes. However, the height of many hill-towns means that temperatures in these are lower than in the surrounding countryside. And if the heat becomes too much, you can always plunge into one of the region's lakes. Summer sun can give way to powerful electrical storms, so be prepared for the occasional cloudburst.

As far as clothing goes, you should expect weather that is basically *hot* from the beginning of May through to mid-October. The likelihood of rain

JD

(apart from thunderstorms) diminishes to almost zero the closer to July and August you travel. Pack accordingly, with a thought for something vaguely warm if you are planning to spend time in the mountains. Dress with some decorum in churches — as little bare flesh as possible being the general rule — certainly no shorts or skimpy tops.

Getting to Umbria

By air

There are rumours of plans to upgrade Perugia's airport to receive international flights. At present, however, they seem to be no more than a twinkle in a developer's eye. Currently daily flights operate only between Perugia and Milan, leaving Rome's Fiumicino or Ciampino airports as the best options if you want to reach Umbria in a hurry. Pisa, which largely serves Florence, is a slightly more distant alternative. If time is short, a **Fly–Drive** deal is the most convenient way of seeing the region. Enquire at travel agents for details of these, and of the numerous flights and packages available to Italy.

By train

Unless you are under 26, trains can be the most expensive way of reaching Umbria. If you are prepared to phone around the bucket shops, flying will always be cheaper.

There are two basic rail routes from London Victoria, each with a journey time of about 24 hours. (i) Paris–Turin–Genoa–Rome. You are required to change trains and station in Paris (Gare du Nord–Gare de Lyon) except during the summer, when through-trains operate uninterrupted. (ii) Lille–Basel–Como–Milan–Florence–Rome. This is the route you should take if you are making

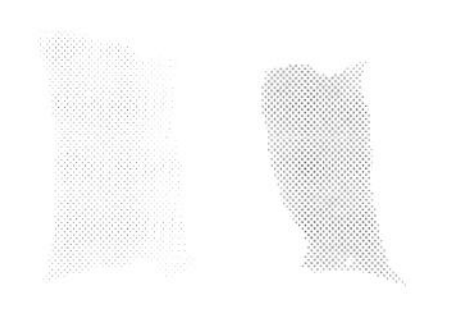

straight for Umbria. It touches the edge of the region, usually stopping at Arezzo, Terόntola, and Chiusi. Check the small print on the timetable at Victoria or with your travel agents. Change to a *locale* (a stopping-train) at Arezzo if you are in any doubt about whether or not your train stops. Couchettes are available on both routes, and should be booked well in advance, especially in the summer. Cheap Transalpino tickets are available for those under 26, and there are reductions for those holding a Family Rail-Card. All tickets are valid for two months from the date of issue, with stopovers permitted *en route*.

By car

A car is obviously the most flexible travel option, and essential if you are to get to grips with the rural hideaways that constitute much of Umbria's charm. However, it is a long 1000-mile (1600-kilometre) haul from Calais to Perugia. The only way of cutting down on time behind the wheel is to take advantage of the French Railway's twice-weekly motorail service from Boulogne to Milan (15 hours, summer only). Trains run overnight and there are connections at Milan with Italian motorail services.

Drivers should take advantage of the reductions on petrol and motorway tolls that Italy offers to foreign tourists. The saving on petrol — currently the most expensive in Europe — is an appreciable 15–20 per cent. Toll vouchers are more of a goodwill gesture. They are worth about 5 per cent off your motorway bill. Both are available at the Italian border, or from British motoring organizations as part of overall travel packages.

As a motorist you will need a red warning triangle, full insurance and registration papers, and an Italian translation of your driving licence (issued by the AA, RAC, or Italian Automobile Club). Speed limits are 100 kph on normal roads, and 130 kph on motorways. After an accident or breakdown the emergency number is 116.

Alitalia, 27 Piccadilly, London W1 (ticket office). Tel. 01-745 8256.
British Airways, 421 Oxford Street, London W1. Tel. 01-897 4000.
London Student Travel, 52 Grosvenor Gardens, London SW1. Tel. 01-730 8111.
Pilgrim Air (charters), 44 Goodge Street, London W1P 1FH. Tel. 01-637 5333.

Eurotrain, 52 Grosvenor Gardens, London SW1. Tel. 01-730 3402.
French Railways (SNCF), 179 Piccadilly, London W1V OBA. Tel. 01-409 3518.
Italian State Railways/CIT, 50–51 Conduit Street, London W1. Tel. 01-434 3844.
London Victoria Station. Tel. 01-834 2345.
Transalpino, 71–75, Buckingham Palace Road, London SW1. Tel. 01-834 9650.

AA, Fanum House, The Broadway, Stanmore, Middlesex. Tel. 01-954 7373.
Italian Automobile Club, Via Marsala 8, Rome.
P & O Ferries. Tel. 01-734 4431.
RAC, 49 Pall Mall, London SW1. Tel. 01-839 7050.
Sealink Ferries. Tel. 01-828 4142.

Getting around Umbria

By train

Rome–Florence

All Umbria's major towns, except for Gubbio and Norcia, are well served by trains. The main Rome–Florence line in the west is perfect for Orvieto. However, it is increasingly the policy of the revamped state network, Ferrovie dello Stato (FS), to run high-speed trains on the route, with just one stop at Arezzo. The chances are your train will be a slower *diretta*, with halts at Orte (connections with the Rome–Ancona line), Orvieto, Chiusi, Castiglione del Lago, and Terόntola (with connections for Perugia, Assisi, and Foligno). Two painfully slow, but very useful, *locali* (stopping-trains) ply the same north-south route, the first from Arezzo to Chiusi (connections for Siena) and the second from Chiusi to Orte. Both, in theory, are timetabled to provide services complementary to the faster *diretta* trains.

Rome–Ancona

This is the most useful way into Umbria if your approach is from Rome and the south. You can take a train either directly from Rome, or pick one up from Orte, where the lines for Florence and Ancona diverge. The major stations *en route* are Narni and Terni (where there are connections for the Abruzzi and the FCU — see below), Spoleto, Trevi, Foligno (connections to Perugia and Assisi), Nocera Umbra, Gualdo Tadino, and thence to Ancona and Marche.

JD

Foligno–Terόntola

A second division branch-line with frequent trains between Foligno, Spello, Assisi, and Perugia. There are direct trains from Perugia to Rome and Florence once or twice a day, and numerous connections for both cities from Terόntola. However, if you are faced with a return journey to Rome from Perugia, the Ancona line via Foligno is about an hour quicker (connections allowing).

Ferrovia Centrale Umbra (FCU)

This is one of a handful of privately owned lines in Italy, a quaint 145-kilometre odyssey from Terni through to San Sepolcro inside the Tuscan border. On its meandering and often scenic course up the Tiber valley, it fills in some crucial gaps left by the state network. Todi, Deruta, Perugia, and Città di Castello, not to mention dozens of tiny halts, are brought within reach of the rail traveller. With lashings of ramshackle charm, it can be an outing in its own right. Facilities are spartan, but services frequent, with buses occasionally replacing the distinctive two-carriage trains.

Note: For obvious reasons, most Umbrian hill-towns are some distance from their stations. Generally buses operate a regular shuttle-service between the station and central piazza of the town in question. Tickets are often on sale in the station bar, and must be purchased before boarding the bus. To save hunting around for a bar later on, buy an extra ticket for the return trip.

By car

The last 10 years have seen a dramatic improvement in Umbria's infrastructure, almost the first since the Romans drove the Via Flaminia through the region in 217 BC. The main route is Italy's premier motorway, the *Autostrada del Sole*, which touches Orvieto in the west. Three important spurs from the motorway (the A1) have prised open the rest of the region. The first is the fast dual-carriageway, the N3 bis, from Orte to San Sepolcro by way of Narni, Todi, Perugia, and Città di Castello. The second is the spectacular road from Orvieto to Todi (the N448) along the shore of Lake Corbora. The third is the motorway link from the A1 to Perugia (the perfect approach if you are coming from Siena or the north). There is then a curving spur from the N3 bis, which follows the course of the old Via Flaminia. This is largely a dual-carriageway, and connects Terni, Spoleto, Foligno, and Assisi, before rejoining the N3 bis at Perugia.

In the more rugged eastern part of the region it is a different story. The ever-expanding road network has yet to penetrate the interior, and gives up somewhere around Spoleto. As a car-owner you will be left to your own devices and a maze of time-consuming but highly scenic roads. Hairpin bends notwithstanding, most are in good condition, even those marked as 'white' unmetalled roads on the map. Unlike in Britain, where they would be tracks or bridleways, in Italy they are well-worn and well-kept lifelines between upland villages.

Opening hours

Shops

Shop hours are normally 9–13 and 16–20, Monday–Saturday, with variations according to season and the mood of the shopkeeper. Almost everything is shut on Sundays, and a great many shops also close on Mondays. Thursday is the most common early-closing day, particularly for food shops. Many establishments, in good Italian fashion, put family holidays before commercial gain, and shut for the whole of August. The following national holidays also bring the shutters down: 1 January, 6 January (Epiphany), Easter Sunday and Monday, 25 April (Liberation Day), May Day, 2 June (Republic Day), 15 August (Assumption), 1 November, 8 December (Immaculate Conception), 25 and 26 December.

Museums

These are tricky, and times given in the text should always be treated as provisional. Many galleries open only in the morning, and most close at least once a week, usually on Mondays. Times become more flexible off-season, especially in the smaller provincial museums. As a general rule, knock off about half an hour from opening and closing times outside the summer months. Many Umbrian museums and historic sites are too small to warrant a full-time custodian. This can mean knocking on some nearby door to summon the caretaker, or, more dauntingly, a trip to the local council offices or the village policeman (who is known as the *vigile urbana*). When in doubt ask at the nearest tourist office, or failing that, in a local bar (always the most sensible thing to do in any emergency).

Churches

The House of God, contrary to its claims, is not always open, and churches keep some eccentric hours. Some close at noon for a couple of hours and then reopen until sunset. Others, sadly, appear to be inexplicably shut for the duration. A trip to the tourist office or a knock on a likely-looking door may occasionally produce a key. On Sundays there is naturally no problem, but discretion and common sense are wanted if a service is taking place.

Banks

Banks are open from 8.30 to 13.30, Monday–Friday, and sometimes from 15 to 16.30. Exchange (*cambio*) facilities tend to follow shop hours.

Post offices

Post offices are open from 8 to 13.30, Monday–Saturday. Stamps may often be purchased from bars displaying a blue 'T' sign.

Tourist offices

Tourist offices usually follow shop hours, but in larger centres during the summer they occasionally stay open all day.

Garages

Garages close for lunch, and tend to shut up shop completely at 19.00. Motorway service stations are open 24 hours.

Money

You may bring 500,000 lire in cash into Italy, plus unlimited amounts of sterling and any number of travellers' cheques. Occasionally you will have

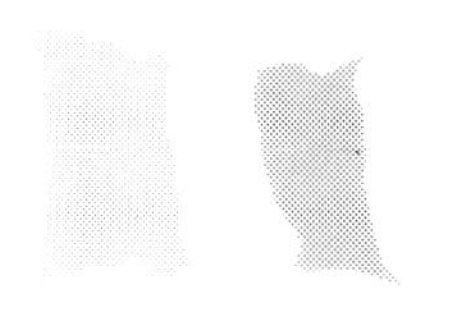

to make a declaration of quantity at your point of entry — the idea being that you cannot take out more money than you brought in.

With tourists now a common sight in Umbria, changing money is becoming less of a problem, as exchange facilities open to meet increasing demand. Italian banking, however, has some way to go before it shakes off its Renaissance counting-house image, so queues and paper-pushing are still the norm.

You should take your passport with you when changing money, check the amount you receive, and count the number of noughts on the receipt. With all the zeros of Italy's notorious toytown money it is sometimes easy to lose track of relative amounts when changing large sums. Keep records of your transactions in the unlikely event that you are quizzed about currency on leaving the country. In an emergency you might be able to persuade hotels and even shops to change money or accept payment by travellers' cheque. However, as a general rule Italy is still a country where **cash reigns supreme**.

This is particularly pertinent when it comes to credit cards. Many of Umbria's rustic hotels and restaurants, financially speaking, are still in the Dark Ages, and very few indeed will want to accept plastic money. All too often fistfuls of cash are the only answer. Larger and more up-market establishments are more obliging, but even where a restaurant indicates outside that it is going to accept your card, that doesn't always mean that it will do so in practice. Always check a proprietor's attitude to credit cards before embarking on a meal.

Make doubly sure that it is impossible for amounts to be tampered with, and give consideration to potential fluctuations in the exchange rate between your signing for something and its appearing on your statement.

Bargaining, except in the odd market or antique shop, is no longer appropriate in Italy.

Prices

Inflation is down from its rampant seventies level, but Italy is far from the bargain holiday destination it once was. Gone, too, are the days when Umbria was unknown and undervalued. Prices in the region may not be as low as you might have hoped, but they are not yet as shocking as they are in Rome and Venice. This said, there are still bargains to be had, especially in more rural outposts, and small luxuries such as wine and coffee are as good value as they have always been. Prices in hotels and bars must be, and usually are, displayed by law.

Tourist information

Any enquiries receiving a blank look from your travel agent should be referred to the Italian State Tourist Office in London. It is an efficient and helpful body, able to deal with most problems, and eager to supply you with armfuls of semi-useful bumf.

The local tourist office (whose full title is the Azienda Autonomia di Soggiorno e Turismo — AAST) should be your first port of call in any town.

Umbria has woken up to its new popularity, and to the fact that this popularity represents an opportunity to improve its economic well-being. Visitors are well treated as a result, and most tourist offices are modern, friendly, and well run. Their room-finding services, in particular, are invaluable, and should you have any complaint they will do their best to provide redress.

Compagnia Italiana Turismo (CIT) is a state-sponsored agency largely designed to co-ordinate group travel. They organize guided coach tours of Umbria. Centro Turistico Studentesco (CTS) is aimed largely, but not exclusively, at students.

CIT UK, Marco Polo House, 3–5 Landsdowne Road, Croydon CR9 1LL. Tel. 01-686 5533.
CIT (Umbria), Corso Vannucci 2, Perugia. Tel. 075 26061.
CTS, Via del Roschetto 21, Perugia. Tel. 075 61695.
Italian State Tourist Office, 1 Princes Street, London W1R 8AY. Tel. 01-408 1254.
Umbrian Regional Tourist Office, Via Pievaiola 11, Perugia. Tel. 075 756845.

Telephones

Telephone services are improving. At one time, most public telephones in bars and on the street only accepted tokens known as *gettone*. Now call-boxes are being built or adapted to take coins (100, 200, and 500 lire), and, in some rare cases, magnetic telephone cards. (Buy them in bars with a blue 'T' sign.) In rural Umbria most telephones are of the old type. The current cost of a *gettone* is 200 lire; they are sold in bars and occasionally given as change. While one or two suffice for local calls, anything up to 10 and over are needed for trunk calls (known as *Inter-urbana*). Sometimes you may be lucky enough to come across a bar with a metered booth (*un telefono a scatti*) — your best bet if you are making an international call. You speak first and pay later, according to the time you have clocked up. Sometimes the barkeeper adds a small fee to the basic flat charge; it is unusual to encounter dishonesty.

More and more towns now have sleek SIP offices (SIP is the state telephone company), each equipped with banks of telephones, change machines, and assistants on hand to help with dificulties. They are centrally sited, and the obvious places to make for if you have a lot of telephoning to do.

Post

The Italian postal service is fairly dire: you will almost certainly reach home before your postcards. Allow about a week for mail to arrive from Britain, and up to three weeks for anything posted in Italy. To encourage speedier delivery you might pay extra for an *espresso*, and more still for a registered

letter, known as a *raccommandata*. Neither necessarily guarantees that the item posted will arrive any quicker.

Mail can be left *poste restante* by marking it *fermo posta*. In large towns your should specify a precise post office. You must collect the mail in person and take along some form of identification. Air mail (it may still go overland) should be marked *via aerea*.

Passports

A valid UK passport, British visitor's passport, or EEC passport is required for entry into Italy. UK, Eire, EEC, US, and Canadian passport-holders do not need visas for stays under three months. However, all visitors are supposed to register with the Italian authorities within three days of arrival in the country. In practice nobody does, and if you try you will probably be told quietly to go away.

Casual visitors should have absolutely no problems with any of the various Italian police forces. If something does go wrong, some immediate form of identification will save a lot of trouble. If possible, any dealings with the police should be with the semi-military *carabinieri* in preference to the *polizia*. (And stay calm when Italian passions are roused.)

JD

Maps

The best single map is the Touring Club of Italy's 1:200,000 sheet of Umbria and the Marche (Reference No. D40). An invaluable purchase, it is widely available in Italy, and is also sold in Britain from larger booksellers and specialist map-shops.

Time

Italian Summer Time is two hours ahead of GMT and runs from the end of March to the last weekend in September.

Electric current

Electricity is 220 volts AC. British electrical appliances require a two-pin continental adaptor.

Water

Water is safe to drink everywhere, though it may be occasionally over-chlorinated. There are plenty of cheap bottled waters, including Umbrian brands such as San Gemini and Nocera Umbra.

JD

Accommodation

Hotels

Generally, hotels (as opposed to *pensione*) in the 'Where to Stay' sections fall into one of two categories. In the first there are the old traditional hotels — usually in a town's central piazza — that for decades have kept up a steady and solid reputation for old-world elegance. These sorts of place are known quantities, with obvious advantages: convenience, reliability, and the chance, more often than not, to stay in the oldest part of town and in some of its oldest buildings. Being old, however, does not necessarily mean that they are tatty; with visitors arriving in greater numbers, many have smartened themselves up (whilst at the same time making sure they retain their antiquated elegance).

Then there is the newer breed of hotel: the freshly converted castles and monasteries, most of them secreted away in superb countryside. Part of a popular and fast-growing trend, many are likely to be busy and booked up well in advance. Though obviously less convenient for sightseeing, they are extremely attractive from the point of view of ambience, and perfect if all you want is a spot of peace and quiet in rural surroundings.

Where hotels do not fall into one or other of these categories they are usually distinguished by some particular quality — charm, cuisine, setting, tennis-courts, swimming-pool — or simply by the fact that there is no other local accommodation available.

General hints

Always make straight for the tourist office if you arrive in a town without having booked accommodation, or if you dislike the look of this guide's recommendations. Most are equipped with a room-finding service and are usually happy to take care of any organizing that needs to be done. Booking ahead, of course, is always preferable, especially in any town such as Spoleto, where an event like the annual festival means that accommodation is often at full stretch. Where possible make bookings by letter — through the tourist office if necessary.

Try to avoid hotels around railway stations, not because they might be squalid, as big-city station hotels can be squalid, but because the station is usually the focus for a new town (Orvieto Scalo and Narni Scalo, for example) and hotels are correspondingly modern and characterless. Always make the winding journey to the old hill-town for a room with a view. As for paying, all the major hotels accept credit cards, though in the more backwoods areas it is probably as well to have cash at the ready.

A single room is *una camera singola*; a double room, touchingly, is still known as *una matrimoniale*. A double room with single beds is *una camera doppia*.

Grading

The grading of hotels is one of the pleasing areas in which Italian bureaucracy has done itself proud. Hotels are checked annually, and awarded between one and four stars (five in exceptional cases) according to their facilities and overall ambience. (This is the rating system followed in the 'Where to Stay' sections in this guide.) The grading of a hotel puts a ceiling on the prices that can be charged, through the rates for individual rooms can vary within the set limits. Inspectors judge each room on its merits, and fix a price, which can only be altered in exceptional circumstances. Thus, if another bed is brought into a double room at your request, the price can be raised by no more than 30 per cent. If only a single room is available and another bed is brought in for a couple, the overall charge cannot exceed that for a single room. The price of every room must be clearly displayed, either in the room itself or in the hotel lobby; if it is not, you should ask to see it. There is nothing to stop a wily proprietor showing you the most expensive room first, so demand to be shown everything available if you are not happy with the initial choice. In many areas, inspectors recognize a high and a low season, so the time of your visit may have a bearing on price. The high season is uniform, and runs from 1 July to 1 September.

On the whole, the system works well. Depending on the grading, you know more or less what you will be paying, and have some idea of a hotel's facilities, or lack of them. It is also unlikely that you will be cheated. If you do have any complaints, take the problem to the nearest tourist office.

Some extras and things to look out for

Occasionally a hotelier may say that he or she has rooms for one night only, or for a maximum of three. This is usually to cover themselves against your being an English football supporter. Rooms often become available when they are persuaded that you are not in some way undesirable. (This is assuming that you are prepared to wait around long enough to be vetted.) Possible legitimate extras include an 18 per cent 'visitors' tax' (a sort of VAT, which may or may not be included in the price of a room), supplements for showers (especially in cheaper hotels), a daily tariff for air-conditioning, and a charge for breakfast (which you might be better off taking in a bar).

Pensione and private rooms

Umbria is particularly well served by the *pensione* type of accommodation. In what is still a comparatively poor region, paying guests are a useful source of extra income. Consequently tourist offices are geared to placing visitors in *pensione* and private rooms almost as a matter of policy. Even the smallest village should have something in this line. Therefore don't waste time tramping the streets — make use of the tourist offices (which in large towns also deal

with the surrounding district).

Pensione, like hotels, are subject to regular inspection (some come within the lowest hotel categories). Prices are similarly fixed and should be displayed in rooms.

JD

Flats and villas

Renting a flat or villa may be the cheapest and most practical way of spending time in one area. The accessibility of towns in Umbria, and their proximity to one another, make a single, central base an attractive and workable proposition. The best places to find villas are the specialist agencies increasingly taking Umbrian properties on to their books. (Check the pages of the Sunday newspapers.) Tourist offices have a surprisingly large number of furnished flats for rent, usually for a minimum period of a week. The office in Castiglione del Lago, for example, a small town on the shores of Lake Trasimeno, offers no fewer than 62 such flats. They are usually snapped up quickly by the Italians, however, so you have to move fast. Write to the appropriate tourist office for details. They will handle the on-the-spot organization.

Agriturismo

Agriturismo is the latest, and fastest-growing manifestation of Umbria's tourist boom. It means, simply, any sort of accommodation with a rural bent, and can include anything from small farms and cabins in the woods, right up to specially converted medieval hamlets. From just 19 such enterprises in 1976, there are now over 100, with a total of 1500 beds, a figure that ranks Umbria fourth by region in the field. Most, but not all, are simple, cheap, and for single overnight stays only. Others offer longer stops and the opportunity to pursue some leisure activity (usually horse-riding). Working farms are obviously an attractive proposition if you have children, and the beauty of all of them is the chance to escape to rural peace and quiet after the day's orgy of city sightseeing.

For further details inquire at tourist offices, or write to:

Agriscambi, Foro Traiano 1a, 00187 Rome. Tel. 06 679 5917.
Agriturist, Piazza Sant'Andrea della Valle, Rome.

Camping and caravanning

Italians are increasingly taking to camping, though their version has little to do with Baden-Powell or singing round the campfire. In Umbria the masses tend to head for the lakes — Piediluco, Corbora, and Trasimeno — partly for the swimming and watersports, but mainly because campsites elsewhere are fairly thin on the ground. (Thus, while there are 14 places to pitch a tent round Trasimeno, there is only one in Assisi, and two each in Perugia and Spoleto.) Like hotels, all official sites are independently assessed and graded (1–3) according to their facilities. All have accommodation for campers and caravans, and some offer caravans or holiday bungalows should you get tired of life under canvas. Bear in mind that shade will be the commodity you come to treasure most, and that, though sites are sociable places, Italian youth is not accustomed to going to bed early; at least, not without numerous and noisy 'Goodnights'.

Much Umbrian countryside — particularly in the Valnerina and the north-east — is perfect for backpacking, and many of the smaller roads ideal for tucking away a camper or caravan. With courtesy and common sense freelance camping away from official sites shouldn't cause you any problems. Fires, given the amount of woodland about, are probably the main thing to watch out for. It is worth remembering that most land in Italy is owned by someone, somewhere. Owing to the odd way in which it is parcelled up, however, it may not be obvious who they are or where they live. Try to find owners where possible, and don't assume that you have stumbled across 'common land', which in Italy is a rare commodity.

The addresses of all the region's major campsites are given in the appropriate 'Where to Stay' sections. For more details try:

Camping and Caravan Club Ltd, 11 Lower Grosvenor Place, London SW1.

Youth hostels

Italy has some 150 youth hostels. You don't have to be a member of the YHA to use many of them. Umbria has just six (in Assisi, Foligno, Sigillo (Gubbio), Todi, Trevi, and San Venanzo (Orvieto)). Full addresses are given in the appropriate chapters.

Youth Hostels Association, 14 Southampton Street, London WC2. Tel. 01-836 8541.
Associazione Italiana Alberghi per la Gioventù, Piazza Civiltà dello Lavoro, Quadrato della Concordia, 00144 Rome. Tel. 06 5931702/758.

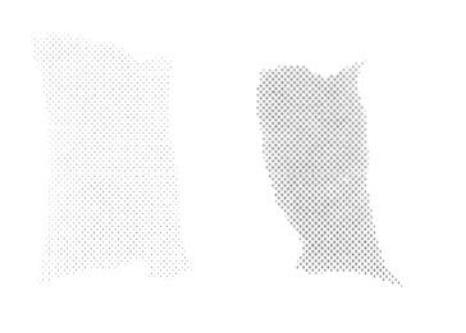

Eating and drinking

Food

Over the centuries it has been the region's position, so close to the south, to the great watershed of the *Mezzogiorno* (the land of the midday sun), that has defined its cooking, allowing it to combine the best of two great culinary traditions: the sophistication of the north, with its French and Austro-Hungarian influences (creams, rich sauces, pastries), and the more rustic simplicity of the south (garlic, olive oil, tomatoes), where poverty has long been the great mother of invention.

Market day in Castiglione del Lago. (JD)

No one, of course, would claim that this happy compromise has made Umbria the country's gastronomic heart; Emilia-Romagna takes that particular mantle. However, it does have the advantage of being wonderfully fertile (remember that it is 'the green heart of Italy'), and boasts an abundance of the very best fruit and vegetables. And as you will see below, it also has a few precious commodities all of its own.

Because the region's rural economy is, for want of a better word, still partly peasant-based, much of what you see growing, however, is going to wind up on some lucky smallholder's table. Some home produce, though, will find its way to market, and wherever possible this is where you should do your shopping. Most fruit and vegetables are organically grown, not because it has suddenly become fashionable to abhor chemicals, but because farming methods in Umbria have not changed in centuries, and this is the way that things have always been done. It is in the market-place, too, that you are most likely to find regional varieties of such things as cheeses and cooked meats (though surprisingly the same variety can be available in supermarkets, where local products often figure prominently).

Umbria's highly regarded olive oil can often be bought from small farms that wouldn't normally trade commercially — the addresses of some of these are given in the text. (Look out particularly for oils that have been flavoured with garlic, basil, and sage.) In fact, you should be able to pick up all sorts of rural produce on your travels — anything from jam, honey, and wine to pork, chicken, and rabbit. You may have trouble tracking down a freshly dug truffle (see below) but you will always be able to find a canned, bottled, or even puréed version. As a general guide, Italian supermarkets sell most things in larger quantities than we are accustomed to. For real bulk-buying you could try local oil presses and co-operative *cantinas*, or the offices of the PCI, the Italian Communist Party, which, as well as offering advice, often sell foodstuffs and agricultural supplies at cost-price.

Truffles

Much has been written about Umbria's most famous speciality, that humble-looking but costly item, the black truffle. To read some books you would think that the Umbrians lived on nothing else, that their cooking was awash with its powerful and piquant presence. Not so; whilst a feature of the region's cuisine, especially in the east, they are not as widespead as you are led to expect.

Umbria's own and rather special version is found in comparative abundance around Norcia and Cascia, where it has been a noted delicacy since Roman times. (The Romans believed that truffles were created at the point at which lightning struck the earth.) Strictly speaking, its colour is grey-brown rather than black, and it is far smaller and less perfumed than the white truffle, which is more common elsewhere in the region. Many are exported and often find their way to Périgord in south-west France, where they are sometimes sold as French truffles in times of local shortage. In Umbria they are used sparingly for their strong flavour in such things as omelettes, or more particularly in specialities such as *crostini al tartufo* — small croûtons with a *tartufo* (truffle) paste. In the heart of truffle country around Norcia and

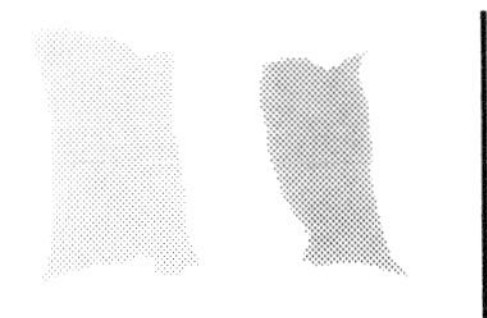

Terni (and, to a lesser extent, Spoleto) they are frequently used to flavour sauces for *tagliatelle, spaghetti*, or *tortellini*. The season, incidentally, runs from Christmas to March, with the best specimens reaching perfumed perfection towards the beginning of Lent (carnival time in Italy). Outside this period you will be eating truffles of dubious origin.

Porchetta

More characteristic of the region as a whole, and of central Italy in general, is *porchetta*, a mouthwatering variation on roast pork. Though ubiquitous around Rome, it was the Umbrians who first came up with the idea. The concept is simplicity itself: succulent slices of meat from a suckling pig that has been stuffed with herbs and spices, and roasted whole either over charcoal or in a large oven. Eaten in crusty white rolls known as *rosette* it is about as close as Italy gets to fast food. (Though the ubiquitous hamburger, of course, is already well-established in Umbria.) Typically *porchetta* is bought from vans placed strategically on busy roads, from local markets, or at any number of summer festivals. The piquancy of the stuffing varies from van to van, and from one jealously guarded recipe to the next. No two rolls will taste alike. Local refinements include *porchetta al finocchio*, where fennel is added to the meat and the whole heavily seasoned with black pepper.

Salami

Pork generally is one of Umbria's staple meats, whether as ham or in the spicy sausages (*salsicce*) and *salami* for which the region is famous. Perhaps the notoriety has something to do with the region's big black pigs, which you see everywhere, not force-fed with grain, but left to rummage free-range for acorns and wild mushrooms. Norcia in particular has a long and proud tradition in the *salami*-making arts, holding a festival in their honour during the autumn. Such is the association of the town with all things sausage that the Italians sometimes call a pork-butcher *un norcino*. The best ham (*prosciutto*) is supposed to come from the mountains (*prosciutto della montagna*). The very best will be cured *al naturale*. (Remember that the ham with which we are familiar (say, Norfolk ham) is known as *prosciutto cotto*. The red, 'Italian' ham is called *prosciutto crudo*.) Look out for the sausages marinated in olive oil to stop them drying out, and for the extraordinary *salame mazzafegato* (an amalgam of pine-nuts, pork liver, candied orange, sugar, and raisins).

Norcia, by the way, is not alone in taking its culinary specialities seriously. Bevagna celebrates the suckling pig with a fair in June, and Foligno honours, of all things, the red potato with a festival in October. Trevi is well known for its celery (*sedano*). (See the list at the end of the chapter for details of festivals with a gastronomic flavour.)

Meat and game

Slightly less eccentrically, game is widely available, often poached out of season. (Is there any Italian law that cannot be broken?) Apart from songbirds — which the Italians really do shoot and eat — the main Umbrian speciality is *palombaccia*, or wild pigeon. The ways to prepare it are legion, but most commonly the bird is roasted and then cooked further in a basic sauce of wine, oil, vinegar, and herbs. Particular variations include *piccione alla Perugina* (pigeon roasted with black olives); *palombe in salmi* (a rather piquant pigeon casserole), and *palombaccia all'umbra* (pigeon stewed in a sauce of sage, thyme, bay leaves, carrots, celery, and onions). In autumn you will find pheasant (*fagiano*), and from time to time guinea fowl (*faraona*).

Plain, roast meats, *al cacciatore* (in the way of the hunter) are the single greatest standby of most Umbrian restaurants. Often there is little to choose between them, though an open grill and the day's cuts on display are usually good signs. (Meat *alla griglia* indicates an open fire.) Dishes to look out for include *capretto a scottadito* and *agnello a scottadito* — spit-roasted goat and lamb respectively. (Lamb is very common.) *Fegatelli di maiale allo spiedo* are grilled pigs' livers, and *carne ai capperi e acciughe* is veal in a sauce of herbs and capers.

Pasta

Umbrici, as the name suggests, are typical of the region, a large heavy pasta, cooked in a sauce of garlic, tomatoes, and cheese. Various *spaghetti* dishes are popular — truffle sauces are a favoured accompaniment — but keep an eye open for *spaghetti con rancetto* (bacon and marjoram), and the thread-like *stringhozzi* found near Spoleto. If you are in Orvieto, try *zuppa di lenticchie*, a lentil soup peculiar to the town. (Lentils, for some extraordinary reason, are synonymous with wealth the length and breadth of Italy. Traditionally they are eaten on New Year's Eve, the received wisdom being that the more you are able to eat, the richer you will be in the coming year.) The tiny lentils of Castellucio, a village in the east of Umbria, are also well known.

Fish

Strangely for a land-locked region, Umbria boasts a wide variety of fresh fish, thanks mainly to the rivers Nera and Clitunno, and the freshwater lakes of Trasimeno, Bolsena, and Piediluco. Eels (*anguille*) and mountain trout (*trote*) are fished in the rivers Scordo and Corno near Norcia. (Local dishes include *trota della Nera* and *anguilla in umido*, eels in a tomato sauce.) Prawns and crayfish are found in the Nera, while Piediluco has tench (*tinche*), often made into a stew known as *tinca in umido*. Other common fish include carp (*carpe*), *cappitoni*, a type of eel, and pike (*luci*), traditionally eaten at Easter. Frozen fish can run the whole gamut. (The menu should specify that they are *congelato*.) Be ready for lobster (*aragosta*), salted cod (*baccalà*), squid (*calamari*), mussels (*cozze*), mackerel (*sogombra*), swordfish (*spada*), and tuna (*tonno*). *Fritto misto di mare* is a selection of fried fish, *pesce arrosto* is roast fish, and *pesce alla griglia*, grilled fish.

Dolci

Where desserts (*dolci*) are concerned, Umbria, like all of Italy, has a sweet tooth. It could even claim to have one of the sweetest of all, for as any Italian child will be able to tell you, Perugia is the home of Buitoni-Perugini, makers of some of the country's best chocolate. The most famous nibbles are the *bacci*, chocolate and hazelnut 'kisses', each wrapped in a pithy quotation on love. Chocolate notwithstanding, try to leave room for one of the many *dolci* that sit prominently oozing calories in most restaurants. It is difficult to pin down specialities, as individual towns make their own cakes for specific events, especially for Carnival (before Lent) and religious festivals. One delicacy

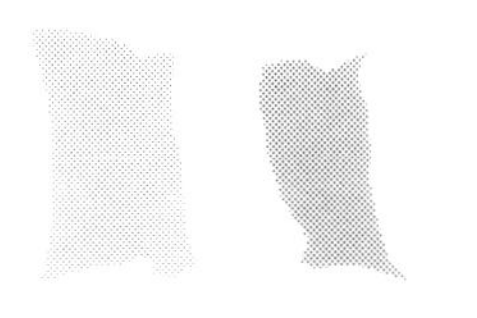

you should track down, however, are the famous white figs (*fichi bianchi*) from Amelia, eaten in a tooth-decaying mixture of almonds and chocolate.

Il brusengolo, a cake based on apples and raisins, is quite common, as is *il torciglione*, which is rather like a Bakewell tart. *Pinocchiate* are small sweets, wrapped in coloured paper, and traditionally eaten at Christmas. They come from Perugia and are made from just three ingredients: water, sugar, and pine-nuts. Also from Perugia are *serpentone* (big snakes), envelopes of pastry filled with dried fruit. The recipe was devised by the nuns of the city's Capuchin nunnery. *Ciarmicola* is a meringue-covered cake based on the spicy liqueur Alkermes (which uses cochineal as a flavouring), and is topped with sugared almonds. *Cicerchiata*, a honey-based Carnival cake, is less exotic, but amongst the best of the purely Umbrian *dolci*. It is a deep-fried concotion of dough, almonds, candied fruit, and pine-nuts. Todi comes up with an eccentric speciality, *pan nociato*, a bread livened up with *pecorino* cheese and raisins, and baked with wine, cloves, walnuts, and vine leaves.

Cheese

As far as cheeses go, Umbria is rather hard done by. Mountain villages will have their secret sheep and goats' milk cheese, but the only readily available speciality is *pecorino*, which is produced throughout central Italy. Made from sheep's milk, and found in a variety of forms, it is best eaten mature, when it is as strong and hard as Parmesan. When young, it is a different cheese, whitish and slightly crumbly, but in comparison with the mature version, bordering on the bland.

Finally, bear in mind that you will find good food and local specialities at all of the local festivals listed at the end of the chapter.

Wine

It is a shame that a region with so much to offer in the way of fine wines should be almost wholly associated with Orvieto, the delicate but half-hearted standby of a thousand supermarket shelves. Where bacchanalian pleasures are concerned, Umbria these days is taking off. No longer is it enough to dismiss her as Tuscany's shabbier sister. With a little searching you will find that there is more to choose from than the handful of passable whites and the pale Chianti imitations of a few years back. Distinctive, not to say exceptional, wines — most notably the Torgiano vintages — are now appearing, the sweet first fruits of a post-war renaissance in Umbrian viticulture.

Producers in the region are some of Italy's most forward-looking, even if at times their approach retains an old-world muddle at odds with the steel-tank and computer-controlled school of production. They have done all the obvious things and done them well; pioneered the new techniques, up-dated methods, and championed the new French grape varieties. The main ingredient of their success, however, has been the quality of Umbria's vineyards themselves. These have long been renowned for being immaculately, even neurotically, looked after, a tradition kept up year in, year out, by an army of men and

Cantina. (JD)

women hoeing or pruning back unproductive shoots through the months of spring and early summer.

Umbria boasts few of the vast estates that characterize the hills of Apulia, Chianti, or the Veneto. Instead, the emphasis is on the small producer, the recent and direct descendant of the centuries-old peasant smallholder. As in the past, little of the wine produced goes beyond the family dinner-table. Any that does, however, benefits from the skills and traditions that necessarily accompany small-scale production. Two-thirds of the region's 70,000 hectares of vineyard are given over to such 'private' or 'secondary' production. All this has an obvious knock-on effect in the commercial sector, as the 1986 figures illustrate. The million hectolitres of wine produced in Umbria ranked it only 16th amongst Italy's 20 regions, but of this 36 per cent was of high enough quality to merit DOC status, an impressive proportion, even given the doubts surrounding the DOC classification (see below). More significant was the rise from the 1983 figure of just 12 per cent, a three-fold increase in as many years. Clearly, as growers are nudged from the private sector (or the submerged black market sector) it appears that they are taking their personal standards of quality control with them.

The Italian background

The wines of Umbria's larger producers have also been improving steadily. This happy state of affairs mirrors the course of events in Italy generally (barring the shameful methanol scandal of 1985) where innovation and new ideas from France are revolutionizing both attitudes and techniques. Fashion, always of the greatest importance in Italy, has made it trendy to produce and consume top-quality wines (Italians anyway are drinking less than they did), and there is now a ready market of connoisseurs eager for the new and audacious vintages that Italian producers have filched from the Médoc or Napa Valley.

In Umbria (as elsewhere) this has meant the appearance of the Chardonnay grape responsible for Chablis, and the Cabernet Sauvignon of Bordeaux fame, first in Lungarotti's Torgiano vineyards, but increasingly as staples throughout the region.

The DOC shambles

Choosing an Italian wine, however, is not an easy business. Classification, like much else in which Latin bureaucracy plays a part, is chaotic, though in Umbria, where quality is fairly clear-cut, things could be a lot worse. Perhaps the first rule to observe when buying wine, whether at home or in Italy, is to hold the *Denominazione di Origine Controllata* (DOC) in at least partial contempt. This supposedly reassuring mark of quality was introduced in 1963 as the first attempt to regulate viticulture in what was then (until France nudged ahead) the world's single largest producer of wine. Modelled on the French *appellation contrôlée*, it attempted to impose legally binding controls on any producers who wanted its blessing. To date some 500 wines from 200 different zones have been awarded certificates. This may well sound a lot, but it still represents only 12 per cent of Italy's total production (which in 1981 was 8 billion litres, two billion of them destined for export).

The real problem with the DOC has been its failure to deliver what it set out to. Restrictions on grape varieties and production practices are all very well, but the all-important promises to guarantee quality have remained unfulfilled. Matters have simply got out of hand. In the Alban hills above Rome there are nine *denominazioni* for what is, effectively, the same wine — plain Frascati to you or me. Obscure, not to say unpronounceable, wines of dubious lineage — Caa'e Mmitte di Lucera is a fine example — have found themselves an undeserved place in the classification.

Against this background some more honourable producers have given up on the regulations altogether, exasperated by the scheme's consensus approach, and the backward-looking techniques that it forces them to adopt. To overcome what they see as barriers to excellence they disdain even to apply for a DOC grading, preferring to present their new wines under the humblest classification of all — plain Vino di Tavola. This confuses an already chaotic situation further, and means that excellent wine is lumped together with the purest plonk — to the frequent perplexity and frustration of the uninitiated.

The DOCG solution

Even the Italians acknowledge that things are a mess, and to try to salvage something from the ruins of DOC, have come up with 'son of DOC' — the *Denominazione di Origine Controllata Garantita* (DOCG), which sets out to guarantee what is, in theory, already guaranteed. The new label applies to wines traditionally and universally acknowledged to be outstanding, and to ensure consistent quality, rigid controls are followed up by regular tastings. That 'king of all wines', Vino Nobile di Montepulciano (made on Umbria's border with Tuscany) received the first DOCG in 1981, and was followed by Barolo, Barbaresco, and Brunello di Montalcino. Few would argue with these, but reputations recently took a nose-dive with the addition of Chianti — which has been going through some difficult times — giving rise to ominous murmurings that similar 'mistakes' will undermine the classification's credibility.

If this all sounds a bit grim, take heart. The DOC mark and quality are not mutually exclusive — excellent wine can be found, and perfectly good wine abounds.

Buying wine

The brief run-down of Umbrian wines in the next few pages is intended to help out on the spot, whether it be in shops or restaurants. If you are a more serious buyer, or simply fancy a morning looking around a *cantina*, then the addresses dotted about the text will be more useful. If you write in advance to producers, prefix the address with 'Azienda Agricola', or, if your Italian is not up to it, contact the Italian Trade Centre at 46 Piccadilly, London W1 (Tel. 01-439 2941), who will be happy to deal with any enquiries. The ultimate authority for Italian enophiles is the *Italian State Official Gazette*, which contains an exhaustive list of producers. It is available from the Italian Trade Centre.

Real pioneers will have to ask in shops and bars for the addresses of farmers who might have a surplus of wine (or any other product) that they would be willing to sell. Finding such information is not too difficult — what is often harder is persuading people to accept money for what they would be willing to give away. When buying in such circumstances, be sure to take along some clean bottles, and allow plenty of time for tasting, and appropriate conversation.

The most straightforward way to buy wine in quantity is to head for the *Cantina Sociale* or *Cantina Cooperativa* of any large town. These are large-scale commercial concerns co-operatively owned by councils and local farmers, a set-up which sometimes (but not always) involves a levelling of standards. (Though it does have the advantage of providing smallholders with a guaranteed income.) Most have small shops or noticeboards to help you choose from the wines in stock.

Umbrian wines

Orvieto (DOC)

Umbria's most famous export, Orvieto, at its very best reflects the character of the region itself — subtle in character, gentle and unassuming in nature, and with a tendency to insinuate rather than shout its charms and reputation. It has been a wine of renown for centuries. Signorelli's great fresco cycle in the town's cathedral, for example, was painted in 1500 with the help of its liquid inspiration. His contract for the work mentioned 'two measures of wine and two quintals of grain' to be paid monthly in addition to his fee. And during some restoration work on the same cathedral in 1492, poor old Pintoricchio

JD

so took to its pleasures that his contract was rescinded after a year, 'for having consumed too much azure, too much gold and too much wine'.

The tipple of masterpiece and undoing was the rich, honey-coloured Orvieto of tradition, the *amabile* or *abbocato*. This ancient wine was born of fine volcanic soil and weeks of mysterious fermentation in the tufa caves below the town — the reason, or so the wily old producers tell you, for its distinctive qualities: the flowery bouquet, pale colour, and marvellously delicate taste. Originally the grapes were left to rot in open casks (unlike French Sauternes, where the fruit is left to rot on the vine) the net result being what the Italians call *muffa nobile*, the French *pourriture noble*, and the English, with characteristic bluntness, 'noble rot' — all names for the same thing — an unedifying fungus, which removes moisture from the grape but leaves its acids and sugars unmolested.

The resulting wine, with its blend of delicacy and sweetness, has now all but disappeared, the victim, like much else, of ruthless economic logic. Orvietan producers were amongst the first to realize that the trend of the market was towards lighter and drier wines, and adapted their methods accordingly. Their perspicacity paid off (in commercial terms at least), and the vast proportion of the 12 million litres of Orvieto drunk annually is the new, mass-produced *secco*. The traditional version, much lamented but scarcely 'viable', however, is still hanging on. The best examples are Bigi's Vigneto Orzalume, Dubbini's Palazzone, or Ducagnano dei Barbi's outstandingly good Pourriture Noble.

The bandwagon effect, enormous demand, and not a little complacency in new producers during the 1970s led to some anaemic and anonymous years for the new Orvieto, but things have recently tightened up. By sticking to names such as Barberani, Ducagnano dei Barbi, Bigi (try their Vigneto Torricella) and the renowned Florentines, Antinori, you should not be disappointed. Both dry and sweet Orvietos use an approximate blend of 60 per cent Trebbiano grapes (so prolific in central Italy that they have been called weeds), 20 per cent Verdello, 15 per cent Malvasia (a variety originally imported from ancient Greece), and just 5 per cent of the sweet, scented Grechetto (more or less Orvieto's secret ingredient). Nowadays the wine is likely to find its way into a standard bottle, rather than the distinctive Orvietan *pulcianella* of the past — a smaller and squatter version of the familiar Chianti flask. Very occasionally you may come across a 2-litre Orvietan bottle known as a *toscanello*.

In addition to the area's whites there is an unexceptional red, similar to Chianti, and a local Vin Santo. Orvieto Classico, incidentally, simply means wine made in the vineyards close to the town, the traditional heart of the production area.

Torgiano (DOC)

The Torgiano group of wines — currently amongst the country's finest — has done more than any other to improve the good name of Umbria's wine in the last 30 years. They centre on a small, but wildly successful, DOC south-east of Perugia, established almost single handedly after the war by Dr Giorgio Lungarotti, one of the great folk-heroes in the far from fairy-tale world of Italian viticulture.

He is very much one of the new breed, and his experiments with imported grape varieties have produced startling results. Almost anything from his model vineyards automatically carries the highest seal of approval. The quality of the house red, the Rubesco, has dropped off recently from excellent to only very good, but the Rubesco Riserva remains one of Italy's outstanding wines, and certainly the best you will drink in Umbria. To reach perfection it needs three years in the cask and at least six in the bottle, which puts the 1982 'harvest of the century' vintage just out of reach. (Though along with the 1985, you might take some home for a rainy day.) The 1971 and 1975 vintages are the ones to treat yourself to on special occasions, but if you want to be kinder on your pocket the San Giorgio is also superb, particularly the 1981. Marvellous things are also expected of the new Cabernet Sauvignon di Miraduolo — even parity with the Rubesco Riserva, though it is still too early to make any concrete predictions. Whites to look out for include the Chardonnay di Miraduolo and the Torre di Giano (the 1983 Riserva for a special treat). Castel Grifone is the house rosé.

Colli Alto Tiberini

This is one of Umbria's newer DOC regions, and one of which great things are expected. It was established in 1980, and covers the hills and valleys of the Tiber around Città di Castello. Large amounts of money need to be invested in new machinery if the wines are to really take off, but what is already being produced is generally good. Some two-thirds of total production is red, the remainder white, which is the reverse of the usual Umbrian proportions. Most of the reds are made in much the same way as Chianti just over the border, and with similar results. The red and white Montecastelli and Fontesagale are both recommended. Sangiustino, made near the village of the same name on the norther edge of the region, is one of the most pleasant whites — dry, full-flavoured, and fragrant. Panicale and Tiferno are more modest wines from the same area, the latter occasionally sparkling and best drunk young.

Montefalco (DOC)

This is another newish and very small DOC, whose wines will take some hunting down anywhere but central Umbria. Its area covers Montefalco itself, along with the neighbouring towns of Giano Umbra and Gualdo Cattaneo. The most famous wine is the quite extraordinary and heavily scented Sangrantino Passito — rather like a strong Vin Santo crossed with blackberry essence. It is to be highly recommended if you can find it — the best producer is Bevagna's Adanti. (Adanti is also responsible for Rosso d'Arquata, one of the region's newcomers, but already shaping up as one of its most outstanding table wines. The Bianco d'Arquata is also well above average. Both need about four years to reach their best.) From the same area, and with qualities of a watered-down Sangrantino, come Piegaro, and the more interesting Scacciadiavoli (whose name — beware — translates as 'the chaser-out of devils'). The plain-sounding Montefalco Rosso is anything but, and rates as one of the best-value reds around. Drink it within four years and look for producers Adanti or Fongoli.

Colline del Trasimeno

The neighbouring Colli Perugini DOC might usefully be tagged on to this shambling DOC around Lake Trasimeno, established in 1972. The wines have for a long time been serviceable and adequate, but these days their star is rising. The most famous (and conspicuous) producer is Lamborghini. After leaving his father's farm on a bicycle, a penniless 16-year-old, and building up a vast business (of which automobiles were only the most glamorous part), the larger-than-life Lamborghini sold up in 1969 and came to Umbria with the intention of making wine the way he used to make cars. He began in characteristic style by bulldozing 450 acres of woodland for his vineyard — without the permission of the local council. Today his only fear is boredom. 'I'll get on one of my bulldozers and spend the day digging a hole', he has been quoted as saying, 'and next day, if I still don't have anything to do, I'll go off and fill it in.' His wine is good as far as it goes,

JD

but it is probably worth combining a tasting with a visit to his *cantina* at La Fiorita. You'll have no problem finding it — the dozens of imploring signs dotted around the lake have seen to that.

Other wines

Other wines to look out for include Ora di Lugnano and Rubino di Lugnano from the area around Terni — soon to be turned into a DOC centred on Spoleto. The star of the new region will almost certainly be the outstanding Castello di Montoro, an elegant red best drunk after five to eight years. A Nebbiolo is made around Gubbio, but can be difficult to find. Though made from the same grape as the mighty Barolo, it is not, sadly, in the same class. Merlot has been produced for over a century, and is always reliable, sometimes excellent. Finally, one of the happiest new experiments, Antinori's 1985 debut, is the Cervaro della Sala, a Chardonnay aged in French oak and already hailed as one of Italy's great future whites — soon, no doubt, to overshadow its more humble but worthy stablemate, the Castello della Sala.

Vin Santo

Made all over central Italy, Vin Santo ('holy wine') most closely resembles sherry, except that it tends to be taken at the end of a meal, or with coffee and pastries. Umbria's version, with its deep golden colour and rich velvety taste, is particularly good. The finer points of production vary, but the best results are obtained by making small amounts, and allowing plenty of time for ageing. This makes it a difficult wine to produce commercially, though the irrepressive Lungarotti manages (his grappa is also good), and Greco di Todi has a fine reputation. Most Vin Santo starts with selected Trebbiano and Malvasia grapes, which are hung in attics or near fires (for a smoky flavour) to dry and gather sweetness. The results are pressed and sealed in the smallest of barrels to ferment and mature for a minimum of four years. While warmth for this length of time would normally be anathema to wine, in the case of Vin Santo it produces the same sorts of change in taste and colour that occur in the making of Madeira. Filtered, aged, and bottled, the wine is then ready for drinking. Should you not stumble across Vin Santo by accident, try asking for it in a restaurant at the end of a meal.

Bars

There is not much, of course, that anyone needs to know in order to enjoy such pleasures — most things about bars are pretty self-explanatory. However, one or two tips could save you some time and trouble. The most important is that in virtually every bar — certainly those in larger towns — you are expected to pay for what you want at the cash desk (*la cassa*), and then take your chit (*lo scontrino*) to the bar and repeat your order. It seems this was originally to guard against light-fingered staff (the owner was the only one who ever got to go behind the till), but now it is really just a habit (or a means of providing employment). It is also more efficient, as it means that there is no hanging about waiting for someone to find their money when you could be getting served. (You soon discover that Italians can be as impatient in bars as they are in cars.)

If you are intimidated by the voluble and assured patrons around you, or the fine disdain with which the barman seems to be viewing both you and his job, then a 100-lire tip (very important this one) slapped down on the bar, or put ostentatiously in the saucer provided, often works minor miracles. And if you have left the phrase-book behind, don't be afraid to point, gesticulate, or otherwise improvise — the Italians do have a sense of humour, and do find (unlike the French) even the most appalling stab at their language endearing.

Sitting or standing

Unlike their British or French counterparts, Italian bars rarely have tables and chairs (inside at least). Where they do, there is no consistent policy on how much they charge you to sit on them — except that it is always going to cost something. The only exceptions are in the smallest villages, where the bar is more a community centre than somewhere to drink. Asking card-playing old men to pay for the privilege of camping all day at the tables would be like asking them to pay for fresh air. Any bar that did so would soon be out of business. Where you do have to pay an extra tariff, then the prices are fixed by law and ought to be prominently displayed.

Coffee

The certainty of an excellent cup of coffee, anywhere, anytime, is one of the small luxuries that gives Italy its character. On the whole, Italians appear to prefer the short, sharp shock of a small *espresso* to the longer, milky *cappuccino* (named after the brown robes and white cowls of Capuchin monks). Its deep, black aromatic kick is usually strong enough for most eventualities, though in times of real crisis a *caffè lungo* (two *espressos*) is what you might take as a 'morning-after' lifesaver. If you prefer carrying on where you left off, then a '*caffè corretto* (coffee and brandy) is the widely taken 'hair of the dog' alternative. *Caffè ristretto* (a concentrated *espresso*) is for real caffeine fiends only. *Caffè macchiato* (literally 'stained coffee') is espresso again, but with an added dash of milk. There is also a *latte macchiato* — milk with a touch of coffee.

At the other extreme, the longest coffee of all is a *caffè latte*, the equivalent of the French *café au lait*. If, for some bizarre reason, you wanted powdered coffee, or one with lots of water, ask for a *caffè americano*. Decaffeinated coffee is becoming increasingly popular and seems to be known everywhere as *caffè Hag*. If you are really particular, the mark of a good bar is one that uses fresh, not UHT, milk. The latter is generally more acceptable to the Italians who have lived for longer without fridges.

Water

A glass of water, not iced unfortunately, frequently accompanies coffee. In Italy this means mineral water — tap water is for the flowers or for washing up with (although mains water is perfectly safe). Ask for *un bicchiere d'acqua minerale*, and specify *liscia* (still) or *gassata* (sparkling). The best-known of Umbria's mineral waters are San Gemini, Fontecchio, Nocera Umbra, and San Faustino.

Beer

Beer is currently fashionable in Italy, and it is becoming a point of honour for bars to stock as many foreign brands as possible. Italians know how to milk a trend, however, and prices, even for national beers, are high. The cheapest and most common thirst-quencher is a small bottle of Peroni, known as a *Peroncino*. Beer from the keg (*una birra alla spina*) comes in two basic measures — *piccola* (25 centilitres) and *media* (50 centilitres). A 1-litre *grande* and you're getting serious. Most of the time you will be served yellow, lager-like beer (*birra chiara*), though brown ('British') beer (*birra scura*) is becoming common.

Other drinks

If coffee pales, there is always tea, usually with lemon (*un tè al limone*) rather than milk (*un tè con latte*), a combination that raises eyebrows in Italy. In summer, iced tea and coffee (*tè/caffè freddo*) are both popular — the former with an added dollop of lemon sorbet as a treat. Otherwise, bars carry all the spirits, liqueurs, and aperitifs you could want (plus a few you wouldn't). Wine by the glass, though cheap, tends to be of the mouthwash red variety. Measures are far from standardized, but always far more generous than in Britain. That 100-lire tip could make all the difference at this point.

Umbria's own specialities include several meads, Vin Santo (see 'Wine') and (the pretty foul) Amaro di Tartufo, a bitter digestif flavoured with Norcia's black truffle. As an alternative to alcohol all bars stock fruit juices (*un succo di frutta*), milk shakes (*un frullato* — or *un frappé* if made with ice-cream) and freshly squeezed orange or grapefruit juice (*una spremuta*).

Food in bars

Cappuccino, usually drunk only in the mornings (Italians think it odd to drink one in the evenings or after a meal) is accompanied by *un cornetto, una pasta*, or *un brioche*, all different names for pretty much the same thing — the Italian equivalent of the croissant. Any bar worth its salt will have a variety of these plain, creamy, or chocolatey pastries, but unless it doubles as a *pasticceria* (a pastry shop) stocks are usually well depleted by mid-morning.

Bars generally have a wide range of freshly made and good-quality snacks. The variety of names is bewildering, so you are probably best off just pointing. A *panino* is any small roll, *medaglione* and *rosette* more ambitious versions of the same. An ordinary sandwich is *un tramezzino*. All of them can be toasted (*tostato*) if you ask. A bar displaying the sign *tavola calda* means that you can expect a few simple hot dishes, something like a pub lunch, with

the important difference that they will be cooked by Italians and not by microwaves. Many bars are also *gelaterie*, and the Italian way is to round off a meal or evening with an ice-cream in the current bar of the moment.

Toilets

It is generally accepted that bars must provide the service no one else wants to. *Il gabinetto* is the functional name; *il bagno*, conjuring up visions of marble and gleaming porcelain, is more genteel. Whatever you ask for, what you will find — once you have waded through the debris in the bar's back cellar — are the more spartan facilities suggested by the former term. The only exceptions are in the larger museums in the main towns, and in these you may have to cross an old lady's palm with silver. Whether this is a gratuity or an admission fee is left deliberately vague.

Restaurants

Umbria has its fair share of excellent restaurants in every price-range, and in every category, from the familiar *pizzeria* to the trendy post-modern. As well as variety, the region is strong on tradition. Restaurants such as Il Tartufo and Il Morino in Orvieto have been in the same families for generations, and appear to be coping perfectly well with the vigorous competition from newcomers such as Lungarotti's Tre Vaselle in Torgiano, and the immensely fashionable Vissani on Lake Corbara. While prices in these sorts of place tend to be in the 'arm and a leg' bracket, eating in Umbria need never be expensive, first, because in Italy generally it rarely is, and second, because many of the region's so-called tourist centres are still relatively unknown. Pay some extra attention, however, in well-known tourist traps such as Assisi, Orvieto, and Spoleto (especially at festival time).

Where costs are concerned, common sense, of course, will take you a long way. Meals remain reasonably priced if you stick, say, to a pasta dish and a salad (*il primo*). They only really become expensive if you start adding all the trimmings. Naturally the meat/fish course (*il secondo*) is the centrepiece (don't expect vegetables to be included), but if you go for antipasti, fruit, coffee, cheese, and liqueurs then the cost starts to spiral. These extras are where restaurants make up their margins, and tend to be comparatively over-priced — it is not unknown for a single apple to set you back as much as a plate of *spaghetti*.

Most types of restaurant are as relaxed as the Italians themselves, and few stand on ceremony (though Italians tend to dress up more than most for social gatherings). They may go under a variety of names, but often the food they serve is very similar. Somewhere calling itself a *pizzeria* will offer no surprises, but what they serve will not necessarily stop at *pizza*. Any of the Italian staples, from pasta to ice-cream, will usually be available. The *trattoria* can be in the same league (but with a wider menu), though here the food can be exceptional — what we might expect of a good restaurant. A *taverna*, or *locanda*, is a more modest version of a *trattoria*; an *osteria* sells the simplest food of all — the nearest British equivalent would be a pub lunch.

Whatever these establishments call themselves,. they should all serve simple but satisfying food in a convivial and easy-going atmosphere. Don't think you have to work through all the courses on the menu. Italians go out and have a *pizza* on its own as we do. If you want a dessert, you will always find ice-cream on the menu, but for a truly impressive range of *gelati*, you would be better off going to a *gelateria*, which sells nothing but ice-cream. There are few Italian towns without one. Otherwise, the more limited selection of a bar is a reasonable alternative. (As a general rule, if a more humble restaurant does disappoint, this is most likely to be at the dessert stage. The majority of them rely on one or two tried and tested standards — often brought in from outside caterers.) Bear in mind that bars are a good source of hearty and wholesome snacks; see the section on 'Bars' for details.

Any restaurant that calls itself such, or has a name (Il Posh), has certain pretensions. This sort of place usually represents the most expensive way of eating out — which is not to say that it will necessarily offer the best food. In Italy you can eat well in every price range.

You should ignore the various recommendations that are sometimes slapped over restaurant doors like wallpaper; with certain honourable exceptions they guarantee very little. Do, however, take note of which credit cards are accepted, and do check to make sure that they will be accepted in practice as well as in theory.

A cover charge (*il coperto*) and a service charge (*servizio*) are frequent additions to the bill (*il conto*). There may also be a surcharge (*un supplemento*), but you would be unlucky (and unlikely) to be landed with all three. Where there are no obvious charges, tip at your discretion, bearing in mind that the service charge is between 12 and 15 per cent. In the larger towns you will find fixed-price 'tourist menus' (*menu turistico*), which simplify pricing if your Italian is not too good. However, they don't always mean that you will pay less than if you had eaten *à la carte*. All bars and restaurants are obliged by law to give you an itemized bill, which includes a VAT number. (An attempt by the state to beat tax evasion.) If they give you a scrap of paper with a scribbled price, they are on the fiddle. If you want a proper bill (and, of course, you are entitled to one) ask for *una fattura* or *un ricevuto* (a receipt). You may even find it has the effect of reducing the bill. Sunday is the most popular day for Italians to eat out *en masse*, so arrive at a restaurant early (12.30 for lunch) or book a table in advance. It is also the day many of them get married, so popular rendezvous may be swamped by wedding receptions. Lunch is generally the main meal of the day, and dinner is taken at around 20.30, though there are no hard and fast rules. Most restaurants (as well as *trattorias* and *pizzerias*) close once a week, usually on Mondays. A great many also close for the entire month of August.

Festivals and cultural events

Some happy combination of history, landscape, ambience, and art, has today made Umbria one of the most important cultural centres in Italy, with something for almost every taste.

The range of events can be broken down into three categories. First, festivals of the performing arts, which are growing in number and popularity every year. Second, traditional pageants and processions, which preserve the region's rituals and historical rivalries. Third, exhibitions of local goods and cuisine, which can include anything from truffles to tractors.

Amongst the first, Spoleto's *Festival dei Due Mondi* (Festival of the Two Worlds) is by far the most famous. Now one of Europe's leading arts festivals, it started life humbly enough in 1958, when Giancarlo Menotti and a group of friends came to central Italy looking for a venue suitable to stage a wide-ranging festival of the arts. They saw more than 60 towns and cities before choosing Spoleto, whose beautiful location, the special something of an old Umbrian town, and its Roman and nineteenth-century theatres, all seemed to make it the ideal setting. Now every summer the town is transformed by two months of exhibitions, films, classical concerts, and all manner of ballet, theatre, and opera. Sibling festivals take place all over the world.

The event attracts a cosmopolitan and sophisticated audience, largely comprising, to the chagrin of some, what the Italians call *la modanità*, and what in the sixties would have been called the jet-set. The tanned, well-heeled, and culture-hungry hordes can make it difficult to find a ticket for some of the more prestigious performances, though not all the events by any means are gala affairs. There are plenty of one-off shows, fringe events, and impromptu concerts, so the occasion is far from being elitist and institutionalized. Furthermore, the festival has recently put its faith in the young and experimental in an effort to regain its original spirit and artistic edge.

No less popular, but far less sedate, is Umbria Jazz, the foremost event of its kind in Italy, and on the verge of international recognition. Concerts are held in Perugia itself, and around smaller venues in neighbouring towns. Recent line-ups have included Miles Davis, Gil Evans, Dexter Gorden, Sting, Stan Getz, and Wynton Marsalis. Perugia also offers outdoor theatre in July (*Teatro in Piazza*) as well as a festival of church music in September, *La Sagra Musicale Umbra* (which in 1986 celebrated its 50th anniversary). For those of a more studious bent, the University for Foreigners holds summer language schools, and the Arts Academy offers courses in sculpture and painting. Elsewhere Umbértide has summer rock concerts and Città di Castello hosts a national festival of chamber music (*Festival delle Nazioni di Musica di Camera*). These are some of the bigger events; numerous Umbrian towns hold their own summer (and winter) festivals of music, theatre, and dance.

On these outdoor occasions Umbria itself is often stage and literal backdrop for the plays or concerts, and sometimes steals the show completely. (The summer opera in Gubbio's Roman amphitheatre, for example, is one such evocative event.) However, there is little chance of this happening with the vast spectacle of traditional ceremonies such as Gubbio's *Corsa dei Ceri* and Orvieto's *Festa del Corpus Domini*. They are never surrounded with quite the same razzamatazz as Siena's *Palio*, but only because they are not as well known outside Italy; as ceremonies thay are every bit as colourful and fascinating. Again, there is a host of more modest events that pay homage to Umbria's rich historical heritage, particularly to her numerous saints. Religious ceremonies — of which Assisi naturally has an inordinate number — are not, however, pious affairs, and the lay elements are many, and vigorously enjoyed. These events are innumerable; even the smallest hamlet has its saint or relic, each the sound pretext for a rousing party. The great majority take place at Easter or during the summer. Most are advertised on church doors, and consist of a special Mass and a procession, after which they are indistinguishable from any other high-spirited Italian festival.

Finally there are a range of shows and exhibitions dedicated to the region's crafts and many products. These are growing in number every year as Umbria becomes more popular with tourists, and as each town tries to exploit or invent its own speciality. Bastia Umbra near Assisi is self-appointed leader in the field, hosting a big agricultural show in September (*Agriumbria*) and a gathering of meat-traders in May (*Umbriacarni*). There are also exhibitions of office equipment and ideal homes — none of them events to set the pulses racing. More in keeping with the region's rural past are Norcia's autumn truffle fair, Città di Castello's horse show, the ceramic markets of Gualdo and Deruta, the nationally famous antiques fairs at Todi and Assisi, a *festa* devoted to the Vale of Spoleto's noted olive oil, and Torgiano's annual homage to Umbria's wines. There are many more, all usually either markets for genuine craftsmen, or continuations of fairs that have been held for centuries.

These are the major Umbrian festivals. The precise dates vary each year, so check with local tourist offices for up-to-the-minute information.

Cultural festivals and traditional events

Assisi

Holy Week. Numerous processions and celebrations.

Calendimaggio. 30 April–1 May. Procession to celebrate spring and St Francis's vision of Lady Poverty.

Festa della Voto. 22 June. Celebrates salvation of the town, with processions in medieval costume.

Perdono. 31 June–2 July. Processions in the traditional costumes of Lazio, Abruzzo, and the Campania.

Festival to celebrate return of St Francis to Assisi. First Sunday of September, but not held every year.

Festa di San Francesco 3–4 October. A celebration of the saint's canonization. Draws religious leaders and pilgrims from all over Italy.

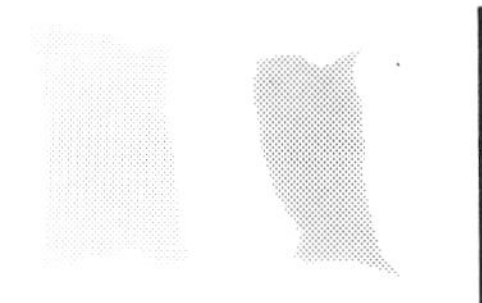

Festa del Corpus Domini. November. Especially large procession through flower-strewn streets.

Bastia Umbra

Bastia Summer Festival. June–August.
Insula Romana. 1 June. National prize-giving for unpublished poetry and prose.
Agriumbria. September. National agricultural show.
Palio dei Rioni. Horse-race between rival quarters of the town.

Bettona

Maggio in Bettona. May. Plays, concerts, and exhibitions.
Festa di San Crispolto. 11–12 May.
Horticultural Show. 29 August–1 September.

Bevagna

Good Friday. Procession.

Calvi di Umbria

Festa di San Pancrazio. 12 May. Procession in medieval dress.

Cascia

Good Friday. Procession.
Festa di Santa Rita. 22 May.
Il Ferragosto. August. Plays, concerts, and exhibitions.

Città di Castello

National Festival of Chamber Music. August–September.

Foligno

Giostra della Quintana. Medieval joust. Second Sunday of September.

Gualdo Tadino

International Ceramics Exhibition. July–August.

Gubbio

Antiques Fair. Second Sunday of every month.
Corsa dei Ceri. 15 May. One of Umbria's most famous traditional events.

Norcia

Fiorito. June. Large horticultural show.

Orvieto

Festa della Palombella. Pentecost.
Corpus Domini. Procession to celebrate the Miracle of Bolsena.
National Festival of Polyphonic Music. September.

Perugia

Amici della Musica. Spring and summer concerts.
Umbria Jazz. July–August. Italy's biggest jazz festival.
Sagra Musicale Umbra. September. Religious music.
Teatro in Piazza. July–August. Open-air theatre.
Desolata. Religious festival on the Friday after the Passion.

Spello

Infiorita. Corpus Domini. Streets covered in extravagant carpets of flowers.

Spoleto

Festival dei Due Mondi. One of Europe's foremost cultural festivals.
Medieval Studies Convention. April.
Organ Recitals. April–June, Held in town's churches.
Festival of Experimental Lyrical Songs. September.

Todi

Pianto della Madonna. Holy Week. Religious festival.
Antiques Fair. April–May.
Todi Artigianata. August–September. An exhibition of wood and metal crafts.
Todi Festival. September. Variety of concerts and exhibitions.

Food, wine, and craft festivals

Listed below are the dates and venues of festivals involving Umbrian wines and regional cooking. The precise times vary from year to year, so check with the appropriate tourist office before setting off. The summary here is far from exhaustive, as even the smallest village seems to have something that demands to be commemorated loudly and extravagantly every year. Festivals like these you have to be lucky enough to stumble across — not that this will be difficult: in the summer they are everywhere; even the Italians get fed up with them.

When you find one, be sure to enter into the spirit of things and have a go at some of the games. Guessing the weight of a live pig is popular — here winning is to be avoided at all costs, unless you want the prize: several hundredweight of petrified pig. Throwing a hoop over the goose's neck is another favourite (there is no equivalent of the RSPCA in Italy). At some point you will doubtless be encouraged to buy tickets for a vastly over-subscribed raffle

(enticed by the prospect of winning a small tractor or the inevitable Fiat). Somewhere in the proceedings there is always, but *always*, an enthusiastically awful brass band — and fireworks to end with on Saturday night.

Città di Castello

Città di Castello	November	Arts, crafts, and agricultural show
Cornetto	August	Festival of Colli Alto Tiberini Wines
Pitigliano	July	*Sagra della Berlingozza* (cake)
Ronti	June	*Sagra della Penne Arrabiata* (spicy pasta)
Trestina	April	Agricultural show

Gubbio

Gubbio	August	*Festa del Colpalambo*
	October	Events centred on the truffle
Montone	July	Wine festival
Pistrino	September	Wine festival
Umbértide	July	Wine festival
	October	*Sagra della Castegna* (chestnut)

Lake Trasimeno

Borghetto	June	*Sagra del Pesce* (fish)
Castiglione del Lago	October	*Cucina Tipica* and wine festival
Città della Pieve	April	*Festa della Fontane* (the town's fountains run with wine)
Panicale	April	*Sagra di Torta di Pasqua* (plus wine in the fountains)
San Feliciano	July	*Sagra del Pesce*
Tuoro sul Trasimeno	August	Tuoro festival

Orvieto

Allerona	May	Town festival
Amelia	June	Festival of food and wine
Narni	May	*Corso dell'Anello*
Orvieto	June	Grand regional festival of Umbrian wines
Piediluco	July	*Sagra del Pesce* and wine-tasting
	October	Wine and chestnut festival
San Gemini	September	Medieval joust with food and wine festival
Terni	May	*Festa* (with local wines)

Perugia and district

Bagnaia	May	*Sagra della Bruschetta* (food and wine)
Capanne	May	*Sagra del Grano* (wheat festival)
Castel Piano	August	*Sagra del Pesce*
Pianello	August	*Sagra dei Funghi* (mushrooms)
Pila	June	*Sagra della Torta* (desserts and wines)
Sant'Enea	April	Festival of food, wine, and local culture
San Martino	September	*Sagra del Grano*
Solomeo	April	*Sagra del Piatto Rustico* (food and wines)

Spoleto

Bettona	August	Festival of food and wine
Bevagna	June	Wine festival
	August	Craft fair and market
Cannara	April	*La Festa della Vernaccia*
Campello	July	Trout festival
Collemancio	July	Wine festival
	September	Festival of the onion (*sic*)
Spello	April	Festival of Umbrian folklore

Todi

Marsciano	September	Grape festival
Montecastello	August	*Festa dell'Acqua* (wine and ham)
Montefalco	April	Wine festival
Signoria	July	Wine festival
Todi	October	*Festa Gastronomica*
Torgiano	August	Torgiano Show (food and wine)
	Autumn	International wine-tasting

HISTORY

Pre-Roman and Etruscan Umbria

Umbria's early history is lost not in those fabled mists of time but in the boggy marshes, rivers, and lakes that criss-crossed and divided the region before the drainage schemes of the Romans. It was near such unlikely places, in the Chiascio and Tiber valleys, that some of the first Italian settlers made their homes over 1500 years before the birth of Christ, nameless and unknown people who formed part of the larger migration of primitive tribes then drifting into Italy from central Europe and the East. Almost nothing of them now remains, save what has been dug or dredged from the mud to be exhibited in the archaeological museums of Rome or Perugia.

Umbria, so soft and benign today, was then a far bleaker proposition, and would have presented those early settlers with the dilemma that has continued to trouble generations of Umbrians ever since: simply to decide on the relative merits of a widely contrasting landscape; whether, on the one hand, it was better to make for the marshy valleys and lakeshores, which, though they hampered movement and were vulnerable to attack, had the advantage of being level and well suited to farming, or whether it was better to choose the mountains — the Apennines to the east or the lower but still inaccessible hills to the west — whose slopes, while barren and inhospitable, were safe from attack and easy to defend.

As time went by — and the legacy of this tendency is still evident today — mountains and hilltops began to take preference, and tribes started to move away from the plains around Terni and Perugia in favour of the upland area around Norcia, giving rise to the first of the hill-towns that were eventually to dominate the entire region.

By the eighth century BC, these early tribes, who had been predominantly nomadic peoples, were absorbed by the larger and more sophisticated tribes that followed them from the north. These gradually formed themselves into three distinct groups: the Samnites, the Latins (who later became the Romans), and the Umbrians (though Umbria was not known as such until several hundred years later). All three had common cultural roots, spoke dialects of a shared language, and between them occupied all but the southernmost tip of the Italian peninsula. The Umbrians' own territory extended far beyond the region's present boundaries, including the best part of what are now Tuscany and the Marche; a vast area for a people of whom almost nothing is known. Only the Eugubine Marbles (a sort of Rosetta Stone of central Italy) found near Gubbio (then probably the Umbrian 'capital') yield any clues as to the religion or language of what was clearly a cogent and self-contained tribe. Beyond these all is mystery, and the Umbrians' only other memorials are the tracts of city walls still standing, more or less intact, in what were the Umbrian cities proper: Otricoli, Amelia, Todi, Terni, Narni, Nocera, Spoleto, Foligno, Assisi, Gualdo Tadino, Bettona, Gubbio, and Città di Castello.

Their erstwhile and ghostly inhabitants were probably peaceful people, shepherds rather than soldiers, with many of the gentle and pastoral qualities that are still characteristic of Umbria today. When the Etruscans began to encroach on their cities, for example, they did not stand and fight, but retreated quietly into the mountains east of the Tiber and carried on life much as they had done before. In time they started to trade and intermarry with their new neighbours, and by about the third century BC the two cultures had become more or less indistinguishable.

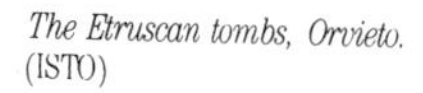

The Etruscan tombs, Orvieto. (ISTO)

The Etruscans are some of the most fascinating and mysterious of all the ancient peoples, and to this day no one is really sure who they were or where they came from (though there has been no shortage of theories). The earliest chroniclers, usually monks, had few doubts. Basing their long-winded and shambling accounts on the Bible (the one great history they possessed) they assumed their strange ancestors to be descended from Noah, who, having taken advantage of the lull in the Great Flood (they said), had climbed the Apennines and pitched his tent on a hill close to the Tiber, thus founding Perugia. What is known for certain is that by 700 BC the Etruscans were the largest and most powerful civilization in central Italy, with an influence in Umbria that extended as far east as the Tiber, and in some isolated cases (Gubbio for example) some way beyond it. All aspects of their life point to a sophisticated and ordered social set-up, with a political system that was formed around a loose, but well-organized, confederation of leading cities, of which two — Perugia and Orvieto — were situated in what is now Umbria. (It is worth remembering that places that are now no more than sleepy villages were once numbered as cities in Etruria — Bettona, for example, south-east of Assisi, which, to judge by its walls, was only a little less important than Perugia itself.) In their art and religion the Etruscans owed a great deal to the East, but they became more eclectic in the wake of trade with Greece and as they assimilated the cultures of near-neighbours such as the Umbrians.

Most of what we know about them comes from the evidence of their tombs, a fact that in the past has led to a one-sided and somewhat necrophilic view of what were a far from gloomy people. There is no doubt that they had an acute sense of death and the unknown — the graves with their powerful, almost brutal, array of painted animals and strange apocryphal figures show this quite clearly — but the same tombs contain scenes of dancing, drinking, and celebration, which, however brooding the graves themselves appear today, would seem to be the work of artists who belonged to a joyful, vibrant, and even wanton race. And turning to the beauty, variety, and craftsmanship of their artefacts and everyday objects, it is impossible to be unaware of a harmony that went far beyond a narrow preoccupation with the afterlife. Even D.H. Lawrence, in *Etruscan Places* (a surprisingly good and detailed introduction to the subject) considered them a 'living, fresh and jolly people' (it was the Romans he had no time for).

Nevertheless, there is no escaping the fact that bleak necropolises are almost all that remains of what was once a great and extensive civilization; there is nothing in the way of sites comparable to the Roman remains at Pompeii or Ephesus, only what has been salvaged from the tombs (and a great deal of this has been, and is still being, lost to thieves and 'amateur' archaeologists). In Umbria the bulk of this treasure (left in the tombs to provide the occupants with all they would need in the afterlife, rather in the manner of the Pharaohs) is in the museums of Perugia and Orvieto (which also have substantial graves). Chiusi and Volterra on its western borders, having also once been Etruscan cities, have further tombs and museums.

Roman Umbria

The first time Umbria appears in Roman records is in 309 BC, the occasion being Perugia's defeat at the hands of the Roman Consul Fabius. Then, for the first time, the city and its fellow members of the Etruscan league were forced to acknowledge the new and ever more powerful influence of Rome. The defeat marked the beginning of the end for the Etruscan cities, and though some continued to cling half-heartedly to independence, most by the second century BC had become powerful, if reluctant, allies of the Romans. Any faint vestiges of autonomy were stripped away in 40 BC, when Perugia was defeated a second time, one of the few occasions on which events in Umbria had repercussions in the Empire as a whole.

The defeat formed part of a bitter power struggle that followed the murder of Julius Caesar in 44 BC. This effectively amounted to a confrontation between the Consul Mark Antony, his brother Lucius, and Octavius, Caesar's great-nephew. In 40 BC the dispute reached crisis-point, and while Antony was amorously preoccupied with Cleopatra in Egypt, Octavius (whose slight appearance belied great strength of purpose) gained the upper hand and succeeded in harrying Lucius from Rome. Lucius, unhappily for the citizens of Perugia, decided to take refuge within their walls. This was the cue for a chain of events that had all the makings of a Hollywood epic.

Octavius followed Lucius and wasted no time in laying siege to the city, which was eventually brought to its knees after seven months of famine and hardship. Beneficent in victory, Octavius surprisingly agreed to spare those citizens who had survived starvation, but — and here was the catch — on the sole condition that 300 of the city's elders be brought before him and killed in their place. With no alternative but to agree, the Perugians surrendered their leaders, who duly met their end, it being said that the future emperor ignored their final pleas for mercy with a toss of his head and the simple and magisterial phrase: 'They must die'.

Octavius, obviously feeling that a memorable victory and massacre

Right *Roman Porta Venere, Spello.* (DL)

Below *Roman amphitheatre, Spoleto.* (DL)

were enough action for one day, planned to postpone the sack of the city until the following morning, but was denied the pleasure by Caius Cestius Macedonius, a citizen of Perugia, who, consumed with the shame and ignominy of defeat and deciding that suicide was the only option for a man of honour, made a funeral pyre of his house. Singing and babbling hysterically while his home crashed around him in flames, he stabbed himself to death. The resulting fire raged through the whole city, which, like all Etruscan cities, was made entirely of wood. By dawn all that remained of Perugia were heaps of smouldering ruins and a lone temple to Vulcan, whose survival of the conflagration was taken as a sign of divine intent. (When the city was rebuilt it was to this robust god that it was dedicated; Juno, its previous celestial patron, whose protective powers had been found wanting, was abandoned). Octavius went on from this victory (though not without more complicated political manoeuvrings) to proclaim himself the Emperor Augustus, and with this proclamation the Imperial Age began.

Under Augustus, Umbria continued to enjoy a period of prosperity that had begun with the opening of the Via Flaminia in 220 BC. The new road linked Rome to the Adriatic coast as well as to the cities of the north, and gave Umbria immense strategic importance. It superseded the Tiber as the focal point of the region and brought in its wake a massive increase in trade and prosperity. Colonies were built, either from scratch or on the sites of Umbrian and Etruscan settlements, land was drained and roads constructed and Umbria (called as such for the first time) became a unified and thriving province.

Early Christianity and the Barbarian invasions

The most important aspect of Umbria's history following the fall of Rome, and up to and including the darkness of the Barbarian invasions, was the growth of Christianity. The new religion spread quickly from the start, thanks mainly to Roman lines of communication, in particular the Via Flaminia, and by as early as the first century AD towns such as Spoleto and Foligno had already become bishoprics. Within another 200 years, helped by a new freedom of worship, most towns had substantial Christian communities. Because, however, religious practice increasingly adhered to the monastic pattern established in the eastern Mediterranean, it was in Umbria's remote countryside, rather than her cities, that Christianity eventually found its most enduring home. The first recorded monastery was founded at Monteluco, near Spoleto, by Julian, a Syrian from Antioch. From this small beginning and many others like it was born the extraordinary religious and monastic tradition in Umbria that was to culminate with St Francis and his Order 1000 years later.

St Benedict, by far the most significant of Umbria's early saints, was born in Norcia in AD 480, within a few years of the deposition of the last Roman Emperor, and at the very moment that the first Barbarian invaders from the north were turning greedy eyes towards Italy. The Order he founded, and the Rule he drew up to guide its members, were of incalculable importance in ensuring the survival of Western culture in the tumult that followed the fall of Rome. The Rule, especially, was crucial. It aimed to move men to a perfect love of God through a combination of prayer, study, and work. This last was vital, for it implied that though one had to leave the material world to reach God, one also had to serve it, enrich it, and leave a mark, however faint or humble, of one's presence in it. Not all monks were to exemplify these tenets as outstandingly as the Venerable Bede, say — some merely copied manuscripts, tilled the land, or repaired buildings — but during the hundreds of years of Barbarian invasions, Benedict's edict ensured that countless monks were quietly working, studying, and preserving aspects of learning that might otherwise have vanished for good.

Once the control and protection of Rome disappeared from Umbria, self-defence and self-sufficiency on the part of individual towns became impossible. As the Goths and Huns plundered the length and breadth of the country,

Palaeo-Christian San Salavatore (fifth century), Spoleto. (DL)

Column from Lombard Ducal Palace, Sant'Eufemia, Spoleto. (DL)

the region, because of its central position, once again became a battlefield, with cities and countryside alike succumbing to the consequences of plague, famine, and poverty. The only order in desperate times came from the clergy, who began to take over the civic functions no longer being carried out by the old Roman state. Bishops, such as Fortunato in Todi, or Ercolano (killed fighting Totila in Perugia), took it upon themselves to become generals, frequently instigating or inspiring resistance to the invaders. While on the face of things their achievements seemed negligible (virtually every Umbrian city was razed to the ground), they started to win increasing respect for themselves and the church they represented.

After the death of their leader, Totila, at Gualdo Tadino, the Goths were replaced by the Lombards, another Teutonic race from the north, who by 571 had established three separate principalities in Italy, the central one of which contained most of Umbria and had Spoleto as its capital. The Dukedom of Spoleto, as it became known, was to achieve great importance throughout central Italy, despite being cut off from the Lombard kingdom to the north (centred on Pavia — present-day Lombardy) by a narrow corridor of territory controlled by the Byzantines — a strange ribbon of land that started on the Adriatic and ran as far south as Rome, including the Umbrian towns of Narni, Amelia, Terni, and Perugia. This buffer-state remained a thorn in the Lombards' side for 300 years, though in Umbria it had the effect of guaranteeing the Dukedom of Spoleto, and the towns in its domain, considerable independence of action, a habit that in the coming years would be a hard one to break.

The new invaders, unlike their uncouth and less-sensitive predecessors, adopted the manners and customs of the local people, establishing an order which brought a short-lived increase in artistic and commercial initiative. Acknowledging the increasing growth of Christianity, they even built monasteries alongside those of the Benedictines; sadly very little evidence of these survives in Umbria, save the styles and techniques bequeathed by their builders to future generations of craftsmen.

In 754 the growing power of the Papacy as a force in Italian politics was illustrated by Pope Stephen III's direct appeal to the Franks to rid Italy of the Lombards once and for all. (Six years earlier he had interceded against the Lombards on behalf of the Perugians, whose semi-autonomous government in the Byzantine corridor had been threatened by the acquisitiveness of the Lombards.) The Franks took up the invitation, first under their king, Pepin the Short, and then under his more famous son, Charlemagne. By 800 Lombards and Byzantines alike had been driven out of the country.

Umbria between the Empire and the Papacy

The Papacy was by now well and truly established, and received great tracts of land from Charlemagne, who in return demanded that Pope Leo III crown him Emperor of the new Holy Roman Empire. Peace reigned while Charlemagne lived, but the harmony between Papacy and Empire, and the unity he had imposed on much of the West, disappeared within a few years of his death. The divisions amongst his successors, and their distant preoccupation in northern Europe, again left much of Italy prey to invasion and conflict. The Papacy was no healthier, weakened by the rival claims of powerful families; with no central authority, it was not long before the whole country reverted once more to virtual chaos.

The anarchy of the next few years provided just the opportunity and impetus that Umbria needed to go its own way, and set the tone of events for centuries to come. Many towns and old Roman centres, such as Arna and Carsulae, unsuited to the rigours of constant invasion and siege, were either abandoned or destroyed, to be replaced by fortified villas and castles, to which the region's hilly terrain was ideally suited. Around these developed independent and self-sufficient communities, and with them all the institutional and commercial structures of civic life, the larger becoming first the economic and then the administrative centres of the countryside around them. Thus was born the pattern of isolated, independent, and ambitious hill-towns, each with an eye to the power and territory of its neighbour, that was to be the basic feature of Umbria's historical development for most of the Middle Ages.

Throughout this whole period, Italy was the scene of a complicated, confused, and constantly shifting series of conflicts between the Empire and the Papacy. For the sake of simplicity, the Pope's party (and that of vested mercantile interests) is usually referred to as the Guelph faction, and that of the Emperors (and old feudal nobility) the Ghibelline, though in practice things were never quite this simple. If the Emperor was in the ascendant, and especially if he was in Italy with a large army, many supposedly Guelph towns often found it politic to change their allegiance (and vice versa if there were a stronge Pope). In addition to this there were the problems of corruption, of rival Popes, rival Emperors, anti-Popes, anti-Emperors, local factions, local feuds — all of which served the emerging Umbrian towns in a variety of ways: for example, amidst the unrest and constant jockeying for position between the super-powers of their day, they were able to take increasing control of their own affairs, simply by exacting new measures of independence from whoever ruled them at the time, in exchange for promises of loyalty and allegiance. But because the balance of power in Italy shifted fairly frequently, and alliances were fickle and short-lived, a promise made to an Emperor one year was easily revoked the next, should he be deposed or called back to Europe by more pressing problems at home. The greater autonomy he might have granted, however, the cities never willingly relinquished.

Against such a background, a powerful and often cynical pragmatism began to operate in Umbrian politics. Cities became fiercely self-regarding and concluded treaties with outsiders individually and with no regard for any unified Umbrian policy. Loyalty became a bargaining counter to be offered to the highest bidder, and the greater rivalry between the Pope and the Emperor simply an excuse for local rivalry and self-assertion. Thus, if Perugia 'sided' with the Papacy (as was usually the case), Assisi invariably sided with the Empire, the final end of all such manouevrings being power at the expense of one's nearest neighbour. The often dazzlingly complicated and short-lived treaties between cities against one another were concluded with precisely the same aim.

As the Middle Ages progressed, communications and commercial interest, and thus real power, began to move north to Tuscany. And yet the presence of a region with such Machiavellian attitudes, and so many well-fortified cities so close to Rome, should still have posed a serious threat to the interests of the Papacy. That it did not was the Umbrians' own fault. Although the cities made useful allies, and could never be ignored completely, they never seriously perturbed the Papacy. Quite simply, Umbria was always too preoccupied with bickering and one-upmanship to achieve the unity that might have made it a real force. Of all its cities (and not only had the large towns become independent communes, but some smaller ones too, such as Spello, Montefalco, Cascia, and Amelia) only one, Perugia, ever really come to merit attention on a 'national' scale.

It had become a free commune in 1139, owing its power and wealth to important trade links with Rome and Florence, and was soon the prime mover in any machinations that affected the region as a whole. But to ensure its continued prosperity and supremacy it was forced to fight off the challenges of other Umbrian cites, which had begun to appreciate that isolationism and constant war-like posturings were of no use when it came to trading. Unlike Perugia, the economic base of most Umbrian cities was agricultural, and, because of poor communications, confined to the countryside in their immediate vicinity. As a result their only option was to trade with each other, no easy matter when they spent much of their time at one another's throats. Excellent hilltop fortresses, as Umbria was increasingly to find to its cost, made far from perfect market-places.

Occasionally, however, Perugians and others alike were distracted from their internal squabbles by events taking place in the world at large. In 1152, for example, the uneasy truce between the Empire and the Papacy produced by the Concordat of Worms in 1122 was shattered by the election of a new and ambitious Emperor, to the imperial throne: Frederich Hohenstaufen. His determination to reassert the power of the Empire in Italy spelt doom for the Umbrian cities, who soon had cause to fear the man better known by his Italian nickname of 'Barbarossa'. As he marched south, some towns, such as Assisi, took his side, others such as Perugia, tried to stand up to him, but the majority (of which Spoleto was the most notable example) were partially or completely destroyed.

On the whole, his campaign was a success, but like Charlemagne before him, he was unable to ensure the survival of the authority and homogeny he had imposed on the Empire. Spurred on by the power vacuum that followed Barbarossa's death, Pope Innocent III set about exploiting the anti-imperialist feeling aroused in Italy by the ferocity of his campaigns, and to ally it with the collective guilt at the capture of Jerusalem by the infidel Saladin in 1187, hoping thereby to resurrect Papal fortunes. When he came to Umbria, however, he met with little success, cities such as Perugia and Spoleto (which had been quickly rebuilt with typical medieval industry) being quite happy to accept new measures of independence, but turning a blind eye when it come to accepting the Papal Government sent to administer them.

The medieval communes, noble families, and *condottieri*

In 1308, with the moving of the Papacy to Avignon, the outlook for the Church grew even more bleak. Europe remained divided in its support for rival Popes until 1417 (the so-called Great Schism). The power vacuum which resulted was the single most important factor in allowing the development of independent and 'democratic' communes in central Italy. At the same time, the influence of the older noble families was eclipsed by the emergence of a new mercantile class, brought to prominence by the increase and diversification of trade. It suffered neither Church nor Empire (both, in any case, too weak to assert themselves) but owed natural allegiance to the principles of self-government and civic autonomy. With the influx of new money and new men, secular building took place on an unprecedented scale, giving the rapidly expanding cities the appearances that they have largely retained to the present day. Liberal and sophisticated constitutions were drawn up to administer the new towns, of which Spoleto's at the end of the thirteenth century serves as a typical example.

Originally civic issues were decided by a show of hands in the *arringo*, a general assemby of all adult males convoked in the city's central piazza. By 1296, when a new constitution was drawn up, the size of the population made such an arrangement impracticable, and the role of the *arringo* (from which we derive our word 'harangue') was reduced to a body that could express opinions, but no longer take decisions; the latter function was taken over by a General Council elected from the 12 *vaite*, or parishes, that made up Spoleto's administrative districts. Final executive and judicial power lay with the *Podestà*, often a kind of troubleshooter elected for a year and brought in from outside the city — a measure designed to keep him at a distance from the town's affairs. As a further check on his powers he was answerable to the *Capitano del Popolo*, a type of senior policeman and appeals judge, also responsible for the day-to-day running of the administration. Below him were a host of minor officials, all of whom were elected, and in the manner of contemporary Italian bureaucracy, constrained by rigid and restrictive job specifications.

This, then, was the theory, but the practice was often rather different, and in some places, as time went by, very different indeed. First, cities spent so much time, if not fighting, then arguing with their neighbours, that their

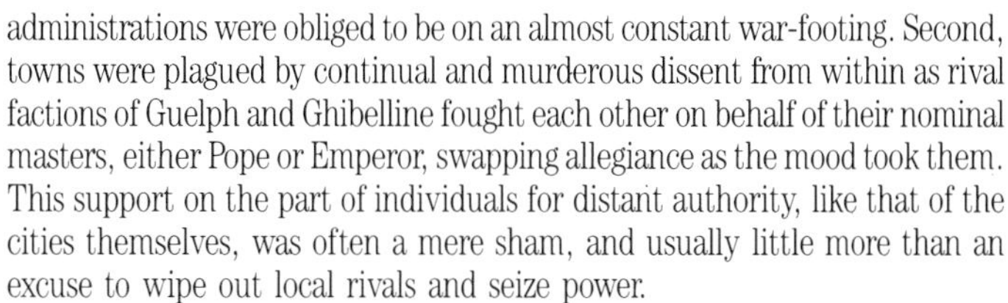

administrations were obliged to be on an almost constant war-footing. Second, towns were plagued by continual and murderous dissent from within as rival factions of Guelph and Ghibelline fought each other on behalf of their nominal masters, either Pope or Emperor, swapping allegiance as the mood took them. This support on the part of individuals for distant authority, like that of the cities themselves, was often a mere sham, and usually little more than an excuse to wipe out local rivals and seize power.

Against this background of almost unending crisis, administrations were expected to make the reforms and take the decisions to ensure the smooth running of the city. Not surprisingly they found it increasingly difficult to do so, and in the face of such unrest a city's democracy and independence were all too often compromised. Citizens soon came to realize that a strong executive was the only means to combat uncertainty and disorder, and began to accept the domination of a particularly forceful individual, usually the head of the strongest noble family of the moment, or the person who could muster the largest private army; in most cases this was one and the same man.

At about the same time, as if the towns did not have enough to contend with, other powerful individuals began to figure in Umbria's affairs: the *condottieri*, or itinerant private soldiers hired by cities to fight battles on behalf of their citizens. There was no shortage of mercenaries drifting around Europe at the end of the fourteenth century, most of them English or French refugees from the Hundred Years' War, or German and Swiss stragglers from the imperial armies. Some were astute enough to form themselves into efficient bands and soon found in Umbria a healthy market for their services.

By 1364, four main groups were operating in central Italy, among them the 'Great Company' of the German Duke Werner, and the notorious private army of Sir John Hawkwood, an Englishman whose name crops up with monotonous regularity in the chronicles of Orvieto, Perugia, and Cortona, one minute helping their citizens with a siege or two, the next terrorizing the same citizens on behalf of some neighbouring city.

Deals made with such men were never anything more than business arrangements, simple contracts of employment that at first sight appeared to suit all parties; only the poor unfortunates on the receiving end seemed to come out of things badly. The citizens avoided danger and the mercenaries got well paid to fight in their place — or not, as the case may be, for the truth was rather different. First, the *condottieri*, in line with their times, were nothing if not cynical. An historian of the time, Sismondi, observed that 'Horsemen who went into battle clad in steel were rarely killed or wounded so long as they kept their saddle. Once unhorsed they surrendered'. Surrender and defeat, however, were of very little consequence as they rarely involved dying. Self-preservation, expediency, and exploitation were the order of the day. Machiavelli, in his *Historie Fiorentine*, wrote that 'Combatants then engaged with little danger, being nearly all mounted, covered with armour and preserved from death when they chose to surrender. There was no need for risking their lives. While they continued to fight their armour protected them, when they could resist no longer, they surrendered and were safe.'

If, as very often happened, two groups of mercenaries had been hired to fight each other on behalf of rival towns (today in Italy this is known as football), they might reach a private agreement before the event, designed to make the occasion as harmless as possible for all concerned. Once fighting started, the battlefield was the scene of much sound and fury, but very little battle. Death, after all, would have been very bad for business. Machiavelli, again, gives a description of the battle of Anghiari, near San Sepolcro, in which only one man died, despite the fact that fighting 'raged' for more than four hours, 'and he not from wounds inflicted by hostile weapons or any honourable means, but who, having fallen from his horse, was trampled to death'. The only damage incurred on such occasions was financial, and when the dust had died down, it only remained for both sides to return to their respective patrons for a renegotiation of terms.

The cities were losers each way in such situations. They wasted money, property was destroyed and land plundered. Neighbours bound by alliance to be allies one year were enemies the next, and at any moment large and fickle bands of armed men could pay a surprise visit and wreak havoc. Added to this, cities had to contend with the everyday chaos produced by warring noble factions, whose disputes were often settled in scenes of bloodshed worthy of the best, or worst, Jacobean tragedy. And all going on year in year out, with no prospect of resolution or stability. Along with the normal range of calamities, such as plague and famine, which could strike the medieval world at any time, life in Umbria should have been intolerable.

But against this background of violence, in one of these puzzling paradoxes of history, the artistic and intellectual life of the region went from strength to strength. The same subtle changes being wrought throughout Northern Italy that were to culminate in the Renaissance, were also taking place in Umbria. Every branch of civilized life blossomed. In religion, St Francis almost single-handedly revitalized man's relations to the divine. In painting, Cimabue, Giotto, and their followers introduced a naturalism that left behind the stilted beauty of the Byzantines. In architecture, the Gothic, but more particularly the Romanesque, flourished as nowhere else in Italy. A university was founded in Perugia as early as 1308, and the first edition of Dante's *Divine Comedy* was printed not in Florence, but in Foligno. Craftsmen excelled in every sphere, particularly in wood and ceramics, and their fame spread far and wide. And all in a region that had become a byword for violence and degeneracy. On one side of a wall in Perugia, Perugino and Pintoricchio were painting soft-faced saints and Madonnas, while on the other the ruling Baglioni slaughtered each other, and the streets quite literally ran with blood. In Orvieto, the only slightly less notorious Monaldeschi funded the city's Duomo with one hand, and calmly but extravagantly massacred opponents with the other.

The Papacy and Risorgimento

Eventually and inevitably, however, the bitter in-fighting between cities left them exhausted and disenchanted. The Papacy, who, out of choice or necessity, had largely stood back from the centuries of bloody disorder, now seized the opportunity to exert its power once and for all. One by one the cities fell. Spoleto, in 1354, to the crusading Cardinal Albornoz; Foligno, in 1439, when the ruling Trinci family surrendered to soldiers of Pope Euginius IV; Spello, in 1535, after 150 years of despotic rule; and Gubbio in 1624, handed over to Urban VIII by the last of the ruling Montefeltro.

It was a familiar story, and one that was repeated all over central Italy. Nowhere did it have the same drama as in Perugia. Over the years the city had been ruled, if that is the right word, by soldiers of fortune, the Viscontis of Milan, the powerful and charismatic Braccio Fortebraccio, and, finally, and most outstandingly, by the infamous Baglioni. These last would have made perfect protagonists in a medieval soap opera, being the incarnation of intrigue, violence, tragedy, crazed ambition, duplicity, lust, and just about any other ignoble impulse one cares to imagine. With a sort of Machiavellian genius, however, they managed to retain control of the city for over 100 years — despite the fact that they spent most of their time devising new ways to kill one another. Their colourful reigns, rather sadly, came to an end in 1535 when Ridolphi Baglioni took his turn at the city's helm. He lacked, to a marked degree, the class and subtlety of his predecessors, and bungled what should have been a perfectly straightforward assassination of the Papal Legate. Unfortunately his lapse came at a time when the Papacy was both powerful and in fighting mood. Paul III despatched a large force to Perugia with orders to disband the Baglioni armies, and to destroy their palaces in and around the city. This they did with a vengeance, Ridolphi keeping well out of the way, and after one further ill-fated and half-hearted revolt, the family's reign was finally over. It only remained for Perugia to join the growing list of Umbrian towns that had become permanent fixtures in the Papal domain.

By 1650, the region could no longer be considered independent of anything. The old Priori and tattered civic administrations were replaced by Papal governors, and for two centuries before unification, Umbria slumbered under the quietly effective rule of the Church. With order restored, people left the security of the cities and ventured back to the newly stable countryside, but here they found that peace and Papal rule were no guarantee of prosperity. The isolation that had once served the region so well now began to tell against it, as successive governors ignored its many problems, and allowed its very existence to be forgotten. Absentee landlords (amongst whom the Papacy figured large) collected rents, but took little interest in drainage projects or land measurement, so that the condition of the soil deteriorated, and with it the agriculture on which Umbria depended. Such industry as existed was agriculture-based and so shared in its stagnation; it was, in any case, cut off from the prosperous markets to the north by poor communications. Even cultural life suffered from the narrow strictures of Papal rule. To any casual observer surveying the Umbrian scene at the end of the eighteenth century it would have seemed as if very little had changed in almost 500 years.

Matters improved somewhat in the upheaval that followed the French Revolution and the rule of Napoleon, when the French organized the region into two districts and tried to encourage and protect economic growth (though there was widespread plundering of art treasures by light-fingered French troops). In the more liberal atmosphere of the times, a new and more free-thinking and prosperous class of merchants emerged, which the return of Papal rule after Napoleon's death could do little to repress. By 1859, and the battle for the unification of Italy, this spirit found broader and more popular support, and Umbria, as caught up in the ideals of liberation as the rest of the country, welcomed Garibaldi's troops into Perugia on 11 September 1860.

Unfortunately, unification did not bring the life of wine and roses for which many had hoped. When trade barriers between the old regions were abolished, the Umbrian economy, always unstable, was subjected to the rigours of free competition — with which it was ill-equipped to deal. Traditional craft and agricultural industries crumbled in the face of new industrialization in the north. Next to nothing was brought in to replace them — a chemical works in Terni, a lignite mine near Spoleto, and an arms factory in Terni. Private wealth remained idle, or was invested in the north, while the state, conspicuous by its absence, failed to make the improvements to the region's infrastructure that might have halted the agricultural decline.

Umbria in the twentieth century

In the first years of the twentieth century, however, the Italian economy as a whole was on an upswing, and for a while things began to look up for Umbria as well. Light industry appeared in the region, most notably in the shape of the famous Perugina chocolate factory (now the massive Buitoni works) and the steel mills in Terni, but such a brief flicker of prosperity was too good to last; it came to an abrupt end when the small Banca di Perugia (which had been largely responsible for funding it) was swallowed by the Banca Commerciale, which preferred to invest in the more profitable and less risky ventures in the north.

Where the capital went, the people went too. Although in 1911, half the region's population could still neither read nor write, they did not need education to know that their future lay outside Umbria. Thousands upon thousands took the familiar route out of poverty and emigrated to America or the new factories of Turin and Germany, leaving a population at home who increasingly saw socialism as the answer to the region's ills. By 1919, Umbria's scattered left-wing parties commanded 48 per cent of the vote, and had established control of many local and regional councils. Hopes of reform however, were quickly dashed by the rise of Mussolini and the right. Even under Fascism

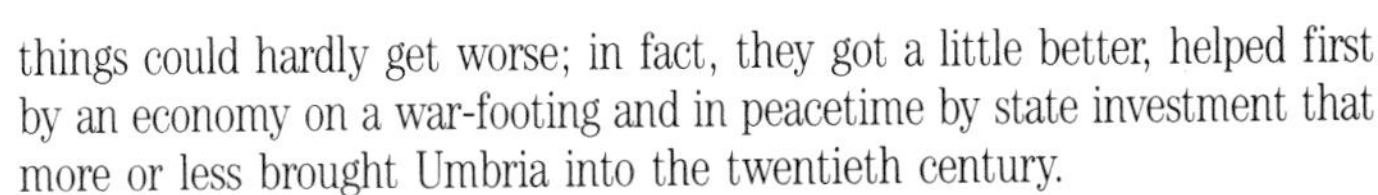

things could hardly get worse; in fact, they got a little better, helped first by an economy on a war-footing and in peacetime by state investment that more or less brought Umbria into the twentieth century.

Even so, for many it was still not enough, and post-war emigration rates were higher than ever. Only when central government devolved more power to the regions did Umbria, left to its own devices, begin to prosper. Political control by now was in the hands of the Communist Party, which carefully directed funds at co-operative ventures and projects appropriate to the region's special needs, with transport, agriculture, and latterly tourism, as the main priorities. Road and rail links, even now being improved, at last provided an economic lifeline to Rome and the north.

Finally, and perhaps most importantly, the last 20 years have seen the birth of what can only be described as new pride and youthful enthusiasm in Umbria. There is still poverty and there are still problems, but there is also a powerful sense of vigour and community, which seems determined to overcome them. It is a spirit that even the most casual visitor cannot fail to notice, manifestly obvious in the region's extraordinary range of cultural events, the diversity and skill of its craftspeople, the Umbrians' own obvious pride in their countryside and their heritage, and a host of more minor hints and signs that at last point to hope and progress being made after centuries of apathy and decline. And, it is worth adding, these are being made without sacrificing any of the strange, mystical, and contradictory qualities that thread their way through Umbria's long and frequently troubled history.

ART and ARTISTS

The Umbrian heritage

In art, as in much else, Umbria is overshadowed by neighbouring Tuscany — unfairly: she has one of the richest and most varied artistic heritages of any Italian region. Here, however, the treasures, unlike Tuscany's, which are largely concentrated in Florence, are scattered far and wide amongst hilltop towns and remote country villages. Far from being a drawback, this is one of the great pleasures of looking at Umbrian art. Rarely are paintings lost to view behind jostling crowds, and never do you have to suffer the jabbing elbows and wearing claustrophobia of the big museums. Instead, paintings and fresco cycles are ranged across Umbria's tranquil countryside, often resting in the buildings for which they were first painted: tucked away in the meditative calm of churches, lost in the intimate simplicity of Romanesque cathedrals, or hanging — usually quite haphazardly (and uncatalogued) — in the quiet of tiny provincial galleries.

The region boasts two of Italy's most famous fresco cycles: Giotto's *Life of St Francis* in Assisi, and Signorelli's *Last Judgement* in the Duomo at Orvieto (which, one should add, also has in Maitini's bas-reliefs some of the country's finest Romanesque sculptures). Giotto's frescoes adorn the great Basilica of St Francis, not only a shrine to Italy's patron saint, but also a monument to the best Italian artists of the thirteenth and fourteenth centuries — Cimabue, Pietro Cavellini, Giunto Pisano, Pietro and Ambrogio Lorenzetti, Simone Martini — as well as a host of unknowns.

There are also minor fresco cycles — those of Gozzoli in Montefalco, Ottaviano Nelli in Gubbio, Pintoricchio in Spello, Perugino in Perugia — the works of the Florentines — Fra Angelico, Ghirlandaio, Fra Lippo Lippi, Benozzo Gozzoli — and, of course, the Umbrians themselves. In the last case, Perugia's Galleria Nazionale is an ideal introduction to the region's schools and cross-currents, though their painters will become more familiar if you discover them for yourself, in the course of a more meandering artistic odyssey through Umbria's towns and villages.

The Umbrian school

The Umbrian school of painting started in the region's remote northern corner (in Gubbio) during the latter half of the thirteenth century, and culminated in the work of Perugino and his contemporaries in the second half of the fifteenth century. Its main themes were devotional, and its painters often servants of the church. For much of its 200-year history it fulfilled a traditional role, reiterating a pious and medieval view of life, long after the Florentines had ushered in the more challenging themes of the Renaissance. Initially influenced by the icons and stylized Madonnas of Byzantium, it also borrowed from the Sienese masters, Duccio and Martini, and in time, from the more forward-thinking Florentines themselves.

What it is that makes an Umbrian painting so characteristically 'Umbrian' can only be described as a sort of mystical impulse on the part of the artist; the paintings have an aura of gentleness and languid calm, with their soft, faded outlines and still, dream-like landscapes, their sense of faint, misty depth and utter delicacy, the placid beauty of their saints and Madonnas. In short, they reflect the qualities of Umbria itself.

Light and landscape

These still and melancholy qualities developed from the school's early Byzantine and Sienese roots. They also stemmed from an affinity between art and landscape peculiar to the region itself. The link shows itself in the pastoral hills and the soft translucent light that so often illuminates Umbrian paintings. Behind foregrounds of soft-faced saints and Madonnas lie backgrounds of calm, almost mystical, grace.

Mysticism is not a quality that readily yields to analysis, yet there is something otherworldly about the atmosphere of Umbria; it can be seen in the proliferation of saints, the strange edge to the light, the tone of its poetry, the extraordinary pale stillness of the countryside. Mysticism was a fact, or feeling, to which most Umbrian painters bore witness, whether because they were imbued with the quality from birth (like the saints?), or simply because they were painting what they saw. They capture, for want of a better term, the landscape's 'religious quality', the something extra that lies in the region's green and benign countryside, a certain abundance, or trick of the light, that points vividly to the hand of its Creator; the quality that St Francis perceived so acutely.

In drawing on the landscape, the Umbrians infused their paintings with its qualities, and more importantly, the reflective state of mind induced by these qualities. Simply put, what we see and feel in Umbria is very often what we see and feel in her art — radiance, harmony, tranquillity, and introspection. In Umbrian paintings, backgrounds become far more than mere settings for the religious drama of the foregrounds. They assume a spiritual and meditative dimension of their own, with subject (always religious) and setting fused into a single, devotional whole.

These refined qualities, which were to culminate in the sublimity of Raphael (a pupil of Perugino), evolved only gradually. For much of the thirteenth and fourteenth centuries, Umbrian art continued to develop along traditional lines. No single great artist appeared to alter its course (as Duccio had done with the Sienese). Even Giotto's powerful example at Assisi made little impression. Indigenous painters preferred to adhere to artists and traditions that more closely suited their own (Umbrian) temperaments. Thus numerous and isolated schools of painting developed, whose exponents looked to the mannered stillness of the Sienese, rather than to the new realism of Assisi. Happy for the most part to follow and adapt, they only slowly began to experiment with those strains that were to be come known as 'Umbrian' — a softening of outline, an air of calm introspection, the strange otherworldliness of the landscape.

Florence and the Church

In many ways the Umbrians were given few opportunities to develop. With no great patrons of the stature of the Medicis in Florence, they had to rely for their commissions on the Church, a body whose natural outlook was traditional and reactionary. Whilst such commissions could occasionally result in revolutionary work, as was the case in Assisi, they more usually required of artists merely a hackneyed treatment of themes already familiar and acceptable.

The more daring Florentines, by comparison, were in the vanguard of the Renaissance. Mostly painting for a small and artistically literate group of patrons, they were able to experiment with new ideas against the background of a blossoming and cosmopolitan city. The Umbrians, in the relative isolation of their provincial hill-cities, could not help but be less adventurous. If they were quieter and safer, however, they were also more in keeping with their times, and probably more in touch with the needs and sensibilities of their contemporaries. Their religious paintings, devout and ingenuous, would have been immediately comprehensible to peasants and nobility alike. Florence's new language of humanism, on the other hand, would probably have seemed alien to all but an educated few.

None the less, as time went by Umbria could hardly fail to be influenced by the Florentines who came to decorate its churches and civic palaces. Local artists inevitably made use of the creative and technical advances of such pioneers as Fra Angelico and Benozzo Gozzoli, at the same time clinging on to those qualities that were still demonstrably Umbrian. It was this moulding of two traditions that allowed artists such as Perugino and Piero della Francesca to forge their own highly individual styles. It also ensured that the creative flow between Florence and Perugia was not all one way. Umbria's greatest legacy to Italian art is the distinctive sense of light and depth — to be exemplified by Raphael — and with it the soft mystical blur, which seems everywhere to soften colour and outline.

The Umbrian painters

The Gubbians

The Umbrian school has its vague origins in the artist Odersi, or Oderigi (1240–99), of whom little is known except that he was a friend of Giotto, and worked mainly in Gubbio. Now only a handful of his miniatures survive, though to believe his contemporaries he was a prolific painter. Dante, for one, called him 'l'onor d'Agobbio', the pride of Gubbio, and stuck him in Purgatory

ladonna del Belvedere *by*)ttaviano Nelli, Santa Maria, Gubbio. (ISTO)

as punishment for an obsession with art that left him no time for anything else.

Odersi was followed by one of his pupils, Guido Palmerucci (1280-1345), who was also apprenticed to Sienese masters, hence the juxtaposition familiar in his and other paintings of the period — a still, Byzantine-tinged mysticism alongside the soft, golden beauty of the Sienese.

Palmerucci spawned many followers, amongst them Martino Nelli, a poor painter, but remembered as the father of **Ottaviano Nelli** (active 1400–44) in whose lovely, brightly coloured canvases the Umbrian school found its first master. He brought the so-called 'International Gothic' to Umbria, a refined, courtly style of painting that flourished throughout Europe at the turn of the fourteenth century. His paintings crop up in Foligno and Assisi, as well as Gubbio, intricate and glittering pieces, worked as if to resemble miniatures or illuminated letters.

With Nelli's death art in Gubbio declined (despite his many pupils), though by then numerous other minor schools had begun to spring up elsewhere. Amongst their most notable artists were Ugolino d'Ilario and Cola Petruccioli in Orvieto, Arcangelo di Cola and Antonio Alberti in Città di Castello, Bartolomeo di Tommaso in Foligno, and Giovanni di Corraduccio in Montefalco. All to a greater or lesser extent continued to paint in the established traditions of the Byzantines and the Sienese; a few, however, began to borrow from other central Italian painters, such as Crivelli and Gentile da Fabriano (1370–1427), the latter a leading and influential exponent of the 'International Gothic'.

By the middle of the fifteenth century Umbrian painting entered a new phase, as its isolated conservatism gave way to the growing influence of Florence. Three painters in particular were responsible for the broadening of its horizons: Fra Angelico, Fra Lippo Lippi, and Benozzo Gozzoli.

The Florentines

Fra Angelico (1387–1453) provided the perfect link between the respective artistic traditions of Umbria and Florence. Although he painted in the region only twice — in Orvieto cathedral (1447) and in Perugia's San Domenico (1437) — his influence was considerably greater than just two visits might suggest.

He was a member of the Dominican Order, which discouraged individual aspiration and sought, against the tide of Renaissance thought, to maintain the tradition of art in the service of the Church. His impulse, therefore, was to paint to the greater glory of God, much as the Umbrians had always done. Innovative and progressive, despite the stance of his Order, his grace and sweetness struck obvious chords in the region. He also brought with him a taste for radiant colour, a clear sense of space, and a more classically inspired concern for elegance. Perhaps most importantly he introduced a refined awareness of the naturalism pioneered by Giotto in Padua and Assisi, still to make an impression on the diffident Umbrians.

Although his paintings do not have quite the same intensity, **Fra Lippo Lippi** (1406–69) also had considerable influence. After being adopted by Carmelite monks as an orphaned 8-year-old, the painter had an extraordinary life (well-documented in Browning's famous poem), and though one of the most outstanding painters of his generation was, according to Vasari, 'a man who would stop at nothing to satisfy his desires'. More often than not the desires were of a carnal variety. Thus it was in the wake of sexual scandal rather than out of any sense of vocation, that he came to Spoleto to paint in the cathedral. (Lippo had forced his patron, Lorenzo di Medici, to send him south after compromising the reputation of a prominent Florentine's daughter.) It was as well for Umbria, which got a superb fresco cycle out of the painter's shame (*Life of the Virgin*). With it came a lesson in Lippi's careful and advanced composition, his use of decorative motifs and something of the bold, three-dimensional style pioneered by Masaccio (1401–28), amongst the most innovative of the early Florentines.

Benozzo Gozzoli (1421–97) was one of the less eminent Florentines to paint in Umbria, but amongst the most influential, mainly because of the sheer volume of work that he left dotted around its churches. His single greatest piece is the fresco cycle in Montefalco on the *Life of St Francis*, in its day a point of pilgrimage for all the region's up and coming artists. He was a pupil of Fra Angelico (whom he assisted in Orvieto), but never matched his divine intensity. None the less he shared the master's highly decorative style — greatly appealing to the Umbrians — and his apparent joy in the beauty and variety of the natural world. His work also displays a particularly strong sense of place. He seems to have been much at ease in Umbria's gracious landscape, finding

in it the perfect setting for his sunny vision of a mellow and untroubled world.

Early painters in Perugia

From about 1460, and with Florentine help, Umbrian painting began to blossom, and to develop an increasingly distinctive style of its own. Benedetto Bonfigli (1420–97) and Bartolomeo Caporali (1420–1503) were the first important artists to work in Perugia, which, with the rise of Perugino and Pintoricchio, was to become the crucible of painting in Umbria. The bulk of Bonfigli's works are still found in the city, including the fresco cycle on the life (and violent death) of St Ercolano, painted in what was once the chapel of the Palazzo dei Priori, but which is now part of the Galleria Nazionale of Umbria. Both he and Caporali are charming and pleasant enough painters, but still, however, largely concerned with the religious themes that had sustained the Umbrian school for two centuries. Despite the odd flicker of innovation (the use of Perugia as a background to supposedly New Testament scenes, for example) both still carry the 'Heavenly chill' that looks backwards to the conventions of Byzantine art. Passion and drama only occasionally break through in their *gonfaloni* (painted banners); otherwise all is restraint and stillness.

Nicolò Alunno

Nicolò da Foligno (1430–1502), or Nicolò Alunno (literally the 'pupil'), on the other hand, was a distinctive artist, whose depth and diversity made him the greatest of the purely Umbrian painters before Perugino. (His are amongst the most precious paintings in Rome's Vatican Museum.) He was probably the pupil of Carlo Crivelli (1435–95), a Venetian artist who worked for long periods in the Marche, and taught Alunno his use of bright colouring and particular sense of precision.

Like most Umbrian painters he has a profound sense of beauty. What sets him apart from his peers is his wider range of feeling, and his willingness to explore the grief *and* the joy in the stories of Christ and the Virgin. He demonstrates an intensity and passion, a darker strand to his character altogether, than, say, Bonfigli or Perugino. This certain bite is most apparent in his backgrounds, which forgo Umbria's dulcet pastorialism for the bleaker and more savage countryside around Gubbio and Foligno. Bernard Berenson described him as 'the first painter in whom the emotional, now passionate and violent, now mystic and ecstatic temperament of St Francis' countrymen was revealed'.

Fiorenzo di Lorenzo

Very little is known of Lorenzo's life (1440–1525) — he may have been a pupil of Bonfigli — and very little of his work survives either inside or outside Umbria. What there is points to a marvellous painter who seems constantly to strive towards new ideas. He casts off the Byzantine stillness of the earlier Umbrians, and bursts with a vitality that communicates the new Renaissance sense of joy and beauty in the earthly life. Naturalistic detail there is aplenty, often in the form of languid youths who loll around his paintings, quite irrelevant to any allegorical or documentary purpose. Everything in his paintings shines: his skies with Perugino's luminous sense of space, his landscapes with the sunniness of Gozzoli.

Piero della Francesca

Whether Piero (1416–92) is an Umbrian is a moot point (he was born in San Sepolcro, on the northern border with Tuscany). In any event he was one of the most important artists to have worked in central Italy during the fifteenth century. (Only recently has his reputation become established. During his own lifetime he was less well regarded, and died, almost blind, in relative obscurity.) He assimilated the new intellectual vigour and innovations of the early Florentines (Veneziano, Masaccio, and Uccello), merging them with his own preoccupation with perspective and the mathematics of composition. This produced strange, sometimes unsettling pictures, which managed to be both dramatic and deliberate at the same time. From his concern for composition evolved a new context for light and space within a painting.

Previously the drama and detail of the foreground had carried almost the full weight of an artist's intention. While Florentine art had developed the compositional possibilities of height and breadth, it had yet to come to terms with depth. To Piero della Francesca and the later Umbrians goes credit for making the eloquence of background space an integral part of a painting's cumulative effect. In reproducing their landscape's misty horizons they automatically evoked an airy sense of perspective. The result was to give the foreground saints and Madonnas an otherworldliness that in isolation they might have lacked. Thus to the cold art of composition, and the new problems of space, they brought the softening, purely Umbrian qualities that were to be the region's chief legacy.

Perugino

Perugino, the adopted name of Pietro di Cristoforo Vannucci, was the greatest of the Umbrian artists, and, with the exception of his pupil, Raphael, the finest painter of these effects in Italy. He was born in Città della Pieve in 1445. Though poor, his family was well placed, and it was decided to educate him as an artist. (The apprenticeship started when he was just 8 years old.) 'He was a child', said Vasari, 'who had been reared in penury and want, and was given as a shop drudge to a painter who was not particularly distinguished in his calling, but held the art in great veneration, and highly honoured the men who excelled therein.'

The 'not particularly distinguished' painter was probably Bonfigli. Other early influences must have been Fiorenzo di Lorenzo, Luca Signorelli, and Piero della Francesca (then working on his masterpiece, the *Story of the True Cross* in Arezzo). Soon advised to train in Florence, he studied alongside Leonardo da Vinci in the workshop of Andrea Verrachio. Here he endured a poverty so acute that Vasari said he had to sleep in a box because he could not afford a bed, and 'knew no other pleasure but that of exhausting himself in the practice of art'.

During 10 years spent in the city his output was prolific, and though he quickly learnt the forms and techniques of the Florentines, his art retained much that belonged to his native Perugia. By 1480 his reputation was such

rugino *(self-portrait), Collegio* *l Cambio, Perugia*. (JD)

that he was invited to paint in the Sistine Chapel. He transformed its entire east wall into a small piece of Umbria, filling it with the gentle melancholy figures tht crop up again and again in his work. (Michelangelo was forced to destroy most of these narrative scenes in 1535 and today only one of Perugino's original three panels remains, *The Giving of the Keys to St Peter.*)

The peak of Perugino's career spanned the years 1480 to 1502, during which time he completely dominated Umbrian painting. In 1500 he executed his greatest work in the region, a fresco cycle commissioned by the Bankers' Guild of Perugia for their Collegio di Cambio. This was probably the first occasion on which he was assisted by his young pupil Raphael, and, ironically, the moment that his own career began to wane.

Perugino paid the price of his own fame (which was considerable: contemporaries spoke of him in the same breath as Leonardo and Michelangelo). It was impossible for one man to produce all that was demanded of him. In old age he increasingly put his name to second-rate copies, or to works that had been executed almost entirely by pupils. Having found success, he was accused of repeating a popular formula, and of somehow 'manufacturing' religious paintings without real personal conviction. The spontaneity of his best work vanished. What in earlier compositions had been profound and innovative, came to seem stilted and insincere. Vasari claimed with horror that he was, if not an atheist, then an agnostic, 'a man of little or no religion, who could never bring himself to believe in the immortality of the soul'.

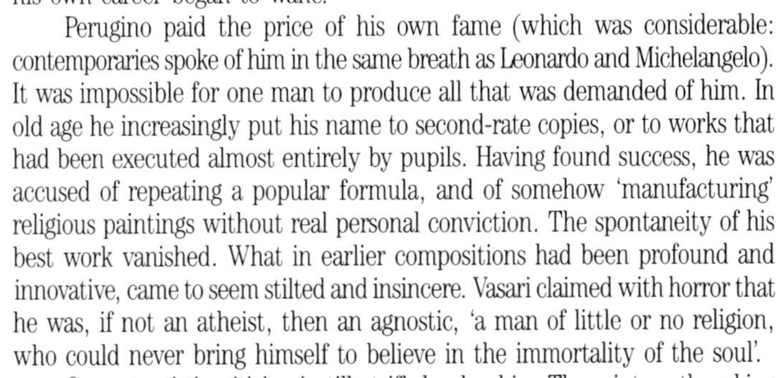

Current artistic criticism is still a trifle hard on him. The point worth making is that while lacking the unimpeachable inner faith of a Fra Angelico, the power of Perugino's technique and his artistic imagination enabled him to *evoke* both religious feeling and conviction. He does become sentimental at times, and does lack passion and movement; his compositions *can* appear static; he does, like most other Umbrian painters, steer clear of the real world; yet he is still amongst the finest and most influential of the Renaissance painters, the catalyst for Raphael, and mentor for a host of Umbrian artists, major and minor.

Pintoricchio

Perugino's most outstanding peer was born Bernardino di Betto (1454–1513), more commonly known as Pintoricchio, and more cruelly as *il sordicchio* (the little deaf one) after Vasari's comment that he was 'deaf,

Nativity *by Pintoricchio, Santa Maria Maggiore, Spello.* (DL)

small and not much to look at'. He was taught by and collaborated with Perugino, and also associated with Fiorenzo di Lorenzo and Eusebio di San Giorgio (another pupil of Perugino). For some reason he has remained in the second rank of Italian painters, and has never been acknowledged as having achieved the greatness that his earlier talents had promised. And yet he is found in all the right places: in Siena's Piccolomini Library, in numerous churches dotted

around Rome, and in the Sistine Chapel, where he painted two panels whilst still in his 20s. (And of course there is the masterpiece in Spello's Santa Maria Maggiore.)

Because he shares a vision of a pretty, untroubled world, he is sometimes known as the Umbrian Gozzoli, and, like the Florentine, revels in any subject that gives him the opportunity to be decorative or ornamental. His landscapes are always full of birds and animals, and bright with intricately woven patterns of wild flowers. His women are invariably pretty (like those of Fiorenzo di Lorenzo), and rarely anything but beautifully dressed (rather like those of Bonfigli). As a result his paintings are some of the loveliest to look at. If they have a fault, it is perhaps that the wealth of ornament and surface detail suggests a lack of deeper feeling.

Minor Umbrian painters

All Umbrian painters in the late fifteenth and early sixteenth centuries were influenced to a greater or lesser extent by Perugino. Even artists older than him, such as B. Caporali and Fiorenzo di Lorenzo, came under his spell. Around Spoleto (where generally he was less well known) his most inspired follower was Lo Spagna (1450–1528), a painter possibly of Spanish origin (hence the name), but based for much of his life in Umbria. Like many of his contemporaries he also came under the influence of Raphael, who spent at least five of his formative years (1499–1504) working in Città di Castello. (A dozen or so of his major works once in the region are now scattered around the world's museums; only two remain in Umbria.)

Around Assisi Perugino's leading protégés were Francesco Melanzio, a painter of beautiful landscapes (and also a pupil of Alunno); Andrea d'Assisi (a mysterious figure known as L'Ingegno — the genius); Tiberio d'Assisi, Sinibaldo Ibi, and Pier Antonio Mezzastris (1457–1506), also tutored by Gozzoli (and a painter of delicate, dreamlike canvases). Eusebio da San Giorgio features more around Perugia, and frequently collaborated with both Perugino and Pintoricchio, though his works are impressive in their own right.

Later painters, though they still owed something to Perugino, were more obviously captivated by Raphael, and it is debatable whether they can actually be called members of the Umbrian school. The best known are Giovanni Caporali, Dono Doni (taught by Lo Spagna), Domenico Alfani, and Giannicola di Paolo (1460–1544).

Luca Signorelli

The singular figure of Signorelli (1441–1523) stands alone in the canon of Italian painting. Born in the ancient town of Cortona, a few miles north-west of Umbria, his artistic allegiance was never firmly pledged to any of the schools or traditions with which he was brought up. Not being Umbrian, Sienese, or Florentine, his comfortable social position allowed him an artistic freedom now always available to his contemporaries. (Much of his long life was spent in the public service of his home town, where he held positions in the General Council and in the Palazzo dei Priori.)

He worked all over central Italy, but is remembered most for his

Cappella San Brizio *(detail) by Signorelli, Duomo, Orvieto.* (ISTO)

extraordinary fresco cycle in Orvieto cathedral (*The Last Judgement*), painted in 1499 when he was 58. Vasari pointed out (and was not the last to do so) the enormous debt Michelangelo's frescoes in the Sistine Chapel (1536–41) owed to the singular treatment Signorelli had brought to the same apocalyptic theme.

His early influences were Perugino, Piero della Francesca, and possibly Donatello, for his main preoccupation was with the human form (as one look at the cathedral's writhing mass of bodies makes clear). Vasari's reverential account of Signorelli (the artist was one of his teachers) claims that 'he showed the true mode of depicting the nude form, and proved that it can be made, although not without consummate art and much difficulty, to appear as does the actual life'. Whilst leaving few of the formal possibilities of the nude unexplored, the frescoes are not simply exercises in draughtsmanship and technical vigour, but powerful works of bizarre invention, the product of an oddly unique and capricious imagination.

The art of fresco painting

From the fourteenth century onwards the most important type of wall painting in Italy, and the one that is found at Assisi and elsewhere in Umbria, is known as *buon fresco*. Frescoes are so familiar a feature of Italian churches that it is easy to take them for granted, but how were they actually painted?

At the heart of the process are a chemical reaction and the drying and fixing qualities of plaster (a mixture of lime, fine sand, and water). As plaster dries on a surface, carbon dioxide is absorbed from the air, converting the lime (calcium hydroxide) to calcium carbonate. This crystallizes around the sand particles, binding them to the wall to be painted. If powdered pigments are mixed with water and applied to the wet plaster, then the carbonization process also fixes the particles of pigment to those of the plaster. In this way a durable surface is created in which the pigment is permanently fixed and resistant to further action by water. Only subsequent crumbling of the plaster, or chemical deterioration of the pigment itself, can then affect the colours of the fresco. (As has happened in the case of Cimabue's frescoes at Assisi, where the original white lead pigments have oxidized and turned black.)

The layers of plaster, or 'ground', were applied in various stages. The first was a rough and quite thick base layer called the *arriccio*, which comprised one part lime to three parts sand. On to this the artist drew a full-scale sketch of the composition in red ochre, and incised lines in the plaster to indicate the picture's main outlines. This sketch is known as the *sinopia* after the red pigment used in the drawing. Some of these original plans have been discovered and left exposed in the Basilica at Assisi.

The artist or his helpers then added a thin layer of plaster, or *intonaco*, to the *arriccio* — but only so much as could be painted in a single day. This obscured part of the *sinopia*, which was redrawn in *verdaccio*, a mixture of lime and black pigment. The surface was then ready to be painted.

Artists had to work quickly, and know exactly the final effect that was desired. Once the plaster was dry there was no room for correction or improvisation. Mistakes could only be altered by removing the day's *intonaco* and repeating the whole process. The range of colours available to painters was initially limited. Only natural pigments were considered suitable, and these complicated the artist's task by drying lighter than the painted colour. The blending of colours was also difficult, making depth of tone hard to achieve. Final effects, therefore, were sometimes achieved by hatching, or through the use of base coats. Any parts of the fresco that were to represent flesh, for example, were given an undercoat of *terra verde*, a green earth pigment, while the skin tone itself was achieved with *cinabrese*, a red pigment composed of *sinopia* and lime-white. Certain pigment colours could not be applied wet, and were painted on to dry plaster using tempera (where egg yolk is used to fix the pigment). Colours added in this way, however, were far less durable than those added to wet plaster; Vasari considered the whole process a 'vile practice'.

As frescoes became more complicated, realistic cartoons were increasingly used as aids to composition. They were transferred to the wall by a variety of methods. Their outlines could be scratched on to the wet plaster, or enlarged from a small drawing on to a wall squared up for the purpose. Alternatively, small holes were made on a full-sized cartoon along the lines of the drawing. Charcoal was dusted through them on to the wall behind.

Gonfaloni

Gonfaloni are painted flags or standards. They have their earliest origins in the *laboro*, a banner painted with the sign of the cross which first appeared during the battles of Constantine (the first Christian Emperor) in the fourth century. The religious revival of the thirteenth century, and a renewed interest in the power of saints, marked their widespread appearance throughout central Italy. Towns and villages began to adopt local saints, invoking their protection against the ills of war, disease, and famine. (Perhaps because of the medieval imagination's need for tangible aids to devotion — a need borne out by the proliferation of holy relics.) Accordingly the images of saints began to take the place of the cross, which by this time had also been adopted by the Crusaders. Eventually a picture of the town or village in question was added to that of the saint. Banners were paraded from church to church on feast days, or when some particular calamity was at hand. Initially, at least, they were the sole reserve of religion.

The thirteenth century, however, was also a period during which the stature and autonomy of Umbria's city states were on the increase. As lay administrations became more powerful, they sought to surround their civic ceremonies with the weight and dignity of church ritual. One way they could do this was to commission *gonfaloni* to be used in exclusively civic processions. When banners were not actually being paraded, they were left to hang in the public palaces as tangible reminders of civic authority. Eventually members of the nobility and the emerging tradesmen's guilds adopted the idea. All parties went to the top artists of the day, the only way to be sure of getting a *gonfalone* commensurate with their own importance.

The basic iconography of the standards varies very little. Usually the figure of Christ, or the Virgin Mary, stands with an open cloak over a picture of the town and groups of its citizens, Saints and angels occupy the space to the side of the Madonna, or hover above the townspeople. Occasionally, as further entreaty, a cluster of angels flutters alongside holding a prayer of supplication. Within the basic scheme, however, there is great variety of treatment, and often considerable artistic merit. (Though many banners, of course, have suffered the effects of time and wear.)

Gonfaloni by Bonfigli can be seen in Perugia, where he probably had a workshop given over to their production and repair. The best examples are in the church of Santa Maria Nuova, and in the Galleria Nazionale of Umbria, which also has a banner by Perugino. Perugia's San Domenico boasts a *gonfalone* by Giannicola di Paolo, commissioned in 1494 in response to a new and particularly virulent epidemic. A *gonfalone* painted by Raphael when he was 17 survives in the art gallery at Città di Castello. The church of Santa Maria Maggiore at Bettona has two banners, one by Perugino, the other by Nicolò Alunno. Bartolomeo Caporali left a *gonfalone* in the small village of Montone near Umbértide; Terni's gallery houses another by Lo Spagna.

PERUGIA

General Information

TOURIST INFORMATION: Corso Vannucci 94/a. Tel. 23327 Located past the Standa supermarket towards Piazza Italia. Small additional office during the summer at the FS station (Tel. 71660)

POPULATION: 130,000

HEIGHT: 493 m

POST OFFICE. Piazza Matteotti

TELEPHONES: SIP Office, Corso Cavour 24. Also Via Marconi 21

STD CODE: 075

POLICE: Questura, Piazza dei Partigiani. Emergencies: Tel. 113

CTGS: Student Information – Accommodation Office, Via del Roscetto 21. Tel. 61695

DISTANCE TO:
Gubbio 40 km Assisi 27 km
Todi 45 km Spoleto 66 km

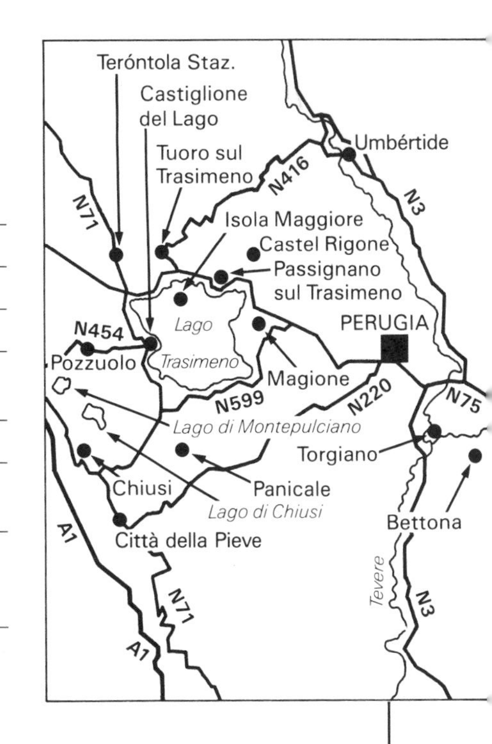

Getting Around

Whatever your approach the main object is to reach Piazza Italia. After that everything is within walking distance. Car drivers should leave vehicles in one of the peripheral car-parks (see below). Roads are busy and poorly signposted, and much of the centre is closed to traffic. Buses (26, 27, 29, 32–6) run from the FS station to the centre (either Piazza Italia or Piazza Matteotti). Tickets are valid for any number of journeys within a 40- or 70-minute time limit. They are available from the booth or small machine in front of the FS station.

Trains

Frequent trains on the state (FS) network to Assisi (25 minutes) and Foligno (for Spoleto, Terni, Rome, Ancona). Also to Terόntola (40 minutes) for Florence (2 hours 30 minutes), Arezzo, Castiglione del Lago, Chiusi (change for Siena), Orvieto, and Rome. Occasional through-trains to Rome and Florence. Connections on private FCU line: (south) to Deruta, Todi, and Terni; (north) to Città di Castello and San Sepolcro. The two lines have separate stations; the FS is at Piazza Vittorio Veneto (Tel. 71660) and the FCU at Sant'Anna on Viale Roma (Tel. 29121). Both lines share the station at Ponte San Giovanni, 8 kilometres east of the city (bus from Piazza Italia).

Buses

The main bus terminal is in Piazza Partigiani, linked to Piazza Italia by strange subterranean escalators (*scala mobile*). Serves most Umbrian destinations, plus Rome, Florence, and Urbino. Local buses leave from Piazza Italia, where there is a board showing all times and destinations.

Parking

Parking in the city centre is a virtual impossibility. Follows signs on the approaches to peripheral car-parks and then walk or take an escalator. Best bets are Piazza Partigiani, Piazza Piccinino, and Piazza Pellini.

Centrally placed, and the hub of Umbrian communications, the provincial capital, Perugia, is likely to be your first taste of the region. However any lesser symbol for its hill-towns and pastoral countryside would be hard to find. For all its popularity and convenience — and the undoubted charm of its medieval centre (which has two days of essential sight-seeing) — the city is a modern horror of service industries, sprawling suburbs, ring roads, factories, and general chaos. Distant prospects and approaches are bleak and unpromising — like a Victorian biscuit factory says one guide. (Foodstuffs — Buitoni pasta and Perugini chocolate — are actually the chief commercial concerns.) Because of this Perugia may well be somewhere you want to visit from elsewhere. (Spoleto is probably the most pleasing overall base.) If you can arrange to stay in the centre, however, much can be overlooked. (You should have no accommodation problems.) The advantages of staying in Perugia are its variety, numerous cultural events, and the usual big-city attractions (though shopping, surprisingly, is poor).

History

Perugia has been dominant in Umbrian affairs since the sixth century BC, thanks to its towering position and command of central Italy's major communication routes. It rose to prominence under the Etruscans comparatively late (fourth century BC), but soon became a member of their 12-strong federation of cities. The Romans arrived in 295 BC, but they largely left the inhabitants to their own devices. The scant records for the period suggest several centuries of quiet prosperity (broken only by Augustus' dramatic attack in 40 BC).

Like most of Umbria, it was a prey to the Barbarian invasions, and in 547 it was destroyed by Totila after a siege reputed to have lasted seven years. Gothic domination, however, was shortlived. Lombard rule in 592 brought Perugia under the control of the Spoletan Duchy, one of the few times the city relinquished tacit control in the region.

The first mention of Perugia's being an independent commune — it was a Papal–Guelph vassal from the time of Charlemagne — comes in 1140.

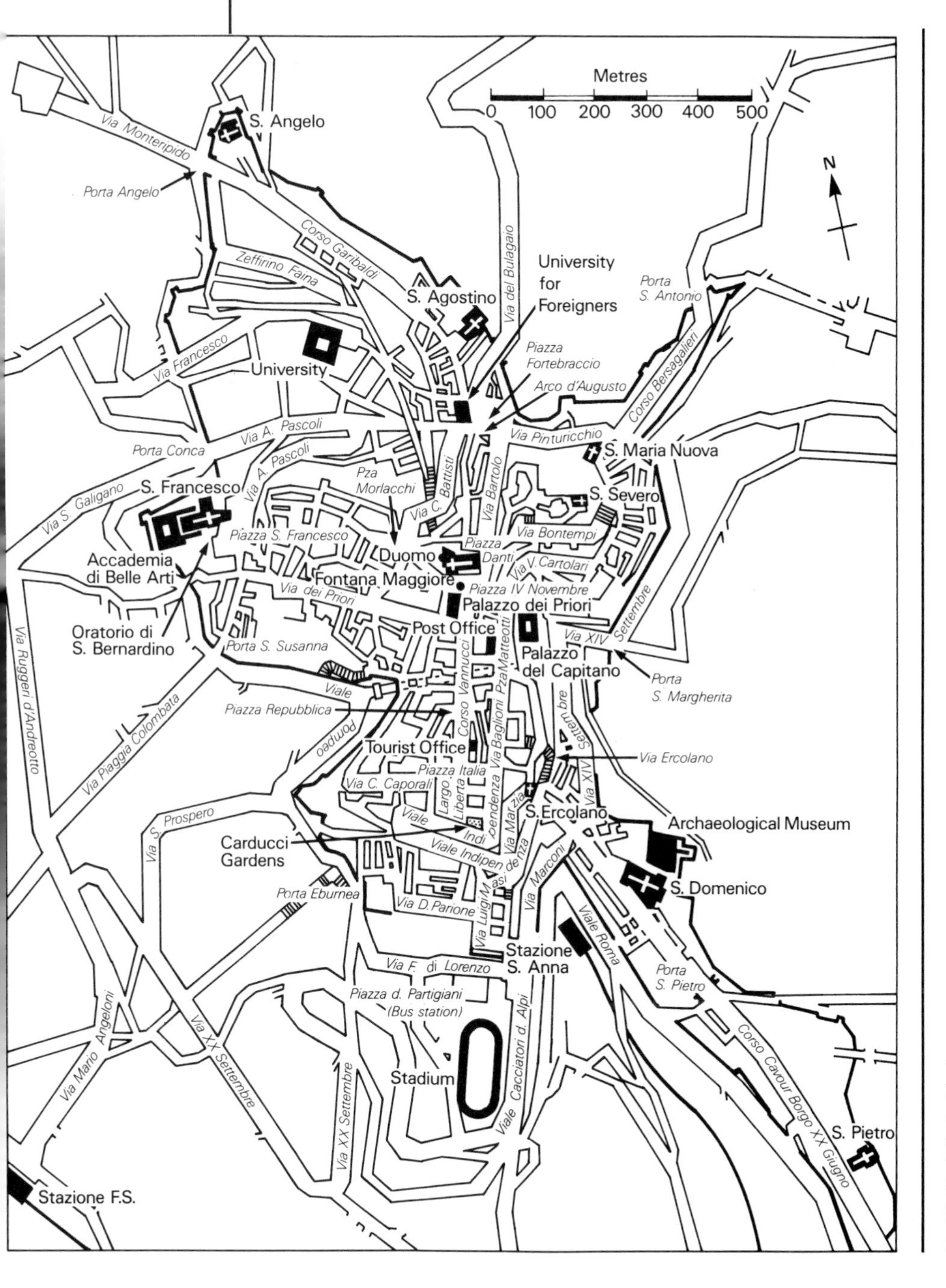
Metres
0 100 200 300 400 500
N
S. Angelo
Via Monteripido
Porta Angelo
Corso Garibaldi
Zeffirino Faina
S. Agostino
Via del Bulagaio
University for Foreigners
Porta S. Antonio
Via Francesco
University
Piazza Fortebraccio
Arco d'Augusto
Corso Bersaglieri
Via A. Pascoli
Porta Conca
Via Pinturicchio
S. Maria Nuova
Via A. Pascoli
Pza Morlacchi
Via C. Battisti
Via Bartolo
S. Severo
Via S. Galigano
S. Francesco
Piazza S. Francesco
Via Bontempi
Piazza Danti
Duomo
Via V. Cartolari
Accademia di Belle Arti
Fontana Maggiore
Via dei Priori
Piazza IV Novembre
Palazzo dei Priori
Oratorio di S. Bernardino
Post Office
Via XIV Settembre
Porta S. Susanna
Pza Matteotti
Palazzo del Capitano
Porta S. Margherita
Via Ruggeri d'Andreotto
Viale Pompeo
Piazza Repubblica
Corso Vannucci
Via Baglioni
Via Piaggia Colombata
Tourist Office
Via XIV Settembre
Via Ercolano
Piazza Italia
Via C. Caporali
Largo Libertà
Viale Indipendenza
Via Marzia
S. Ercolano
Archaeological Museum
Via S. Prospero
Carducci Gardens
Viale Indipendenza
Via Marconi
S. Domenico
Porta Eburnea
Via D. Parione
Via Luigi Masi
Viale Roma
Stazione S. Anna
Via F. di Lorenzo
Porta S. Pietro
Piazza d. Partigiani (Bus station)
Via Mario Angeloni
Via XX Settembre
Corso Cavour Borgo XX Giugno
Stadium
Via XX Settembre
Viale Cacciatori d. Alpi
S. Pietro
Stazione F.S.

Thereafter it rose to prominence through unremitting aggression, and dozens of shifting, Machiavellian alliances. The zenith of its influence came with the defeat of Siena in 1358. Decadence followed, with Perugia going the violent way of most surrounding towns. 'Democracy', so-called, gave way to involved and bloodcurdling disputes between noble families, each clan accumulating in their 'despotic individuality', says J.A. Symonds, 'the privileges previously acquired by centuries of consuls, *Podestàs* and captains of the people'. It was an age, reported one chronicler, 'when perfect pandemonium reigned in and about the city'.

The Papacy, to all intents and purposes, was powerless. When Cardinal Albornoz bore the keys of his subdued cities to Urban V — after Papal exile in Avignon — those of Perugia, according to legend, were the only ones left behind.

The stricken city turned to the *condottiere* to arbitrate in its affairs. Leading soldier of fortune was the popular Biordo Michelotti (1393), who lasted five years before being stabbed to death by jealous conspirators. Visconti, the Duke of Milan, tried his hand, but was removed by the plague in 1402. The most famous of all, Braccio Fortebraccio (literally 'strongarm') arrived in 1416. He cut through Perugian politics with the sword, driven by an ambition that extended to the domination of all Italy. The eight years of rule before his death brought a measure of rare unity.

Obviously an extraordinary and swashbuckling figure, he alone seems to have had the measure of the Perugians ('the most warlike of the Italians', wrote Sigismondi, a people 'who always preferred Mars to the Muse'). Braccio was a hater of idleness, of 'i consummatori della piazza' — the wearers out of pavements — and reintroduced a game that had been unique to Perugia since Roman times. In the Battle of the Stones two teams fought for control of a square, the *campo di battaglia*. Combatants padded themselves with deer hair as protection, and dressed in beaked helmets to resemble birds. The object was to kill or maim the opposition by showering them with rocks. Children were encouraged to join in for the first two hours to promote 'application and aggression'.

With Braccio gone there began the bloodiest and most colourful period of Perugia's history — the infighting of the Oddi and Baglioni nobility — 70 years of soap opera and Italian *Morte D'Arthur*. There were mass slayings, desperately involved vendettas, incestuous marriages, lions kept as pets, hearts torn out of bodies (and then eaten), sisters who looked like angels of Paradise, couples slaughtered on their wedding night. The 100 murders following one betrayal resulted in the bloodied cathedral being washed down with wine and reconsecrated. Another Baglioni, Malatesta IV, entrusted with the defence of Florence in 1530, simply sold the city to the enemy (Pope Clement VII), earning from the Doge of Venice the title of the 'world's greatest traitor'.

In the end the family simply ran out of members. When the surviving and lacklustre Ridolpho murdered the Papal legate (1535), a bellicose Pope Paul III sent in the troops, razing the Baglioni palaces, and burying them under the Rocca Paolina, a huge fortress that guaranteed Church supremacy for the next three centuries.

With Italy's struggle for unification in 1859 Pope Pius IX dispatched the Swiss Guard to quell Perugia, which it did with a ferocity and carnage still remembered in local folklore. A year later the city was liberated by the *bersaglieri*, the pick of Garibaldi's Republican troops.

What to see

Corso Vannucci

A first glance at a map of Perugia shows a frighteningly complicated street pattern. In fact, almost everything you will want to see is on or near the central Corso Vannucci, named after the painter Pietro Vannucci (better known by his nickname of Perugino). A broad pedestrian thoroughfare, it bisects the city's medieval heart, and, but for a brief lull in the afternoon, is constantly crowded with a babbling and excited throng. Like some slick, cosmopolitan cat-walk, Corso Vannucci is one of Italy's finest spots for watching the world go by, a perfect stage for the ritual of the evening *passegiata*. Probably the best place to survey the goings on is from one of several bars along the way. Nicest by far is the small Pasticceria Sandri, easily missed at No. 32. It is an

ontana Maggiore, Piazza IV Novembre. (JD)

atmospheric wood-panelled hideaway, with gleaming brass, red-coated waiters, and frescoed ceilings, and is not, despite appearances, expensive. Café del Cambio opposite at No. 29 is trendier — all marble, glass, and mirrors — but preferable to Ferrari up the road, which is washed out and expensive. (Though the upstairs lounge is not too bad.)

Duomo

The climax of the Corso is the big Piazza IV Novembre, a glorious medieval antidote to the nineteenth-century Piazza Italia at the other end of the street. (4 November 1918 was the date of the Italian armistice with the Austrians.) Tourists gather here on the cathedral steps, and it is where most of the town's voyeurism and social action takes place. It was once the site of a Roman reservoir.

Facade

There has been a church on the site since the ninth century. The present cathedral was started in 1345 — at least that is when the foundation stone was laid. Virtually nothing else happened for another 100 years. It was eventually completed in 1490, though the Gothic facade remains unfinished. The bronze statue to the left of the (side-) entrance is of Pope Julius III (sixteenth century). The pulpit to the left was built specially for the roving San Bernardino of Siena. From here he urged the Perugians to burn their books and fine clothes (and the women their wigs), all of which they did, though they did not stop killing each other. Four arches to the left of the steps comprise the over-praised Loggia di Fortebraccio, all that is left of the *condottiere*'s house, built in 1423 and destroyed in the sixteenth century.

Interior

The spacious interior is warm and graceful, but dull, a disappointment after a promising exterior. Seventeenth-century Perugia was rich enough and willing enough to indulge in baroque renovations, and many local churches — including the Duomo — were sacrificed to the dubious taste of the day. It has only recently been reopened after damage suffered in the 1983 earthquake — one or two of the pinkish octagonal columns are still very much askew. Large, pleasing, and dappled in soft light, the church is nevertheless low on works of art. The most famous possession is the Virgin's 'wedding ring', a one-inch piece of white onyx that is meant to change colour according to the character of the person wearing it. Originally held in Chiusi, it was 'piously stolen' in 1473, and has since resided behind the wrought-ironwork of the Cappella del Sant'Anello (first chapel, left-hand nave). The Perugians keep it locked up inside 15 boxes, the keys of each held by separate people (for 'security' reasons). They come together on 30 July, the only time the ring is brought out for public edification.

Elsewhere look out for the *Madonna delle Grazie* by Giannicola di Paolo (third pillar in the right-hand nave). An appealing work (except for the Virgin's silly crown), it is covered in votive offerings, tinselly testaments to its supposedly 'miraculous' powers. Mothers still bring their newly baptized children to kneel before it. The rear right-hand chapel contains an impressive work by Baraccio, the *Deposition* (1569). (Apparently much admired by Rubens, and painted under the effects of poison administered by a jealous rival.) The third chapel on the right-hand side has a pleasing carved arch, spoilt only by a very grim nineteenth-century fresco below. On the left of the church, embedded in the wall, are some easily missed fragments of an old altar by Agostino di Duccio (1473). To their left (fourth arch) is a lovely painting by Berto di Giovanni (1526). (Notice the view of Perugia in the background.) The work in the lunette above is by Giannicola di Paolo. The choir, as ever, is excellent.

Also in the Duomo are the urns of two Popes who came to grief in Perugia. One, Martin IV, died after gorging on eels; the other, Urban IV, was poisoned with *arquetta*, a particularly unpleasant medieval potion made from smearing arsenic into pig fat and distilling the mess that oozed out. Pisano built a magnificent tomb for Martin, later ransacked by Mommaggiore for his fortress at Porta Sole (see below). The two pulpits beside the altar are reputedly made from its fragments.

Museo Capitolare

As so often, the cathedral museum contains more of interest than the cathedral itself. The entrance is via the cloisters, reached through the sacristry (right transept). (Five medieval Popes were elected in conclaves held in these cloisters.) Highlights are a *Pietà* by B. Caporali (1486) and a *Madonna and Saints* by Signorelli, one of the painter's earliest and most important works. There is also a *Madonna and Saints* by Meo Guido da Siena, plus manuscripts and miniatures from the sixth to the thirteenth century — Perugia was renowned throughout Italy for her miniaturists. Additionally there are several lesser Umbrian paintings (schools of Perugino, Lo Spagna, etc.). On coming out of the Duomo you might want to explore the streets to its left, particularly the Via delle Volte, all high arches and medieval vaults. It was once part of the Palazzo del Podestà, burnt down in 1543.

Fontana Maggiore

This Gothic fountain (1277), one of the loveliest and most graceful in Italy, has a serenity that contrasts with the bloodshed that must have gone on around it. It was designed by the Sylvestrian monk, Fra Bevignate (who supervised early work on Orvieto cathedral), and sculpted by Nicola and Giovanni Pisano, possibly with the help of Arnolfo di Cambio.

Water supply in this highest of hill-cities was always a problem. In 1254 an obscure wandering monk, Frate Plenario, conceived the then rather outrageous idea of bringing water by aqueduct from Monte Pacciano (3 kilometres away). When built, neither materials nor design were up to the concept, and his causeway quickly fell into ruin. However, a stronger version was constructed in 1274, and the fountain commissioned to receive its waters. Sophisticated holding reservoirs were created at the end of the thirteenth century.

There were strict laws regarding its use. The historian Bonazzi says it was 'the subject of grave solicitude . . . beasts, barrels, unwashed pots and unclean hands were forbidden the use of the water, and indeed it was guarded with such jealous care that it seemed as though the people of Perugia had built their fountain for the sake of beauty only'.

The outstanding bas-reliefs are detailed and complicated, though badly faded in places. The **Lower Basin** has eight groups of three compartments, each individual compartment divided into two, making 48 pictures in all. (From the side facing the Duomo they are: Adam and Eve; Expulsion from Paradise; Samson (2); Allegory of the Lion and Dog (2); David (2); Romulus and Remus; the Wolf of Rome and Twins; Vestal Virgin (holding a cage, symbol of virginity); Aesop's Fables — the Crane and the Wolf, and the Wolf and the Lamb; 24 panels showing the months of the year and agricultural work appropriate to each; Guelph lion; Perugian griffin; 7 panels describing the liberal arts — Grammar, Dialectic, Rhetoric, Arithmetic, Geometry, Music, Astronomy, and Philosophy. The **Upper Basin** consists of 24 statues, starting with Salome and the head of John the Baptist facing the Duomo. Then follow mainly saints, with Moses, Solomon, and David, and a nymph of Trasimeno thrown in. Atop everything are three bronze nymphs by Giovanni Pisano in 1272. One mark of the fountain's harmonious subtlety is the lack of correspondence between the two basins. The upper and lower panels never quite match, inviting you to walk round the sculptures, your eye searching for a point of repose that never comes.

Palazzo dei Priori

Dominating the Corso, and rightly celebrated as one of Italy's most beautiful public buildings, the Palazzo is a huge, rambling, and somewhat gaunt affair, owing much of its effect to harmonious medieval surroundings and some fairy-tale refinements: stairways, balconies, mullioned windows, and castle-like crenellations (from which criminals were thrown summarily to their deaths). Started in 1293 (probably to a design by Fra Bevignate), it was built piecemeal over some 130 years; hence the curving line of its wall along the Corso. Dozens of churches and houses came down during the early stages, and as with the Duomo, much use was made of ransacked materials. Nearby Bettona, for example, sacrificed many of its Roman and Etruscan marbles.

Sala dei Notari

Open 9–13, 15–18.
Admission free.

Started in 1297, this is one of the palace's earliest and most appealing parts,

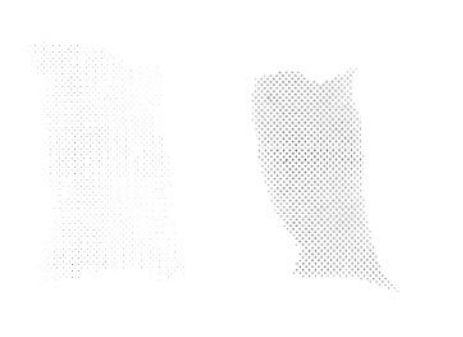

erugian Griffin and Guelph ion. (JD)

a large council chamber bought by the city's lawyers as a meeting place in 1583. Orientation around the palace's various components can be confusing. The Sala is a large single hall above the fan-shaped steps that spill out on to the piazza (opposite the Duomo). Above the doorway are bronze figures of the Guelph lion and the Perugian griffin — once thought Roman, but actually the first pieces of large-scale casting in medieval Italy (1274). The chains are from the gallows and gates of Siena, snatched during a raid on that city in 1358.

Inside, lavish frescoes (1297) cover every available space — impressive enough, but striking more for their decorative than artistic effect. They are the work of the important Rome-based painter Cavellini (or his followers), who also painted in the Upper Church in Assisi. Amongst his tales from the Old and New Testaments are interspersed the heraldic arms of Perugia's successive *Capitani del Popolo*. They were added until 1499.

Sala del Collegio della Mercanzia

Open 9–12.30, 15–18; Sunday 9–12.30.
Closed Monday.

Entrance to this single room is via a small door on the Corso frontage of the palace (after the main door). Every surface is covered with a magnificent display of intricately carved and inlaid wood. It all dates from the beginning of the fifteenth century, and was commissioned as a meeting place for the Merchants' Guild.

Collegio del Cambio

Open 1 March–31 October 9–12.30, 14.30–17.30; 1 November–27 February 8–14.
Closed Monday.
Admission price also allows entry to the Sala del Collegio della Mercanzia.

The entrance is via another of the palace's side-doors, a few metres down from the above. The Collegio is undoubtedly one of Perugia's main sights,

The Nativity *by Perugino, Collegio del Cambio.* (ISTO)

a single hall built between 1452 and 1457, and used by members of the city's medieval exchange. Its walls contain a series of superb **frescoes by Perugino**, executed at the height of his powers, and considered by many to be his masterpiece.

He was offered the commission in 1496, a time when he was also considering a contract to paint in the Duomo at Orvieto. The subject was given to him in advance. Members of the Bankers' Guild, wanting the best of all things for their rooms, consulted a leading humanist scholar, Francesco Maturanzio, who proposed the curious mixture of pagan and Christian elements. The idea was to suggest that human perfectibility was attainable through Christ's example, that there was unity in variety, and that a harmony resulted from the fusing of Christian feeling with ancient culture. The work took Perugino until 1500, during which time he was assisted by pupils, including, it is thought, Raphael.

The figures are melancholy, idealized, and beautiful, as they always are in Perugino; only a scowling self-portrait on the left-hand wall detracts from the mellowness of mood. The ceiling vaults contain the leading gods of the classical world: Apollo on his chariot in the centre; Saturn, Jupiter, and Mars above the rear wall; Mercury, Venus, and Diana towards the window. On the walls (moving right from the window) is the lone figure of Cato (symbol of wisdom), above him Prudence and Justice, below him Greeks and Romans, including Socrates and Trajan. All is backed by limpid Umbrian countryside. Then comes Perugino's self-portrait, followed by Strength and Temperance, with Greek figures below. The end-wall contains the Transfiguration and the Nativity (both damaged by smoke from the room's former oil-lamps). The right-hand wall shows God amongst the angels, with sybils above and men below (Isaac, Moses, Daniel — possibly a portrait of Raphael — David, Jeremiah, and Solomon).

The smaller adjoining chapel to the right, also striking, is frescoed by Giannicola di Paolo (1515–18), a pupil of Perugino, but influenced by Raphael and Andrea del Sarto.

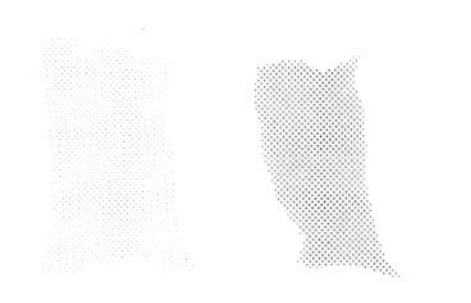

Galleria Nazionale dell'Umbria

Open 9–14; Sunday 9–13.
Closed Monday.
Admission charge.

Reached through the magnificent main doorway on the Corso and located on the Palazzo's fourth floor. Take the lift or stairs to the right of the vaulted stone entrance hall. (Nobles used to ride their horses up these stairs.) The intermediate floors are given over to council business.

One of the biggest galleries in central Italy, it boasts 33 rooms of Umbrian painting — a perfect summary and history of the school, though you may suffer a surfeit of saints, altarpieces, and chubby-legged cherubs. The presentation is rather bleak, and the admission charge high, but these aside it still forms an essential part of any itinerary. Room VII alone is worth the visit for the sublime masterpieces of Fra Angelico and Piero della Francesca, the highlights of this or any other gallery.

It is impossible to list the many hundreds of works, and it is unlikely that you would want, or be able, to take them all in. Numbers are found above the various rooms, which proceed in a clockwise and chronological order. The earliest (bear to the left in the large opening hallway) are some of the best, with a large *Crucifixion* by the Maestro di San Francesco, Sienese pieces (Duccio, Meo da Siena, Bartolo di Fredi, Taddeo di Bartolo), and sculptures by Arnolfo di Cambio and Pisano (removed from the Fontana during restoration in 1949). Room VI is outstanding, with works by Gentile da Fabriano and Ottaviano Nelli. After Boccati in Room VIII things begin to go awry (with the exception of some works by Bonfigli), picking up again in Rooms XI and XIII (Caporali and Fiorenzo di Lorenzo) and XIV–XVIII, those given over to Perugino and Pintoricchio (the subject, be warned, of frequent reordering and restoration).

Subsequent rooms contain works by followers of these painters, most notably Eusebio di San Giorgio and the occasionally impressive Sinabaldo Ibi. Room XX has a marvellous ceiling, which surprisingly turns out to be a late-nineteenth-century work. Room XXIII, too, is out of the ordinary. Until incorporation into the Galleria, it was once the Palazzo's chapel, and preserves original and rather good frescoes by Bonfigli. They form an account of Perugia's patron saint, Ercolano, and are especially interesting for the detailed picture they give of the city in the fifteenth century — all towers, walls, and monuments, most now long vanished. In the remaining rooms and corridors, paintings largely give way to *objets d'art* — gold, silver, and ivory assortments, ceramics, and suchlike — many very lovely. By this point, however, your attention may well be flagging.

Via dei Priori

Via dei Priori, a perfect little medieval street, strikes off the Corso to the left of the Palazzo dei Priori. Attractive in itself, it also leads steeply and conveniently to one or two of Perugia's better monuments, and — if you wish — makes up the first part of a coherent walk around the city. (Note that logical itineraries are difficult to follow, given Perugia's many hills and its maze of streets.)

The first right turn, Via della Gabbia, used to house dungeons and a large cage in which criminals were hung to be reviled by passing pedestrians. Not even the clergy escaped its clutches: in 1442 the unfortunate priest Angelo di Ferolo was 'once again put in the cage at mid-day and it was very cold and there was much snow, and he remained there 'til the first day of February both night and day and that same day he was brought out dead'.

The first of several minor churches on the street, fourteenth-century **Sant'Agata**, is worth a quick peek for faded frescoes (the story of San Severus on the left-hand wall) and the fragment of a notable Umbrian *Crucifixion* behind the main altar. Baroque San Filippo Neri further down on the right is of little interest. To its left runs Via della Cupa, leading to Via Deliziosa, with Perugino's house thought to have been at No. 17. The unmistakable tower is the Torre degli Sciri (46 metres), one of the few to have survived Perugia's medieval squabbles. The city was reputed — probably without too much exaggeration — to have had 700 such look-outs. One of the largest was on the Duomo, destroyed in 1375, and rather fancifully believed to have stood for 3500 years. The church of Santi Stefano e Valentino on the right is rarely open; it is a quiet, musty place, its flowers haphazardly arranged, the occasional fresco on its medieval walls.

After just two or three minutes the road bends right at Piazzetta della **Madonna della Luce**, passing a tiny church which gives the quaint little piazza its name. Look inside the chapel for an impressive and incongruous altarpiece by Tiberio d'Assisi, *Madonna and child with St Francis and St Ludovico*. The ceiling is by G.B. Caporali. The church is so called (Madonna of the Light) because on 12 September 1513, a young barber named Fallerio swore so colourfully on losing at cards that a Madonna in a wayside shrine closed her eyes in horror — and kept them closed for four days. The miracle caused celebrations, processions, and the building of a new church. To its left stands the Etruscan arch, Arco di San Luca, gateway to the ancient road to Lake Trasimeno.

Oratorio di San Bernardino

Via dei Priori then opens out on to a pleasant patch of grass, where you can share a five-minute sit-down with students from the Arts Academy behind. (The Academy offers summer courses in painting and sculpture; details from the tourist office.) This is also the spot to admire the finest piece of sculpture in Perugia, Agostino di Duccio's vivid **facade** to the Oratorio di San Bernardino. It was built by the city's magistrates in gratitude for the saint's efforts to bring peace to their habitually warring townspeople. Duccio decorated the facade from 1457 to 1461 with an odd, almost Art Deco touch, producing an early Renaissance mixture of bas-relief, sculpture, and brightly coloured marbles.

In the tabernacles on either side are depicted Gabriel and the Annunciation. Below are the saints Ercolano and Costanzo. In the lunette Bernardino ascends to Heaven, whilst in the architrave above the doorways, in delicately finished panels, are five miraculous episodes from his life. Inside the (rarely open) oratory is a fourth-century Christian sarcophagus, used from 1260 (when it was found in the church next door) as the coffin of Egidio, an early and important follower of St Francis.

The church in question is **San Francesco al Prato** (1230), once vast but now long ruined by years of landslips and neglect. An early church of its type (built four years after Francis's death) it repeats the single-naved pattern of Santa Chiara and the Upper Church in Assisi. Most of the interior has collapsed, though the facade has been reconstructed from a plan of the original, making a strange but evocative patchwork of style and sculpture. *Al prato* means 'in the field' and refers to the Franciscan habit of preaching out of doors; in this case on the quadrangle of grass that still survives.

Arco d'Augusto

From the Oratorio the straightforward but dull walk along Via A. Pascoli to Piazza Fortebraccio is an ideal way to see a secluded part of the city. The best part is where the road passes under Perugia's famous raised walkway, Via del Aquadotto, a much-photographed medieval link from Via Battisti to the north of the town. The grim buildings hereabouts are part of the state university.

treet scene. (JD)

On reaching the piazza, the eighteenth-century Palazzo Gallenga (at No. 4) houses the famous **University for Foreigners** (Università Italiana per Stranieri). Mussolini set it up in 1926 to promote Italian culture overseas, and it survives today, drawing thousands of students from all over the world — one of the reasons for Perugia's cosmopolitan, if occasionally hectic, atmosphere. The bar is friendly (obviously a good place for contacts) and the foyer usually has details of English-language films, as well as lists of the city's numerous plays and concerts. The Information Desk (left off the foyer) gives details of the myriad courses available, but is sometimes not too informative. (Open April–December.)

The Arco d'Augusto (or Arco Etrusco) looms unequivocally over the piazza, the towers and lower half Etruscan (second–third century BC) — it was then the main gateway to the city — and the upper part added by Augustus after his sack of Perugia in 40 BC. (Inside the arch you can still make out his new name for the colony: Augusta Perusia.) A sixteenth-century loggia tops the whole thing off.

Sant'Agostino

Pass under the Arco d'Augusto and there is a good (but steep) walk back to the Duomo. Take Corso Garibaldi in the opposite direction and two minutes brings you to the thirteenth-century church of Sant'Agostino. In the Middle Ages this part of town had a reputation for being inhabited by the most violent and dissolute of Perugians. Any discontent and revolt usually originated here. While the church's facade is pleasing enough, the interior is partially and badly converted baroque, a terracotta pavement and odd patches of fresco the only reminders of what must once have been a lovely, airy building. Sad signs dotted around tell of the paintings that used to reside in the church — Peruginos and Raphaels, spirited away to France by Napoleonic troops, now replaced by the most horrendously inappropriate 'modern' art imaginable. All, however, is not lost. The inlaid choir (1502), possibly carved from a drawing by Perugino, is wonderful (it took 30 years to complete) and there are two good frescoes immediately to the left of the nave on entering: a *Crucifixion* by Pellino di Vannuccio (1387) and a late-sixteenth-century *Nativity*. The first chapel on the right has an altarpiece by Giannicola di Paolo.

Next door on the right lies the **Oratorio della Confraternità di Sant'Agostino**. If closed enquire in the sacristry of the church. Its main appeal is a riotous ceiling of gilt, plaster, and general froth, showing just how far the baroque style could be taken. Confraternities were rather like religious guilds, and had their origins in the Flagellants, another Order in which Perugia — along with Provence — took an early lead. The movement dates from about the middle of the thirteenth century. Its advocates took to abnegation, excessive privation, and hearty scourging as expiation for the sins of the world. The age's rash of death, disease, and famine they took as signs of an offended deity; theirs, they thought, was the way of appeasement. Other behaviour designed to please included clanging human bones together, dressing up in white sheets, and taking to the streets wailing dirges on moonlit nights. Confraternities had similar aims, but were generally calmer. With their works of mercy and aid to criminals they operated more as medieval charities.

Sant'Angelo

In a tranquil, leafy spot at the end of Corso Garibaldi, Sant'Angelo was originally a fifth-century church, almost certainly built on the site of a circular pagan

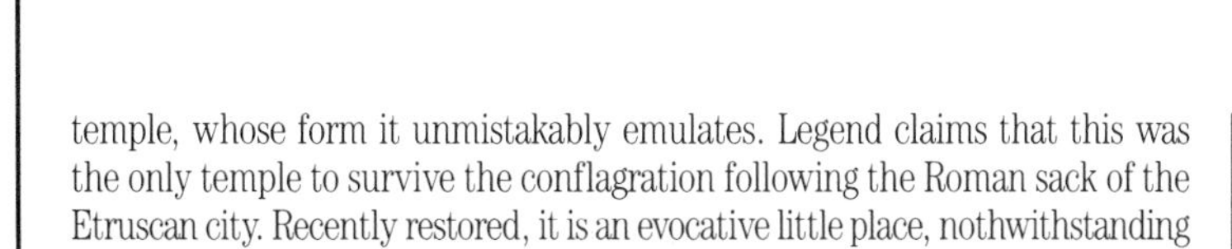

temple, whose form it unmistakably emulates. Legend claims that this was the only temple to survive the conflagration following the Roman sack of the Etruscan city. Recently restored, it is an evocative little place, nothwithstanding its uncertain history and distance from the city centre.

Inside, the two rings of columns probably survive from the earlier building. Each pillar of the inner ring is made of a different stone. (Look out for a whitish-grey marble known as *cipollino* — little onion — so named because of its veined, greenish markings.) A third ring of columns was removed by the Benedictines to build the church of San Pietro (see below). Its only notable work of art is a very early and faded Umbrian (Sienese?) fresco, *La Madonna del Verde*.

Convento di Sant'Agnese

This fourteenth-century convent, a little further up Corso Garibaldi, is worth a look given that you have already walked this far. Ring the bell and a nun (a Poor Clare) will take you to the chapel and a fine work by Perugino (the *Madonna delle Grazie*, painted in 1522, a couple of years before his death). Two nuns pray to either side of the Virgin: they are cousins of the painter, and both sisters at the convent. (There were about 50 convents in Perugia during the sixteenth century.) Across a courtyard and a garden of old-world flowers lies a chapel with another fresco, *San Sebastiane* by Eusebio di San Giorgio (1519).

Porta San Angelo

A short way beyond the convent, Corso Garibaldi ends in this striking gateway in the city's old medieval wall. It was rebuilt in 1326 by Lorenzo Maitini, leading architect of the Duomo in Orvieto. Just outside to the left is the small Gothic church of San Matteo. It is notable for some early frescoes, thirteenth-century works on the rear wall, which show the influence of Torriti, one of the important Roman artists to have painted in the Basilica at Assisi. Lesser Umbro-Sienese pieces adorn the side walls.

Crucifixion *(thirteenth century)*, Galleria *Nazionale*. (ISTO)

South Perugia

The nineteenth-century Piazza Italia forms the starting-point for a second, reasonably self-contained, walk around the rest of Perugia's monuments. Most of what you will want to see is on the Corso Cavour, a narrow and frenetic road that in summer can become wearing and claustrophobic. Start in the **Carducci Gardens** behind the piazza, small but well kept, and usually home to dozens of romantically intertwined couples. The panorama here is superb — Henry James called Perugia 'the little city of the infinite views'. Too often, however, much of the prospect is lost in haze.

Porta Marzia and the Rocca Paolina

Beneath the piazza — and literally supporting it — are the remains of Pope Paul III's huge fortress, the Rocca Paolina, built in 1540 to keep Perugia in check, and enthusiastically pulled down by her citizens in 1848. 'Few buildings', wrote Trollope, 'have been laden with a heavier amount of long-accumulated popular hatred than this.' The demolition — of what must have been an astounding construction — went on for 30 years.

Four hundred houses and ten churches had been razed to accommodate the Rocca, though the architect, Sangallo, managed to incorporate the second–third-century BC Porta Marzia — or at least its arch — as part of his defensive scheme. (He had to move it 4 metres, stone by stone, to do so.) The three statues above are probably Roman divinities, though popular legend has it that they are a Perugian family who died from eating poisonous mushrooms.

Through a door in the gate you can enter the subterranean **Via Baglioni**, an evocative collection of medieval houses preserved when the Rocca was built over them. *Open 8–14. Closed Monday*. Drop down from the side of Piazza Italia on Via Marzia, the site of an open market on Tuesday and Saturday mornings, or from Via Oberdan on the steep Via Ercolano.

Sant'Ercolano

A strange, octagonal church, rarely open (it has been adopted as a war memorial), built on the site where Bishop Ercolano, helping to defend the city, was decapitated by Totila. (See Bonfigli's frescoes in the Galleria Nazionale.) When the townspeople came to claim the body, his head had miraculously reattached itself. (This is one reason why he is Perugia's patron saint.) His annual *festa* has two processions. In the first, the saint's statue sports a wooden head, in the second he graduates to silver. (One old Perugian proverb aptly describes the city's credo as the three Ps: *Processione, Persecuzione, Protezione*). A liar in Perugia is said to be like the two-faced St Ercolano.

San Domenico

Midway down Corso Cavour proper, Umbria's largest church San Domenico, rises on the left, a vast, somehow derelict, building of warm orange stone. Grass grows from between cracks in the mortar, there are birds nests in odd places; the effect is rather appealing in a forlorn sort of way.

Inside there is no such charm, just a cold, cavernous warehouse of space and mud-coloured paint. It was started in 1305, from a drawing by Giovanni Pisano, fell down in the sixteenth century, was rebuilt, fell down again, and was eventually left unfinished, the money and enthusiasm presumably spent. Surprisingly, however, there are one or two quite exceptional works of art hidden in the dull gloom. The first, in the fourth chapel on the right, is an unusual carved archway by Agostino di Duccio (1459), only mildly spoilt by some chintzy nineteenth-century frescoes and a cheap, doll-like Madonna.

The undoubted highlight, in a chapel to the right of the main altar, is the **tomb of Pope Benedict XI** (1324), the greatest Gothic sculpture of its kind in Italy, and about the only thing that Benedict left to posterity. He ruled for eight months, was the last Pope before Papal exile to Avignon, and died in Perugia after eating poisoned figs. The work's sculptor is unknown. Tradition attributes the piece to Giovanni Pisano, but Maitini or followers of Arnolfo may also have been involved. It is interesting to note that the tomb made use of precious Roman marbles removed from Gualdo Tadino. Some of these are missing, picked out by Napoleonic troops when a regiment and its horses were quartered in the church. (The naves are 122 metres long.)

Other chapels to either side of the altar contain substantial early frescoes, hints as to how beautiful the church must once have been. They are votive paintings, commissioned by private individuals as thanksgiving offerings. The choir (1470–98) is notable, like many in Perugia; this one, however, is a trifle gloomy. The organ looks as if it has come straight out of a cinema pit. There is an interesting *gonfalone* by Giannicola di Paolo (1494) in the third chapel on the left. The stained-glass window — a welcome splash of colour — is the second largest in Italy. Only those in Milan cathedral are bigger.

Museo Archeologico Nazionale dell'Umbria

Open 9–14; Sunday 9–13.
Closed Monday.
Admission charge.

Unmissably located in the cloisters of San Domenico, immediately to the left of the church. (Take the stairs to the upper tier.) It is an extensive and important museum, and has an interesting prehistoric section, but it is mainly given over to the Romans and Etruscans. The eight rooms of the former collect finds from all over central Italy. The exhibits — tools, weapons, jewellery — are initially displayed chronologically; from Room V onwards they are arranged according to their place of discovery. In the Etruscan and Roman collection proper (miscellaneous urns and suchlike line the cloisters and corridors) look out for a *stele*, or headstone, in Room I, decorated with two warriors (sixth century BC); the sixth-century BC sarcophagus in Room II; the small bronzes and statues of Room III, (some of the most important such remains in existence);

the so-called *cippo Perugino* outside Room VI containing one of the longest inscriptions in Etruscan. Finally, it is worth looking at at least some of the countless vases and assorted ceramics.

Continuing up Corso Cavour you pass through a double-arched **Porta San Pietro**, apparently a wonderfully preserved Roman gateway, but in fact a superb piece of work started by an unknown architect in 1147 and (almost) finished by Arnolfo di Cambio 30 years later.

San Pietro

This is by far the most fascinating and idiosyncratic of Perugia's churches, and a visit here is highly recommended. Identified from afar by its pointed campanile, the entrance is somewhat hidden in a group of buildings belonging to the university's agricultural department. The doorway is actually in the far left-hand corner of the first courtyard off Borgo XX Giugno.

The interior is one of the most beautiful (and tastefully) decorated churches you could hope to find — sumptuous, even by Catholic standards, but with a spiritual rather than a showy air. Started in 926 by the Benedictine abbot of the city, it was built over an Etruscan temple and on the site of Perugia's first cathedral. Despite the weight of (mainly High Renaissance) artifice added since, it still preserves its original basilica form, and with it a sense of harmony free of mere size and splendour for its own sake. The abbot was a friend of Emperor Otto III, who shared a common expectation of the imminent end of the world. He provided money for the church as a sort of insurance policy for his soul.

The number of treasures is overwhelming, though it is a case of the whole being greater than the sum of the parts. The number of real masterpieces is actually very small. That so much survives is due to events at the time of the unification of Italy. When rampaging Papal troops entered Perugia in 1859, the church's monks opened their doors to the townspeople; they even joined in the fighting (ignoring the fact that they were siding with the 'opposition'). Loyalty to the Republican cause was not forgotten. When religious houses were broken up by the state a year later, San Pietro was designated a 'national monument', and allowed to keep its patrimony.

The **choir** (1526), indeed all the woodwork, is exceptional. It has even been described by the Touring Club of Italy guide — not one given to hyperbole — as the finest in all Italy. Bizarre and otherworldly creatures divide each stall (with the Perugian griffin omnipresent). Six panels on the rear door (1536) are particularly good. They describe the Annunciation, Moses Saved from the Flood (a recurring theme), and the Heads of St Peter and St Paul. If open, this door leads out to a loggia, with some superlative views. Look out too for the intricately gilded side-pulpits.

Thereafter, the overall effect is more impressive than individual details. The 11 large frescoes around the upper walls are by Vassilacchi (1592), a disciple of Veronese. The largest, on the rear wall, crowded with faces, is a genealogical

Tree of the Benedictines. It collects together the most eminent members of the Order. The greenish-tinged frescoes on either side of the door are by Orazio Alfani. The third altar down has a picture attributed to Eusebio di San Giorgio, *Benedict Giving the Rule to his Followers*. The figure being boiled and roasted above is St Cristina.

At the very top of the left-hand nave is a *Pietà with St Girolamo and St Leonardo* by Bonfigli (or Caporali), which is one of the best things in the church. Next to it on the left is the Cappella Vibi, with a fine altar tabernacle by Mino da Fiesole (1473) and works by Giannicola di Paolo and Caporali (lunette and left-hand wall). Passing down the right-hand wall, next to the final side-altar (which has an *Assunzione* by Alfani) is one of Eusebio's best works, the *Magi* (1508). The big chapel on its right has three canvases by Vasari. Between altars one and two is a late work by Perugino, *Pietà*, much in need of a clean.

Other sights

The church of **San Severo** is a short walk from Piazza Dante, the smallish square behind the cathedral. (It is the site of an occasional open-air ceramics market.) Underneath it lies a large **Etruscan Well**, which, like the traces of Perugia's walls and gateways, is constructed from huge uncemented blocks of travertine marble. The entrance is at Piazza Dante 18. *Open 9–12.30. Closed Monday*. Via Bontempi leads off from the right, followed by the tiny Via Raffaello soon after, curving left towards San Severo. Most of the church's interior is eighteenth century, though the original building dates from 1007. Legend has it this was the site of a pagan temple to the sun, a building that gave its name to the *rione*, or district — the Porta Sole. (Note the area's east-facing location, perfect for a temple to the rising sun.) There were originally five such *rioni*, spreading from the temple (the highest point of the city), down to the five different gateways of the old city. This particular *rione* probably formed the heart of the Etruscan settlement.

The main reason for a visit, apart from the quiet charm of the spot, is to see Raphael's first complete work. It is a large, but in parts poorly preserved, fresco, located in a small chapel that survives from the earlist church. The top half of the painting, which is dividied horizontally, is by Raphael (1505); the lower half — depicting six saints — is by Perugino (1521). There is a certain pathos in Perugino painting a year after the death of Raphael, having seen his own (obviously) declining fame surpassed by that of his former star pupil. *Open summer only 9–12, 15.30–18.30. Closed Monday; winter Tel. 284295.*

Return to and follow Via Bontempi downhill to **Santa Maria Nuova**, a rambling fourteenth-century church, refitted many times, but recently returned to its Gothic original. You could also reach it from Piazza Fortebraccio and the Arco d'Augusto (on Via Pintoricchio). The second chapel on the right has a *gonfalone* by Bonfigli (1472), with Jesus directing thunderbolts at Perugia, and saints interceding to placate the divine ire. The choir (1456) is magnificent. Patches of early fresco compete with a good cycle of paintings by Lazzaro Vasari, great-grandfather of the Vasari who wrote *Lives of the Artists*. It is in a chapel to the right of the apse.

In the streets above — Porta Sole proper — once stood the palace of Cardinal Mommaggiore of Cluny, the city's Papal governor from 1372. Chroniclers described the palace as the most splendid in Italy, and the Cardinal as 'that French Vandal, that most iniquitous Nero'. The citadel was linked by passageway to the Palazzo dei Priori, the corpulent cleric not hesitating to knock down parts of the cathedral to accommodate his folly. He stored enough wine and provisions to last him 10 years.

In 1375 the townspeople revolted, with help from as far afield as Florence and Siena. An enormous catapult, the *cacciaprete*, or 'priest-hunter', was brought to bear on the palace. The *condottiere*, Sir John Hawkwood, who had been employed by the Cardinal, was bribed, and when needed, was otherwise indisposed. Surrounded day and night, Mommaggiore concluded peace, and was escorted from his palace in full armour (hardly able to move), accompanied by jeering whistles and helped across the muddy ground by the obliging Sir John.

Where to stay

Brufani Palace
★★★★★

Small, well-appointed, and highly luxurious hotel. Also, of course, highly expensive. Located in a nineteenth-century palace built over the ruins of the old Papal fortress, the Rocca Paolina. Superb views from the right rooms. Central, with all facilities, including air-conditioning, garage parking, etc. Piazza Italia 12. Tel. 62541. Rooms 24. Bathrooms 17. Showers 7.

Tre Vaselle
★★★★★

Out of the city in the town of Torgiano, 11 kilometres to the south-west. Possibly a more attractive option if you want to escape Perugia's bustle. Set in a converted villa, it is a beautiful and renowned *Relais* hotel–restaurant complex (created by wine-producer Giorgio Lungarotti). It is used for conferences, and can seem business- and expense-account-orientated; despite this, it remains popular and can be recommended. Expensive. Via Garibaldi 48. Tel. 075 982447. Rooms 48. Bathrooms 43.

Hotel Bellavista
★★★★

Annexed to the Brufani Palace. Bigger and cheaper, but enjoys the same excellent views and central location. One of the few Italian hotels to offer three grades within its four-star listing (standard, medium, and superior). Piazza Italia 12. Tel. 20741. Rooms 81. Bathrooms 47. Showers 26.

La Rosetta
★★★★

Reliable, long-established hotel divided into old and modern wings, with wide range of rooms in varying states of decoration. Excellent restaurant and summer terrace. Central location. Piazza Italia 19. Tel. 20841. Rooms 96. Bathrooms 57. Showers 33.

Della Posta
★★★

Oldest hotel in the city. Goethe stayed here during his Italian journey. Little more than adequate for all that, but cheapish, and with a perfect central

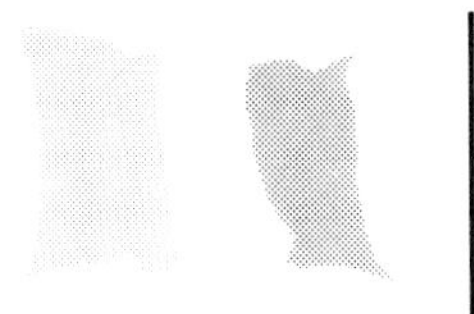

location. Corso Vannucci 97. Tel. 61345. Rooms 56. Bathrooms 9. Showers 45.

Signa ★★

In a quiet and characteristic side-street close to San Domenico. No restaurant. Garden. Via del Grillo 9. Tel. 61080. Rooms 21. Bathrooms 5. Showers 15.

Fortuna ★★

Central, functional hotel with garage, garden, and most facilities. Via Bonazzi 19. Tel 22845/6. Rooms 32. Bathrooms 32.

Lory/Rosalba ★

Two simple, central *pensione* at the same address. The Lory is marginally more appealing. Corso Vannucci 10. Tel. 24266/28285. Rooms 11/9.

Anna ★

Pensione in central, medieval street. Two minutes from the Corso Vannucci. Via dei Priori 48. Tel. 66304. Rooms 9. Bathrooms 2.

Youth hostel

Centro Internazionale di Accoglienza per la Gioventù

Midnight curfew. *Closed daily from 9.30 and 15 December–15 January*. YHA membership not required. Pleasant and central position. Via Bontempi 13. Tel. 22880.

Camping

Paradise d'Ete ★★

(650 metres). Out of town at Colle della Trinità (36 bus and a short walk). *Open all year.* Places 50.

Il Rocolo ★★

(378 metres). Also at Colle della Trinità. *Open June–September.* Places 100.

Note: There are more campsites dotted around the nearby Lake Trasimeno (see below).

Where to eat

Falchetto

A small, but excellent restaurant two minutes from the Duomo. Single-vaulted room, with more intimate stone-walled dining area to the left. Unfussy, with an open-plan kitchen at the rear. Sparkling white-washed walls, crisp linen, and amiable service. Many specialities: try *i falchetti verdi*, the house pasta, the old-world *pasta e fagioli*; the lamb or grilled trout, and any of the homemade *dolci*. A selection of Umbrian cheeses (try Norcia's *pecorino* or the *caciotta* from Ascagnano). Regional wines. Reasonably priced. Via Bartolo 20 (off Piazza Dante). Tel. 61875. *Closed Monday.*

La Rosetta

Long-famous restaurant annexed to venerable hotel of the same name. Located in roomy, medieval chamber, with plants, tasteful paintings, and cool pastel decoration. Good, traditional Umbrian cooking, with little attempt at originality. Excellent roast meats and a single out-of-the-ordinary pasta: *tagliatelle di castagne alla crema di funghi* — tagliatelle with chestnuts and cream of mushrooms. Adequate wines. Can be expensive. Piazza Italia 19. Tel. 20841. *Closed Monday.*

Aladino Recent and eccentric addition to city's restaurants. Deliberately down-at-heel, and tongue-in-cheek atmosphere — ties are forbidden — but extraordinarily good food. Hosts' Sardinian background gives added dimension to already adventurous cuisine. A plate of more than 35 cheeses to finish. Via Santa Elisabetta 16/a. Tel. 20938. *Closed Tuesday.*

La Taverna In a picturesque corner of the city. Old bottles and fittings provide the somewhat arcane atmosphere of a chemist's shop. Broad range of standard Umbrian and Italian dishes. Wine list extensive but not always well chosen. House wines perfectly acceptable. Via delle Streghe 8. Tel. 61028. *Closed Monday and 15–31 July.*

Del Sole Large (300 places) but elegant, and with some fine views. Restricted regional cuisine, but extensive wine list. Via della Rupe 1 (off Via Oberdan). Tel. 65031. *Closed Saturday.*

Cavour Small, cheap, down-market, and away from centre on the approach to San Domenico and San Pietro. Corso Cavour 28. Tel. 61214. *Closed Monday.*

Peppino Five-tabled, 'greasy spoon' café straight out of a fifties film. Simple, functional, very cheap, and — though hidden — surprisingly central. Via Danzetta 9 (opposite the Banco Commerciale on Corso Vannucci). Tel. 61570. *Closed Monday.*

Pizzeria/Student Fratelli Brizi (Via Frabretti 75) and Pizza Grimana (Via Scortici 6). Both close to the University for Foreigners. Pizza Medioevo (Via Baldo — off Piazza della Repubblica). *Tavola Calda* (Piazza Dante 16).

Note: The historian Bonazzi gives a description of Perugia's medieval fare: 'Victuals were of a coarse description; more lard and pepper were eaten in those days than coffee and meat in ours. But at the feasts of the priests and nobles an incredible quantity of exquisite viands was consumed; great animals stuffed with dainties were cooked entire, and monstrous pastries served at tables, from which, when the knife touched them, a living and jovial dwarf jumped out.'

AROUND PERUGIA

Lake Trasimeno

Perugia's immediate countryside is fairly bleak. By far the best spot to make for locally is Lake Trasimeno, the fourth largest lake in Italy. Subtlely beautiful in itself — with miles of placid water, ringed by low hills, olive groves, and vineyards — the lake is wonderful for swimming (a welcome pastime in Umbria's stifling summers), and also for sailing, water-skiing, and wind-surfing.

ake Trasimeno. (ISTO)

Nowhere is it deeper than 7 metres, so that in summer the water temperature is like that of a warm bath. There is little problem with pollution. Fishing and tourism being the mainstays of local economy, it is in everybody's interest to keep things clean. Large, clogging banks of weed are the only problem, and these the council largely keeps in check. (The lake has been silting up for centuries. Note that the Vale of Spoleto and the Tiber valley below Perugia are both ancient lake-beds. Drainage — started by the Romans — was not completed until the Middle Ages. Napoleon at one time planned to drain Trasimeno itself.)

Magical and tranquil, the lake can also become gloomy and melancholy, evoking memories of the days when it was ridden with malaria. Nor it is uniformly pretty. The southern and western shores — those furthest from Perugia's new motorway spur — are, generally speaking, more appealing. The numbers of tourists are increasing (you will find all the summer campsites busy) but most visitors are still Italians, and the area has some way to go before it becomes irrevocably spoilt. Bear in mind that much of the shore is marshy and reed-lined, so it is quite difficult to find isolated and deserted nooks and coves.

Castiglione del Lago

TOURIST INFORMATION: Piazza Mazzini 10. Tel. 075 952184

Castiglione, its fortified promontory visible from afar, is the largest and most pleasant of the lake's towns. With one street and one square, there is little to see, but with its friendly and unpretentious atmosphere it is an ideal base for swimming or relaxing. Hotels, *pensioni*, and private rooms are plentiful without being obtrusive. (The tourist office has a good room-finding service.) It is easy to reach by rail (with a newish town inevitably reaching out towards the station, 2 kilometres from the lake). Fewer and fewer trains are now stopping on the Rome-Florence run, though there are plenty of slow *locali* from either Chiusi or Terόntola. There are several small beaches to choose from; the public lido on the southern side of the castle is best. In summer there are lakeside fish restaurants, most of them on the other side of the castle from the lido. The bar–restaurant alongside the landing stage is modernish, and slightly expensive, but good, with a fine, sunny lakeside terrace. Most of the campsites are ranged along the shore south of the town, with little to choose between them. The one-star **Lido Trasimeno** is the best in the town itself. Close by is a wind-surfing school. From Castiglione you might want to visit the Etruscan tombs and museum in Chiusi.

Where to eat

La Cantina

The best restaurant in the old town itself and highly recommended. Co-operatively run, it is at the lower end of the main street. Excellent food, charming, and cheap. Via V. Emanuele 89. Tel. 922163. *Closed Monday except in summer.*

Isola Maggiore

Boats run out to the lake's three islands, and to other points on the shore (Passignano, Montone, San Feliciano), all making for cheap and enjoyable outings. Most popular is that to the Isola Maggiore (a good day-trip). There is a pleasant stroll around the island perimeter, and a couple of churches to see. San Michele Arcangelo, at the highest point (fine views) is the most interesting, with patches of fresco (fourteenth–sixteenth century) which include a fine *Crucifixion* by B. Caporali (1460). In 1211 St Francis spent 42 days fasting on the island (it was then deserted — today the population is about 100). During this time, it is said, he ate just half a loaf of bread. A small chapel marks the spot of his disembarkation; another, some way above, that where

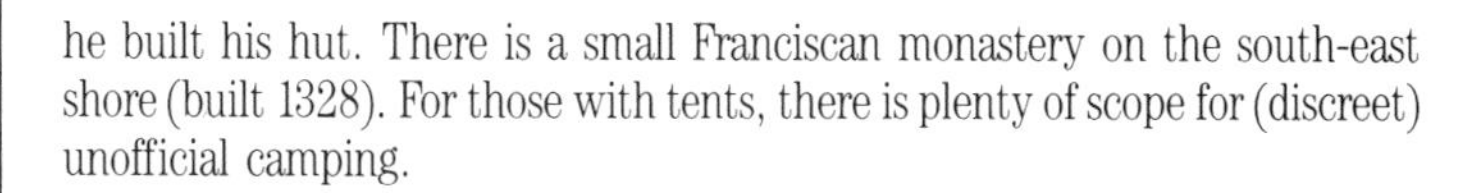

he built his hut. There is a small Franciscan monastery on the south-east shore (built 1328). For those with tents, there is plenty of scope for (discreet) unofficial camping.

Where to eat

Sauro

Of the two restaurants that do a roaring trade with the captive audiences on Isola Maggiore, this is the best, a little gem, with a limited but superb menu given over mainly to fresh fish (with the usual varieties of pasta for those that want it). It doubles as a two-star hotel, offering 11 rooms that are much in demand. Via Guglielmi. Tel. 075 846168.

The tree-covered Isola Polvese, largest of the islands, has recently been bought by the Provincia of Perugia. (The third island is in private hands.) It too is being opened up to visitors. There is a church, a restaurant (summer only), a medieval castle, and after that — nothing; just the simple charm of being on an island.

Passignano sul Trasimeno

Passignano on the northern shore is a favourite destination of Italian summer and Sunday drivers. As a result it is sometimes completely clogged with traffic. It has a negligible medieval centre (still walled), and a long promenade (no swimming) with all sorts of seaside-type attractions. Good for children perhaps. It is not ugly, or tacky, but it is probably not somewhere in which you will want to spend very much time. None the less, the place is lively, with dozens of restaurants, boats trips, and, if you want it, plenty of hotel and camping accommodation. It is also easily accessible (perhaps too accessible) both by road and rail (hourly trains from Perugia). There is swimming at the Lido Passignano.

Where to stay

Camping

Europa ★★

In the village of San Donato. Tel. 075 827403. *Open April–September.* Places 108.

Kursaal ★★

San Donato. Tel. 075 827182. *Open April–September.* Places 90.

Where to eat

Cacciatore

By far the best restaurant, but exotic and expensive. Via Nazionale 11. Tel. 075 827210.

Castel Rigone

The little-known countryside behind Passignano is some of the best within easy reach of Perugia. The road 4 kilometres east to Castel Rigone offers marvellous views of the lake, and, as you approach the village, a fine panorama over the hills of southern Tuscany. Castel Rigone itself is a small, pretty place (geraniums, well-kept medieval streets) frequented mainly by elderly people taking the air. Hence two luxurious and gentle-paced hotels, and a peaceful, off-the-beaten-track atmosphere. Unexpectedly the village also boasts one of Umbria's most important Renaissance churches, Madonna dei Miracoli, built by Lombard masons in 1494. The road east towards Umbértide is wooded and scenic, with a worthwhile detour to the small and charming village of Preggio, a good base for some easy walking.

Where to stay

La Fattoria ★★★

Via Rigone 1. Tel. 075 845197. Rooms 27.

Villa La Castellana ★★★

Via Matteotti 4. Tel. 075 845249. Rooms 9.

Both hotels have gardens and restaurants open to non-residents. The latter, by virtue of its smaller size, is preferable.

Tuoro sul Trasimeno

Tuoro sprawls over olive-coloured hills some way from the lakeshore and 5 kilometres west of Passignano. (FS station.) This sleepy village is best known for being the site of one of the bloodiest and most shaming battles in Rome's history, though a more unlikely scene for a summer afternoon of carnage would be hard to imagine. Somewhere to the west — either at Sanguineto, the place of blood, or Ossaia, the place of bones — a Roman force under the Consul Flaminius met Hannibal, just 30 years old, and marching on Rome. Already behind him were the crossing of the Alps and a sweeping victory at Placentia. (By this stage just one of the famous elephants was still alive.) Hannibal knew he could not break the Empire by force alone. Instead he was hoping for a popular revolt in his favour, encouraged by the fact that it was but 90 years since the loss of Etruscan independence.

As dawn broke on 24 June 217 BC the countryside was still hidden in mist. Under its cover, Hannibal concealed the bulk of his troops in a horseshoe of hills north of the lake. (A spot described by Livy as 'formed by Nature for an ambush'.) As the mist cleared he ordered a small company of men to march slowly towards the northern rim of the basin. As intended, Flaminius (camped on the lakeshore) saw the men, and with the military orthodoxy that was to be his downfall, assumed them to be the rearguard of Hannibal's army. If, he concluded, these were stragglers from the enemy force, then the bulk of their companions must have already crossed the hills. If this were the case, he would be safe in marching his men away from the boggy lakeside. He could then occupy the valley 'vacated' by Hannibal. This he did, dispatching a small force to scout after the 'army' disappearing over the hills.

Things might have gone better for Flaminius if he had heeded the malevolent omens that piled up on the morning of battle. The ceremonial banners stuck in the mud, he fell off his horse, and — most worrying of all — the sacred chickens refused their breakfast. Poultry accompanied all Roman armies into battle. According to their behaviour, or, for the unlucky ones, the spread of their entrails, commanders decided on the disposition of the gods.

Happily camped in the valley, the Romans were surrounded by hills bristling with Carthaginian troops. Not only had Hannibal held the upper hand from the outset, but his men had been primed for battle since dawn. The Romans had broken formation, and were setting up camp, waiting for news of Hannibal's 'retreating' army. At a given signal this army poured down from the hills into the mass of helpless legions, who, surprised, surrounded, and disorganized, were swiftly and bloodily defeated. The few who survived the initial onslaught could only retreat to the narrow lakeshore, and here they were trapped and hacked down in their turn. Sixteen thousand Romans, including Flaminius, were killed.

I roam
By Thrasimene's lake, in the defiles
Fatal to Roman rashness, more at home;
For there the Carthaginian's warlike wiles
Come back before me, as his skill beguiles
The host between the mountains and the shore,
Where Courage falls in her despairing files,
And torrents, swoln to rivers with their gore,
Reek through the sultry plain, with legions scatter'd o'er.

Like to a forest fell'd by mountain winds;
And such the storm of battle on this day,
And such the phrenzy, whose convulsion blinds
To all save carnage, that, beneath the fray,
An earthquake reel'd unheededly away!
None felt stern Nature rocking at his feet,
And yawning forth a grave for those who lay
Upon their bucklers for a winding sheet;
Such is the absorbing hate when warring nations meet!

Byron, *Childe Harold's Pilgrimage* (Canto IV, 62–4)

Despite the decisiveness of his victory, Hannibal's hoped-for uprising did not materialize. When it came to the crunch, the Etruscans preferred the familiar domination of Rome to the uncertain rule of Carthaginian foreigners. Having been checked at Spoleto, and then cut off from fresh supplies in southern Italy, Hannibal and his dilapidated army were forced to flee the country.

Two unmetalled roads strike off up the valley in question: one to Sanguineto, the other from Tuoro itself. (Turn left and then right in the centre of the village.) Forgo the battlefield, and you could take the high, picturesque road to Umbértide (N416). While in the area, it is worth visiting the marvellous Tuscan town of Cortona, 20 kilometres to the north.

South of the lake

Around the lake the countryside generally is nothing special, and is best treated as scenic backdrop. The coast road touches a couple of quiet, largely modern villages. The largest, Magione, has a grand fifteenth-century castle, La Badia, property of the Knights of Malta. Hilltop Panicale, with its tiny medieval heart, most deserves a visit, partly for a broad panorama of the lake, but also for two little known Peruginos. They are in the church of San Sebastiano off the central Piazza della Vittoria. If you are lucky enough to be here for the April *festa*, you will see the town's fountains running with wine. The road to the south — the N220 from Perugia to Città della Pieve — is a long, tedious drive with nothing to recommend it. The only minor point of interest is the Santuario della Madonna di Mongiovino (7 kilometres south-west of Panicale). It is a noted but rather cold Renaissance church built in 1513.

Where to eat

Il Settimio

This famous fish restaurant is genuinely outstanding, but pricey and popular. Lungolago 1, San Feliciano. Tel. 075 849104. *Closed Thursday except during the summer.*

Torgiano

Torgiano, an easy 16-kilometre hop from Perugia on the N3 to Todi, has been made famous by the superb wines of Dr Giorgio Lungarotti (see 'Wine'). The same man has also created the **Tre Vaselle** hotel and restaurant complex (see p.92) — excellent, but slick and expensive eating in a converted villa. The town's **wine museum** is worth a diversion in its own right. It is another Lungarotti enterprise, and a cut above the usual predictability of such

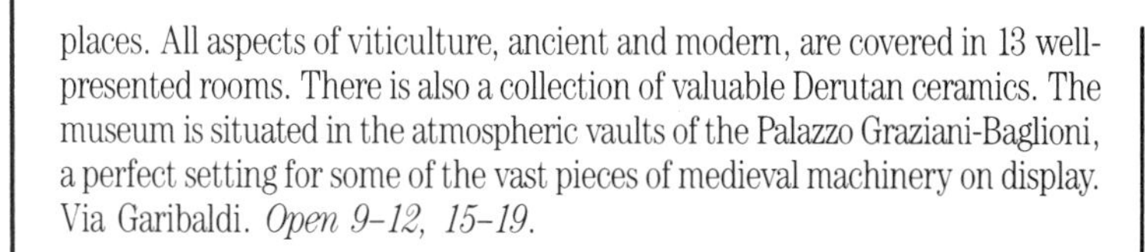

places. All aspects of viticulture, ancient and modern, are covered in 13 well-presented rooms. There is also a collection of valuable Derutan ceramics. The museum is situated in the atmospheric vaults of the Palazzo Graziani-Baglioni, a perfect setting for some of the vast pieces of medieval machinery on display. Via Garibaldi. *Open 9–12, 15–19.*

Bettona

Local literature promises much of Bettona, which in reality does not quite live up to expectation. It was once an extremely important Etruscan city, of which only occasional traces of wall remain. One or two quite good paintings are to be found around its (moderate) medieval streets. Santa Maria Maggiore in the main Piazza Cavour has a *gonfalone* by Perugino, and a *Crucifixion* by Nicolò Alunno. Both are in the Cappella di Santa Rita, to the right of the main door. The Pinacoteca, also in Piazza Cavour, has minor works by Perugino, Tiberio d'Assisi, Fiorenzo di Lorenzo, and others, plus Roman and Etruscan fragments.

ASSISI

General Information

TOURIST INFORMATION: Piazza del Comune 12. Tel. 075 812534

POPULATION: 25,000

HEIGHT: 424 m

POST OFFICE: Piazza del Comune. Open 8–19

TELEPHONES: SIP office, Piazza del Comune

STD CODE: 075

DISTANCE TO:
Perugia 25 km Spoleto 47 km
Gualdo 31 km Orvieto 90 km

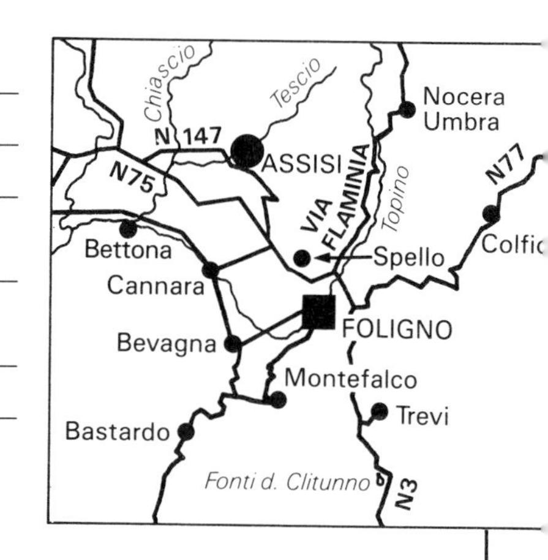

Trains There are trains approximately hourly to Foligno via Spello (30 minutes) and Terόntola via Perugia (30 minutes). The station (next to an ugly brick-works) is 5 kilometres from the town, with a half-hourly bus connection to Piazzale Unità d'Italia.

Buses Frequent buses to Perugia and many surrounding towns and villages leave from Piazza di Santa Chiara. Daily buses to Rome and Florence depart from Piazza San Pietro.

Road Fast dual-carriageway connections to Todi (N3 bis), Perugia, and Foligno (N75).

Parking Very limited town-centre parking. Best bets are Porta Nuova, Piazzale Unità d'Italia, and Piazza Matteotti.

Taxi Tel. 812600/812606 (expensive).

The world's best-loved saint, St Francis, was born and is buried in Assisi. He it is who has brought an otherwise sleepy spot its considerable fame. Over and above being one of the country's chief shrines (only St Peter's ranks higher), the rosy-pink town harbours some of Italy's most famous paintings — Giotto's enthralling frescoes on the life of the saint.

Inevitably there is a price to pay for this embarrassment of artistic and spiritual riches. With several million visitors annually it could not be any other way. Monstrous tourist buses crash into the town on their whistle-stop tours; baubles, trinkets and sheer trash from gaudy shops regale visitors. At (almost) every turn the cult of the saint is milked for its considerable commercial potential.

Yet Assisi is one of those rare towns that's able to absorb visitors and still retain its charm. Even without St Francis it would still be one of Umbria's medieval highlights. Narrow streets and alleyways spirit you away from the crowds in seconds; geraniums adorn many a window, and while the approaches resound to the grinding of gears, small piazzas echo to the sound of nothing more piercing than the trickle of fountains. And come evening, when the shops shut and the trippers go home, Assisi again becomes a quiet and fitting shrine to St Francis.

History

Despite being somewhat off the beaten track, and having almost inextricable links with St Francis, Assisi still manages to have an independent history of sorts. Its origins are Umbrian; those of Perugia, which was its almost constant enemy, were Etruscan. Even today, though only a few kilometres distant, the two towns are clearly a civilization apart and still carry the different spirits of their respective founders.

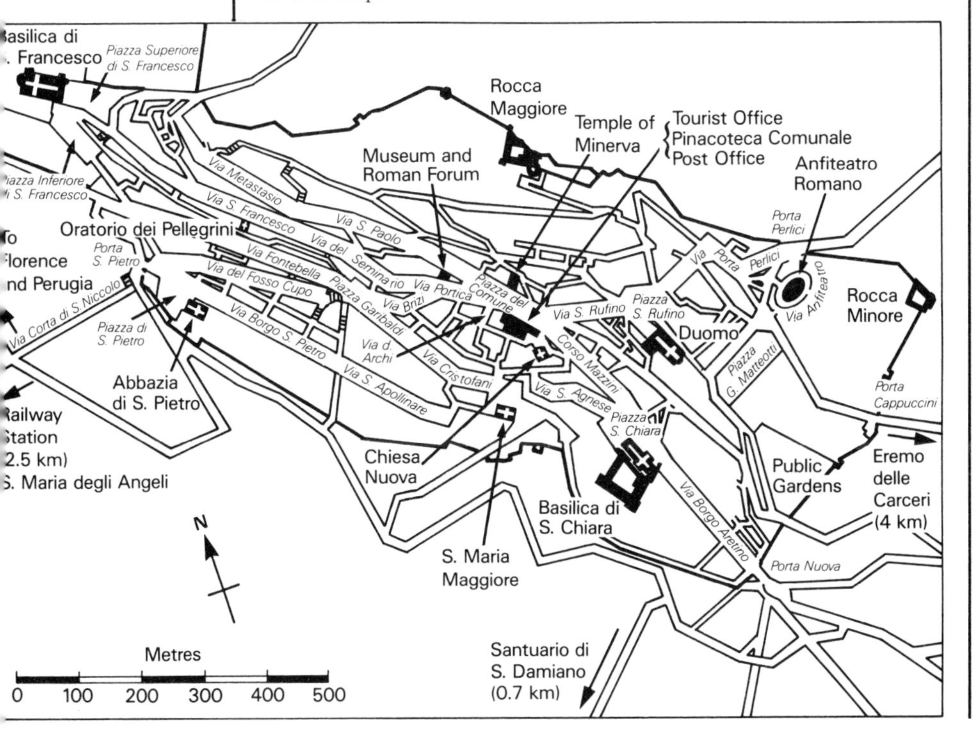

Until it fell to the Romans in 309 BC, the town, like Gubbio, was a key centre of Umbrian religious worship. Thereafter it flourished, though rarely made waves; the main event of note was the birth of the great Latin love poet, Propertius.

The arrival of Christianity, creeping up from Rome and Spoleto, turned it into a sort of third-century Beirut, with pagans and believers fighting one another for control of the city. Huns, Franks, and Lombards passed it by with scarcely a sideways glance; only Totila laid serious siege to its walls, and he, like many others, was quickly distracted by the prospect of richer pickings in Perugia.

For years Assisi was annexed to the Dukedom of Spoleto and often strayed from Papal allegiance, which is perhaps why Charlemagne and his 'terrible and fierce followers' came to teach it a lesson. Having all but flattened the old colony, they brought in Lombard craftsmen to rebuild it. One small door in Piazza delle Rose is almost all that remains of their work. The Rocca, their other legacy, saddled the town with a new, and not entirely welcome, strategic role.

The Middle Ages proceeded with many a Perugia–Assisi confrontation, none more stirring than an episode in 1321, when the resources of both sides were at a low ebb. Perugia sold its fishing rights on Lake Trasimeno to raise cash, and Assisi followed suit by selling treasures from the Basilica of St Francis. Unfortunately they were not the town's to sell; they belonged to Avignon's exiled Popes, who excommunicated the entire population for 38 years as punishment for the theft.

Church doors remained locked, and bells silent, though the townspeople seem to have cared not a whit. They flogged half to death the two friars who brought the Bull of Excommunication, making them swallow its heavy lead seals for good measure.

Inter-family disputes involving the Sforzas and Montefeltro added to already considerable confusion. The arrival of Perugia's Baglioni only made things worse. They were men, according to one Franciscan, 'who did not shudder to murder men, cook their flesh, and give it to the relations of the slain to eat in their prison dungeons'. What with plague and famine, life became fairly grim — so grim, in fact, said one chronicler, that 'people sustained themselves with three or four cooked nuts dipped in wine, and with this they made good cheer'.

Even such limited good cheer evaporated with the arrival of Church control. Until 1923, and the 700th anniversary of St Francis's death, Assisi was the blandest of Papal backwaters. Celebrations then boosted the cult of the saint, and when Pope Pius XII made him Italy's patron saint in 1939, Assisi was finally on the map. Annual numbers of tourists and pilgrims run to several million, and are increasing.

St Francis

'Il più santo dei Santi' — the most saintly of the saints — Mussolini said of St Francis, not an epitaph (at least not coming from a Fascist dictator) that Francis would have relished. It is a true one, however: Francis is amongst the most evocative and influential of characters, an extraordinary man, who, with no greater tools than preaching and personal example, turned medieval religion on its head.

Pope Pius XI's encyclical on the 700th anniversary of his death said: 'It seems unnecessary for us to affirm that there has never been anyone in whom the image of Jesus Christ and the evangelical manner of life shone forth more strikingly than in St Francis . . . appearing to his contemporaries and to future generations as though he were the Risen Christ.' Dante, in the *Divine Comedy*, placed Francis alongisde that other great Messianic figure, John the Baptist.

He was born in 1181, the son of a cloth-merchant father and Provencal mother — presumably this is why he picked up the nickname 'Francesco' — little Frenchman. (He was baptized plain Giovanni.) Richard the Lionheart was on the throne at the time in England; Saladin and Genghis Khan were both contemporaries.

He enjoyed a rakish early life of drinking and womanizing (as future saints usually did), which he gave up at about 20, following a year in a Perugian gaol. Captured in one of Assisi's frequent skirmishes with the town, he fell ill, and with time to reflect, decided that he would abandon his plans to become a crusading knight. On being released he also began to abandon worldly habits (such as eating and dressing properly) and instead took to hours of silent and solitary contemplation.

The culmination of several visions (and the one that tipped the balance) was that in the semi-derelict church of San Damiano, in which God commanded him to 'Go and repair My Church', an injunction that the ingenuous Francis obeyed to the literal letter. Travelling to Foligno, he sold his father's entire stock of cloth (and his horse), and offered the proceeds to San Damiano's priest to help rebuild his shattered church.

Soon after he renounced his inheritance, and in Assisi's Piazza del Comune, before a gathered crowd and his outraged father, stripped naked in a symbolic casting off of wealth and worldly shackles. Dressed in the coarse grey garb of the lowest peasant (the brown Franciscan habit came later), he began to beg and to work with lepers, a conscious embodiment of Christ's invocation to His Apostles 'to heal the sick and carry neither purse, nor scrip, nor shoes'.

In time, he gathered 12 followers (another deliberate echo of Christ), and after some difficulty obtained permission from Pope Innocent III to found a monastic Order based on poverty, chastity, and obedience. He began to preach, and covered vast distances, roaming through Umbria and Tuscany, attracting an enormous following, after initial ridicule and opprobrium. (Today the Italian equivalent of the colloquial term 'Shanks's pony' is still 'Il cavallo di San Francesco', after the many miles Francis covered on foot.) In 1212 he created a second Order of Franciscans, the Poor Clares, and in the same year took off to Spain to continue preaching.

He visited Egypt in 1219, having been previously thwarted by illness, and in the midst of the Crusades tried to convert the 'infidel', Sultan Melekel-Kamel. With characteristic directness, he marched through the battle-lines to address the enemy leader in his tent, offering to undergo an ordeal by fire to prove his faith. The sultan was captivated (though unconverted) and told Francis to go on his way in peace. Francis subsequently travelled as far as Antioch and the Holy Land.

Back in Italy he met St Dominic in Rome, and, in a famous episode, initiated the first ever Christmas crib at a service for peasants in the village of Greccio. (Perhaps the most striking example of Francis's earthy, anti-intellectual style.) In 1224 he founded a monastery on Mount della Verna, near Arrezzo (where he received Christ's stigmata in a dream). After years of punishing his body, however (he called it 'Christ's donkey'), his health was failing badly. He virtually withdrew from an active life, easily abdicating 'leadership' of his Order (having never, in any case, been much concerned with the trappings of power).

After being treated for glaucoma in Rieti and Siena, he slowly worked his way back to Assisi via Gubbio and Nocera. In his home town, and feeling close to death, he refused treatment amidst the pomp of the bishop's palace, and returned to the mud floor of the Porzuincola, where he died in October 1226.

It is difficult to pinpoint Francis's precise importance. On one level, he was a fine poet, and the founder of a great Franciscan literary tradition. His French ancestry made him familiar with the ballads of the influential Provencal troubadours who drifted south into Italy during the thirteenth century. His famous 'Canticle to the Sun', a hymn to the beauty of nature, stands comparison with the best of medieval verse (see also the *Fioretti*).

On another, more profound, level, he brought a purifying and uplifting breath of air to a medieval church that was on the verge of moral bankruptcy. Jacques de Vitry, a member of Innocent III's court, was not alone in believing that priests of the day were 'deceiving as foxes, proud as bulls and as avaricious and insatiable as the minatour'. The church was also wealthy, corrupt, and, more to the point, elitist and aloof. 'Ah, Constantine,' wrote Dante of the first Christian Emperor, 'of how much ill was cause, / Not thy conversion, but those rich domains / That the first wealthy Pope received of thee.'

Francis's mass-appeal (generated, incredibly, in an age without mass-communication), his lack of dogma (he never became a priest), and a return to first principles could not put everything to rights, and a great deal of his teachings were subsequently institutionalized and watered down by the Papacy. (A testament to their veracity and their threat to the established order.) However, his humility and sunny optimism captured a medieval imagination still spiritually floundering in the Dark Ages, and in a way, and to a degree, that is almost impossible to comprehend today.

Finally — and this underpins every article of his faith (and message) — Francis saw the natural world (of which man was a supreme expression) as a joyful, radiant thing, an earthly paradise and myriad reflection and expression of God in all His glory. Francis's deity was a mirror of nature, a benign force, which the saint was able to describe to the poor in ways they understood. This view, commonplace today, was then bordering on the revolutionary, a turning away from nature as some malign, threatening force oozing with superstition. It was also, of course, a precursor to the 'humanist', man as divine, strand of thinking that was to run right through the Renaissance.

What to see

Basilica of St Francis

The artistic and architectural splendour of the Basilica — St Francis's burial place and spiritual home to his Order — make it one of the greatest buildings of the Middle Ages, and the single most important 'sight' that Umbria has to offer.

The idea of building a church to house the body of the saint was conceived by the Franciscans' new Vicar-General, Brother Elias, the son of a Bolognese mattress-maker. It quickly received approval from the Order's Vatican protector, Cardinal Ugolino del Conti (the future Pope Gregory IX). Funds flooded in from all over the world, and the scheme received considerable support. It also, however, aroused hearty opposition. The more zealous and honest of

he Basilica of St Francis. (ISTO)

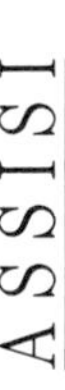

Francis's followers pointed out (correctly) that the proposed magnificence was at odds with everything the saint had stood for. They quoted Francis, who had said that, 'small churches should be built, for they ought not to raise great churches for the sake of preaching to the people or for any other reason, for they will show greater humility and give a better example by going to preach in other churches'.

Work started regardless, and was well under way by the time of Francis's canonization in 1228. This was a decorous affair, conducted by an emotional Pope Gregory. Observers talked of his eulogistic and extensive tribute, delivered in a mournful and booming voice, and broken intermittently by uncontrollable sobs. Accolade, apparently, followed accolade, as he compared the saint to 'a full moon, a rising sun . . . the morning star hovering above dawn mists'. A sub-deacon read a extended list of Francis's miracles, while a learned cardinal ('not without copious weeping') provided a running commentary on his deeds, the Pope listening, with 'rivers of tears punctuated by deep-drawn wails'. Priests and the attendant entourage wept so piteously that 'their vestments were in great part wet and the ground was drenched with their tears'.

(There is a myth that Francis had asked to be buried in the most despised spot in Assisi, the Colle del Inferno, or Infernal Hill, the town's place of execution. Although he granted the request, Pope Gregory insisted that the name be changed to the Hill of Paradise.)

The identity of the Basilica's architect is much in doubt. Vasari's charming but fanciful account would have him as Arnolfo di Lapo, the man who designed the Duomo and Piazza della Signoria in Florence. Many original drawings and documents were lost when the archives were burnt during a Perugian raid, so we will probably never know the truth — a shame because architecturally the building is extraordinary. One of the earliest examples of Italian Gothic, its single-naved Upper Church set a precedent for countless Franciscan churches that were to follow. The idea of having two churches, one literally on top of the other, was audacious by itself, even without the practical engineering problems that such a scheme presented. (The massive arched buttressing that was the answer to the problem — it effectively props up the western end of the town — is one of the wonders of early medieval architecture.) The design is thought to have been the work of Lombard masons, who would have drawn for inspiration on the Gothic models of southern France. The cathedral of Albi in Aquitaine, for example, is strikingly similar to the Basilica in Assisi.

While building proceeded, the political background became increasingly murky and tangled. The final twist came on the day of the funeral itself. Elias by this time had been ousted as Vicar-General, but still retained control of all that went on in the Basilica. He saved his final *coup de théâtre* for the big day. The saint's hearse, drawn by white oxen, proceeded through the streets of Assisi. Onlookers hung from every vantage-point, showering it with wild flowers. Suddenly, as it neared the Basilica, Elias and a posse of soldiers burst on to the scene and seized the body. Ignoring the anger of the crowd, and the indignation of the Papal entourage, they hurried the coffin into the Lower

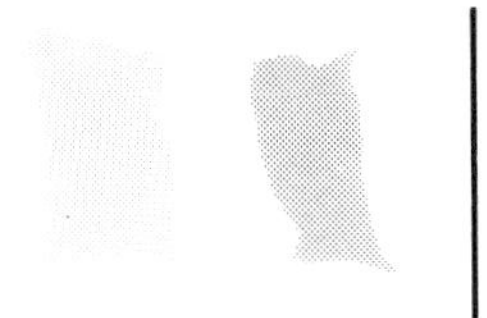

Church and bolted the doors behind them. Elias, prompted by the fear that his master's remains would be stolen or desecrated (medieval relics had enormous financial and spiritual value) had decided to bury Francis in a secret, Pharaoh-like tomb deep within the Basilica.

The episode gave rise to a myth (believed by Vasari), that a vast hidden church had been built below the Basilica, far greater in beauty and grandeur than the churches above. Inside this vast, sealed chamber it was believed the body of the 'almost alive saint' hovered above the altar awaiting his call to Heaven. The tomb actually remained undiscovered, or at least unreached, until a concerted two-month search in 1818.

Elias himself, described in the *Fioretti* as 'one of the most intelligent men on Earth' remains a fascinating and equivocal figure. On the one hand, he is credited with the drive, energy, and ambition that produced the Basilica; on the other, he is viewed as the Judas who betrayed Francis and compromised his ideals. Apologists claim that in 'selling out' the original movement he was guaranteeing its survival as something more than an heretical cult. In a sense this line is justified by the current status of the Order as the biggest in the world, and by the fact that many subsequent splinter groups (such as the Fratricelli) *did* end up on the wrong side of the Inquisition. Sooner or later the Vatican would have been forced to deal with a group whose ideals of poverty sat ill alongside its own extraordinary wealth. (It is worth noting that the contemporary Franciscans have lost none of their vigour, and that they have come into conflict with the present Pope for their outspoken espousal of the church's commitment to the poor.) The Papacy eventually sent Elias to intercede with Frederick II as a diplomatic envoy. He became instead the Emperor's lifelong friend, even accompanying his court into battles against the Church. As a result, he was excommunicated, and languished in a hermitage near Cortona until pardoned just before his death.

Painters in the Basilica

Probably nowhere outside an art gallery is there such a remarkable and influential collection of paintings as in the Basilica. Over a period of 150 years some of the most outstanding artists of the day decorated its walls, turning it in the process into one of the watersheds of Western art.

Early painters

Work on the Basilica progressed extremely quickly after its foundation. By 1230 it had been completed in its basic form, and within only another six years artists had begun to paint in the Lower Church. There is natural confusion over the identities of the earliest painters. A great deal of their work has deteriorated, or was painted over by the artists who followed them. Amongst the first on the scene was the anonymous Maestro di San Francesco. Much emulated, his work, and that of his followers, is found all over the region, though the man behind them remains a stubborn mystery. For a long time his frescoes in the Lower Church were attributed to Giunto Pisano (1202–56), another elusive character. Now it is thought that the Maestro was simply a pupil of Pisano. The same hand may also have been responsible for designing the stained glass in the Upper Church, some of the oldest in Italy. (At this stage, the work in the Basilica, apart from the odd flicker of innovation, was still within the distinctive and stylized Byzantine tradition.)

Cimabue

Cenni di Pepo, or Cimabue (1240–1302), was the last great artist to operate within this tradition, and one of the first to push tentatively beyond it. Vasari's *Lives of the Painters* opens with this artist, and describes him as the father of Italian painting, the man who brought 'first light' to the art. Contemporaries considered him a prodigy, but he was also possessed with a fanatical perfectionism, and often destroyed work with which he was not completely happy. Such uncompromising standards and the effects of time, mean that few of his paintings have survived outside Assisi (the Uffizi has the lion's share of those that have).

Very little is known about his life, and many of Vasari's ruminations on the subject are not always to be believed. He was probably painting in the transepts of the Upper Church between 1270 and 1280, and in the Lower Church some time later, though it is difficult to be precise. The greatest work is the majestic *Madonna and Child, Angels and St Francis* (*c.*1290) in the right transept of the Lower Church, a painting of which John Ruskin wrote: 'among all the Mater Dolorosas of Christianity, Cimabue's at Assisi is the noblest; nor did any painter after him add one link to the chain of thought with which he summed the creation of the earth and preached its redemption.'

These days Ruskin may not be regarded as much more reliable than Vasari, but there is little doubt that the picture marks the dividing line between the old and new art at Assisi. There is an attempt at drama and emotion (witnessed again in the *Crucifixion* upstairs, where Mary throws back her head in visible grief for her dying son), and a tentative use of light and shade to add verisimilitude to figures. Finally, there is an attempt to create a coherent three-dimensional sense of space and location in buildings — all first steps on the path trod later with more certainty by Giotto and the Sienese.

Rome-based painters

Working in the Upper Church at the same time as Cimabue were three Rome-based painters, Jacopo Torriti, Filippo Rusuti, and (possibly) Pietro Cavallini (1250–1330). Again, precious little is known about when they were in Assisi, or for which paintings they were directly or partially responsible.

Before coming to Assisi all three had worked primarily in mosaic, very much a medium in the Byzantine tradition. Giotto had almost certainly seen Cavallini's mosaic in Rome's Santa Maria in Trastevere, a work already showing hints of the new art. In the Basilica they turned to fresco, moving, like Cimabue, with cautious innovation, interpreting old themes more freely, and painting with a greater feeling for space and with a concern for the play of light. The *Four Doctors of the Church*, especially (in the vaults of the Upper Church), shows a narrative sense absent in the earlier paintings: cloaks are left thrown over chairs, books lie open as if half-read. The Doctors, moreover, are depicted

as characters in their own right, distinct *individuals* rather than the bland representatives of artistic convention.

The picture is attributed to Rusuti, but could as easily be by the young Giotto. It underlines the sorts of problem that have plagued art historians for centuries. Given the large number of artists working in the Basilica at the end of the thirteenth century, many were invariably present in the building at the same time, literally painting side by side. Over a period of 30 years their styles naturally altered in the wake of experience, or innovation by others, or became blurred by the effects of collaboration. Frescoes on the scale found in the Basilica, in any case, were rarely the work of a single artist, and could often be finished and even copied by pupils. Hence the historians' considerable difficulties.

Giotto

The role of Giotto in the Basilica has been one of the most contentious issues in the history of Italian art. The scholarly intricacies of the debate are complicated, but for most of this century critics have argued — to general dismay — that Giotto never set foot in Assisi at all. Current opinion is now reattributing to him more of the disputed works, though others are still seen as collaborations, or the fruit of a distinct and unknown hand.

To whatever extent the frescoes may or may not be his, Giotto was by far the most important artist to work in the Basilica. Dante immediately recognized his superiority over Cimabue, and in a famous passage (actually intended to illustrate the hollowness of earthly glory) wrote: 'Cimabue thought to lord it over painting's field / And now his fame is obscured and the cry is Giotto.' The Victorian critic Roger Fry singled him out as the 'supreme epic painter of the world', but he was also a miniaturist, a mosaic artist, a sculptor, and an accomplished architect. He was probably also a close friend of the age's other great iconoclasts, Dante and Petrarch.

Giotto was born the son of a peasant in the Tuscan hills above Florence. His early life, according to legend, was spent tending his father's flock. It was thus, apparently, that Cimabue found him, scratching pictures of his sheep on to pieces of rock. Whether or not this is true (and it sounds fairly unlikely), the young Giotto was apprenticed to Cimabue in Florence, soaking up that something in the city's air that Vasari said 'generates a desire for glory and honour, and gives a natural quickness to the minds of men'.

Up to this point, no attempt had been made to depict the life of St Francis in the Upper Church. It was obvious that such a life had to be the Basilica's artistic centrepiece. The problem was that no painter had yet shown himself worthy of the commission. It is thought that Cimabue himself put forward the name of Giotto, ignoring the fact that his pupil had yet to prove himself on a major work. One way or another, however, possibly by doing some test-pieces in the Lower Church, Giotto must have persuaded the friars that he was equal to the task. He probably started painting some time around 1296, aged just 29.

The frescoes reveal a profound sympathy on the part of the painter for the spirit of St Francis, and, like many writers and artists, it was fitting that Giotto should have become a member of the Third Order of lay Franciscans. (Dante, Michelangelo, Leonardo, Velazquez, and Cervantes were some of the others.)

The old artistic language of the Byzantines — still current despite the work of Cimabue and the Romans — was totally unsuited to the subject at hand. Its images were beautiful but lifeless icons; reverent and devotional, but also remote and stylized — highly inappropriate for Francis's very human message. They made no concessions to real life, had no earthly element, and lacked any real sense of movement, dimension, or shadow. To a forceful thirteenth-century society in a state of material and spiritual flux they were limited reminders of an age considered long past.

Giotto's response was a new artistic language, one whose vocabularly was to be used and added to for nigh on 200 years. Its basic grammar was naturalism. Any account of St Francis, almost by definition, had to take account of the natural beauty that moved the saint to such profound joy. Giotto's vision is just a faintly more austere mirror of Francis's own. Vasari wrote that Giotto 'deserves to be called the disciple of Nature, rather than of other masters, for Nature was to him a never failing source of inspiration'. Hence Giotto's figures have a naturalness and grace missing from the stiff saints and Madonnas of the Byzantines. He attempts to give movement and proportion to the human form, and to imbue the face with character, straining to convey complex human emotions in a simple and straightforward way.

In the unfolding of his Franciscan story, Giotto displays a new feeling for narrative, introducing a greater variety of subject and character than had been seen previously. At the same time he cuts straight to the heart of the matter, paring an event down to its most important details. (Consider, for example, the eloquent simplicity of a panel such as the famous *Sermon to the Birds*). The frescoes display a wealth of colour, of clothes, of carefully considered architectural detail, of scenes from everyday life — in short, an informality and naturalism that make them immediately comprehensible (just as Dante's poetry was accessible to anyone with a command of the vernacular). They acknowledge and involve the individual in a recognizable world, they become 'available' to ordinary people in a way that more ethereal Byzantine art does not. St Francis's message was addressed to the predominantly illiterate poor. It is always necessary to remember (difficult in our largely literate world) the impact of the painted surface on a medieval imagination denied books.

In this respect, Giotto's paintings show a subtle intertwining with the message of Francis himself. Technically innovative, they are at the same time humble and popularist. By the standards of later Florentine works, of course, they are also quite crude, but in them religion, life even, is being looked at and depicted in a completely new way. Apparently simple paintings to us, in their day, and for the first time, they gave forms and feelings the depth and dignity of real experience. The beautiful but stylized Byzantine gloss did not disappear overnight, but the Franciscan cycle marked clearly the arrival of an art that was to be revolutionary.

Simone Martini

Simone Martini (*c.* 1284–1344) has been called 'the most lovable of all the Italian artists before the Renaissance'. One of the first artists to paint in the Basilica after Giotto, he was a pupil of Duccio, and after him the greatest of the Sienese painters. He left work in Siena, Pisa, and Orvieto before moving to Assisi.

Martini was directly or indirectly responsible in the Lower Church for all aspects of the decoration in the Chapel of St Martin, right down to the marble inlay of the floors and the stained glass of the windows. With the 10 frescoes on the *Life of St Martin*, this makes the chapel one of the most complete and unified decorative schemes from this period in Italy. Its sunny frescoes have all the mellow and intimate loveliness characteristic of the Sienese school, and a remote and gentle beauty more in keeping with the spirit of Umbria than with the new and austere realism of Giotto. (Perhaps this is why the early Umbrian schools took Martini and the Sienese as models rather than Giotto, whose influence in Umbria was never as great as it was in Florence.)

St Clare *by Simone Martini*. (ISTO)

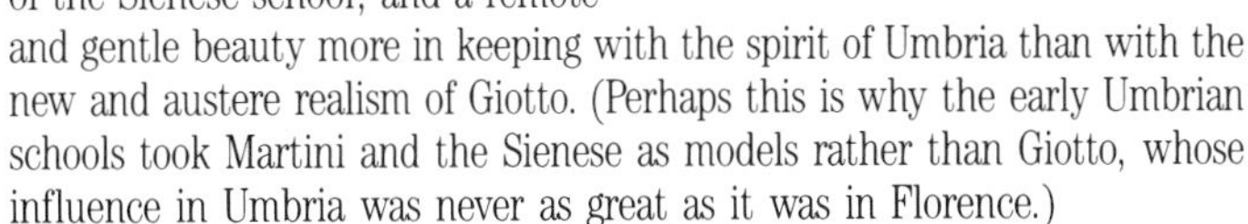

Martini's painting of figures occasionally shows Giotto's influence, but his incidental detail is more delicate, and his tone more lyrical. He is also sweeter and more obviously 'pretty'. His characters trip from the pages of medieval romance, rather than from any recognizably 'natural' world; he deals only in joy, rarely touching on pain or tragedy. He continued to develop the decorative effects of outline and sophisticated patterning that were Duccio's hallmarks, and shared his love of pure and harmonious colour. Everything combines to produce paintings that are brilliant with colour and decoration, magnificent and delicate by turn.

Pietro Lorenzetti

Less famous than Martini, but in many ways his equal, was fellow Sienese painter Pietro Lorenzetti (*c.*1280–1348). He painted in the Lower Church at about the same time as Martini, and his frescoes in the left transept are some of the most striking in the Basilica. Of eleven scenes from the Passion, five are by Lorenzetti, the *Descent from the Cross* and *Crucifixion*, with its vast crowd scene, being the greatest of his works dotted over central Italy.

He was more heavily influenced than Martini by Giotto, and his paintings, though undeniably beautiful, are less so than those of his Sienese contemporary, exhibiting more of a Giottesque preoccupation with narrative than a concern for the decorative possibilities of ornament. What he lacks in loveliness, however, he makes up for in emotional intensity, and his range of feeling is greater than any other artist represented in the Basilica.

He paints with great decorum and a careful attention to every aspect of his subject. Everything in his frescoes has clarity; his faces in particular, grave and realistic, are minutely observed. Every detail has its proper place and purpose. He died, along with his brother and fellow painter, Ambrogio, in the plague epidemic of 1348.

Lorenzetti was the last great artist to decorate the Basilica. There are, however, paintings by a host of others, great and small, scattered around the walls and in the Tesoro adjoining the Upper Church.

Lower Church

Most people walk straight through the Basilica's Gothic doorway into the Upper Church, lured by Giotto's frescoes and by the fact that it is the first thing they see at the end of Via San Francesco. Ideally, however, a visit should start in the Lower Church, which is at the bottom of some steps to the left of the main facade. It comes first, both architecturally and artistically, and many visitors find it ultimately more rewarding than the bustling, more famous church upstairs.

Little prepares you for what is inside. The atmosphere is calm, gloomy, crypt-like — deliberately conceived centuries ago to provoke meditation and introspection. Monks wander the solemn shadowy corners, candles usually light the low, claustrophobic vaults (the complicated floor-plan was also deliberate). Visitors are kept firmly within bounds — no noise, no photographs. Every inch of wall, pillar, or ceiling seems covered in fresco or decoration, every part of the church touched with a sort of darkened hush. 'One of the most impressive buildings in the world', said Edward Hutton, at the turn of the century; a masterpiece of architectural and artistic achievement.

Initially the church consisted of a single nave. The numerous side-chapels were added some time later to accommodate the vast numbers of pilgrims coming to Assisi. The basic style (and gravity of feeling) are Romanesque, though they are interrupted (particularly near the entrance) by some of the first Gothic touches in Italy. Note that the nave falls almost imperceptibly towards the main altar to give worshippers at the back a raised view of the Mass — a measure of the skill and thought that went into the Basilica's planning and construction.

The walls of the nave contain the frescoes of the Maestro di San Francesco, the earliest in the Basilica, and the first attempt to portray the Franciscan story. Many, of course, were lost when the side-chapels were opened up.

Below are the rest of the church's (major) paintings and treasures. The scheme runs anticlockwise (see plan), though it is difficult to follow any sort

The Lower Church. (ISTO)

of coherent route. The gloom, by the way, is not the problem some books suggest it to be. The lighting in the church was deliberate, and artists painted and chose their colours with the dimness in mind. (Works of outstanding merit in the Upper and Lower Church are indicated by **bold** type.)

1 Cappella di San Sebastiano. A seventeenth-century altarpiece and *Madonna delle Salute* (fifteenth century), the only known work by Ceccolo di Giovanni, a follower of Ottaviano Nelli.

2 Pulpit (1459). It contains five mirrors decorated with Subasian 'marbles' (actually normal polished stone), above which are three Papal Bulls depicted in gold — copies of the Bulls that assigned privileges to the Basilica.

3 Tomb of Filippo di Courtenay (beginning of the fourteenth century), titular head of Jerusalem and Emperor of Constantinople. By a follower of Pisano.

Basilica of St Francis: Lower Church.

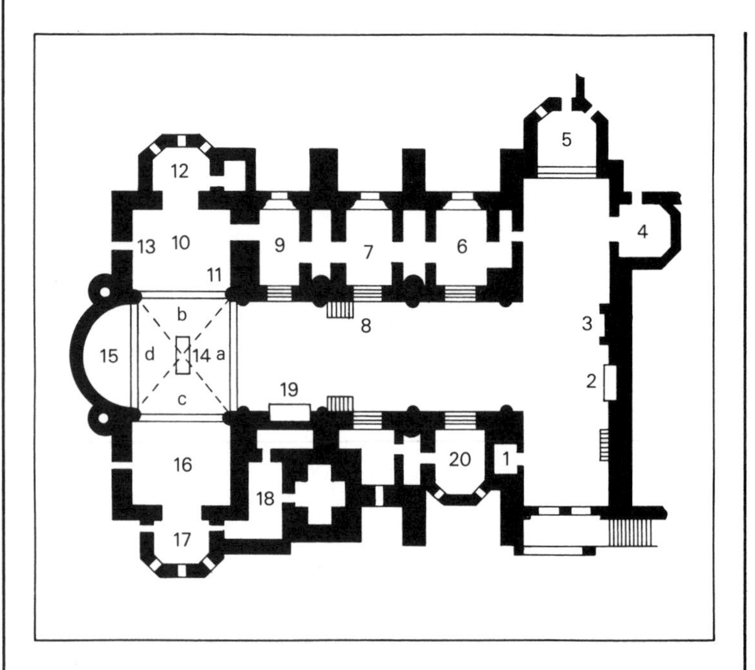

4 Tomb of Blascio Fernandez, Duke of Spoleto, and his son, Garcia (assassinated in 1367). A doorway leads out to some small cloisters, attractive for their cypresses, thirteenth-century cemetery, and general air of tranquillity. A second door from the cemetery opens into a small garden with an interesting external view of the superimposed structure of the two churches. (Note that a Napoleonic ordinance of 1806 decreed that all Italian cemeteries should be outside the towns proper. This was the last date on which the cemetery was used.)

5 A chapel built by Matteo Gattapone of Gubbio (responsible also for the Palazzo dei Consoli in Gubbio and the Ponte delle Torri in Spoleto). It was commissioned by Cardinal Albornoz, who was buried here in 1367. (He was the Papal agent responsible for the castles in most Umbrian towns.) The body was eventually removed to Toledo cathedral. Walls: *Scenes from the Life of St Catherine* (1368) by Andrea da Bologna. Left wall: *Portrait of Alboronoz Kneeling before Saints* (1368). Beautiful stained glass depicting 18 saints, possibly from drawings by Andrea da Bologna.

6 Cappella di San Stefano. Walls: *Life of St Stephen* (1575) by Dono Doni. Stained glass (*Virgin and Saints*) from a design by Simone Martini or his school. Passage: *Martyrdom of San Lorenzo* and *Capture of Jesus* (1360s), probably by Andrea da Bologna.

7 Cappella di San Antonio di Padova. Frescoes (1610) by Cesare Sermei da Orvieto.

8 Crypt of St Francis. The present crypt dates from 1925–32. Searchers found Francis's body in December 1818, concealed in blocks of travertine marble, after 52 consecutive nights of digging. Above the main altar is the simple

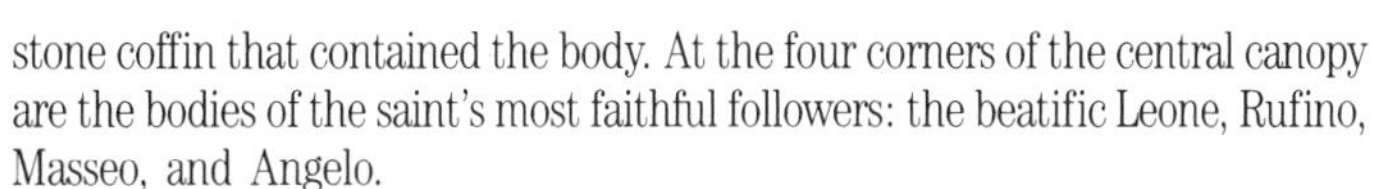

stone coffin that contained the body. At the four corners of the central canopy are the bodies of the saint's most faithful followers: the beatific Leone, Rufino, Masseo, and Angelo.

9 **Cappella della Maddalena.** The whole chapel is decorated — on a commission by Trebaldo Pontano, Bishop of Assisi (1296–1329) — with frescoes either by followers of Giotto, or (in the case of the best pieces) by Giotto himself. Arched vaults: *12 Saints*. Vaults: *Jesus, Mary Magdalene*, *Martha*, and *Lazarus*. Left wall (from the bottom): an excellent *Portrait of Trebaldo Pontano, protected by San Rufino* (claimed to be the first 'portrait' ever painted); *Supper in the House of the Pharisees*; *Resurrection of Lazarus*; *Mary Magdalene taken to Heaven*. Right wall (from the bottom): *Pontano at the feet of Mary Magdalene*; *Noli me Tangere*; *Mary Magdalene*; *Mary Magdalene and Angels*. Stained glass (1324): *Scenes from the Life of Mary Magdalene*.

10 **Right Transept.** The ceiling comprises two groups of frescoes. Right group: **Madonna, Child, Four Angels and St Francis**, a work by Cimabue, but much repainted. (It contains one of the best-known portraits of the saint.) *Jesus in the Temple*; *Nativity*; *Flight into Egypt*; *Dispute in the Temple* and the 'miraculous' scene of a child falling from a house and remaining unhurt. The second group is the work of Giotto and assistants. Left group: *Crucifixion*; *Epiphany*; *Visitation*; *Massacre of the Innocents*; *Holy Family leaving Jerusalem to return to Nazareth*; *St Francis*.

11 Tomb of Five Companions of St Francis and their portraits. To the left of the door, *Madonna, Child and Saints* by Simone Martini. The frescoes high on the rear wall are also by Giotto and assistants. To the left, a depiction of a child pulled alive from a fallen house; the figure on its extreme right may be a portrait of Giotto, and the man next to him, Dante. Lower down are *Five Saints* attributed to Simone Martini. The fourth is a lovely (and very famous) **Portrait of St Clare**.

12 Cappella di San Nicola. Built by Napoleone Orsini towards the end of the thirteenth century. Tomb of Giovanni Orsini, possibly by a Roman craftsman, but with the influence of Arnolfo di Cambio. Followers of Giotto painted the wall frescoes, *Scenes from the Life of San Nicola* (1330–40).

13 The door in the rear wall opens out to a terrace and the main **cloisters**, with a small shop selling trinkets to the right. Next to the shop is the entrance to the treasury (see below). A staircase from this point leads to the Upper Church.

14 **Vaults of the High Altar**. For years these celebrated frescoes were attributed to Giotto. Now the experts are not so sure, and the artist goes under a flag of convenience: the 'Maestro delle Vele' (literally the master of the 'sails' or 'vaults'). The paintings depict the three virtues on which St Francis founded his Order.

a *Allegory of Poverty*. Poverty in the centre, with Christ and St Francis behind. Christ hands Francis a ring to symbolize his marriage to 'Lady Poverty', who hands it in turn to the figure of Hope. Charity offers her heart to Francis and Poverty. In the right-hand corner, three youths, representing Pride, Envy, and

Avarice, disparage Poverty. At the feet of the 'couple' a dog barks and two children torment Poverty, one with a stick, the other with a stone. Above, angels offer God a cloak and a building, symbols of material possession.

b *Allegory of Chastity*. A look at medieval morals. Chastity stands between a tower topped with a white banner (a symbol of purity) and the walls of a turreted castle. Soldiers stand guard at the corners of the castle. The figures of Purity and Fortitude offer a shield and a white banner to a man, who, assisted by four angels, is trying to enter the castle (by taking a morally cleansing bath). In the left-hand corner, St Francis and two angels welcome into the castle three figures who represent the three Franciscan Orders. One is a Friar, another a Poor Clare, and the third, Dante, a Tertiary, or Lay Franciscan. Behind St Francis stand two virgins (and three figures who may be the Wise Virgins of the New Testament). In the right-hand corner the figure of Penitence puts Love to flight, along with Death, Immodesty, and Concupisence.

c *Allegory of Obedience*. The figure of Obedience raises her forefinger to command silence. To either side are Prudence and Humility. An angel below the figure of Humility blocks a centaur, the symbol of pride and violence.

d *Apotheosis*. St Francis enthroned and surrounded by angels.

15 **Choir** (1471). A beautiful, three-tiered work by the Florentine, Tomaso di Antonio, Andrea da Montefalco, and others.

16 **Left Transept**. The two groups of frescoes are both by Pietro Lorenzetti and assistants (and possibly his brother, Ambrogio). Right vault: *Capture of Jesus*; *Last Supper*; *Flagellation*. Left vault: *Entry into Jerusalem*; *Calvary*; *Washing of Jesus' Feet*. On the left of the transept are two of the church's highlights: Lorenzetti's **Madonna and Child with St Francis and St John**, and his remarkable (but damaged) *Crucifixion*. The rear wall contains more works by the same artist: a superb *Deposition*, and, to its right, a lesser *Resurrection*.

17 Cappella di San Giovanni Battista. The chapel was founded, like its opposite number, by Napoleone Orsini (1288). Above the altar is an outstanding triptych by Lorenzetti, **Madonna and Child with St Francis and John the Baptist**. The stained glass in the chapel is believed to be some of the oldest in the church. Its design is attributed either to Cimabue or one of the Roman painters.

18 Sacristry. The room was damaged by fire in 1952. The main work of art is the **Madonna and Child with St Francis and St Clare** (1320s) by an unknown Umbrian artist, the Maestro di Figline. Under the painting is a door which leads to the so-called 'secret sacristry'. This contains a vast number of relics associated with St Francis (already catalogued by 1338). Among the more interesting and bizarre are: the Papal Bull approving the Order (1223); the white shirt used by Francis during his final illness; the special sandals made for Francis by Clare to relieve the pain of his stigmata; the stone on which the saint's head rested in the tomb, and many more.

19 Pulpit (thirteenth century). In a niche above are the **Coronation of the Virgin** and the *Miracle of St Stanislao*, frescoes attributed to Puccio Capanna di Assisi, one of the most important local followers of Giotto.

20 **Cappella di San Martino.** The **frescoes** by Simone Martini — *Scenes from* *the Life of St Martin* — (1322–?6) are the high point of the Lower Church. Stained glass: 18 *Saints*, probably from designs by Martini. Entrance arch: *Saints*. Rear wall: *St Martin and Cardinal Partino*. Left wall (from the bottom): *The Saint Divides his Cloak with a Poor Man*; *The Saint Revives a Child*; *The Saint at the Funeral of St Liborious, Bishop of Tours*; *Death of the Saint and his Assumption*; *Emperor Valentine Pays Tribute to the Saint*. Right wall: *The Saint Renounces Arms and Leads with a Cross*; *Christ appears to the Saint*: *The Saint leaves St Hilary, Bishop of Poitiers*; *Celebration of Mass*; *The Saint is made a Knight by Emperor Constantius*.

Museo-Tesoro della Basilica

Open 9.30–12.30, 14.30–18.
Closed Monday and November–March.
Admission charge.

The entrance to the Treasury — home to works of art given to the Basilica over the centuries — is on the terrace behind the apse. It can also be entered from the Upper Church. There is a broad selection of paintings, including a collection of modern art inspired by Franciscan themes, as well as the noted **Perkins collection**, a bequest of 57 fourteenth- and fifteenth-century masterpieces comprising paintings by Lorenzetti, Masolino di Panicale, Signorelli, Fra Angelico, and others. Also expect to see works by Gozzoli, Bonfigli, the Umbrian and Sienese schools, Dono Doni, Lo Spagna, and the Maestro di San Francesco. The range and number of the other exhibits is enormous — too large to be catalogued here. For the most part they consist of silverware — chalices and reliquaries, religious paraphernalia — copes, vestments, tapestries, and the like, plus a fair sprinkling of miscellaneous 'precious objects'.

Upper Church

Few contrasts can be more marked than that between the Upper and Lower Churches. Upstairs everything is big, bright, and airy, majestic even, as if in celebration. The floor-plan is simple and straightforward: a single nave and transepts, with the soaring Gothic ceiling (and every other surface) glitteringly decorated. All eyes inevitably turn to Giotto's fresco cycle, far bigger than all the postcards and reproductions prepare you for, and then — nothing. The church is curiously empty, almost as if the paintings were the only reason for its existence — but what paintings! The squabblings of the art historians, or the many restorations over the years cease to matter — these paintings are unquestionably some of Italy's finest.

The 28 frescoes of **Scenes from the Life of St Francis** start on the right-hand wall in the corner nearest the altar.

1 The saint is honoured by a simple man in Assisi's Piazza del Comune. Notice the artistic licence taken with the Temple of Minerva — five columns instead

The Upper Church. (ISTO)

of the actual six.

2 The saint offers his cloak to a poor man. To the left is a view of Assisi from Porta Nuova, with a view in the distance of Subasio's Benedictine Abbey.

3 The saint dreams of a palace full of weapons, each with the sign of the cross.

4 The saint in San Damiano, where he hears the voice of God telling him to repair the Church.

5 **Francis strips in front of his father and the Bishop of Assisi, who covers the saint with a cloak.**

6 The saint appears to Pope Innocent III in a dream.

7 Pope Innocent III approves the Franciscan Order.

8 Francis appears before his companions in a flaming chariot.

9 Brother Leone sees the celestial throne for which Francis is destined.

10 **The saint chases the Devils from Arezzo.**

11 **The saint proposes a trial by fire before the sultan.**

12 The ecstasy of the saint.

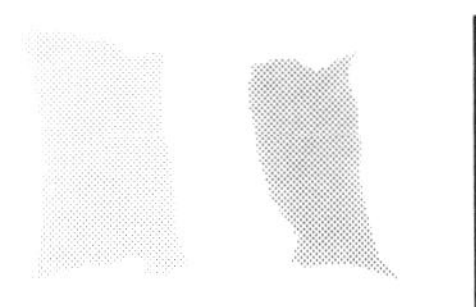

13 **Francis performs a service at Greccio with the first Christmas crib.** One of the most outstanding frescoes from the point of view of perspective depth and narrative power.

14 **The saint causes a fountain to flow.**

15 **The Sermon to the Birds** — possibly the most famous fresco of all.

16 **The saint predicts the death of a man.**

17 The saint preaches at the (spellbound) Court of Pope Onorio III.

18 The saint appears to the Franciscan friars at Arles.

19 Francis receives the stigmata. (The iconography of this fresco continued to appear in Italian art for centuries.)

20 The death and funeral of the saint.

21 The saint appears to Brother Augustin and the Bishop of Assisi.

22 The truth of the stigmata is confirmed.

23 Clare's lament over the corpse of Francis at San Damiano. (Notice the church's elaborate but actually non-existent facade.)

24 The Canonization of St Francis (partly lost).

25 The saint appears to Pope Gregory IX to dispel doubts over the stigmata. (This, and the remaining frescoes are not attributed to Giotto, but to a painter known only as the Maestro della Santa Cecilia.)

26 The recovery of the gentleman of Ilerda from a mortal wound.

27 The triumph of a woman after confession.

28 Pietro d'Alife, accused of heresy, is released from prison.

Left transept

Crucifixion (?1277) One of Cimabue's most striking frescoes, despite the damage caused by oxidation of its lead-based pigments. Giotto, and possibly Duccio, may have assisted Cimabue as pupils. The five *Apocalyptic Scenes* next to it have been reduced to little more than their bare outlines.

Apse

Faint frescoes by Cimabue of the *Life of the Virgin*. Below them, the Papal throne (fourteenth century). (The Basilica is the only Papal See outside St.Peter's in Rome.) The apse is dominated by a stunning **choir**: 105 intricately carved and inlaid stalls. The majority of the figures represent history's more illustrious Franciscans. The frescoes in the vaults above the main altar (consecrated in 1253) are by Cimabue.

Right transept

The frescoes here — also by Cimabue — are in very poor condition. They are a *Crucifixion* and *Scenes from the Life of St Peter.*

Nave

Giotto's are not the only frescoes in the nave. The first set of ceiling vaults (starting from the facade) depicts the *Four Doctors of the Church*, attributed to either Rusuti, Giotto, or a follower of Giotto. The figures in the third set of vaults — *Jesus*, *Mary*, *John the Baptist*, and *St Francis* — are by Jacopo Torriti (1290).

The walls contain another fresco cycle, a much damaged and, of course, overshadowed sequence depicting stories from the Old and New Testaments. Vasari believed they were by Cimabue; today they are attributed to the Roman school (Torriti, Rusuti, and Cavallini) and to pupils of Cimabue (possibly including the young Giotto). They start on the right-hand wall towards the altar.

Right-hand wall: 1. *Separation of Light from Darkness*; 2. *Creation of Adam*; 3. *Creation of Eve*; 4. *Original Sin*; 5. *Expulsion from Paradise*; 6. (Lost); 7. *Sacrifice of Cain and Abel*; 8. *Cain Murders Abel*; 9. *Building the Ark*; 10. *The Flood*; 11. *Sacrifice of Isaac*; 12. *Abraham and the Angels*; 13. *Deceit of Jacob*; 14. *Esau and Isaac*; 15. *Joseph*; 16. *Brothers of Joseph in Egypt*.

Left-hand wall: 1. *Annunciation*; 2. *Visitation* (lost); 3. *Nativity*; 4. *Epiphany*; 5. *Presentation in the Temple*; 6. *Flight into Egypt*; 7. *Jesus* (from the *Dispute in the Temple*); 8. *Baptism of Jesus*; 9. *Wedding at Cana*; 10. *Resurrection of Lazarus*; 11. *Arrest of Jesus*; 12. *Flagellation*; 13. *Journey to Calvary*; 14. *Crucifixion*; 15. *Deposition*; 16. *Mary at the Tomb*; 17. *Ascension*; 18. *Pentecost*.

The Rest of the Town

Temple of Minerva

'It is impossible to describe the deep impression I received from the contemplation of this edifice, and it will produce everlasting fruit', said Goethe of the temple. It was the 'first complete monument of ancient days' he had seen since crossing into Italy, and the only thing in Assisi he had time for. The Basilica he dismissed as those 'monstrous bowels of churches on top of each other in a Babylonian pile', an excessive, but perhaps understandable, reaction from a man reared on the eighteenth-century taste for classicism.

The temple formed part of the old Roman forum which was situated on the site of the present Piazza del Comune. All that now remains is the porch, or *pronao* — six genuinely impressive columns from the first century AD — the rest was destroyed by the Barbarians or converted into Santa Maria sopra Minerva, a sixteenth-century baroque church of no interest whatsoever.

Pinacoteca Comunale

Open Tuesday–Saturday 9–12, 16–19, Sunday 9–12.
Small admission charge.

The small, six-roomed gallery is housed in the thirteenth-century Palazzo Comunale, four linked buildings rather knocked out of joint by the twentieth-century neo-Romanesque post office next door. The Basilica would be a hard act for any gallery to follow, but the pinacoteca still merits a visit, with some excellent little works by Nicolò Alunno, Ottaviano Nelli, and L'Ingegno. (L'Ingegno, or 'the Genius', is another of Umbria's mysteriously elusive painters. All we know is that he studied alongside Raphael and under Perugino, helping the latter paint the Collegio di Cambio in Perugia.) All the best paintings are

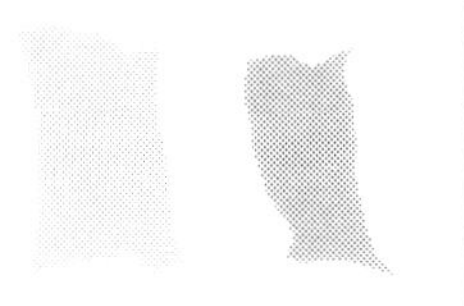

in Room II, where you should look out especially for a fifteenth-century picture describing the story of San Guiliano. He slaughtered his parents in bed, believing one to be his wife and the other her lover (his wife is actually behind him in the picture, screaming blue murder). He built a hospital to try to make amends. Room I houses earlier works — school of Giotto for the most part, along with the poorish remnants of some detached thirteenth-century frescoes.

Museo Civico

Open 9.30–12.30, 16.30–19.

The museum stands at the entrance to the Piazza del Comune (Via del Seminario 2) and is housed in the eleventh-century crypt of what was once the church of San Nicolò.

The main reason for a visit is the opportunity to see the partly excavated remains of the old Roman forum, still extant under the bars and restaurants of the piazza above. H. V. Morton in *A Traveller in Italy* called this 'one of the most surprising experiences I had known in Italy'. The entrance comprises fragments and a second-century sarcophagus, followed by a headless Apollo (or Castor), probably from a group that formed the centrepiece of the forum. Alongside is an Etruscan statue of Charon (note the pouch used to collect money for conducting the dead over the River Styx). There are also parts of the old travertine pavements, the bases of monuments, fountains, urns, gravestones, and a long stone dais with fittings for seven chairs: the spot where magistrates — or the tribune — sat in session.

Duomo di San Rufino

Exterior

Though in a quiet and restful corner, and in the centre of ancient Assisi, there is a slight air of gloom about the Duomo, as if it knows that it is not the focal point it might have been in any other town. It was built between the twelfth and thirteenth century, with a beautiful, if typical, Umbrian facade (the usual three tiers) and a vast blockhouse of a tower dating from the eleventh century. The central door is extraordinary, guarded by two red marble lions — one eating a man's head — and framed by a straggling pattern of lilies, leaves, faces, penguins, winged crocodiles, masses of intertwined finery, and two lolling griffins, one chewing pieces from its neighbour.

Interior

The interior was remodelled to predictable effect in the sixteenth century and is extremely tedious. Most of the works of art date from the nineteenth century, and could be cheerfully consigned to oblivion. At the back right-hand corner of the three naves is the porphyry font used to baptize Saints

The Duomo. (ISTO)

Francis, Clare, and Agnes, and the future Emperor Frederick II, who, by strange historical coincidence, was born prematurely in a field outside the town. You can also see the stone knelt on by the angel who attended Francis's immersion (disguised as a pilgrim). It contains the imprint left by his knee. After a word with the saint's mother he apparently vanished.

The wooden choir stalls (1520) pass muster — they are by a pupil of the man who carved the finer stalls in the Basilica. Left of the altar in the Cappella della Madonna is a German terracotta Virgin. A tablet records the fact of its bursting into tears in 1494.

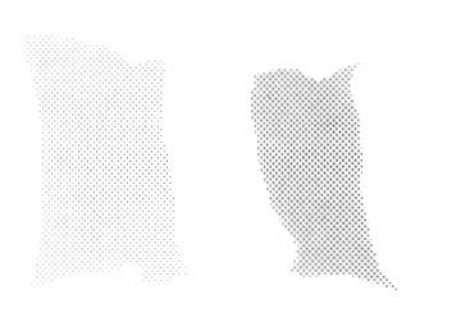

Museo Capitolare

Via the sacristry on the right-hand side of the apse is the cathedral museum, its handful of works worth more than all of those in the interior. The collection is dominated by a triptych, *Madonna and Child and Four Saints* by Nicolò Alunno. Make a point of checking the exquisite miniature work in the predella above, which details San Rufino's extravagant martyrdom. There is another, lesser, triptych by Matteo da Gualdo, and one rougher still by Maso, or Giottino, an anonymous painter who also crops up in the Lower Church.

Equally interesting is the descent into the crypt (ask in the sacristry). It is entered from a small piazza outside the Duomo to the right. Here are the remains of the church's second incarnation, built by Bishop Ugonia in 1028. The faint vestiges of fresco — *St Mark and the Lion* — were once thought to be some of the oldest in Italy, third only to those in the catacombs in Rome, and St Celso in Verona. They are not, of course, but are still fairly venerable. The Roman sarcophagus, with its racy story of Diana and Endymion, was San Rufino's first tomb; he is now thought to lie upstairs under the main altar.

Rocca Maggiore

Open summer 9–12, 14–18.
Admission free.

It is difficult to miss the well-preserved castle, which dominates the broad crown of Assisi's hilltop. The best time to see it is probably after a visit to the Duomo. Opening times, seem to vary according to the custodian's mood.

It was reputedly built on the site of an ancient burial ground, where Umbrian seers used to perch and look out for whatever signs and omens seers looked out for. During its long history it has entertained a colourful collection of characters ranging from Popes, Emperors, Viscontis, and Medicis to the pampered Lucrezia Borgia, who received it from her father as part of a wedding dowry.

Defensive walls first rose after Charlemagne rebuilt Assisi in 733, and were designed to help Papal emissaries keep the town's citizens in check. Albornoz arrived on the scene in 1367 to reclaim the castle for the Popes. He repaired the walls, which had been damaged through repeated skirmishes with Perugia, only for disgusted townspeople to pull them down a few years later. From time to time it was used as a prison. Executions took place for the lucky ones in Piazza del Comune; if the governor was impatient, however, malefactors could just as easily be hung from the battlements, or simply thrown out of a window into the ravine.

It finally became less important with the building of the Rocca Paolina in Perugia, and the firm establishment of Papal power. By the eighteenth century it had fallen into almost complete disrepair. A supplication from the city governor to Rome in 1726 asked that, 'the strong and ancient castle of Assisi, which had always been the chief fortress of Umbria, should be saved from ruin', but to no avail; many of its stones found their way in wheelbarrows to new houses being built around the station. What survives today are the evocative, but much restored remains.

Basilica di Santa Chiara

Chiara, or Clare, St Francis's doting companion from the age of 17 and the founder of the Poor Clares (the female wing of the Franciscans), was buried in 1253 with all the pomp and splendour that had surrounded her mentor's funeral 27 years before. She was canonized in 1255 and two years later work began on a basilica designed to replace her tomb in San Damiano. It was built on the site of San Giorgio, where Francis had gone to school, and where his body had lain for two years during construction of the Basilica. It was a virtual copy of the Upper Church with the important difference that it was not as well built, hence the flying buttresses, which support walls that would otherwise have collapsed into their crumbling foundations.

The Poor Clares moved from San Damiano with Clare's body, and in the process lost their Franciscan links (they had used to beg for the friars). They became a comtemplative rather than an active Order, under the jurisdiction, what is more, of the Papacy, which demanded (and still demands) a pound of candles as tribute on the feast of St Francis.

The church is physically large, and an important point of pilgrimage, though it may be a disappointment for the casual visitor. After a sumptuous rose window, the interior is dark and bare, with scant colour, and a few patches of faded or ruined fresco. The ruin is attributed partly to a seventeenth-century German, Bishop Spader, who, fearing that the nuns, peering through their grating, might see too much of the wordly tourists who came to admire the church's frescoes, whitewashed the paintings over.

Some works of art, however, survived his self-righteousness. Right of the main altar is the entrance to the Cappella del Sacramento — part of the old church of San Giorgio — dotted with several patches of fresco. The best is an Umbrian/Giottesque *Madonna, Child and Saints* on the left-hand wall. The adjoining chapel (the Cappella del Crocifisso) houses the famous twelfth-century crucifix said to have bowed its head to St Francis and told him to go and repair God's Church.

The most startling sight is the body of St Clare itself. Like St Francis she was buried in secret and only found in 1850. When her coffin was opened, sprigs of wild thyme placed there hundreds of years earlier were said to have kept their fragrance. Her body, long blackened by age and less wholesome agents (weevils), was not so inviolate. The flesh was more cotton wool and rotten bindings than saintly substance — and full of very much alive insect life. She recently paid a long-overdue visit to a Roman saint-restorer for patching up. Nor was that the end of her indignities; she was made patron saint of *television* in 1958, something to do with a vision she had of a Christmas service taking place a mile away in the Basilica.

an Damiano. (ISTO)

San Damiano

San Damiano is the church where St Francis received his calling to repair God's Church. It was also the home he gave to the Poor Clares, and where Clare herself lived a pinched and frugal life from the age of 18 to her death. The nuns left seven years after their mistress's departure, and the church now belongs to the Friars Minor, who have kept it in much the same state as it was centuries ago. Alone amongst the spots in Assisi with Franciscan associations, this one preserves something of an ideal or spirit that is recognizably Franciscan — rural peace and quiet, groves of olives, cypresses, wild flowers, summer's drowsy humming, and the pastoral Vale of Spoleto stretching away into the haze below.

It was one of the saint's favourite retreats. He came here sick and half-blind towards the end of his life and composed the 'Canticle to the Sun'. Thereafter he returned only once, in death, fulfilling a promise to Clare that she might see him for the last time before he was buried.

Above the door is the small balcony where Clare stood in 1241 to turn back a Saracen army that was pursuing Assisi's Guelphs. In a closed chapel to the left are some unremarkable paintings by Tiberio d'Assisi, and on the left-hand wall a fresco of St Roch proudly displaying a large black plague-spot — he is the patron saint of, or rather against, infectious skin diseases.

Inside is a single, sparsely decorated nave of utter simplicity. On the right-hand side is the small window where San Damiano's priest threw the money that Francis offered him to repair the church. Nearby you can see the tiny hole where the saint hid 'for a month' from the wrath of his father. The large crucifix here was made in 1634. The friar who carved it had worked for nine days and had only the head to finish. Leaving it overnight, he returned next morning to find that 'mysterious hands' had completed the work. Christ's face is said to show agony, death, or peace, depending on the viewer's standpoint.

Beyond some stairs leading to a terrace and small garden is a vestibule with a woodwormy choir and two frescoes, one an altarpiece by Mezzastris (1482), the other a lovely *Madonna and Child* by a unknown Giottesque artist. Up the stairs you reach the oratorio, and then a small dormitory, with a small cross and flowers marking the spot where Clare died. A door to the right leads to the cloisters; to the left of a fresco by Eusebio di San Giorgio (*St Francis Receiving the Stigmata* — 1507) another door opens on to the refectory. Its low, smoke-darkened vaults perhaps evoke the sheer simplicity of the monastic life more effectively than anything else in the town. The chairs, table, and oak benches are all origninal. Flowers, again, usually mark Clare's own place.

Santa Maria degli Angeli

The church is in the slightly squalid lower town, and all accounts, even those of baroque sympathizers, agree that it is a mess, and an extremely large one at that. It was built in 1569 with the simple purpose of protecting the Porzuincola (literally 'little portion'), the small chapel where Francis founded his first monastery, and where he died in 1226. It is an important point of pilgrimage, particularly on 1–2 August, the so-called 'Pardon of St Francis'. (The saint had a vision of Christ, who asked him what might be best for the human soul. Francis replied forgiveness for all who crossed the threshold of his chapel.) The already vast numbers of pilgrims were swelled in the 1920s by the supposed movement of the 8-metre high bronze Madonna that crowns the facade.

Legend has it that the first retreat on the site was built by four pilgrims from Jerusalem. They buried a fragment of the Virgin's tomb and then went home. St Benedict repaired the walls in the sixth century, and spent time in the chapel. On establishing Monte Cassino he sent a handful of monks to look after the building. They eventually moved on to a larger monastery east of the town, and in time made it over to Francis as a base for his newly founded Order (1209). The Franciscans, not allowing themselves property, paid rent in the form of a basket of carp; the tribute is still observed.

Most of the key events in the Franciscan story occurred around this early home. It was to here in 1212, for example, that Clare came when she ran away from her family. Francis himself cut her hair, removed her jewellery, and clad her in the Franciscan habit. A settlement of mud huts sprang up to accommodate the rapidly growing Order. In 1221 the community played host to the first Franciscan convention, a jamboree that attracted 5000 followers and sympathizers from all over Europe.

bove and right *Umbrian ineyards near Perugia.* (JD)

ight *Market-day, Castiglione del ago.* (JD)

Above *Fontana Maggiore, Perugia.* (JD)

Right *Oratorio di San Bernardino, Perugia.* (JD)

bove *Farm near Pozzuolo, rugia*. (JD)

ight St Francis Preaching to the irds *by Giotto, Upper Church, ssisi*. (JD)

Right *Eremo delle Carceri, Assisi.* (JD)

Opposite *The Duomo, Spoleto.* (DL)

Below Crucifixion *by Pietro Lorenzetti, Lower Church, Assisi.* (ISTO)

Above *The facade of San Pietro, Spoleto.* (DL)

Right Coronation of the Virgin *by Fra Lippo Lilli, the Duomo, Spoleto.* (ISTO)

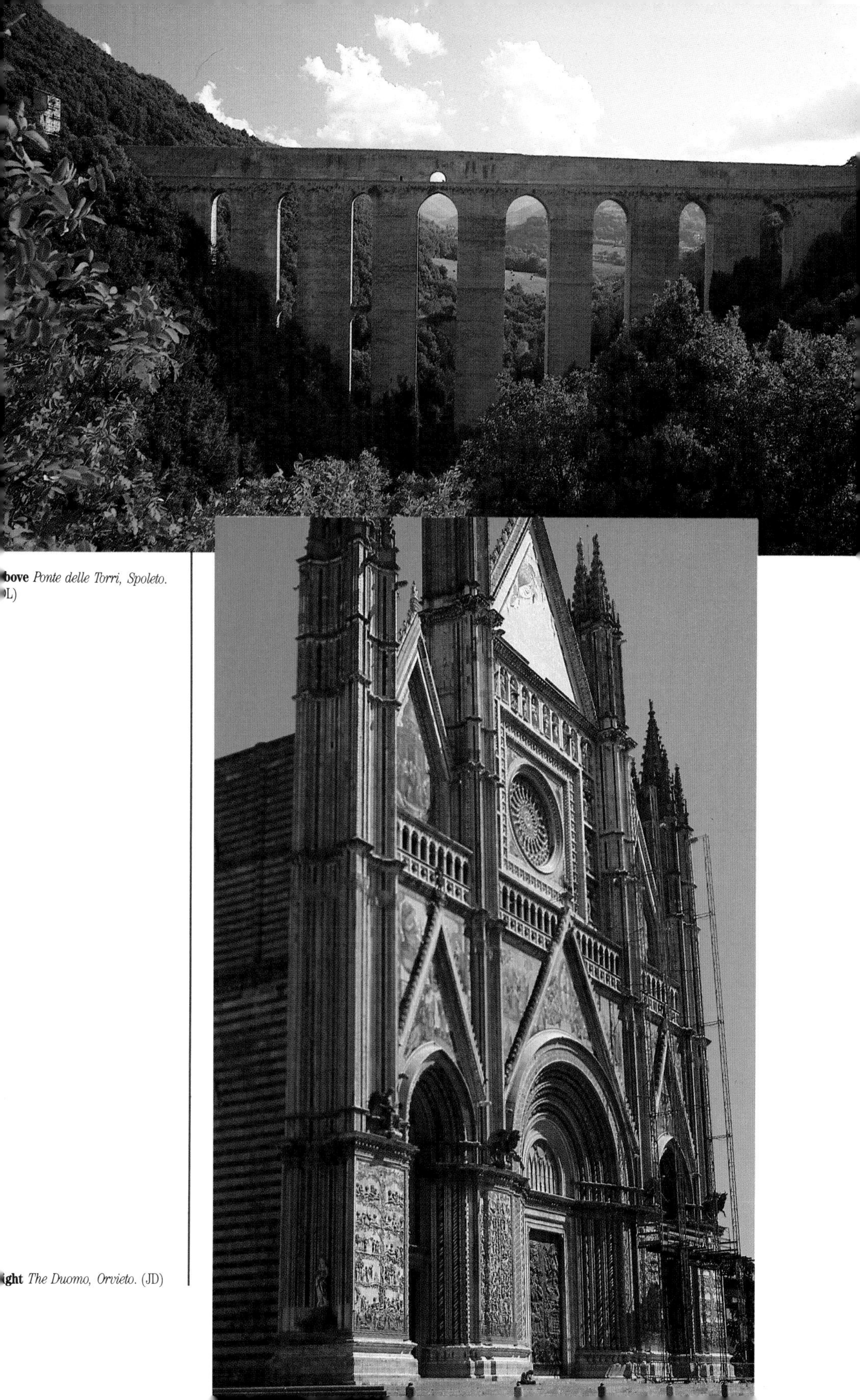

bove *Ponte delle Torri, Spoleto.*)L)

ight *The Duomo, Orvieto.* (JD)

Above *The Duomo, Todi.* (JD)

Right *Medieval street, Todi.* (JD)

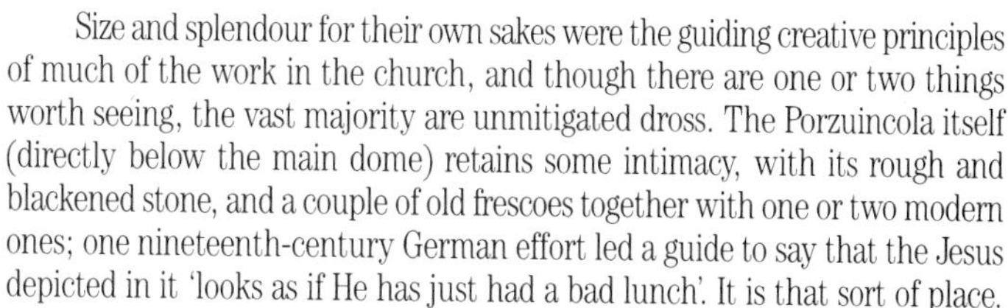

Size and splendour for their own sakes were the guiding creative principles of much of the work in the church, and though there are one or two things worth seeing, the vast majority are unmitigated dross. The Porzuincola itself (directly below the main dome) retains some intimacy, with its rough and blackened stone, and a couple of old frescoes together with one or two modern ones; one nineteenth-century German effort led a guide to say that the Jesus depicted in it 'looks as if He has just had a bad lunch'. It is that sort of place.

Buried in the chapel is Brother Cataneii, one of the earliest Franciscans. He performed so many miracles from beyond the grave, and attracted so many expectant crowds as a result, that Francis implored him in prayer, 'now that we are infected with all these people of the world, I enjoin thee by obedience to make an end of thy miracles and allow us to recover in peace'. The miracles stopped. Beyond, on the right, at the beginning of the presbytery, is the small Cappella del Transito, with some dubious frescoes by Matteo da Gualdo and a noted fifteenth-century terracotta statue of St Francis by Andrea della Robbia. (Though his six bas-reliefs in the apse are actually more genuinely noteworthy.)

Beneath the big choir there are some remnants of the thirteenth–fifteenth-century churches, which were uncovered in 1966, and are occasionally open to the public. Enquire about current arrangements for a visit in the sacristry (through which you should go to reach the Cappella della Roseto — frescoes (1518) by Tiberio d'Assisi). The garden here contains the rose-bushes into which St Francis threw himself one night whilst wrestling with a particularly tempting temptation. The thorns obligingly dropped off on coming into contact with Francis's flesh, and the bushes have been thornless ever since. The leaves, however, are a variegated red, permanently stained with that evening's blood.

Moving back to the church, the cloisters contain a small museum (*open 9–12 and 14–18*, but liable to vary). Among a predictable collection of vestments are books of Gregorian chants, a rare *Crucifixion* by Giunto Pisano, a delicate work by Mezzastris, and a fresco of St Francis by the Maestro di San Francesco.

Eremo delle Carceri

The Eremo delle Carceri is a captivating monastery in enchanting countryside, and the subject of many a photograph and picture-postcard. It is set in a wooded cleft on the side of Mount Subasio, a sudden splash of white stone in a blanket of green, and looks very much as you imagine a monastery should. Reached by a rough but much-travelled road that leaves Assisi by Porta Cappuccini, it is only 4 kilometres away, a proximity that rather takes the edge off its sense of monastic isolation. Even so, the spot exudes a genuine Franciscan charm — tempered only by the cars during busy periods. (For which reason the steep, but pretty, walk from the town is not what it might be.)

The Benedictines, who held spiritual sway over Umbria before the Franciscans, probably gave Francis a small church on the site, though the monastery's precise origins are obscure. So too is the derivation of its name, the 'monastery of the prisons'. *Carcere* in modern Italian means 'prison' in

Eremo delle Carceri. (JD)

the literal sense, but in the past it referred to a place enclosed by a fence some distance from human habitation (such as a monastery). Perhaps, as some have suggested, the name was prompted by the idea of a place in which people were 'imprisoned in prayer'; Francis and his followers, after all, spurned the church in favour of local caves and hollowed out 'cells' in the surrounding hills.

On a good day a friar should show you round the buildings, which for the most part are comparatively modern. There is first a courtyard and a well, whose waters, you learn with no surprise, Francis caused to flow. Opposite is a small fourteenth-century church containing the Oratorio Primitivo, the saint's original cell, with his stone bed and the piece of wood he used as a pillow. The crucifix on the wall is one presumed to have been used by Francis. An eighteenth-century chronicler reports an event the century before in which the cross 'was seen by Brother Silvestro to detach itself from the wall, and with most gentle slaps on the face, warn a worshipper to be reverent and vigilant while praying in this sacred Oratory'. The chapel also contains a cupboard full of the usual relics, including part of the saint's pillow and a piece of the Golden Gate through which Jesus passed into Jerusalem. Sadly, the collection is now missing the hair of the Virgin Mary, and some of the earth that God used to create Adam. On the other side of the church, you see a dry river bed, once a torrent until Francis told it to hush because it was spoiling his prayers. It fills up today only when some public calamity is at hand. One of the walls here was built over the so-called *buco del diavolo*, a crevice into which Francis had cast a devil by the power of prayer. The old holm oak, kept upright by iron stakes, is said to have shaded the saint, and been the spot where birds collected to hear his sermons.

Other churches

San Pietro

Though you may feel that the Basilica is religion enough for one town, Assisi has a couple of churches that are worth a look if you have time. San Pietro, a stone's throw from the Basilica, is the most appealing, with an austerity that might have been more appropriate in San Francesco itself. There is reputed to have been a chapel on the site since the second century, which, if true, would make it the town's oldest church. The present building was started in 970, with the main body dating from the mid thirteenth century.

The front of the church has an unusual six-sectioned facade, as distinct from the customary three, while the interior was well restored in 1954 to its Romanesque original. There is little to see in the way of frescoes, but the place's charm is its simplicity, a refreshing change after the sumptuousness of the art further along the road.

Santa Maria Maggiore

A walk along Borgo San Pietro to the left of the church, brings you to this other simple Romanesque building. It dates from 963, but was rebuilt after a fire between 1212 and 1228. St Francis is said to have reconstructed the apse personally. Until the consecration of San Rufino it was the town's cathedral. The plain facade, divided oddly and vertically, is in the familiar red and white stone that lends character to much of Assisi. The interior is similarly humble, and contains an interesting crypt with remains of the old church and fragments of a Roman house.

Where to stay

Note: In Assisi, more than any other Umbrian town (including Spoleto), it is advisable to book accommodation in advance. Hotels are under assault not only from tourists, but also from a year-round army of pilgrims. The tourist office operates a useful room-finding service that should usually be able to help you, but in emergencies you might be forced to try hotels in nearby towns such as Foligno, Spello, and Bevagna. Avoid Bastia, however, at all costs, and only settle for the cheap modern rooms around the station in the last resort.

Hotel Subasio
★★★★

Since its foundation in 1868, all sorts, from Marlene Dietrich to Charlie Chaplin, have stayed in this converted thirteenth-century monastery next door to the Basilica. It boasts a garden and vine-covered terraces with views down over the Vale of Spoleto. It is larger, but cheaper, than Assisi's other famous four-star hotel, La Fontabella (Via Fontabella 23. Tel. 812883). Via Frate Elia 2. Tel. 812206. Rooms 66.

Umbra
★★★

A favourite amongst Assisi old-timers, and highly recommended. It is medieval, smallish, with a peaceful location in a pedestrianized area close to Piazza del

Comune. Some rooms have nook-and-cranny *en suite* arrangements; others balconies looking out over a patchwork of tiled roofs. Excellent restaurant. Via degli Archi 6. Tel. 812240. Rooms 27.

San Francesco ★★★

A sixteenth-century townhouse close to the Basilica, with large rooms and good views. A slightly down-market version of the Subasio. Via San Francesco 48. Tel. 812281. Rooms 45.

Castel San Gregorio ★★★

Located in the hamlet of San Gregorio 12 kilometres north-west of Assisi on the Valfabbrica road, this twelfth-century castle is set amidst the rural peace and quiet of an Azienda Agricola. Facilities run (incongruously) to a solarium. Via S. Gregorio 16. Tel. 8038009. Rooms 12. Bathrooms 3. Showers 10.

Ideale per Turisti ★★

Despite the absurd name, this is a small, modern and well-furnished hotel, with the bonus of a garden and good views. Piazza Matteotti 1. Tel. 813570. Rooms 9. Bathrooms 2. Showers 8.

Sole ★★

Five minutes to the Basilica. Restaurant, but no telephone reservations. Corso Mazzini 35 (with an extension at No. 20). Tel. 812373. Rooms 30. Bathrooms 9. Showers 16.

Lo Scudo ★★

Very central. Via San Francesco. Tel. 813196. Rooms 8. Showers 8.

La Rocca ★

On a street that runs through a quieter part of town from the Duomo to Porta Perlici. Large rooms and a well-sited restaurant. Via di Porta Perlici 27. Tel. 812284. Rooms 15. Showers 8.

Camping

Fontemaggio ★★

Located in the tourist village complex of the same name on the road out to the Eremo delle Carceri. *Open all year.* Tel. 813636. Places 100.

Hostels

Hostel Antonelli ★★

Aimed at the large pilgrim market. Via Los Angeles 25, Santa Maria degli Angeli. Tel. 8401901. Rooms 105.

Cenacolo Francescano ★

Likewise aimed at a mass market. Via Porta d'Italia 70. Tel. 8041083. Rooms 130.

Youth Hostel

In Fontemaggio, under the same management as the campsite. Tel. 812317.

Where to eat

Buca di San Francesco

Bustling, busy and up-market, the best restaurant in Assisi, and justifiably renowned. Has a large medieval cellar (120 places), which generates a suitable atmosphere, plus a gracious garden in the summer (80 places). Try the *bruschette, cannelloni alla Maddalena, filetto al Rubesco*, pigeon, the truffle sauces, and any of the varieties of homemade *pasta*. A prized and praised selection of wines and rare brandies. Via Brizi 1. Tel. 812204. *Closed Monday and from 1 to 20 July*. Expensive.

Umbra

Affiliated with the hotel of the same name. It shares the honours with La Buca as the town's best, though has a smaller and more classical interior (80 places). Shaded and delightful *al fresco* eating in the summer under a large pergola. Draws together various regional specialities — white Gubbian truffles, Norcia *salami*, Castellucio lentils, and so on, but often gives them an interesting twist. Via degli Archi 6. Tel. 812240. *Closed Tuesday and all of November.*

La Fortezza

There is little to choose between La Fortezza and La Buca, though prices here are a little lower. It is very central, and again has plenty of medieval charm. (Parts of the building are actually Roman.) Meat dishes (rabbit in asparagus sauce, for example) are a speciality. Regional wines. Vicolo della Fortezza 2/b. Tel. 812418. *Closed Thursday (except during August–September) and for the whole of February.*

La Stalla

A simple, charming and rustic restaurant that has been converted from a set of old stables. It is out of the town proper on the road to the Eremo delle Carceri. Has a lovely flower-strewn pergola/garden setting in the summer with seating for 300. Hearty, down-to-earth cooking and good local wines. Look out for the home-produced oil, honey, and cheeses, the *tagliatelle della casa* and the old peasant dish, *polenta con salsicce*. Via Eremo delle Carceri 8. Tel. 812317. *Closed Monday. No holidays.*

Other safe bets if the above are full include: **La Fontana da Carletto**, Via San Francesco 8. *Closed Tuesday/February*; **Il Frantoio**, Via Fontabella 25. *Closed Wednesday and November* and **Il Medioevo**, Via dell'Arco dei Priori 4.

Pizzeria

Via Italia 34. *Closed Monday.*

Pizzeria Il Pozzo Romana

Also a *birreria*. *Open late*. Via Sant'Agnese (near Piazza Santa Chiara).

AROUND ASSISI

Spello

TOURIST INFORMATION: Via Garibaldi 17
POPULATION: 7000
HEIGHT: 280 m
STD CODE: 0742

History

Originally Umbrian, Spello came into its own under the Romans, mainly as a result of Augustus granting large tracts of land in the area to his pensioned-off legionaries. This turned the town into a sort of Roman retirement home, adding a strange geriatric dimension to its importance as a staging-post on the Via Flaminia. (The main section of the road swung north at this point towards Nocera, with a secondary spur branching off to Perugia.) It was also a major religious centre: Constantine built one of Umbria's biggest temples in the vicinity (now vanished without trace).

Spello then became part of the Dukedom of Spoleto, was absorbed into the Church, and later experienced the usual dizzying vicissitudes between tyrants, rival families, and neighbouring towns, of which Perugia, naturally, was the most predatory.

The town was, to all intents and purposes, finished after the Romans, and even today it has scarcely strayed beyond their substantial walls. Still self-enclosed, it retains a thoroughly medieval appearance, the only detractions being a faintly messy twentieth-century sprawl outside, and a rash of well-intentioned but garish yellow signs erected by the tourist office. Its cluster of pink stone buildings rises gently on terraces — hardly a hill-town by Umbrian standards, though still rather striking (as any place lifted from the Middle Ages is bound to be). Spello is one of the gently appealing smaller towns, highly accessible, and surprisingly quiet — and with the bonus of an exceptionally beautiful fresco cycle. You will probably need little more than an hour to do it justice.

What to see

Roman Spello

Ignoring the odd remnants of frieze and fragment embedded in buildings, the most obvious traces of the Roman colony are the walls, 2 kilometres in length, and built in the reign of Augustus. There are five gates along their course, of which the most interesting is the Porta Venere, lonely, overgrown, and largely overlooked. It was named after a nearby temple to Venus, long vanished. Though now leading sadly nowhere it still at least manages to look the part. Whether the imposing twin towers are Roman or twelfth-century additions is unknown. Porta Consolare was where the Via Flaminia came into the town, and where you will probably enter as well. These days it is in a sorry state, ineffectually propped up, and rather lost in the modern bustle below. (Take a peek into the wonderful old bakery beyond it on the left.) Well outside the walls are the anaemic remains of the Roman amphitheatre, hardly worth the walk — though if you do venture forth, make the trek worthwhile by visiting the twelfth-century Romanesque church of San Claudio. It was raised from the ashes of a Roman building, and has a higgledy-piggledy asymmetry inside and out.

ppella Baglioni. (DL)

Santa Maria Maggiore

This twelfth-century church, remodelled five centuries later, is the town's highlight. Two columns languish from some forgotten temple in front of the campanile, overshadowed by the striking Romanesque door, which is decorated with characteristically bizarre carvings and surmounted by the remains of a Roman frieze. A serene but dull baroque interior unexpectedly harbours a stupendous **fresco cycle** (1501) by Pintoricchio (behind glass in the Cappella Baglioni to the left). Recent restoration has brought out the colours to quite breathtaking beauty, but inflation means that you now need a 1000-lire note for the pleasure of having them illuminated. The left-hand wall contains the *Annunciation* (with a self-portrait in the lower right-hand corner), the right-hand wall the *Dispute in the Temple*, the rear wall the *Adoration of the Shepherds* and the *Coming of the Magi*. The ceiling depicts four sybils (prophetesses to whom parts of the world were portioned off — there were ten in all). Pintoricchio was working in Spello, incidentally, at the same time as Perugino (his erstwhile teacher) was painting the Collegio di Cambio. (If you are a fan of this under-rated artist, note that only in his Sistine Chapel frescoes will you find him painting to better effect.) The chapel also has a much-lauded sixteenth-century floor of Derutan majolica. Sadly it does not quite live up to expectations. Over the centuries thousands of feet have worn away its once-gorgeous colours.

Elsewhere in the church, to the right and left of the altar, are two rather weak works by Perugino (1521), said to be the last signed and dated by the artist. Beyond the apse to the left there is a chapel with a faint angel, and in the chapel beyond a lovely *Madonna and Child*, both by Pintoricchio. There are further treasures in the right-hand transept, now screened off after recent thefts, and unlikely to be seen for some time.

Via Cavour and Via Garibaldi

There are more works by Pintoricchio a short way up the road in San Andrea. Its simple thirteenth-century facade hides a dark, atmospheric, and highly decorated interior. Few of the paintings and frescoes are of a high standard, but the overall effect is colourfully striking. The glorious exception is Pintoricchio's *Madonna, Child and Saints* in the right transept, painted in 1508 with the help of Eusebio di San Giorgio. Recent restorations have also revealed a worthy *Crucifixion* (second niche on the left) by an early thirteenth-century Umbrian hand.

Some ill-judged twentieth-century buildings have inexplicably compromised the medievalism of the central Piazza della Repubblica further up the hill. The arched Palazzo Comunale (1270) in the corner has a small gallery with one outstanding painting, the *Crucifixion and Coronation of the Virgin* (1391) by Cola Petruccioli, and a lesser *Crucifixion* by Nicolò Alunno. The modest fortress next door (1358) was one of the church's earliest attempts to strengthen its hand in Umbria.

A few doors beyond the Palazzo on the right is a seventeenth-century facade fronting the twelfth-century church of San Lorenzo. It is noted for a vast baroque altar canopy, modelled on Bernini's bronze enormity in St Peter's, Rome. There are also one or two patches of easily overlooked fresco. Onwards and upwards, the road enters the oldest part of the town, San Martino, with a belvedere offering a reasonable view over the factory-spotted Vale of Spoleto. You can look down on the grassy and overgrown remains of the amphitheatre (easier than walking to them), and, if the haze permits, on to Perugia and the dome of Assisi's Santa Maria degli Angeli.

If you have time you might take the road north-east to Collepino (5 kilometres), an outlying and picturesque village that once formed part of Spello's outer defences. Views and tranquillity are its sole satisfying attractions.

Where to stay

Dal Cacciatore ★★ In the central, upper part of town. Restaurant and parking. Via Giulia 42. Tel. 651141. Rooms 17. Bathrooms 1. Showers 16.

Julia ★★ Via San Angelo 22. Tel. 651174. Rooms 22. Showers 22.

…llepino. (JD)

Where to eat

Il Molino ★★

This is the best restaurant for several miles around; smartish, but relaxed, and with an attractive medieval vaulted dining-room. The food is traditional, perked up by the occasional novelty: *zuppa di legumi ed erbe*, *faggottino agli spinaci*, excellent *crostini*, wild mushrooms, and fine meats roasted on an open grill. Piazza Matteotti 6–7. Tel. 651305. *Closed Tuesday.*

Il Bastaglia

Less salubrious, and a good deal cheaper than Il Molino. A superb view from the terrace spices up the standard menu. (There is a 15-roomed, two-star hotel upstairs.) Via Salnitraria. Tel. 651277. *Closed Wednesday.*

Bevagna

TOURIST INFORMATION: 'Pro Mevania', Piazza Silvestri

History

Hardly ever visited, quiet and unspoilt, Bevagna can be seen in the blink of an eye. And yet it is amongst the most characteristic of the smaller

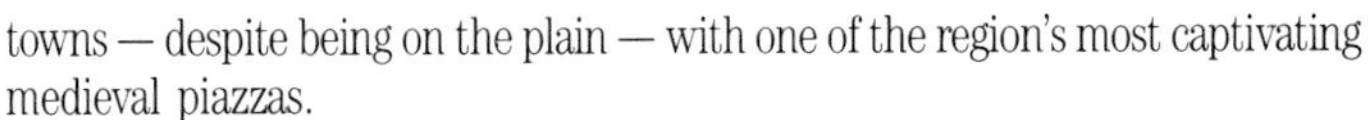

towns — despite being on the plain — with one of the region's most captivating medieval piazzas.

It was yet another staging-post on the Via Flaminia, fading in importance when a new spur to Spoleto was built in the third century. The subsequent decline was never reversed. Bevagna's Roman confines were larger than its medieval limits, and depopulation since the Second World War has left the present town still sealed within its thirteenth-century walls. It was famous in antiquity for its white bulls: Virgil describes how they were dipped into the sacred water of the Clitunnus, and herded to Rome to take part in triumphal processions.

A bishop, San Vincenzo, arrived as early as the third century, but was soon martyred — the usual lot of bishops at that particular time. The town has remembered him by turning his church into a cinema. Bevagna was burnt down by Barbarossa in 1152, and again by a captain in Frederick's II's imperial army in 1249, and then again by Foligno's ruling family, the Trinci, in 1375. What remained was handed to the Church for safe-keeping in 1439, lapsing therafter (inevitably) to Perugia's Baglioni.

What to see

Corso Matteotti

Corso Matteotti is Bevagna's main street; orientation could not be easier — it simple bisects the town from end to end. There are odd flakes from the Roman era fossilized in various buildings, and the remains of a second-century bath-house mosaic at Via Porta Guelpha 2 (off the narrow Piazza Garibaldi). It is well preserved and depicts Triton riding sea-horses accompanied by various creatures of the deep. A little further along the same piazza is the church of San Francesco, its best feature a linear and unfinished thirteenth-century facade. In the baroque interior is a memorial to one of the most famous episodes in the Franciscan story, the Sermon to the Birds. The *Fioretti* tells how Francis, 'came to a place between Cannara and Bevagna, and as with great fervour as he was going on his way, lifted up his eyes and beheld some trees hard by the road whereon sat a great company of birds . . . "ye shall wait for me here upon the way", he said, "and I will go to preach to my little sisters the birds" '. The medieval imagination tended to see animals of all kinds — pigs, cats, toads, bats — as harbingers of evil and foreboding, so this episode was more than just charming; it was trying to tell people something. Even St Dominic saw the Devil in something as innocuous as a sparrow. And the interior's memorial? The stone on which Francis stood to preach the sermon.

Continuing along the street there are other churches and minor distractions — thirteenth-century Santa Marguerita, with its baroque reworking, the Palazzo Comunale, with a first-floor picture gallery (*open 9–13*), and, immediately before Piazza Silvestri, the fourteenth-century church of SS.

Domenico e Giacomo. It too fell victim to the seventeenth-century taste for the baroque, but there are one or two patches of early fresco in the choir, and a crucifix that has apparently been known to ooze blood. It is interesting to note that the commune gave the Domenicans this privileged central position in which to build their church in gratitude for their help in rebuilding the town after its various batterings. It ceded the whole area to them in 1291.

Piazza Silvestri

This **medieval piazza** is undoubtedly the town's highlight; a bare, windswept but perfectly formed vision of what the Middle Ages must have looked like. It starts above the broad flight of steps with the Palazzo dei Consoli (1270), built by Prode, the architect responsible for the Palazzo Comunale in Spello. It bears an obvious resemblance to other civic palaces from the same period, most strikingly to the Palazzo del Capitano in Todi, started in the same year. The interior houses a theatre, restored in 1976, and considered to be the most beautiful in the region.

Next to it is **San Silvestro**, a superb and completely unadulterated example of early Umbrian Romanesque. It was built in 1195 — you can see the date and the name of the builder, Binello, in an inscription to the right of the main portal. The cornice above contains unmistakable Roman fragments, and the remains of an abortive attempt to build a bell-tower. The blunt and sombre interior feels extremely old, with the presbytery well raised above the nave, the crypt below, and just a few traces of early Umbrian fresco around the walls.

Directly opposite is the far larger San Michele, a more mature example of the Romanesque, but almost certainly by the same architect, Binello (another of the great army of unknown Umbrian architects). There is a lovely door with Cosmati mosaic work in the surrounds, and two macabre staring bas-

iazza Silvestri. (DL)

San Michele. (DL)

reliefs to either side. The over-large rose window was added in the eighteenth century. Notice the two sets of trefoil windows above the side-naves, a typical Umbrian motif. Inside, the ancient-looking columns were much abraded in the eighteenth century to take stucco; restorations in 1954 saw most of the damage undone.

Around Bevagna

The most appealing trip, at least for art-lovers, is to take the minor road north-west towards Bettona, turning right after 7 kilometres to the tiny church-filled village of **Cannara** (FS station 4 kilometres). It is stranded somewhat forlornly in the middle of the plain, sheltered by trees from what would otherwise be a desolate solitude. Don't be put off; make for Piazza Marconi, where San Francesco has a *Madonna and Saints* by Nicolò Alunno (1482), and San Giovanni next door, frescoes attributed to Lo Spagna. San Matteo has another triptych by Alunno, and there is a range of fourteenth–sixteenth-century paintings hung in the Palazzo Comunale in Piazza Umberto.

You might then return to the Bettona road and take the dead-end lane to **Collemancio**. About 300 metres north of the village are the virtually unknown and unexcavated ruins of Urbinum Hortense, a Roman (and possibly Etruscan) settlement destroyed by Totila in 545 and never rebuilt. Although hardly a second Pompeii, there are none the less interesting hints of a temple, pavements, and mosaics, with much more, presumably, still to be turned up.

Where to stay

Il Rientro ★

A small *pensione* in Collemancio, should the village's views and tranquillity appeal. There is also a restaurant. Tel. 075 72420. Rooms 6. Bathrooms 1. Showers 6.

Bizzari ★

Via Emanuele 10. Tel. 075 72314. Rooms 7. Bathrooms 1. Showers 3.

Camping

Camping Bevagna ★★★

Pian di Boccio, Caglioli. Tel. 0742 62391; *Open 15 March–30 September.* Places 120.

Where to eat

Del Cacciatore

Traditional Umbrian cooking, with homemade *dolci* and local wines. Piazza Garibaldi 5. Tel. 0742 62161. *Closed Tuesday and November.*

Where to buy wine

Adanti

Outstanding new-wave producer. Recommended buys: Sangrantino, Rosso di Montefalco, Grechetto, Rosso/Bianco d'Arquata. In the village of Arquata. Tel. 0742 62295.

Domenico Benincasa

In the village of Capro. Tel. 0742 602307.

Foligno

TOURIST INFORMATION: Porta Romana. Tel. 60459
POPULATION: 53,000
HEIGHT: 234 m
STD CODE: 0742

Trains

The town is at the junction of the Rome–Ancona line and the Foligno–Terόntola branch-line. Hourly trains to Perugia, Assisi, and intermediate stations. Fast connections north to Gualdo and south to Spoleto, Terni, Orte, and points in between.

History

Foligno is one of Umbria's biggest towns. There is nothing terribly wrong with it; nor, however, is there much particularly to recommend it. The

main problem is that many of its former Roman and medieval glories were bombed to oblivion in the Second World War. What is left is a spacious, sometimes graceful, old-time provincial town, boasting a barracks and prosperous commercial centre, but little of interest, even for a half-discerning visitor. However, it is a major communications centre, so you will find it difficult to move around this part of Umbria without giving it at least a passing glance. You will have nothing to lose by spending an hour or so in its shopping streets — and you could also take in the attractive Piazza della Repubblica.

There must have been plenty here once. It was an Umbrian settlement, and then a Roman colony, doubling in importance with the martyrdom of Bishop Feliciano (251), whose tomb became a venerated point of pilgrimage. After thumpings from the Saracens, Goths, and Barbarossa, it turned into one of the Empire's most reliable strongholds, finding itself, as a result, in almost perpetual opposition to Perugia. From 1310 to 1439, the time of the commune and the bloodthirsty Trinci family, its broad sphere of influence included Nocera, Trevi, Montefalco, and even Assisi. The 11th of April 1472 saw the first printing of a book in Italian — 300 copies of Dante's *Divine Comedy*. The drainage of surrounding marshland (the Vale of Spoleto was once a huge lake), started by the Romans, was completed in the sixteenth century.

What to see

Piazza della Repubblica

The piazza is the kernel of what medievalism remains in Foligno. The Duomo is the earliest building (1133), but it was radically transformed in the sixteenth century. (The facade is from 1904.) The worst horrors of the baroque interior have been removed, but there is still nothing of overwhelming interest to see. The sacristry has a *Crucifixion* by Nicolò Alunno, but little else, apart from the standard fittings. You should leave by the left transept for a view of the 'secondary facade', built by Binello and Rodolpho in 1201. (The same team of architects who were responsible for churches in Spello and Bevagna.) It is far superior to the main facade around the corner, though it too has felt the restorer's hand. To its right, past the Palazzo Orfani and the remains of the Palazzo Pretorio, you come to the **Palazzo Trinci**, occupying one side of the square, and once home to the great medieval family. It was started in 1389, a fact disguised by the neo-classical facade of 1847. The exceptional interior has seen much restoration, though the worst of the work is now over. After a fine courtyard and superb frescoed staircase, there is an above-average picture gallery on the second floor. Probably you will first want to admire the carved ceiling of the vestibule and the room known as the Hall of the Planets and Liberal Arts, decorated, by an unknown artist, with some extravagantly painted women. The adjacent chapel has a series of frescoes by an aged Ottaviano Nelli, the *Life of the Virgin* (1424), striking, but not

amongst his best. In the gallery proper there are works by Alunno and Nelli, their followers, an *Angelo Anunziante* (Room II) attributed to Gozzoli, and then a tailing off into less significant baroque pieces. There is also a small museum comprising a modest collection of mainly Roman exhibits.

Santa Maria Infraportas

There are poor pickings to be had walking around the streets (though you might pop into San Salvatore — ignoring the interior — and make for the sacristry. It has a *Madonna, Child and Saints* (1437) by Bartolomeo di Tommaso, teacher to Nicolò Alunno).

The church of **Santa Maria**, however, is the best thing in the town and is well worth a visit; it is one of those places that feels as old as it claims to be. By some miracle it survived heavy bombing and passed unscathed through the baroque excesses of the seventeenth century. St Peter himself is supposed to have celebrated Mass here, and before him the site was reputedly occupied by a temple to Diana. (You can find it by walking the full length of Via Mazzini from the lower left-hand corner of Piazza della Repubblica.) Many of the columns and niches have faded frescoes by local painters. The more accomplished patches are by Mezzastris (a *Crucifixion* in the first left-hand niche, and *St Jerome and Two Angels* on the right-hand wall of the presbytery). The most captivating aspect of the church is the Cappella dell'Assunta at the beginning of the left-hand nave. Behind the altar is an important Byzantine fresco, probably from the twelfth century, though the chapel itself may date back as far as the eighth century.

Nearby, San Nicolo has two further paintings by Alunno: one above the altar in the second chapel on the right, the *Nativity and Resurrection* (parts of the painting ended up in the Louvre), and the other — an impressive late work — the *Coronation of the Virgin* (1492) in a chapel to the right of the main altar.

Around Foligno

Although disappointing, given its size, Foligno is nevertheless a point of departure for short excursions. Obvious trips are to the coronet of small towns close-by — Trevi, Montefalco, Spello — but in addition, some of Umbria's least-known countryside lies to the east, bisected by the highly scenic N77 to Camerino. Wild, high, and remote, this landscape repays those with a sense of adventure and whose approach is one of random exploration. Unmetalled roads lead off into small valleys; some to dead-end one-horse hamlets; others virtually to the tops of mountains.

If this sounds unappealing, one trip that is definitely worth taking is the one to the **L'Abbazia di Sassovivo** 6 kilometres east of the town. You should leave by Porta Ancona and follow the N77 to where it crosses the main

Perugia–Spoleto road. A small road branches off at the junction to the right, signposted to the abbey. This is set in timeless, wooded countryside, and was established as a Benedictine centre of studies in 1070. The church (apart from an eleventh-century crypt) is of little interest; the **cloisters**, however, are wonderful — the best in Umbria. Dating from 1229, their 58 arches and 128 pillars decorated in mosaics and coloured marbles create an atmosphere of elegance, solitude, and silence.

The road to Camerino itself passes through some fine scenery. Some 6 kilometres out of Foligno you come to Pale, graced with a castle, but better known for the Grotta di Pale, a cave full of stalagmites and stalactites, whose fame over the years has attracted the likes of Catherine of Sweden and Tuscany's Cosimo III. A path from the village climbs to the Sasso di Pale (959 metres), a walk that is rewarded with some sweeping views. Scopoli, at 532 metres, is little more than a well-preserved castle dating from 1460. The road starts to climb tortuously from here on, but you can avoid the hairpin bends by turning off at this point on to a lovely mountain-lined road that runs along the Menotre valley. Midway up the hairpin itself, another enticing road, mostly unmetalled, makes its precipitous way through complete wilderness towards the peaks of Mount Tito (1043 metres) and Mount Pizzuto (1267 metres). (For the adventurous only.) Playing it safe by staying on the N77, you come to the quietly picturesque town of Colfiorito, the site of an important Iron Age settlement, which controlled the nearby mountain pass — one of the lowest and easily surmountable routes between the Marche and the west. Beyond the village are 12 square kilometres of upland plan — Il Piano di Colfiorito — similar, in many ways, to those of the Valnerina. The land is given over to fields of cereals, with scarcely a tree or house in between. Only the circling peaks of Mount Profoglio offer visual relief.

Where to stay

Villa Roncalli
★★★

Central, old-style hotel in fifteenth-century building. Via Roma 25, Foligno. Tel. 670291. Rooms 10. Bathrooms 4. Showers 10.

Villa Fiorita
★★★

Colfiorito, at 760 metres, is cool in the summer, off the beaten track, and as a result becoming ever more popular with visitors. This fine hotel has every facility, including tennis-courts and the obligatory swimming-pool. Via del Lago 9, Colfiorito. Tel. 681125. Rooms 30. Showers 30.

Il Valico
★★

Five kilometres from Colfiorito at Valico, and a more intimate alternative. Restaurant and garden. Tel. 681140. Rooms 8. Showers 7.

Del Pavoni
★

Small *pensione* with no restaurant, but a pleasant garden. Viale Mezzetti 29, Foligno. Tel. 56263. Rooms 12. Showers 7.

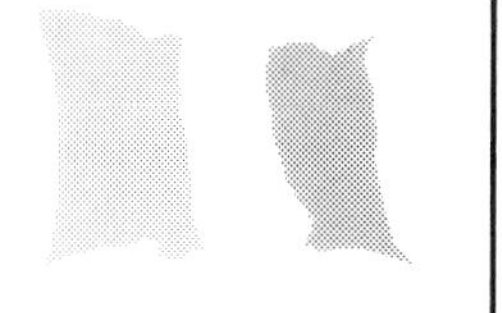

Youth hostel

Ostello Fulginium

Piazza San Giacomo, Foligno. Tel. 9170307.

Where to eat

Dell'Hotel Post ★★

Long-established and dignified restaurant. Game, fresh fish, depending on season. Via Oberdan 1. Tel. 50529. *Closed Sunday.*

Da Remo

Via Battisti 11. Tel. 50079. *Closed Monday.*

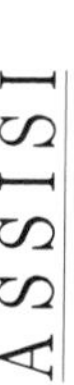

GUBBIO

General Information

TOURIST INFORMATION: Piazza Odersi 6. Tel. 075 927 3693

POPULATION: 32,000

HEIGHT: 522 m

POST OFFICE: Via Carioli 11

TELEPHONES: Via della Repubblica 13

STD CODE: 075

POLICE: Via Matteotti. Tel. 927 3731

DISTANCE TO:
Foligno 60 km Umbértide 26 km
Perugia 40 km Gualdo Tadino 24 km

Trains

Gubbio's nearest station is at Fossato di Vico (19 kilometres) on the Rome–Ancona line. There are 10 connecting buses daily. Trains to Gualdo, Nocera, Foligno, and Fabriano in the Marche.

Buses

Ten buses every day make the run from Perugia, and there are frequent connections to Assisi, Umbértide, Gualdo, and Fabriano.

Road

Road links to Gubbio are comparatively poor. The easterly N3 follows the course of the old Via Flaminia and is still the best approach from Foligno and the south. The N289 from Perugia is a minor but highly picturesque route.

Parking

The town's biggest and most convenient car-park is in the Piazza Quaranta Martiri.

There's no Umbrian town, perhaps no Italian town, as thoroughly rooted in the Middle Ages as Gubbio. It runs Spoleto a close second as many people's favourite. 'The dream of some medieval miniaturist', Edward Hutton called it at the beginning of the century; a 'city of silence', said D'Annunzio, poet and sub-Wildean character of dubious political affiliations. It is a long way from anything, a remote mountain outpost, tenuously linked to the outside world by the poorest of roads. This hasn't prevented tourists arriving in some force. Some whisper that the town is to become the Umbrian Siena. Maybe. Up to now its charm has remained miraculously intact.

Much of Gubbio's beauty, as so often in Umbria, comes from a marvellous setting — the juxtaposition of a stone-built town with beautiful countryside. Here the backdrop is provided by the Apennines rearing up to the north, a deep, tree-filled cleft in the mountains and by the waters of the Camignano gorge, noisily tumbling from the slopes of Mount Ignino.

History

Gubbio, according to the dubious wisdom of the ancient chroniclers, was one of the first five towns built after the Great Flood. The earliest settlement for which there is solid evidence, Tota Ikuvina, belonged to the Umbrians, and, with Spoleto, was one of the most important strategic points in the eastern part of the region — more important even than Perugia, as its command of the Camignano Valley gave it control over all traffic that passed between Rome and Ravenna.

The building of the Via Flaminia brought in the Romans, whose main legacy was a sprinkling of monuments and today's simple street-plan. The colony performed a key role in central Italian affairs until its destruction by Totila.

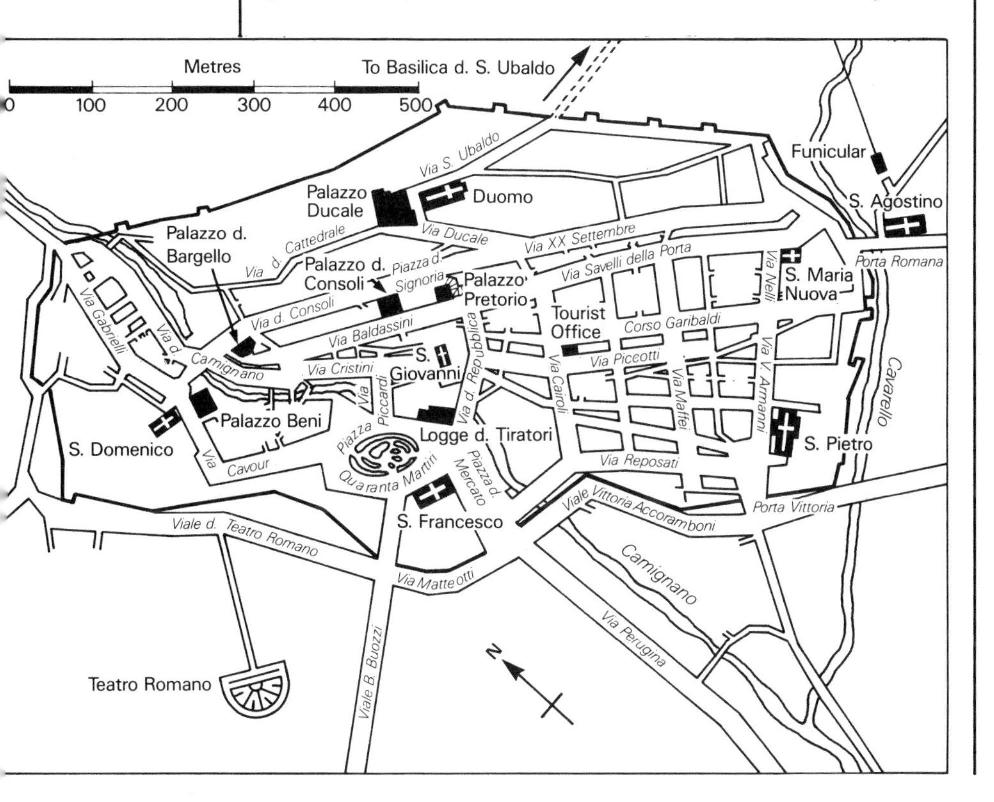

Further attacks over the next few years saw the centre of the town edge from the plain to a more secure position on the slopes of Mount Ignino, where it remained until the urban expansion of the fourteenth century. (This is the reason why today the Roman amphitheatre is some way from the rest of the town.)

As early as the tenth century Gubbio had managed to re-establish itself, and by 1163, after a fierce struggle with Barbarossa, succeeded in securing its independence. The following three centuries saw a period of expansion during which the various mendicant Orders (as elsewhere) built churches in the town, civic palaces sprang up to accommodate the new communal administrations, and a fresh set of walls rose to enclose a population that, by 1300, had risen to 50,000, almost double its present size. (By some freak of communal rule at the time, a special *Conestabile* was elected annually, and for 10 days at the beginning of May had dictatorial powers throughout the town. Remarkably the system continued until as recently as 1817.)

An artistic awakening accompanied the new prosperity, with Guido Palmerucci and then Ottaviano Nelli guiding the first truly Umbrian school of painting. A multitude of minor painters followed (amongst them Petruccio di Luca, Angelo di Maso, and Donato d'Andrea), though as the Middle Ages progressed the focus of artistic endeavour moved to ceramics. The leading exponent of the art was Giorgio Andreoli da Intra, or Maestro Giorgio. He owed what was international success to a glazing process that enabled him to produce a startling array of colours, ranging through ruby- and blood-reds to mother-of-pearl whites. (He took the secrets of his technique to the grave.) The craft still flourishes in many a local workshop.

Gubbio was also home to the Maffei family, whose beautiful wooden carvings grace churches and palaces all over Umbria, and to the monumental architect Matteo Gattapone, responsible for some of the region's most audacious buildings.

The town had had its heyday by the middle of the fourteenth century. Power ebbed gradually from the communes to assertive noble families, with one clan, as usual, achieving supremacy. In this case it was the numerous and fecund Gabrielli, unusual at the time for the broad base of their power, and their genuine fidelity to the Church.

In 1354 Giovanni Gabrielli, in line with the family's honest church-going principles, handed the town over to Cardinal Albornoz, the Papal agent who crops up in Umbria's history as often and with as much popularity as Totila. He delivered it to the Vatican. By 1376 the inhabitants had had enough of Church rule and demonstrated their displeasure in the time-honoured way by indulging in violent rebellion. All they got for their trouble was another Gabrielli, this time Bishop Gabrielli, who, to general disgust, returned Gubbio to the Popes after just five years of independence.

This was the final straw for the hapless citizens. They staged a second and more successful uprising in favour of Duke Montefeltro of Urbino, whose rule brought a period of social calm and cultural growth that survived the

increasingly harsh regimes of his successors. The last of these, Francesco Maria II, handed the reins over to the Papacy, who this time managed to hold on to their bequest, incorporating Gubbio into the Marche, where it remained until reinclusion into Umbria in 1860.

The town was in the path of the retreating Germans in the Second World War and suffered heavy shell-fire, coming within a hair's breadth of being destroyed altogether. It was also the headquarters of partisans operating in the mountains hereabouts. In one tragic episode (22 June 1944) the Germans murdered 40 women and children in reprisal for a guerrilla raid in which just one German was killed. The event is remembered by a memorial next to the church of Madonna del Parto, close to where the massacre took place.

Background

Corsa dei Ceri

Gubbio's *Corsa dei Ceri* is by far the most famous of Umbria's many festivals. It has been taking place every 5 May for something like 800 years, but still no one knows how it came about or what it all means. For some it is the development of a sylvan rite going back thousands of years; for others, a war-dance or pagan fertility ritual that has been cannily commandeered by the Church. At its heart are the *ceri*, or candles, three decidedly phallic pillars of wood, each 8 metres high and weighing several hundredweight. They are kept for most of the year in the Basilica di Sant'Ubaldo, church of Gubbio's patron saint, remembered for persuading Barbarossa to spare the town in 1155. After hours of involved ritual and much drinking, teams chosen from three of the town's old Guilds (stonemasons, merchants, and farmers) race with the *ceri* from Piazza della Signoria back to the Basilica. Each candle bears a different wax saint, though victory always belongs to Sant'Ubaldo and the stonemasons. The race element comes in because Ubaldo must be bundled through the Basilica doors before the other two teams can reach the church. A dramatic and unforgettable day to be in Gubbio — though be warned that the town and its hotels are packed to the gunwales.

Palio della Balestra

The *Palio*, Gubbio's other important festival, is held twice, once on the last Sunday in May, and again in September, and is an archery competition between the town and neighbouring San Sepolcro. On 15 August there is a contest between the town's different quarters in flag-tossing (really), and at Christmas lights are strung across the woods of Mount Ignino to form an illuminated fir-tree, with a star crowning the summit ('The Biggest Christmas Tree in the World'). Easter processions are accompanied by white-robed penitents (with a disturbing resemblance to the Ku Klux Klan), all singing thirteenth-century songs of mourning.

Porte della Morte (Doors of Death)

Somewhere in the course of a walk around Gubbio you are bound to notice curious narrow archways set into the walls of houses, either bricked up or too small to serve much practical purpose. These are the famous and much-discussed *porte della morte*, the 'doors of death', so-called because according to tradition they were used to allow the passage of a coffin after a death in the house. Being tainted by death they were then sealed up. A nice theory, and with its morbid overtones quite an Italian one, though probably a little wide of the truth. A more likely explanation is that they were used in times of attack, when the main doorway could be barricaded, leaving the narrow *porta della morte* as the only, and more easily defended, access to the house.

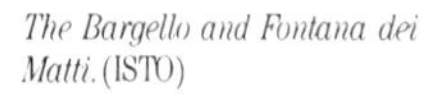
The Bargello and Fontana dei Matti. (ISTO)

Behind the doorways there were tortuous staircases, which led directly to the first floor, avoiding the courtyard and ground floor and further increasing the difficulty of frontal attack. In more genteel times they had the added advantage of allowing a lady to step directly from her carriage into the house without dirtying her skirts.

The doors are almost unique to Gubbio, there being just a few other examples in Assisi and in parts of Provence. The best places to see them are in one of the town's prettiest corners, **Via dei Consoli**, at Nos 49 and 61. Whilst in the street look out for the **Bargello**, the thirteenth-century equivalent of a police station. Staying in the realms of superstition, notice the nearby **Fontana dei Matti**, the fountain of the mad. Here, apparently, rabid madness awaits anyone foolish enough to walk around it three times. The only time you will get away with it is if you are being honoured for services to the town. More often than not there are groups of hesitant people hanging around, wondering whether to tempt fate. It was once the town's only water supply.

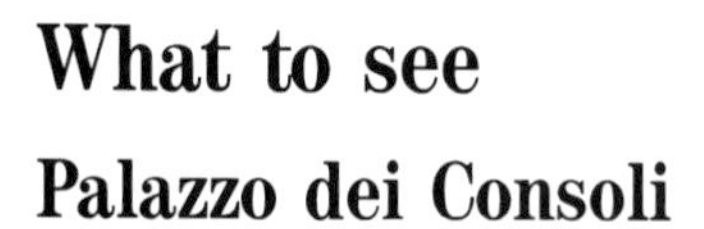

What to see

Palazzo dei Consoli

Open 9–13, 15–17.
Admission charge.

No building better expresses the power, pride, and spirit of the medieval communes than Gubbio's gaunt and imposing Palazzo dei Consoli. The normally restrained Touring Club of Italy guide describes it as 'uno tra i più bei palazzi publicci d'Italia' — one of the most beautiful public palaces in Italy. Its almost

Mount Ignino. (ISTO)

Roman grandeur has dominated every view and aspect of the town for 600 years, rising far above the vast and windswept Piazza della Signoria and dwarfing the huddle of medieval houses clustered below.

Plans for its construction were first mooted in 1321. Gubbio was then at the height of its powers, and in the process of drawing up a programme of redevelopment aimed at giving the town the appearance its new democratic respectability and economic strength were thought to merit. The palace was intended to be the eventual centrepiece of the scheme — a monument to the virtues of self-government, and a much-needed replacement for the somewhat squalid municipal offices in Via Ducale, then still ironically and embarrassingly overshadowed by Church authority in the shape of the Duomo.

Considerable importance was attached to the project, and neither expense nor existing buildings were spared during 11 years of preparatory work. Whole quarters were levelled, and a vast terrace (Piazza della Signoria) carved out of the hillside to provide enough level ground for the proposed palace.

Controversy shrouds the identity of the architect responsible. The name of Angelo da Orvieto appears above the main door, though this may mean only that he designed the door itself, and possibly the short staircase in front of it. More likely is that the overall design was left to the local architect, Matteo Gattapone, a master of other monumental projects, such as Spoleto's Ponte delle Torri. Work, inevitably, did not proceed smoothly. It was frequently interrupted by changes of administration, most damagingly by Giovanni Gabrielli's *coup* in 1350, when there was a pause (if a gap of 150 years can be called a pause) during which all progress on the palace came to a complete halt. After the lull, work resumed (only the first floor had been completed) and surprisingly, given the changes in architectural taste, was rounded off in line with the original plans.

Three pairs of windows, whose design, repeated in other palaces around the town, is peculiar to Gubbio, are almost the only feature that disturbs the facade's severe *ad quaratum* square. To their right is a small hole where once hung the *gogna*, or pillory (from the word *vergogna* — shame), a cage in which criminals were displayed for the gloating benefit of the public below. To its left, rather more obviously, is the palaces's original 2½-ton bell, rung by the town's young bloods during festivals. They stand precariously at the top of the minaret-like campanile and push it back and forth.

Pinacoteca and Museo Civico

Open 9–13, 15–17.
Admission charge.

These are housed inside the palace, which is no longer used as the town hall, a function taken over by the lesser **Palazzo Pretorio** on the other side of the piazza (finished in 1149 and built to the same architectural plan). Inside, there is a single cavernous hall, the Salone dell'Arengo, once the meeting place for consular officials and the town's leading citizens. (It was intended as a

place for 'discussion' though it is interesting to note that the English word 'harangue' derives from *arengo*, so possibly political debate was not always terribly civilized). Today it houses a miscellaneous collection of Roman and medieval remains taken from the Roman amphitheatre, tombs, and local monuments. The most important exhibit is a rare eighth-century sarcophagus, either Byzantine or Barbarian in origin. There are also novelty exhibits — what we would call toilets, but which are here rather politely called *necessari*. (There are 26 in total, a tribute to medieval plumbing.) The building is supposed to have been the first in Italy with piped running water.

Alongside the steep stairs leading to the picture gallery is a much-repainted *Madonna and Child* by Palmerucci, and at the top a small window used by the consuls as a crude megaphone to address their public.

Eugubine Marbles

Pride of place in the museum goes to the Eugubine Marbles, or Tablets, a sort of Italian Rosetta Stone, and the most important (and puzzling) archaeological discovery ever made in Umbria. The seven bronze tablets — there were originally eight but one has been 'lost' — were found close to the Roman amphitheatre in 1444 by an illiterate shepherd (later duped by the commune into exchanging his priceless discovery for a worthless piece of grazing land).

The tablets, the deep, dark green of oxidized bronze, fall into two distinct groups. The first, and more recent, dates from the first century BC, and consists of three slabs inscribed on both sides with a text that approximates to Latin. The second group is a century older and has a text of bastardized Etruscan. Both appear to have had the same purpose: to render the Umbrian dialect — as far as we know a purely vernacular tongue — into a written form using the two most common languages of their day. Thus Latin and Etruscan characters were used, albeit crudely, to produce a type of phonetic translation of Umbrian, rather in the manner of the ill-fated seventies' method of teaching children to read.

One of the Eugubine Marbles (fourth century BC). (ISTO)

The purpose of the tablets was similarly instructional. Most probably they were the work of Etruscan and Roman priests, who wished to introduce new religious practices into an area where their own languages were not understood. They translate a text believed by archaeologists to be either a prayer divided into stanzas, or a series of instructions in minute detail relating to the conducting of particular religious services. Possibly they were concerned with augury, foretelling the future from the flight of birds, for example. These things had to be just so; if the priest was even slightly out of place then the divination was worthless and the whole liturgy had to be repeated.

That they should have been found in Gubbio is no surprise. The town had been a vital religious centre long before the arrival of the Etruscans. Somewhere in the barren mountains to the east was the shrine of the so-called Apennine Jove, or Giove Grabovio (*graba* meant 'stone' or 'rock'), a major and all-powerful deity similar to the Greek Jove of Mount Olympus. People flocked from all over Italy to worship at the shrine (doubtless adding to Gubbio's early growth in the process) and it was natural that new settlers seeking to impose 'foreign' cults should take advantage of the region's already considerable fame.

The bronzes refer to one particular sect, a fraternity of brothers known as the Atiedii, who worshipped a trinity of gods, which included Mars and Vofione as well as Jove. They also list Gubbio's enemies, and the extent of the town's influence. However, just as interesting as the linguistic and incidental detail is the fact that they were found together. The juxtaposition of Umbrian, Etruscan, and Roman suggest, first, that the Etruscans penetrated as far east as Gubbio, and second, that the cultures were in some way linked. Their proximity refutes the idea held for many years that the Umbrians were a distinct people displaced and destroyed by the Etruscans. The same goes for the Romans. It seems unlikely that the Romans would have taken the trouble to impart religious ideas if they then proposed to wipe out their protégés. Seen from this point of view, the tablets provide the single most convincing piece of evidence for the continuity and interdependence of pre-Christian cultures in central Italy.

Other exhibits in the museum include a late-Roman bust, a collection of coins from the same period, and a *stele*, or headstone, from the tomb of an Umbrian magistrate from Bevagna. There is also a range of gorgeous, if somewhat sturdy, fourteenth-century furniture.

Madonna del Melograno *by Fiorentini, Pinacoteca.* (ISTO)

Pinacoteca

Gubbio's art gallery is located in the Palazzo dei Consoli on the second floor. Admission is included in the ticket for the museum. Most of the works, naturally, are by Gubbian artists, but there are also Sienese and Byzantine pieces, paintings by Crivelli (an artist from the Marche) and his school, and a variety of less-interesting works from the sixteenth and seventeenth centuries. The rooms are arranged in roughly chronological order. Be sure to try the door at the rear of the gallery for access to the **Loggia** and a lofty view over the town.

Duomo (Via Sant'Ubaldo)

Gubbio's simple, rosy Duomo, a little overshadowed by the Palazzo opposite, is not as striking as some in Umbria. It dates from the beginning of the fourteenth century, and was built on the site of a much older church, of which only the Lamb of God and the rose-window's Evangelists survive. The facade was restored in the sixteenth century, though the short flight of steps is the only obvious Renaissance addition.

The **interior** is formed from a large single nave, supported by 10 Gothic arches, bowed in a local style said to imitate the joining of hands in prayer. It is graced with fine twelfth-century stained glass, some awful paintings and

terior of the Duomo. (ISTO)

one or two good ones. Look for the Sinibaldo Ibi *tavola* (1507), in the eighth niche on the left, and a *Maddalena* by Timoteo Viti (1521) in the niche next to it. There are some patches of early fresco, but these are almost lost — more than can be said of the baroque chapel of sumptuous but sham splendour that leads off from the right-hand side of the nave. The beautiful organ-lofts to either side of the nave, and the bishop's throne (1550 and 1557 respectively) are the work of Luca and Giralmo Maffei. The altar rests on one of several ancient sarcophagi in the church; no one knows its precise age.

The adjoining **Museo Capitolare**, recently reorganized, has a mixed collection of paintings and sculptures given to the cathedral over the years. For a visit ring the bell outside the sacristry. Included are two works (doubtfully attributed to Palmerucci) and a quite outstanding *piviale*, or sixteenth-century cope, extravagantly embroidered in gold with seven stories from the Passion. Of Flemish origin, it was presented to Gubbio by Pope Marcellus, one of the town's more moderately famous sons.

Palazzo Ducale (Via Ducale)

Open 9–13.
Closed Monday.
Admission free.

The Palazzo is directly in front of the Duomo. For a long time it was in private hands, and many of its more precious treasures were auctioned off, mainly to America. Now the state has intervened, called a halt, and started a long process of restoration. This being completed, the building, and in particular the **courtyard**, with its intricately worked pillars and capitals, will be returned to the beautiful state that made it renowned during the Middle Ages. Medieval writer Sanzi described it as 'facing south-east and flanked by mountains on the north, over-looking fertile valleys and smiling champaigns and excelling the attractions of Urbino in charming prospects and pleasant pathways'. The comparison with Urbino was apposite, as the palace was commissioned by Federico da Montefeltro in 1476 as a scaled-down copy of that town's famous Palazzo Ducale.

It was built on the site of a far older palace whose origins dated back to the Lombards. The Duomo and Palazzo occupy a site which was the centre of the town following the Barbarian invasions (after the old Roman settlement had been abandoned for good). Tradition has it that Charlemagne stayed in the earlier building, and that Barbarossa refreshed himself there before ravaging half of Umbria — its remains are still clearly visible in the exterior walls of the present palace.

Be sure to visit the adjacent gardens for good views over the town.

Churches

San Francesco (Piazza Quaranta Martiri)

Note that churches in Gubbio's golden age were an afterthought, an incidental part of an immensely wealthy lay town, whose energies were devoted to self-aggrandizement and trade rather than pious contemplation. This tall, simple, even austere church is the first thing to catch the eye in the large piazza, which is otherwise given over almost entirely to parked cars. Its design has been attributed to Fra Bevignate (though with little certainty), who in his time was also responsible for the Fontana Maggiore in Perugia and early supervision of work on Orvieto cathedral. The **interior** was transformed in the seventeenth century though recent restoration has returned it to something like its thirteenth-century state.

Its chief attraction is Ottaviano Nelli's cycle of **frescoes**, 17 paintings (there were originally 20) on the *Life of the Virgin Mary*. Located in the left apse, they date from 1408 to 1413, but were only brought to light during renovation work in 1942. The small chapel nearby is thought to be the spot where St Francis stayed when he visited Gubbio (and tamed the famous wolf that had been terrorizing the town). Remnants of an older building are incorporated into its walls, which many believe, or would have you believe, are the remains of his room.

Through the sacristry, a fine example of thirteenth-century architecture (and in this instance known to have been converted from the house of Francis's hosts, the Spadolagne) are the cloisters, with a few traces of the fourteenth-century frescoes that once adorned its four walls. On the right as you look into the courtyard are two rooms lodged in the monastery's old refectory, now home to a small collection of paintings.

Note: Opposite the church is the distinctive fourteenth-century *tiratoio*, or weaver's loggia, one of the few such buildings to have survived. Wool was stretched out in the shady arcade to dry and shrink evenly away from the heat of the sun.

Santa Maria Nuova (Via Savelli della Porta)

This is a far smaller church (actually an ex-church) at the eastern end of the town close to the Porta Romana. If it is closed, contact the custodian at Via Dante 66. Inside, on the rear wall, is another fresco by Ottaviano Nelli, the *Madonna del Belvedere*, its rich colours sparkling like some jewelled mosaic and with the clarity of embroidery. Many consider it amongst his best works. Alongside it are other recently discovered fourteenth-century frescoes and an *Annunciation* attributed to Palmerucci.

Sant'Agostino (Via Dante–Porta Romana)

Rising, as usual with the Augustinians, near the town walls, this church is close to Santa Maria Nuova, through the Porta Romana, and immediately alongside the funicular station to Mount Ignino. More frescoes by Ottaviano Nelli make up for an ugly and unpromising facade, which was tacked on at the beginning of this century. Everything in the presbytery is by him. (The interior, you will notice, is modelled on that of the Duomo.) The main arch is painted with scenes of the *Last Judgement* (1420) and the vaults with the figures of the *Evangelists* and the *Four Doctors of the Church*. The walls contain 24 straightforward panels describing the *Life of St Augustine*. There are further paintings by Nelli above the second and fifth altars on the right-hand side of the nave. Otherwise the building has the sober and restful atmosphere typical of this Order's churches.

San Pietro (Via Vincenzio Armarni)

The church has thirteenth-century roots, though alterations in the sixteenth and eighteenth centuries gave it a liberal coating of baroque gloss. The facade, however, is original and studded with fragments from an earlier building. The best of the paintings is a *Visitation* attributed to Giannicola di Paolo, which you will find above the fourth altar to the right of the nave. The organ-loft (1598) is again the work of the local Maffei family.

San Domenico (Piazza Giordano Bruno)

This is Gubbio's largest church, but that is about all that can be said for it. The facade is dull in the extreme, and the interior poor baroque. There is, however, a faded fresco by Nelli in the second chapel on the left, and the two chapels opposite have a few fourteenth-century frescoes by anonymous members of the Gubbian school. An *Epiphany* in the second is particularly pleasing.

San Giovanni Baptista
(immediately behind the weaver's loggia in Piazza San Giovanni)

The church has been restored to its thirteenth-century state after baroque depredations. The exterior is distinguished by an enormous door and elongated tower, both out of all proportion to the church itself. Inside there is little of note, but the church's age makes it charming enough.

San Secondo (outside Porta Castello)

Although the church contains virtually nothing in the way of art, its peaceful interior has its own appeal.

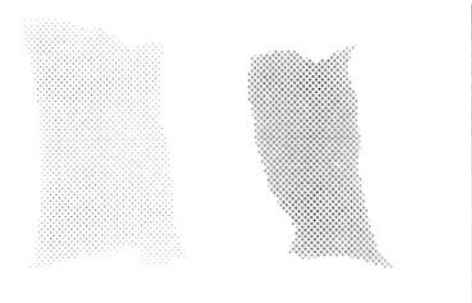

Roman Amphitheatre
(off Viale del Teatro Romano)

The theatre, 112 metres in diameter, and one of the biggest in the Roman world, is a little way out of the main town. If you are parked, as you probably will be, in Piazza Quaranta Martiri, then you should make it the first or last thing you see.

It dates from the first century AD, and is well preserved, especially in its lower sections, though there have been extensive restorations over the years. Recent excavations have uncovered some almost perfectly preserved mosaics, and further archaeological work is still in progress. To judge by the importance of the Roman colony there is probably much more still to be unearthed. In the summer it is used as a stage for concerts and plays.

Close by there are other Roman fragments, many haphazardly scattered and awaiting excavation. The best is the ruined **mausoleum**, easily reached from Piazza del Mercato.

Basilica di Sant'Ubaldo

The Basilica is several hundred metres above the town and there are three ways of reaching it. Most dramatic is to take the funicular from the Porta Romana, a six-minute journey; most exhausting is to emulate the teams in the *Corsa dei Ceri* and follow the track that strikes off from the Duomo; most laborious is to go by car and approach the church from behind, taking the road from Porta Metaurio, the town's northernmost gate.

There is not much to see in the Basilica itself (built in its present form in 1514) except for the *ceri*, and the Renaissance urn containing the body of St Ubaldo. The saint, brought here in 1194, is missing three fingers, 'piously' hacked off by his French manservant (were saints meant to have manservants?). The loyal factotum bore the trophies to his home-town of Thann, in the Vosges, where a church was built to honour the sacred digits.

Outside the Basilica there are several pleasant leafy walks — it is a favourite Sunday morning jaunt for the Gubbians — and some magnificent views. There is also a not-too-incongruous bar-restaurant, and, above all, a welcome and cooling breeze. Higher still, around the **Rocca** (880 metres), there is an even more impressive panorama.

Where to stay

Grand Hotel ai Cappuccini ★★★★

Located in the lower town, and Gubbio's leading hotel. It takes its name from the old Capuchin monastery in which it is situated. The conversion is a tasteful one. Via Cappuccini. Tel. 9273441. Rooms 44.

Bosone ★★★

Standard, very central hotel, just 100 metres from the Duomo and Palazzo dei Consoli. No restaurant. Via XX Settembre 22. Tel. 9272008. Rooms 35. Bathrooms 28.

San Marco ★★★

Larger but slightly cheaper than the Bosone, and with an above-average restaurant and a good garden terrace. Via Perugina 5. Tel. 9272747. Rooms 52. Bathrooms 8. Showers 37.

Gattapone ★★

Splendid central location with a restaurant and small garden. Via G. Ansiei 6. Tel. 9272489. Rooms 13. Showers 13.

Dei Consoli ★★

Cheap, small, and convenient, and therefore often busy. Via dei Consoli 59. Tel. 9273335. Rooms 10. Bathrooms 3. Showers 6.

Galleti ★

Small *pensione* with restaurant. Closed the first and second weeks of June. Via Piccardi 1. Tel. 9274247. Rooms 6. Bathrooms 4. Showers 2.

Out of town

Montegranelli ★★★

The hotel is a lovely country villa in beautiful surroundings some 4 kilometres from Gubbio itself. It is an ideal out-of-town base, but a popular one, so booking is recommended. Via Buozzi in the hamlet of Monteluiano. Tel. 9273372. Rooms 20.

Della Rocca ★★

On Mount Ignino, near the Basilica di Sant'Ubaldo. Cooler in the summer, views, walks, and fresh air. Restaurant and garage parking. Rooms 15. Bathroooms 4. Showers 10.

Catignano ★★

In the hamlet of San Marco 3 kilometres south-east of the town on the N219 to Gualdo Tadino. Restaurant, garage, and a garden. Hills to the rear, but somewhat dull plain to the fore. Rooms 29. Showers 29.

Where to eat

Taverna del Lupo ★★★

Gubbio has perhaps more top-quality restaurants than any other Umbrian town; this is the best. There is seating for 200, so things can become hectic, but otherwise the thirteenth-century medieval surroundings provide the perfect setting. The cuisine is traditional, with the occasional and usually successful excursion into the experimental. Via G. Ansider 21 (off Via Repubblica). Tel. 9274368. *Closed Monday except during the summer, and for the whole of January*. Expensive.

Porta Tessenaca ★★/★

Loses to the Taverna del Lupo by a short head, but still excellent. Central (below the Palazzo dei Consoli), slightly smaller (180 places) but in similarly ancient surroundings — an old guard-hall that belonged to the Dukes of Urbino. It can be swamped at times by visitors. Cooking is a mixture of the traditional and fantastic, with an unfortunate nod to the foreigner in the shape of cocktails and 'scampi'. Via Piccardi 21. Tel. 9272765. *Closed Wednesday*.

Fornace di Maestro Giorgio ★★

Situated on the site of the workshop that belonged to Maestro Giorgio, most famous of the town's medieval ceramic craftsmen — he of the ruby-red glaze. The epoch and ambience have been recreated, if a little theatrically, in the

restaurant. Traditional cuisine with good local specialities. Fresh fish and seafood on Thursday and Friday. A long wine list, including Ascagnano, a leading local vintage. Via M. Giorgio 2. Tel. 9275740. *Closed Monday.*

Grotta dell'Angelo ★

Not as central as some of the above, but a nice setting and a relaxed atmosphere. Cuisine simple and regional. Via Gioia 47. Tel. 9271747. *Closed Tuesday except during the summer.*

Alla Balestra ★

On one of the town's main streets, but with a lovely terrace and garden in which to escape the throng. Via Repubblica 41. Tel. 9273810.

Pizzeria Il Bargello

Best *pizzeria* in town in one of its prettiest streets. Via dei Consoli 37.

Trattoria Fiorella

Central and friendly *trattoria*. Corso Garibaldi 86. *Closed Monday.*

San Martino

At the far (San Domenico) end of the street. The appeal here is the *al fresco* possibility. Via dei Consoli 8.

AROUND GUBBIO

Gubbio, despite its medieval importance, is today out on a limb, a strangely isolated place, remote from most of the region, and in an area that seems to belong neither to Umbria nor the Marche. Ridges of mountains to the east and west cut it off from the rest of the world — it shares something of the Valnerina's bleakness, something of its air of desolation. Here the road system is poor, the soils scanty, the plains empty. The forests are thick, home to rare birds and wild animals, the countryside depopulated, the villages few and far between.

The scenery, however, is very lovely. Particularly notable are the famous woods around Pietralunga to the north-west, rich in plants and wildlife, the more severe, but more accessible, forests of Monte Catria to the east, and, most impressive, the spectacular **gorge** between Catiano and Cagli on the new road north to Urbino. In its early reaches the gorge has some fine spots in which to swim and picnic. Later on, access from the twisting road is more difficult. It is also extremely popular with weekending Italians and can be busy in the summer.

The landscape most visitors will see, however, is south of the town, on the long, winding N298 road to Perugia. It seems much further than its actual length of 31 kilometres, but is striking in places, offering excellent retrospective views of Gubbio before losing itself for good in the hills bordering the Chiáscio valley. There is, too, more to see on this road in an area where 'sights' are few and far between. (The only disappointment locally is perhaps the plain in front of Gubbio itself.)

Gubbio to Perugia

Just 12 kilometres south of Gubbio is the village of **Mengara**, and from here a poor but pretty road strikes off along the ridges of Mount Urbino (836 metres). After 10 kilometres it reaches **Santa Cristina** and **Alcatraz**, where Jacopo Fo, son of the comic and playwright Dario Fo (*Accidental Death of an Anarchist*), has opened a successful hotel and restaurant. The farm adjoining the hotel sells a comprehensive range of home-grown or homemade products — wine, fruit, honey, oil, vegetables — all used, of course, in the restaurant next door. In the summer Fo also holds residential courses in the performing arts (Tel. 075 920052).

Back on the Perugia road, another 5 kilometres brings you to **Vallingegno**, which has a good castle and thirteenth-century Benedictine abbey, San Verecondo. Here, too, you may also buy a variety of local products — a light, red wine, preserves (look out for the fig jam), and a selection of honeys scented with the lime-flowers and sunflowers of the local fields. (It is also possible to stay in new, purpose-built apartments.)

Further down the road (7 kilometres), after the drastic hairpin bends and before the village of Piccione, turn right to **Montelabate**, once one of the most powerful and imposing of all the medieval monasteries in the area. It controlled 20 castles and 30 parishes before decline set in during the fifteenth century. The last monk left in 1860. The large church is not especially enthralling, though there is part of a fresco by Fiorenzo di Lorenzo on the right-hand side. The thirteenth-century cloisters, by contrast, are amongst the most beautiful in central Italy. The eleventh-century crypt nearby, part of a primitive church, is also well worth a look.

The much longer route to Perugia (or Gualdo and Assisi) via **Branca** and **Valfabbrica**, being less remote, is moderately pretty and less bleak — once you have passed the cement works and old lignite workings at Padule — weaving through a succession of small villages and a patchwork of fields given over to wheat and the vivid green of tobacco. Dante is believed to have spent time at one village, Castello di Colmollaro; another, Castel d'Alfiolo, has a tower and chapel built by Cardinal Cervini, later Pope Marecello II, while Branca boasts a good castle. At **Rigali**, recent restorations have cancelled out the sixteenth-century additions to the old church of San Pietro, while the Romanesque parish church at **San Facondino** has a number of frescoes, among them one by the prolific local painter Matteo da Gualdo (1435–?1503).

From here onwards the road skirts the hills of Monte Maggio, and passes through some fairly pretty countryside. Look out for La Vena, known for its mineral waters. Gracious **San Pelligrino**, a little way off the road, and 6 kilometres from Gualdo, is a medieval hilltop village (536 metres — good views) in whose church are several outstanding frescoes, including a precious triptych by Giralmo da Camerino (1465), and more paintings by Matteo da Gualdo. The church of San Cristoforo in nearby **Caprara** has further frescoes by the latter.

aldo Tadino. (ISTO)

Gualdo Tadino

TOURIST INFORMATION: Via Calai 39. Tel. 075 912172

Gualdo is a high hill-town (536 metres) on the edge of the Apennines, tinged with the desolate air of a mountain outpost, and famous for its ceramics, its metalwork, and for an exceptional art gallery. It is also noted for a pottery exhibition, *La Mostra Concorso Internazionale delle Ceramiche*, held annually every summer.

History

Gualdo is very old, Umbrian in origin, and may be one of the towns referred to in the Eugubine Marbles in Gubbio. In Roman times it was called Tadinum, and was situated on the plain close to the Via Flaminia. During the Middle Ages large quantities of precious marbles from the former colony were taken to Perugia, where they were recycled in various churches. Large parts of Benedict XI's tomb in San Domenico, for example, started life in Gualdo. Destroyed by Totila, the town had the satisfaction of seeing the scourge of half Italy killed and defeated in 552, virtually under its walls. Narses, the

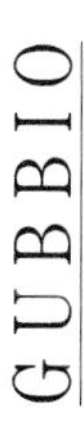

victorious Roman commander, was a eunuch — which must go to prove something. The town moved up on to the hill under the Lombards, and was gives its present name: 'Gualdo' derives from *wald*, meaning 'wood' or 'forest'. From 1251 it was under the Perugian yoke, passing to the Church with dull predictability in the sixteenth century.

What to see

Gualdo has an appealing medieval centre, wonderfully set off by its wooded and mountainous surroundings, though as usual there is some modern development around the station and a sprinkling of light industry on the plain below. The **Duomo** (always odd to think of these tiny towns having cathedrals) in Piazza Martiri della Libertà has a lovely facade — something like a more modest version of that in Todi — with a particularly striking portal (1256). The exterior is far more captivating than the interior, which was spoilt by disastrous restorations in the last century. Notice, amongst a rash of twentieth-century paintings, however, a Renaissance font and a gold-leafed tabernacle painted by Matteo da Gualdo, all of which have survived the cascade of gilt and fake marble.

Still in the heart of the medieval quarter, in the nearby Via della Rocca, is the oddly named **Rocca Flea**, built by Frederick II in the thirteenth century, but since 1977 a cultural centre and site of the town's small civic museum.

The jewel in Gualdo's humble crown, however, is the thirteenth-century church of **San Francesco** (Piazza dei Martiri), which, like its namesake in Montefalco, is home to a collection of paintings remarkable in a town of such modest size. (It may be closed, in which case ask at the AAST or the offices of the *Polizia Urbana*.) Outstanding amongst its many works are a thirteenth-century *Crucifixion* by a follower of the mysterious Maestro di San Francesco, and a magnificent *polittico* by Nicolò Alunno (1471), viewed by many as his greatest work. Then there are three triptychs and a large number of frescoes by Matteo da Gualdo, including his most charming painting, a *Madonna, Child and Four Saints* (1477). (Matteo, whose works are scattered around the churches of the town, and those of the neighbouring countryside, was one of the many Umbrian painters influenced by Benozzo Gozzoli, if not directly, then through his pupil, Mezzastris of Foligno, with whom he worked in the Cappella dei Pellegrini in Assisi.) Finally there is a bewildering array of anonymous works and comparatively minor paintings by artists from the Gubbian, Umbrian, and Sienese schools, for example Sano di Pietro, Antonio da Fabriano, Avanzino Nucci, and Bernardino di Mariotto.

Where to stay

Gigiotto
★★

Details as for restaurant (see below). Rooms 30. Bathrooms 7. Showers 14.

Dal Bottaio ★★

Via Casimiri 17. Tel. 913230. Rooms 12. Bathrooms 9.

Centro Sociale Verde Soggiorno ★

Young, outdoor types here for the grounds and the tennis-courts. Via D. Bosco 50. Tel. 916263.

Da Anna ★

Small *pensione* in the hamlet of Boschetto, 6 kilometres south of Gualdo on the Nocera road. Rooms 5. Bathrooms 1.

Where to eat

Ristorante Gigiotto ★★

The restaurant has been in the same family since 1875, and serves up excellent, if predictable, food in cavernous surroundings (260 places). The *pasta* is all homemade — try the *ravioli verdi* — and roasted meats, especially lamb, are the house speciality. A good cellar and wide range of cheeses — the *pecorino* and *canestro* are recommended. Via Morone 5. Tel. 075 912283. *Closed Wednesday except during July and August, and from 5 to 20 November.*

Nocera Umbra

TOURIST INFORMATION: Largo Bisleri 22. Tel. 0742 81273

Nocera is included here, as it fits into a straightforward itinerary (either by car or by rail) south from Gubbio or Gualdo to Foligno. You could, however, just as easily make it part of a trip from Assisi, just 20 kilometres over the hills to the south-west. The town, almost a carbon copy of Gualdo, is best known for its mineral waters, which are bottled and exported world-wide from a plant near the railway station (well distant, as usual, from the historic hill-town itself). It sits in a fairly picturesque position on the summit of a spur above the River Topino. Wooded hills again provide a rugged backdrop to a town far bleaker than those of the pastoral valleys to the west. It is also growing quickly and is already a busy tourist destination. The main attractions are the springs and mountain scenery to the east.

History

Nocera was initially an Umbrian settlement, Noukria, and then a staging-post on the Via Flaminia, under the Romans. At this time the town was almost certainly located on the plain, only moving up to its hilltop in the wake of the Barbarians. Recent discoveries have uncovered the remains of

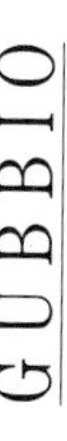

an important Lombard colony — the town was part of the Dukedom of Spoleto — though most of what has been found is now in the Museo dell'Alto Medioevale in Rome. Foligno's Trinci family took control in 1492, just 50 years before the town lost its independence and passed to the Church.

What to see

The main highlight is the church of **San Francesco** in Piazza Caprera, home to another surprisingly good art gallery. (It is possible that St Francis was in Nocera as early as 1215; certainly by 1221 the town's bishop, San Rinaldo, had asked him to establish a convent, a building destroyed in 1248 by Frederick II's Saracen army, and replaced by the present church in 1336.)

If the gallery is shut you may need to negotiate a visit through the *Comando dei Vigili* in Largo Bisleri. The main paintings to look out for on the large bare walls are a *Crucifixion* by Cimabue (or an Umbrian follower of the Maestro di San Francesco) and a broad *polittico* by Nicolò Alunno, which is almost overshadowed by its glitteringly elaborate frame. There are also a few archaeological odds and ends.

The **Duomo** (Via San Rinaldo), built in the fifteenth century from the shell of an eleventh-century church, should be the other point of interest; unfortunately it was ruined by eighteenth-century restoration. Opposite lies all that remains of the town's Rocca. Notice the almost complete absence of a piazza dominated by civic palaces — the church jealously guarded all the key spots. Although there is not much to see in the town, it is a pleasing, peaceful place.

Again, Nocera is an excellent base, either for walks or tours, with mountain roads striking off both east and west. There is a good three-hour walk up Mount Pennino (a minor winter resort) from Bagnara, 7 kilometres from the town on the N361 to Matelica. A road from Colle Croce to the south, however, will take you to within a lazy 20 minutes of the 1571-metre summit. An earlier right turn off the N361 heads towards **Bagni**, a much-frequented spa — remember, the Italians take these sorts of thing very seriously — with accommodation for 500; they enjoy company. Its spring, the Sorgente Angelica, has been famous since the seventeenth century, when people came from as far afield as Portugal and Constantinople to take the waters or soak away their aches and pains in the ample baths. The season runs from June to October.

West of Nocera is a quieter pocket of countryside dissected only by a scattering of white roads. Try the one to **Rocca di Postignano** (which has a castle that belonged to the Trinci family) and you will be retracing St Francis's steps as he returned home to die in Assisi. **Boschetto**, off the main road to the north, has a few Umbrian frescoes, most notably a *Madonna* by Matteo da Gualdo.

Where to stay

Europa ★★

Restaurant. Largo Bisleri. Tel. 0742 81274. Rooms 20. Bathrooms 2. Showers 18.

Casa Soggiorno Bagni di Nocera ★★

A big hostel run by the Church aimed at those taking the waters. Restaurant and grounds. In the village of Bagni. Tel. 0742 819240. Rooms 107. Bathrooms 8. Showers 99.

Where to eat

Albergo–Ristorante Pennino

Out of town in the village of Bagnara, with a peaceful, rustic setting and places for 200. The truffle, in season, is omnipotent, otherwise the cooking is standard Umbrian. Home-produced olive oil and local cheeses. Tel. 0742 81391. *Closed Wednesday.*

Gualdo Tadino to Gubbio

This section largely covers the mountainous area bisected by the N3 (the old Roman Via Flaminia) from Gualdo north into the Marche.

One of the best options locally is the hill-resort of **Valsorda**, 8 kilometres north-east of Gualdo. It is the reward at the end of a beautiful road, which climbs steeply through meadows and wooded slopes to a height of 1000 metres, with wonderful views over Mount Maggio and the Serra Santa. There is plenty of good walking hereabouts, including the popular pilgrimage trek to the top of the Serra Santa (1421 metres). The track, pounded by thousands of feet annually, is virtually a road, and very easy to follow. A popular but unspoilt spot, and highly recommended.

Returning to the main road north you soon reach **Fossato di Vico** (8 kilometres), where you should ignore the jumble of houses that makes up the new town, and head for the medieval town on the hill, Fossato Alto. Following the steep road between the two, you will pass the Cappella della Piaggiola (Via San Pietro), which is adorned with numerous frescoes by Ottaviano Nelli and members of his school. At the top of the street there is an outstanding Romanesque church, **San Pietro**, restored to its eleventh-century glory in 1971.

From Fossato it is a short, 5 kilometre hop to **Sigillo**, a Roman centre of Umbrian origins, conserving the partial remains of a Roman bridge, the Spiano, from the Augustan repairs to the Via Flaminia. The village lies in the shadow of **Mount Cucco**, which at 1556 metres is the highest point in Umbria. The local wines have a certain renown, and were mentioned in 1540 by Sante Lancerio, wine-taster to Pope Paul III. 'Sigillo fa un buon vinetto,' he said (Sigillo makes a good wine), 'ma in questo luogo non ha pari bellezza

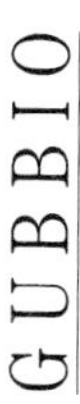

di donne' (but in this place it doesn't have the beauty of the women).

Expect to meet hang-gliders and cavers in the friendly and no-nonsense restaurant (watch out for Uncle Zio's singing, however), all taking time off from the slopes of Mount Cucco, whose summit can be reached reasonably easily. Take the road east from the village (Via del Ranco), which, after 9 kilometres gives way to a footpath to the top. The drive on its own, if you don't have the legs for a walk, is itself very picturesque.

A short detour (turn right off the road after 5 kilometres and follow the signs for Ranco di Sigillo) will bring you to the famous **Grotta di Monte Cucco**, which, it comes as some surprise to discover, is the fifth-deepest cave system in the world (at 922 metres below sea level), and the single deepest in Italy. For a long time only accessible to trained divers, and until recently not even fully explored, it is now gradually being opened to the public, a fact that, when coupled with the area's outstanding natural beauty, is making it an increasingly popular tourist destination. For details of trips into the caves, and of other outdoor activities in the region, contact the **National Speleology Centre**, who have their headquarters in **Costacciaro**, 5 kilometres north of Sigillo (Corso Mazzini 9. Tel. 075 9170236). Their administrative offices are in Perugia (Via Fabretti 6. Tel. 075 28613).

Costacciaro itself, a far more pleasant centre than Schéggia, which follows, nestles on a hill amidst ruined walls, and harbours a tiny church full of frescoes by Matteo da Gualdo. A staggeringly precipitous road strikes off from the village for the northern slopes of Mount Cucco, and links with a less hair-raising route from Schéggia 11 kilometres to the north-west.

At Schéggia you might want to take the Sasso Ferrato road east into the Marche, striking off left at Isola Fossara (9 kilometres) for the important **L'Abbazia di Santa Maria di Sitria** (2 kilometres on semi-metalled roads). The abbey is a ruined eleventh-century Romanesque gem (only the church and sixth-century crypt have been restored) but there is better still (if you are prepared to suffer further hairpin bends) at **L'Abbazia di Fonte Avellana**, one of the Marche's most notable monasteries, 680 metres high and set amid gorgeous mountain scenery.

In the Middle Ages great swathes of the region around Gubbio were administered by such monasteries, which is one of the factors that has given the land the sparse and depopulated appearance it has today. A full account of these would need the application of a monk; suffice it to list some of the many ruins. **Camporeggiano**, midway between Gubbio and Umbértide, is the best, but there is also twelfth-century **Alfiolo**, partially converted into a castle; **San Bernedetto di Monte Pellio** and **Sant'Emiliano**, both now little more than their respective Romanesque churches; and **Vallingegno** and **Montelabate**, already described above.

Where to stay

Narciso
★

In Valsorda itself. Gardens and a restaurant. Tel. 075 913282. Rooms 19. Bathrooms 7.

Camping

Valsorda
★

(1000 metres). A high, breezy site with 40 places. Tel. 075 913261. *Open 20 May–10 October.*

Where to eat

Da Zio Brando

Via del Ranco. Tel. 075 917131. *Open from May to September.*

Città di Castello

TOURIST INFORMATION: Via Raffaelle di Cesare 2b. Tel 075 8554817

The countryside in the low hills on either side of the Tiber valley around Città di Castello is good standard Umbrian. It is quiet enough — nothing out of the ordinary — though it has been one of the destinations for the first wave of foreigners buying into the region's property market. Communications are good: the private *Ferrovia Centrale Umbra* (FCU) runs up from Perugia to San Sepolcro, accompanied by a fast dual-carriageway on one side and the old secondary road on the other. The chances are you will only be coming this way to reach Tuscany and Urbino, or to see the influential pictures of the early Renaissance painter, Piero della Francesca. His masterpiece is the fresco cycle in Arezzo's San Francesco, but there are outstanding works in Monterchi and San Sepolcro (just over the border in Tuscany). As usual there are plenty of roads that repay aimless exploration. Particularly noteworthy are the N257 to Appechio and the N73, which reaches 1049 metres as it climbs over the hills to Urbino.

Plain-bound Città di Castello sneaks a mention by virtue of its size. It is a provincial town, busily getting on with its own business, and the most important spot in the northern part of the region (at least from an industrial point of view). Its present prosperity is based mainly on tobacco — the town is one of Italy's leading centres of production. However, the price to pay is the proliferation of sixties' industrial estates, which mar the northern and southern outskirts.

Though the medieval centre is not without charm, when all is said and done, Città di Castello is a second-division Umbrian town of little real interest.

However, an above-average art gallery redeems things slightly, and there are plenty of civic attempts to spruce up the town's image. Most famous is the Festival of Chamber Music in August, along with a horse show in November and international canoe race down the Tiber in April.

History

Città di Castello was Umbrian, then Roman, and is mentioned by Pliny the Younger — but he was biased: he had a villa and substantial landholdings in the area. Legend has it that the town was razed by Totila and then rebuilt under the guiding hand of the Church, which rechristened it Castrum Felicitas — the castle of happiness. In time it lost this appendage and became plain Civitas Castelli. Cesare Borgia appeared on the scene after spells of domination by the Florentines, invited the head of the ruling Vitelli family to a conference, had him strangled, and by this simple expedient won the town over to the Papacy.

What to see

Pinacoteca Comunale

(Palazzo Vitelli, Via della Cannoniera)

Open 9–13, 15–17; Sunday 9–13.
Admission charge.

Rich in works from the fourteenth to sixteenth century this gallery is considered the most important in Umbria after the National Gallery in Perugia. It is located in one of four palaces built by the Vitelli family before the Borgias put a damper on their career. Laura, one of the Vitelli women, used to throw her rejected lovers to their deaths from its windows.

The town gave birth to no great indigenous painter, but the Vitelli family did patronize both Raphael and Luca Signorelli; Raphael in fact produced his first solo painting (1501) for Vitellozzo Vitelli, a highly Peruginesque *Crucifixion*, now in London's National Gallery.

The gallery is divided into 10 rooms in roughly chronological order. Room I contains one of the highlights, a *Maestà* by the so-called Maestro di Città di Castello, an anonymous follower of Duccio. There is also a *Madonna and Child* attributed to Pietro Lorenzetti, two bronze statues by Ghiberti, and a highly prized silver reliquary of Florentine origin. Room II is given over to Signorelli and his school, with pride of place going to the *Martyrdom of San Sebastian* (1490). Room III contains a *gonfalone* attributed to Raphael, but it is a very early (and damaged) work (1501). Ghirlandaio's *Coronation of the*

Virgin vies for attention in the same room, along with an accomplished *Head of Christ* by a follower of Piero della Francesca. After some fifteenth-century frescoes in Room IV, the collection becomes less interesting, though there are works by Andrea and Giovanni della Robbia, and a selection of average seventeenth-century offerings.

Duomo and Museo

The Duomo occupies Piazza Venanzio, named after a partisan who was shot by the Nazis in the Second World War. On its left is the large and only moderately striking Palazzo Comunale, a Gothic pile 20 years in the building, designed by Angelo da Orvieto. (He was also responsible for the Palazzo del Podestà in Piazza Matteotti, and parts of the more impressive Palazzo dei Consoli in Gubbio.)

The cathedral is a long way from being in the same league as others in the region. It has a nondescript, not to say unfinished baroque facade, grafted on to the fourteenth-century original. Only a slender campanile survives from the earlier church. The interior owes much to Renaissance Florentine churches and is not particularly interesting — you should make directly for the small museum in the sacristry. It contains a collection of rare Palaeo-Christian silverware known as *Il Tesoro di Canoscio* — nine plates and eleven spoons for use during the Mass. After being found in 1935 they were moved to Rome, until a personal appeal to Mussolini by the town's bishop brought them back. Believed to originate from sixth-century Constantinople, it is one of the most precious Byzantine hordes in existence. There is also a *Madonna and Child* attributed to Pintoricchio, and a ravishing *paliotto*, or silver bas-relief, designed as the frontispiece for an altar.

Churches

If you have taken the trouble to stop in Città di Castello you might want to look into the Gothic **San Domenico** (1424), a grandiose affair with several fourteenth- and fifteenth-century Umbro-Sienese frescoes along its restructured nave. Works by Raphael that were once in the church have found their way to the National Gallery in London. **San Francesco** (Via Albizzini) from 1275 has the classic Franciscan form, a single-naved Latin cross, but it was remodelled with seventeenth-century baroque fittings in a manner that is far from the Franciscan ideal. Only the severe Cappella Vitelli (1563) stands out, and this by virtue of its 26 inlaid choir stalls. **Santa Maria delle Grazie** lies northwards on the broad Via XI Settembre, and is a late-fourteenth-century Gothic edifice, which has somehow held on to a minor fresco by Ottaviano Nelli (right-hand wall), and a fine *Madonna and Child* by Giovanni da Piemonte, a collaborator of Piero della Francesca.

Where to stay

Hotel Garden ★★★

Not central, but modern, slick, and in a leafy situation. Parking, restaurant and garden. Viale Bologni (on the Fano road). Rooms 61. Bathrooms 6. Showers 53.

Il Bersaglio ★

Small *pensione* with restaurant and garden. Via V. E. Orlando 14. Tel. 075 8555534. Rooms 7. Bathrooms 2. Showers 1.

Villa San Donino

Small, luxurious hotel with all facilities (swimming-pool, tennis-courts, restaurant, parking, and conference rooms). Good out-of-town location. San Donino. Tel. 075 8578108. Rooms 24. Bathrooms 6. Showers 21.

Camping

Montesca ★★★

Cross the river after leaving the town by Ponte Flurido, pass under the dual-carriageway, turn right after the bridge and then first left. Swimming-pool. *Open 1 May–30 September.* 40 places. Tel. 075 8558566.

Where to eat

Tiferno

This restaurant, part of a three-star hotel, is one of the longest-established in Umbria. It is located in a medieval palace, where comfort is somewhat sacrificed for atmosphere though it is safe to eat in. Piazza R. Sanzio 13. Tel. 075 8550331. *Closed Sunday evenings.*

North to Tuscany

Città di Castello is 55 kilometres from the source of the Tiber, Rome's river, or more properly, Umbria's river, because its character-building stretches are almost entirely within the region — half of its 405 kilometres to be precise. However, it has few attractions, and the two Tuscan towns of Anghiari and San Sepolcro are the main reasons for persevering with the meandering valley to the north. In the latter be sure to visit the Pinacoteca (Palazzo Comunale, Via Aggiunti) for the striking and mystifying works of Piero della Francesca. The former is more recommended for its general and little-known medieval charm.

In this northernmost tip of the region there are still one or two things of minor interest, best taken in on the way to the two key centres nearby, Arezzo (39 kilometres) and Urbino (70 kilometres). Remember the two scenic

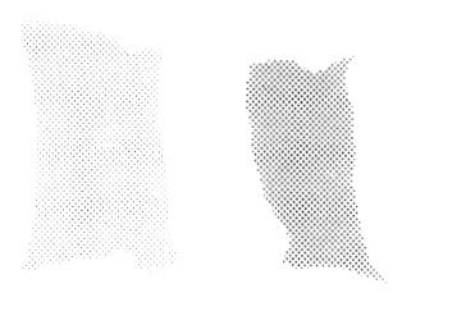

roads that cut through the countryside to the east, the N257 and N3 bis.

North of Città di Castello is the new **Museo di Garavelle**, a folk-museum that faithfully recreates a period rural farmhouse. The display extends to all areas of country life — weaving, agriculture, the blacksmith's forge, viticulture — as they were practised at the turn of the century. Still on the San Sepolcro road, near **Lama** you can see the faint remains of what is believed to have been Pliny's villa (at Colle Plinio) — parts of walls, mosaics, and odd fragments of marble. **Sangiustino**, 5 kilometres further on, is more or less modern, but for the imposing Castello Bufalini, a fifteenth-century fortress partly transformed by Vasari into a villa, and stuffed with paintings and a wealth of antiques. Visits are at the discretion of the owners; enquire at the tourist office in Città di Castello for details. Samples of Colli Altotiberini **wine** may be bought at Azienda Silvio Nardi, Sangiustino/Selci, Tel. 075 8582180. A kilometre beyond the town is the anomalous **Cospaia**, a hamlet on a hill, and until 1826 a tiny independent republic. At its foot is a fishing centre where devotees can go after trout and carp.

Strike off west from Città di Castello on the N221 for Arezzo and you will pass **Citerna** (480 metres), just on the Umbrian side of the border, and one of the best short trips you can make in the Upper Tiber. An almost perfect fortified village, it has had a long history, mainly by virtue of its powerful position — even the Germans were obliged to destroy the strategically placed Rocca in 1944. As a small added bonus, the church of San Francesco (built in 1316, but revamped in 1508) has a modest collection of Umbrian works, and a bell from 1269, still ringing the changes.

From here it is only a short jump to hilltop **Monterchi** and Piero della Francesca's famous and haunting *Madonna del Parto* — the only pregnant Madonna in the canon of Italian art. The artist's own mother was born in the village. The picture is in a chapel at the foot of the hillside, lodged — ironically (deliberately?) given the subject — in a cemetery marked, as so often, by a long avenue of cypress trees. Two angels draw aside a pair of curtains to reveal the Virgin's swelling stomach — an odd but curiously dignified effect. Expectant mothers still come to ask the blessing of the Madonna before they are due to give birth.

From Monterchi you might continue southwards towards **Monte Santa Maria**, an appealing and sleepy hamlet dominated by the large Palazzo Bourbon del Monte. The minuscule road makes tortured and twisting progress through countryside of vast but beautiful barrenness, eventually linking with the old main road at San Secondo, 7 kilometres south of Città di Castello. Turn right and then right again after 1 kilometre at Fabrecce (FCU station) for the Nestore valley, and an alternative, minor route to Arezzo. It is a little-travelled road with a couple of points of interest over and above the scenery: the eleventh-century **L'Abbazia di Santa Maria** at Petroia, with a crumbling crypt and oddments from an earlier building, and the church of San Crescentino at **Morra**, known for its Signorelli frescoes.

Where to stay

Sabaria ★★★

An excellent and small hotel in this most appealing of villages. Garden, restaurant, and above-average facilities in rooms (TV and telephone). Via della Pineta, Citerna. Tel. 075 8592118. Rooms 10. Bathrooms 10.

Serana ★

Via Umbria 37, Sangiustino. Tel. 075 856112. Rooms 8. Bathrooms 1. Showers 1.

Camping

San Pietro ★★★

(700 metres) Near Monte Santa Maria. 47 places. Tel. 075 8570123. *Open 15 June–31 August.*

Umbértide

TOURIST INFORMATION: Via Andreani 48. Tel. 075 934180

Umbértide, dull as its name and bombed flat in the war, is not somewhere you will want to linger (though look out for occasional music festivals); it is more a base for a couple of excursions into the surrounding countryside. As a town, its only attractions are the Palazzo Comunale (the best baroque 'conversion' in Umbria), and a painting by Luca Signorelli, the *Deposition of the Cross* (1516), in the church of Santa Croce. You could, however, make it a stop for lunch.

The impressive **Castello di Civitella Ranieri**, 5 kilometres to the north, is an overbearing example of fifteenth-century military architecture, at present in private hands, and so only open to admiration from outside. **Montacuto** has some panoramic views, and is a good starting point for several easy walks (nearby Mount Acuto, 926 metres, for example). Follow the tiny road beyond the village towards Castel Rigone for a roller-coaster and scenic drive along the ridges of Mount Murlo.

Montone, in the other direction, 6 kilometres north of Umbértide, is the best immediate target, mainly by virtue of the paintings in San Francesco. There are important frescoes of the *Life of St Francis* by Antonio da Ferrara (1422) and a notable *gonfalone* by Bernardino Caporali.

Where to stay

Fortebraccio ★★

Restaurant and garden. Via dei Magistrati, Montone. Tel. 075 9306184. Rooms 10. Bathrooms 10.

Corlo
★★

In the hamlet of Corlo between Montone and Umbértide. Restaurant and garden. Tel. 075 9306146. Rooms 11. Bathrooms 2. Showers 9.

Where to eat

Dell'Hotel Capponi

Good, standard Umbrian cooking. *Claims to be always open.* Piazza XXV Aprile, Umbértide. Tel. 075 932256.

Where to buy wine

Enoagricola

In the village of Montone/Caigatti. Tel. 075 8507213.

Castello di Ascagnano

In the village of Pierantonio. Tel. 075 6040119.

Carlo Polidori

Colle del Sole, Pierantonio. Tel. 075 939156.

SPOLETO

General Information

TOURIST INFORMATION: Piazza della Libertà 7. Tel. 23190

POPULATION: 37,000

HEIGHT: 396 m

POST OFFICE: Piazza della Libertà 12

TELEPHONES: SIP Bar Mancini, Corso Mazzini 72; open daily 7–9

STD CODE: 0743

POLICE: Via Cerquiglia 36 Tel. 49044

DISTANCE TO:
Florence 212 km Perugia 62 km
Rome 126 km Norcia 49 km
Gubbio 93 km Todi 44 km

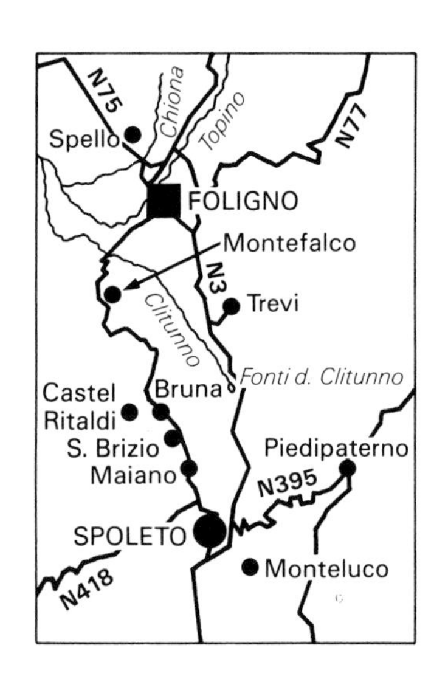

Trains

Spoleto station is in the lower town, 15 minutes' walk from Piazza della Libertà. There are six fast trains a day to Rome (2 hours) with connections at Terni for Todi, Perugia, and Rieti, and at Orte for Orvieto and Florence. Ten trains daily serve Perugia (70 minutes), calling at Trevi, Foligno, Spello, and Assisi. Ancona trains stop at Gualdo Tadino and Fossato di Vico (for Gubbio).

Buses

Four buses — A, B, C, D — ply circular routes around the town, all of them calling at the station and Piazza della Libertà. Local services leave from Piazza della Libertà or Piazza Garibaldi. The No. 9 makes the trip up to Monteluco.

Road

Roads north to Foligno and south to Terni are fast dual-carriageways. The N395, virtually the only link to Norcia and the Marche, is tiny and very pretty, but scarcely level or straight for its entire 25 kilometres. The N418 to Acquasparta and thus Todi, is only marginally better.

Parking

As usual, it is advisable to park in the lower town, and then to either walk or take a bus to the medieval centre. Otherwise try Viale Martiri, or the sports ground south of Piazza della Libertà.

Taxis

At the station. Tel. 28289. In Piazza della Libertà. Tel. 35248.

Festival information

The Box Office is at Piazza del Duomo 9. Tel. 40396. Tickets and information are also available from the tourist office. The press office is in Via del Duomo 7. Tel. 33111.

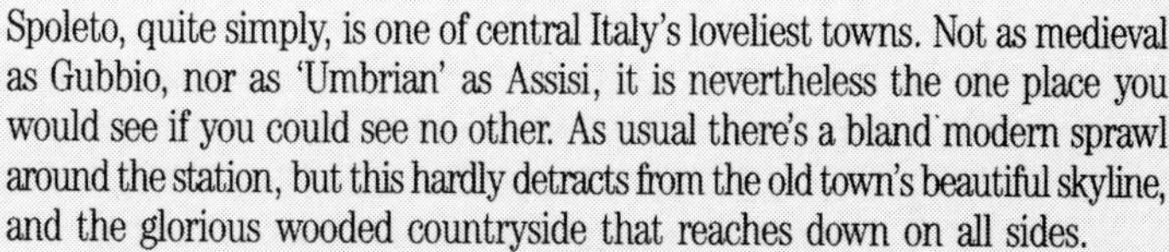

Spoleto, quite simply, is one of central Italy's loveliest towns. Not as medieval as Gubbio, nor as 'Umbrian' as Assisi, it is nevertheless the one place you would see if you could see no other. As usual there's a bland modern sprawl around the station, but this hardly detracts from the old town's beautiful skyline, and the glorious wooded countryside that reaches down on all sides.

The privilege of hosting one of Europe's leading arts festivals has bought with it some unfortunate cultural pretensions. These are manifest in a few appalling modern sculptures scattered hither and thither. (The worst — be prepared for it — is outside the station.) This is a shame because they are at odds with what is a pleasant and quite unpretentious place. The quaint thirties station itself actually sums up much better what the town is all about.

Apart from the captivating scenery on its doorstep, Spoleto claims some of Italy's oldest and most fascinating churches. There's also a cathedral that without being grandiose, manages to be Umbria's most enchanting — as well as an extraordinary novelty, the 'Bridge of Towers'. Other miscellaneous monuments span every era of Italian history, from the Middle Ages to the Lombards, from the early Christians to the Romans and mysterious Umbrians.

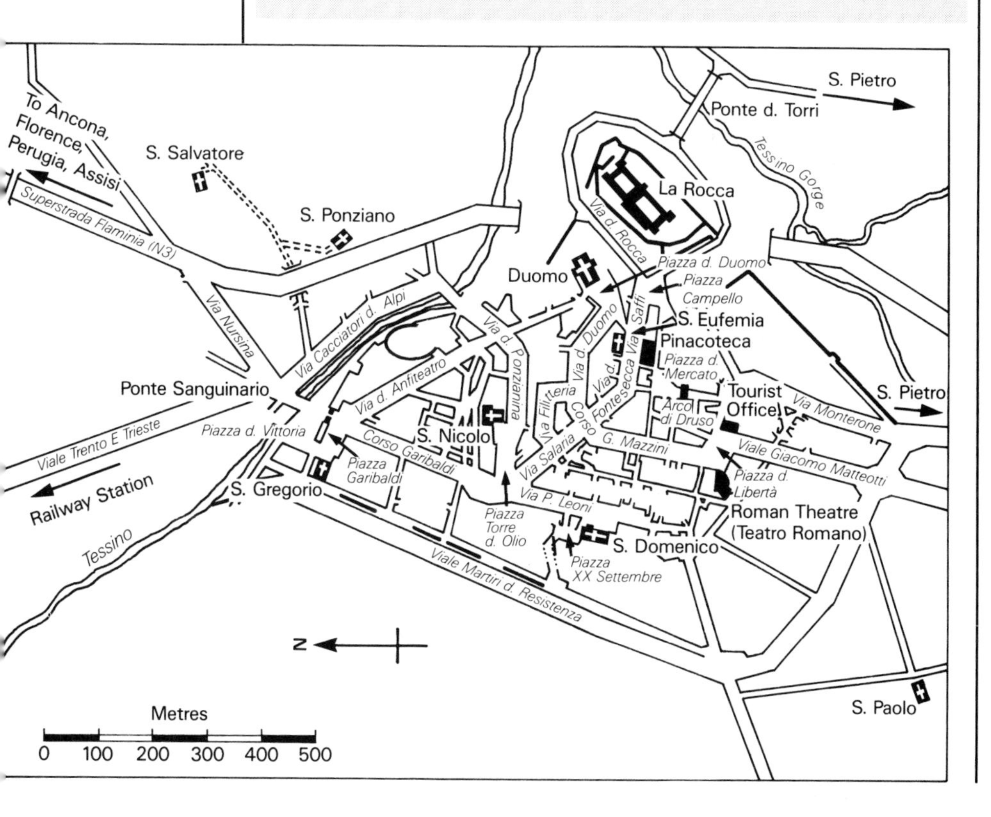

History

In the centuries before the Roman occupation, Spoleto was already an important Umbrian centre, though, tantalizingly, all that remains of its mysterious earliest inhabitants are 2-kilometre tracts of city wall, still standing despite the efforts of sieges, earthquakes, and Second World War bombing.

The Roman colony, Spoletium, was founded in 241 BC, became a vital centre of communications, and remained faithful to Rome through some difficult times. It supported Octavius in his struggle with Antony (and was so spared the fate that befell Perugia) and checked Hannibal's progress south after his victory at Trasimeno. (The event is celebrated by the arch in Via Garibaldi.)

By 90 BC it had risen to become one of the most illustrious towns in Italy, and saw its status raised to *optimum jure*, a position that made it a judicial centre with its own magistrates. Despite the ravages of civil war and the earthquakes that affected this whole eastern part of the region, it continued to prosper until the arrival of the first wave of Barbarians under Theodoric in 493.

Theodoric was followed by Belisarius in 536 and by Totila nine years later, though just when it seemed that the city was in danger of being reduced to rubble, its fortunes took a dramatic turn for the better. The Lombards arrived and made Spoleto the capital of a new Dukedom, soon to be one of the most important in Italy. The principality reached almost to Rome and was powerful enough to survive the fall of the Lombards and Charlemagne's Franks. In fact, it was so powerful that in 890 its then ruler, Guido III, and his son, Lamberto, were able to seize the imperial crown and declare Spoleto the imperial capital.

Occupying such a key position, the city could not fail to flourish. Its eventual fall from grace came in 1155, when it was virtually razed to the ground by Frederick Barbarossa during his sojourn in Italy to restore imperial authority. The following 200 years saw the familiar tussle between the Empire and the Papacy for supremacy, a struggle eventually won in 1354 by the Papacy, when Cardinal Albornoz (who seems to have had the ability to be in several places at the same time) delivered it into the hands of the Church, and built the Rocca, the most imposing in Umbria, to make sure that it stayed there.

Once under firm Church control, Spoleto again became a stable centre of trade and commerce. One of its Papal rulers (between 1499 and 1502) was the 19-year-old, thrice married but otherwise underqualified, Lucrezia Borgia. Such aberrations aside, however, the city seems to have avoided the worst disorders of its neighbours, the most powerful of which, Perugia, laboured on for another two centuries before Papal control brought it to heel.

Under Napoleon it continued to dominate the eastern part of the region and was made capital of the *Dipartimento di Trasimeno*, an administrative district that also included Perugia. In the battle for the unification of Italy, it remained loyal to the Pope right up to 1860, when it was captured by Piedmontese troops. (Its garrison at this time was commanded by a certain Major O'Reilly, whose troop of 300 Irish mercenaries, combining Irish

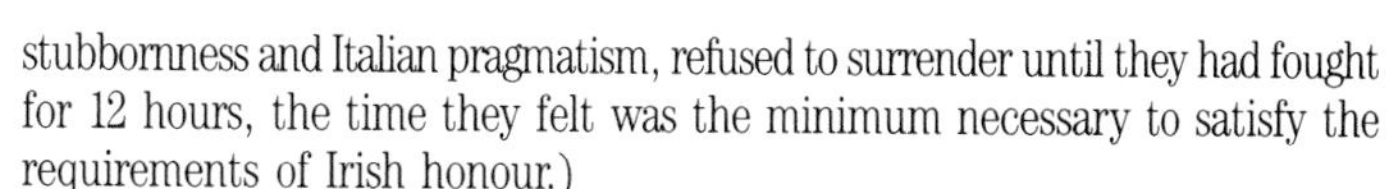

stubbornness and Italian pragmatism, refused to surrender until they had fought for 12 hours, the time they felt was the minimum necessary to satisfy the requirements of Irish honour.)

In the Second World War, the city's importance unfortunately attracted some heavy bombing, during which large areas of the lower town were destroyed. More recently, its history has been happier, having been largely dominated by the Festival of Two Worlds, an event that has brought it renewed prosperity and international renown.

What to see

Ponte Romano

Spoleto is the most Roman of the Umbrian towns, preserving much from the period that elsewhere has disappeared into the fabric of more recent buildings.

The road from Perugia and the north crosses the *Torrente Tessino* into Spoleto via the Porta Garibaldi (though the *Torrente* is more of an unpleasant dry river-bed than a torrent now that the waters have receded). In Roman times it was preceded by a vast bridge, part of which can still be seen under the modern-day piazza. Facing Porta Garibaldi, there are some metal railings on the left-hand side of the road from which steps lead down to the bridge. Nothing else in the bustling square gives any indication that the thing ever existed. If the gate is locked, as is frequently the case, try asking for the key at the nearby Bar Lilli.

The bridge formed part of the improvements to the Via Flaminia ordered by Augustus, and was used until the river was diverted to make way for a new city wall in the fourteenth century. By that time, a large part of it had been buried in silt, and once abandoned it gradually disappeared, both from sight and memory, and was only 'rediscovered' in 1817.

Its nickname, 'Porta Sanguinaria' — the bridge of blood — is colourfully attributed to the rivers of Christian blood that were said to flow into the Tessino from the nearby amphitheatre through runnels thoughtfully constructed for the purpose. More prosaically it probably derives from a corruption of 'Sanapilaria', the name of one of the gates in the same amphitheatre.

Roman Amphitheatre

Traces of this building are still visible nearby. Take Via dell'Anfiteatro, the road opposite the church of San Gregorio (which you might want to look in first — see below), leaving Piazza Garibaldi on the left. Two minutes' walk brings you to Spoleto's barracks, La Caserma Severo Minervio, situated in the grounds of a former monastery. In the courtyard, and to the right of the main building (don't be put off by its severe and imposing outside walls) is all that remains of the theatre, which once measured 115 metres by 85 metres.

It has had a chequered career since the passing of Rome, first being used as a fortress by Totila and then being dismantled by Albornoz, who used its stones to build the Rocca in the upper town. What was left was converted into the medieval equivalent of a shopping precinct in the thirteenth century, and the remainder simply incorporated into the courtyard you see today.

Amphitheatre (Piazza Libertà)

This is a smaller but much better preserved theatre at the opposite end of the town, built in the first century but subsequently swallowed up by the surrounding buildings. It was only fully extricated in 1954. The original stage area has been lost for good to the church and ex-monastery of Sant'Agata, but the theatre is still used as a setting for plays and concerts during the summer festival.

Events here were just as bloodthirsty as those that took place in the other amphitheatre. In 1319, for example, 400 Guelph supporters of the Pope were rounded up and imprisoned in the arena. All then had their throats cut and, dead or not, were thrown on to an enormous human bonfire in the middle of the stage.

Arco di Druso and Roman Temple

The amphitheatre is almost at the heart of the old Roman city. Fifty metres away, through Piazza Fontana (with probably the smallest fountain ever to lend its name to a piazza) and Piazza San Ansano, is the Arco di Montone. The city is full of arches but only a handful are of Roman origin. This one dates from the third century BC. The Arco delle Felice, embedded in the wall behind it, is more recent (sixth century), though the road to the right, Via delle Felici, contains some of the city's oldest sections of wall.

By far the most important of the arches (none are as impressive as those in Rome) is the Arco di Druso, which now straddles the narrow entrance to the Piazza del Mercato, once the entrance to the old Roman forum. It was built by the Senate of Spoleto to commemorate the victorious battles of the general, Drusus, son of the Emperor Tiberius (AD 14–37), during his campaigns in Germany.

To its right is a long, narrow trench below the level of the road, the entrance to what is rather grandly known as the Roman temple. The church above is San Ansano, with access to more of the temple and the fascinating Crypt of St Issac. It needs a very vivid imagination to reconstruct anything from the temple's rather paltry remains, which are almost completely overlooked by the Spoletans hurrying to shop in the Piazza. Outside, all that survives is a single column, half lost in the wall of the church; everything else is half-hearted plaster imitation. Inside, the massive foundation block for the vanished columns is still visible, along with the remains of two Roman streets, which once ran either side of the building. There are also traces of a semicircular apse from the early Christian church that was later built on the same site.

The door on the left upon entering the church leads to the Crypt of St Issac and St Marziale, two sixth-century monks who fled from persecution in Syria to settle down on the slopes of Monteluco. The room's walls are decorated with recently restored frescoes from the eleventh and twelfth centuries, which include the *Beheading of John the Baptist*, *Jesus Enthroned* and the *Last Supper.*

Duomo (Piazza del Duomo)

Spoleto's cathedral is one of the loveliest things in Umbria, thanks largely to its beautiful setting. Blue sky and wooded hills frame it from behind and in front there rises a gently sloping, fan-shaped piazza (extravagantly large for an otherwise fairly cramped hill-town), whose elegant medieval buildings and hanging gardens lead the eye to a simple and harmonious facade.

It was built at the end of the twelfth century on the site of a seventh-century church destroyed by Barbarossa in 1155. Until 1198, when it was consecrated by Innocent III, the facade consisted of only two tiers; the third,

The Duomo: campanile. (DL)

that which contains the largest of the seven rose windows, was added in the second phase of building in the thirteenth century. The campanile, made from old Roman materials, is from the same period.

Facade

The main door, inside the Renaissance portico (added between 1491 and 1504 by Ambrogio Barrocci and Antonio Florentino), has a beautiful and intricately carved architrave. Note also the easily overlooked and rather strange pulpits to either side of the front arches. The cluster of rose windows is an unusual feature in what is otherwise a typical Umbrian facade; the largest is surrounded by the figures of the Evangelists. Above it, the central gently curved Gothic arch contains a Byzantine-inspired mosaic, *Christ between the Virgin and St John*.

Interior

One Luigi Arrigucci, architect to Pope Urban VIII, was responsible for the interior alterations in 1644. 'Improving' work of this kind was common in towns with a measure of prosperity that they wished to make conspicuous. Despite the baroque gloss liberally applied by Arrigucci, the interior has held on to a few things of substance, notably the floor of inlaid marble and Fra Lippo Lippi's frescoes in the apse. The best of the additions is a small bronze bust of Urban VIII by the irrepressible leading light of the baroque, Bernini. You'll find it tucked away above the main door, to the right of which, at the beginning of the three naves, is the Erioli Chapel, or Chapel of the Sacred Heart.

In the first, and smaller, of its two rooms are two frescoes by Pintoricchio. The one above the altar, *Madonna and Child with St Stephen and St John* is the best preserved.

The larger room to the right is the Erioli Chapel proper. It was commissioned (with considerable foresight) by Constantino and Francesco Erioli, bishops of Spoleto between 1449 and 1550. Frescoes, mediocre for the most part, cover its every surface. The artist responsible for the ceiling, with its extraordinary blue background, is unknown, but the wall paintings have been attributed to a sixteenth-century Sicilian painter, Jacopo Santori. The frescoes on the left-hand wall as you face the altar are by far the best, but don't overlook the shattered, though still beautiful, marble-framed Madonna above the altar itself.

The Duomo's most striking feature is the presbytery, where you will find **Fra Lippo Lippi's frescoes**, painted between 1467 and 1469 with the help of Fra Diamante and Piero Matteo d'Amelia. (The latter unsuccessfully submitted plans for the decoration of the Cappella Nuova in the Duomo in Orvieto.)

The frescoes start on the left-hand wall with the *Annunciation*; then comes the *Passage of the Virgin* (with the painters and Lippo's son, Filippino Lippi, in a group to the right), and conclude with the *Nativity*. Above them,

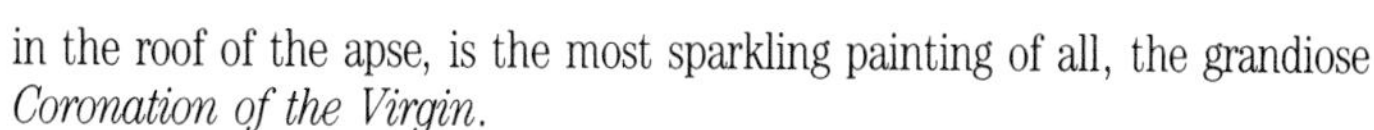

in the roof of the apse, is the most sparkling painting of all, the grandiose *Coronation of the Virgin*.

These frescoes were Fra Lippo's last. He died and was buried in Spoleto, the city's magistrates refusing to return his body to his erstwhile patron, Lorenzo di Medici, in Florence, giving as their reason according to Vasari, the fact that 'they were but poorly provided with ornaments, above all with distinguished men' and so 'consequently begged permission' to keep the artist's remains. Lorenzo eventually agreed and a tomb, designed for the painter by his son, was installed in the right-hand arm of the transept. With quite incredible carelessness, however, the bones were 'mislaid' during the seventeenth-century restorations, and the tomb now is completely empty.

Some say their disappearance was the result of a long-standing vendetta conducted against Fra Lippo by a local family. This is quite possible, as the painter, despite his monkish habit, was a notorious womanizer, and it is thought that the bones may have been spirited away by the descendants of some poor girl whose reputation he had irremediably compromised. It is even said that he was poisoned as punishment for the same crime.

Elsewhere in the Duomo, notice the Chapel of the Sacred Icon in the arch below the organ-loft. The icon in question is a twelfth-century Byzantine Madonna reputedly stolen from Constantinople and given to the Spoletans by Barbarossa as a token of peace in 1185 (rather small amends for his having almost completely destroyed their city a few years earlier). The sixth chapel in the left of the three naves contains a lovely choir of inlaid wood, and frescoed panels executed by local artists between 1548 and 1554, as well as the Duomo's oldest possession, a *Crucifixion* painted on wood and parchment that dates from 1187. The *Madonna and Child* here, by a gifted but unknown fourteenth-century sculptor, is also worth looking out for. (If the chapel is locked ask for the key in the sacristy. Ask at the same time if you can see the ninth-century crypt of St Primiano, which contains traces of early fresco.)

Opera del Duomo — Museo Civico

Open 10–12, 15–17.

The museum is on the ground floor of the unfinished Palazzo della Signoria (1330–1419), on the left of the Piazza del Duomo. Finding the way in can be a problem as the entrance at No. 3 is shared with the elegant four-tiered theatre built in 1880 and named after the Spoletan writer, Caio Melisso. (It is one of the venues for the summer festival.) Ring the bell and, as you are shown to the museum, try to catch a glimpse of the theatre as you walk past. (There is another entrance in a small lane to the left of the Palazzo.)

Both Albornoz and Gattapone had a hand in constructing the Palazzo, which started life as the seat of the town's civic administration, but was left unfinished and eventually abandoned until its transformation into a museum in 1903.

Like its counterpart in Orvieto, it consists of a single hall, in this case the former guard-hall, and similarly has an enormous variety of interesting objects, such as glassware, cannon balls, fragments from tombs and monuments (notice the casts taken of the architrave around the doors of the Duomo and the church of San Salvatore in the entrance hall) as well as the more substantial pieces listed below.

1 Two famous stone tablets, *Lex Spoletina*, from the third century BC. The text, in archaic Latin, is a law that forbade the cutting down of trees in the sacred woods around Spoleto. They were discovered in 1913.

2 The Sarcophagus of St Issac (twelfth century), taken from the crypt next to the Arco di Druso. It is decorated with reliefs representing Christ and the symbols of the Evangelists, with the figures of the Madonna and monks on either side.

3 The Sarcophagus of St Gregory, a fifteenth-century monk who, like St Issac, was a hermit on Monteluco.

4 A bas-relief from the twelfth century, with five scenes from the martyrdom of St Biagio.

5 A sixteenth-century chimneypiece taken from the Palazzo Arroni, opposite the museum and now part of Perugia University. It is worth popping into the palace to see its lovely small courtyard and carved main door.

Ponte delle Torri

During the 109 years of anarchy that accompanied the exile of the Popes to Avignon, its was left to Pope Innocent VI's legate, Cardinal Albornoz, to make sense of the political and administrative chaos in the Papal domain. The key factor in his campaign to restore order was the construction of a series of heavily fortified castles at strategic points throughout central Italy. Of all such works still standing in Umbria (and there are many) the Rocca and Ponte delle Torri in Spoleto are amongst the most striking, and certainly the most enduring. (Just how enduring is illustrated by the fact that until recently the Rocca was used as a high-security prison, numbering amongst its inmates leading ex-members of the Red Brigade and the current Pope's would-be assassin.)

That both have survived earthquakes and bombing without so much as a scratch is due partly to luck and partly to the skill with which they were designed. They are the work of the Gubbian architect Gattapone (precise dates unknown), who was also responsible for the Palazzo dei Consigli in Gubbio and the graceful Loggia in Narni. (One of his most notable buildings, the Perugian fortress at Ponte Sole, was destroyed by the infamously volatile Perugians within a few years of being built, but if records are anything to go by, must have been as impressive of any of his works that have survived. Like the Rocca, it was built at the highest point of the city and seems to have been connected to key buildings, such as the Duomo and Palazzo Comunale, by a complicated series of secret underground passages.)

His plan for the fortress in Spoleto was far more simple, but no less a feat of architectural and engineering ingenuity. Documents suggest that the Rocca was already in existence some time before the Ponte, and it is probably only by chance that the two came to form part of a single defensive scheme.

The Ponte was probably built on the site of an old Roman aqueduct, which almost certainly served as a model for Gattapone (it has a striking resemblance to a Roman aqueduct of antiquity). The Ponte had the original purpose of bringing water from the Patrico and Cortaccione springs on Monteluco (a function that, if necessary, it can still perform). With the building of the Rocca in 1355 it also became a useful means of escape in the event of a siege, for by that date the only access to the bridge was via a covered walkway that descended from the fortified walls of the castle. (Remains of this link are still clearly visible on the rocky hillside between the two.)

Today the bridge is one of the most extraordinary things in Umbria, and has quite rightly become a picture-postcard favourite. Its size and scope would be impressive in modern engineering terms; the fact that it was built over 600 years ago is little short of miraculous. Ideally it should be seen from below, but this being difficult, the next best thing is to include it on a straightforward walk from the town. From Piazza Campello take Via del Ponte, a quiet lane that leaves the town behind almost immediately, and you are soon in beautiful open countryside with marvellous views down into the Tessino gorge and south towards the mountains of Castelmonte. The bridge comes into view soon afterwards. Ten massive arches, 230 metres long and 80 metres high (the Ponte is a notorious lovers' leap), span the holm-oak-covered gorge, linking Monte Sant'Elia (the hill on which Spoleto is built) with the wooded slopes of Monteluco. It is still possible to cross the upper walkway on foot, from where you can see that the two central pillars are actually hollow towers with access to the valley bottom below. Continue over the bridge and turn right, and the wooded road brings you to the church of San Pietro — a walk of about 2 kilometres. Alternatively, return to Via del Ponte and continued to follow the road around the base of the Rocca until you find yourself back in Piazza Campello (a circular walk of around 20 minutes).

Pinacoteca (Piazza del Municipio)

Open 10–13, 16.30–19.30.
Closed Tuesday.
Admission charge. Check details with the tourist office.

Strangely, for a town that seems keen to attract visitors, it rather seems as if someone somewhere doesn't want you to see the Pinacoteca. This may have something to do with the fact that it is housed in four delicately beautiful rooms (worthy of a visit in their own right) that they are reluctant to have trampled by thousands of visitors, or it may simply be a case of bureaucratic obstinacy. In any event, you are expected to negotiate the outer limits of the

Palazzo Comunale, the town's council buildings, before you are shown to the gallery itself. Tickets are bought from a small office on the right of the main door, after which you must wait for a custodian to accompany you to the paintings on the first floor.

The Palazzo itself was started in the thirteenth century but has been greatly altered over the years, especially during the seventeenth century. Only the tower is original. The left wing of the building was added as late as 1913. In front of it, in what is otherwise a more than pleasant piazza, is another of those not terribly impressive sculptures. This one is called *The Tree* and has been here since 1963.

As to the paintings themselves, it makes chronological sense to start in the last of the gallery's four main rooms, that is, in the one furthest from the entrance (Room I). This, moreover, with Room II, also has the better pictures. The best are those by Lo Spagna, many others are older and often anonymous; all are worth the trouble it can take to see them. Amongst the most important are:

Room I

1 *Crucifix* by Maestro di Cesi. An important work on wood by an unknown Umbrian artist from the first half of the fourteenth century. (Two other crucifixes are by earlier Umbrian artists.)

2 *Polittico* of four saints from the Umbrian school.

3 *Madonna della Grazie*. A triptych (with Madonna, Child, and St John the Baptist) attributed to Nicolò Alunno.

4 *Madonna, Child and the Miraculous Well* (1502) by Bernardino Campilli, a follower of Pintoricchio.

5 *Madonna, Child and Angels* (fifteenth century) by a follower of Gozzoli, likewise a *Madonna, Child and Saints*.

Room II

1 *The Virtues — Charity, Clemency and Justice* (1512) by Lo Spagna, originally painted in honour of Pope Julius II, but adapted to include the bust of Pope Leo XII in 1824.

2 *Mother, Child and Saints* (1514–16) by Lo Spagna, with the influence of Raphael, and containing the coat of arms of the Ridolphi family. (Ridolphi was Governor of Spoleto at the time.)

3 *Mother, Child, St Augustine and St Stephen* (1530) by a follower of Lo Spagna. Likewise the fresco of *St Sebastian*.

Churches

San Gregorio Maggiore (Piazza Garibaldi)

A large, but nevertheless intimate church, built in 1069, possibly earlier, consecrated in 1146, and well restored to its Romanesque form after damage over the years from fire, flood, and, more recently, from Second World War bombing. The simple and pleasing exterior looks almost modern, but dates from the twelfth century, and is now a clean and startling white as a result of the years of restoration. The tower to its right was built at the same time, and its lower half, like the facade, is made from large blocks of stone taken from old Roman buildings. The top, of notably different origin, is a fifteenth-century addition.

n Gregorio Maggiore: crypt. (DL)

The facade itself is an attractive patchwork of styles, with a Renaissance porch of three arches, again made of old Roman materials, added when the church was heightened to imitate the Duomo in the sixteenth century. Notice the destroyed but still effective fresco in the Chapel of the Innocents to the left of the porch. It depicts St Abbondanza, who is buried in the church, along with, so popular legend has it, 10,000 Christian martyrs slaughtered in the nearby amphitheatre.

Inside, the church is in the form of a basilica divided into three naves, in itself not unusual, though what is striking is the 3-metre difference in height between the naves and the presbytery. There are fragments of fresco everywhere, with the best pieces in the higher presbytery to the rear. All are by local artists, and date from between the twelfth and fourteenth centuries. Notice the square stone confessionals set into the walls of the naves — rather unusual, and beautiful in their elegant simplicity. Beyond a pair of these on the left is the Chapel of the Sacrament, with a fine marble relief attributed to Benedetto da Rovezzano.

The **crypt**, whose entrance is halfway down the left of the three naves, is one of the best things in the church, intimate and curious with over 20 tiny vaulted ceilings supported by dozens of small columns of widely differing age and origin. The large sarcophagus here is reputed to be the tomb of St Abbondanza.

Sant'Eufemia (Via Aurelio Saffi)

Sant'Eufemia: interior. (DL)

This extremely interesting church was built in honour of a local bishop and saint, St Giovanni, martyred by the Goths and reputedly buried here in 980 when the site was the home of a Benedictine monastery. It dates from the first half of the twelfth century, possibly earlier, was well restored between 1907 and 1953, and is one of the most important Romanesque buildings in Umbria. As well as being in the grounds of the old archbishop's palace, excavations have suggested that the church is sited above an old Lombard palace, probably the ducal palace itself. The same excavations have brought to light the remains of an even older, third-century, building, and one look at the interior of the church is enough to show that its builders made good use of both the site's previous constructions.

It is high, spacious and almost completely bare, with just a few patches of fifteenth-century frescoes above the altar and on several of the church's strangely mismatched columns, no two of which are the same. (Notice especially the square carved column, second on the right, which is particularly beautiful and was clearly never intended for the purpose to which it has been put.) The high-arched gallery above the side-naves, the *matronei*, or woman's gallery, is the only one of its kind in Umbria and was added in the sixteenth century. The altar and the strange stone chair behind it, which look almost modern in contrast to the rest of the church, actually date from the thirteenth century and were brought here from the Duomo.

San Domenico (Piazza San Domenico)

A thirteenth-century church, and restored like San Gregorio Maggiore (though not quite as well) to its original, pre-baroque, state. Outside, it is finished in alternating stripes of extraordinary, but beautiful, pinky-orange stone (recently cleaned) and covered with filled-in arches and windows, all making for a strange but striking exterior. Inside, the large single nave has none of the intimacy of San Gregorio or Sant'Eufemia. Small fragments of fresco are oddly preserved in the new yellowy plaster and only one or two substantial paintings have survived, most important of which is the large fresco on the right-hand wall, found immediately upon entering the church. It is an early-fifteenth-century work, the *Triumph of St Thomas Aquinas*, enclosed in an impressive frame, and showing the saint surrounded by bishops, cardinals, and his disciples. At the rear of the church, on the right-hand side beyond the baroque chapels, is a small room lodged under the bell-tower. The fifteenth-century frescoes here, some of them rather crude, were restored in 1972, and include a *Crucifixion*, *Christ in Glory* and *Stories from the Life of St Mary Magdalene*. In the Capella dei Montevecchio in the left transept, is a silver reliquary (1726) reputed, like rather a lot of other reliquaries dotted around Christendom, to contain one of the nails of the Cross.

Santi Giovanni e Paolo (Via Filitteria)

Scarcely bigger than a very modest chapel and currently being extensively restored, its walls are covered in the remains of frescoes dating from the twelfth century onwards. One of the best, and the thing that draws your attention to the church in the first place, is actually on an outside wall under the eaves; a *Madonna and Child* painted in the thirteenth century.

San Nicolo

A hundred metres down hill from here (off the main road and through the small lanes and gardens opposite) is the vast ex-Gothic church of San Nicolo. The church and cloisters next to it are still being restored (the work has been going on since 1966) but both are now beginning to return to their original appearance. After ceasing to be a church and before falling into almost complete ruin, it was variously used as a truffle market, a bronze foundry, and a workshop for repairing steam engines. It is now a little less imaginatively given over to antique markets, concerts, and exhibitions.

San Pietro

In a town with several more than usually interesting churches, San Pietro, with its fascinating facade, is one of the most outstanding. It can be seen from several points of the city and is easily reached. If you are on foot, cross the Ponte delle Torri and turn right, following the twisting road for about 2 kilometres (be careful as there are no pavements). It is a pleasant and shaded walk, with occasional glimpses of Spoleto and the Ponte through the trees. By car it is no distance. Remember, however, that it is impossible to drive over the Ponte. Leave the town via Porta Monterone, its southernmost exit, and turn left, crossing over the dual-carriageway. You will see the church directly ahead of you.

The church, apart from suffering the noise from the nearby road, is in a lovely position, out of the town proper, privy to wonderful views, and close to the lower slopes of Monteluco. There has been a church here since the

San Pietro: detail from the facade. (DL)

fifth century, when Bishop Achillus built the first San Pietro to house St Peter's Chain, a holy relic that he had smuggled from Rome (and which has long since disappeared). Before this, the site had been in almost continuous use as a cemetery from the time of the Iron Age. The church was enlarged and virtually rebuilt at the beginning of the fourteenth century, but to no avail, alas, for in 1393 it was practically destroyed by fire. The facade and its sculptures (whose precise dates are unknown) were overlooked in the restoration that followed, and later escaped the baroque alterations made to the interior in 1699.

The **facade** like that of the Duomo and many other Umbrian churches, is divided into three horizontal tiers. The uppermost two are ordinary and self-explanatory, save for the symbols around the main rose window, which are those of the Evangelists. The lowest tier, however, is far from ordinary and contains, after the bas-reliefs of Orvieto's Duomo, the finest Romanesque

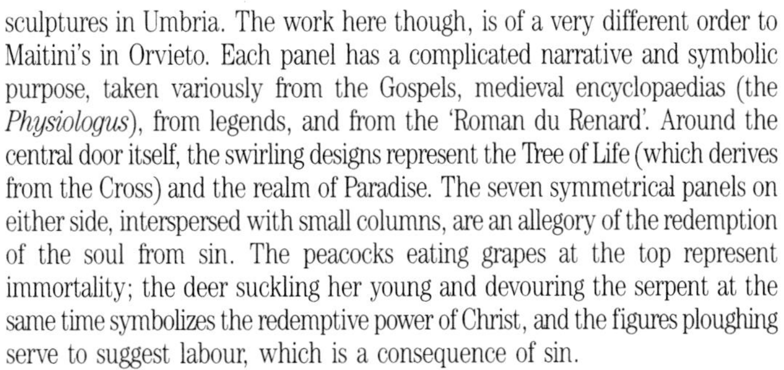

sculptures in Umbria. The work here though, is of a very different order to Maitini's in Orvieto. Each panel has a complicated narrative and symbolic purpose, taken variously from the Gospels, medieval encyclopaedias (the *Physiologus*), from legends, and from the 'Roman du Renard'. Around the central door itself, the swirling designs represent the Tree of Life (which derives from the Cross) and the realm of Paradise. The seven symmetrical panels on either side, interspersed with small columns, are an allegory of the redemption of the soul from sin. The peacocks eating grapes at the top represent immortality; the deer suckling her young and devouring the serpent at the same time symbolizes the redemptive power of Christ, and the figures ploughing serve to suggest labour, which is a consequence of sin.

Next to these are ten larger panels, five on either side. Those on the left, from the top to bottom, represent the following:

1. The death of a just man. St Peter frees the man of his chains while the Archangel holds the man's soul in his scales. The Devil, lashed by the keys of St Peter, tries to weight the scales in his favour. He holds a scroll that reads: 'I mourn because before he was mine' — 'Doleo Quia Ante Erat Meus'.
2. The death of a sinner. Here, by contrast, the Archangel Michael withdraws, and two demons bind and torture the sinner before throwing him into a pot of burning oil.
3. The lion and the woodman. Some symbolic detective work is required here. The lion (perhaps the power of God) is trying to free its paws from the tree, which is about to be felled by the forester. The panel probably deals with the ability of man to free himself from the corrupting influence of the Devil. (Notice here, and elsewhere, how the lion's tail ends in a serpent's head, a common feature of Lombard sculpture.)
4. A man kneels before the lion. Man kneels before God to receive the grace and forgiveness that first have to be asked for.
5. A soldier challenges the lion and is attacked by it. This symbolizes the opposite of the above, and man provokes the wrath of God.

The panels on the right, from top to bottom, represent the following:

1. Christ washing the feet of St Peter.
2. Christ calming the waters of Lake Tiberias for St Peter and St Andrew.
3. A fox feigns death before two ravens. Here the fox is the Devil, or the Flesh, and the ravens the Soul tempted by the flesh.
4. A wolf disguised as a friar and a fleeing ram. This is a dig at loose monastic morals; the wolf is doing its best to study but cannot keep its eyes off the ram.
5. A lion chases a dragon. The lion is Christ and the dragon is evil. The dragon is in the process of being banished.

San Salvatore

Like Sant'Eufemia, San Salvatore is one of those notable exceptions to the rule that says churches claimed in guide-books to be very old rarely seem

San Salvatore: interior. (DL)

that way once you are inside them. Here the sense of antiquity is tangible, almost disturbingly so. Many consider it to be one of the oldest churches in Italy.

No one, however, is really sure of the building's precise age. The chances are that it was consecrated in the wake of the new freedom of worship introduced by Constantine the Great at the end of the fourth century, and built on a site chosen for its proximity to some existing Christian catacombs. What makes it so interesting is that large parts of the first Palaeo-Christian church are still intact, despite centuries of restoration, leaving us with a building of considerable architectural interest. When the idea of a Christian church was conceived, the dominant form of religious practice was still pagan, and it was natural therefore for those involved in its construction (probably Eastern Mediterranean monks), to adopt the prevailing 'pagan' architecture of the day; the result is a Roman temple only faintly disguised as a Christian church. Not the mock Roman temple of the Renaissance, where pagan and classical ideas were used to evoke antiquity, but the real thing, complete with Doric and Corinthian columns, 'borrowed' from nearby Roman buildings.

The effect is almost impossible to describe; the church is cold, bare, and austere, its atmosphere redolent of age. Centuries ago the ancient columns in the nave were filled in to keep the roof from collapsing, in the presbytery newer pillars are wedged between older ones, and everywhere stone fragments lie scattered in a kind of dusty gloom. At some point, a more Christian apse was added (though on a different alignment), giving the upper half of the church a crowded and lop-sided appearance.

The facade also bears all the signs of extreme old age, and even seems in danger of imminent collapse. Although the whole exterior is badly damaged, and the original marble facing is missing completely, some idea of its late Roman splendour can still be gained from the curved architraves around the main door, and the strangely mismatched windows (the central one of which contains elements not found in any other church from the same period).

San Ponziano close by is unexceptional unless you are able to descend into the thirteenth-century crypt. Propped up by strange columns, there are also several well-preserved Byzantine frescoes.

San Paolo inter Vineas (Via San Paolo)

The church is quiet and simple now that it has been restored (1966) to its twelfth-century Romanesque state. It was consecrated in 1234, but, as is so often the case with medieval Umbrian churches, it was a place of worship long before this date, and some of the capitals in the nave are from an earlier tenth-century building.

The ulterior motive for visiting San Paolo is for its frescoes, which are some of the oldest in Umbria. They were painted before the church was consecrated, and in view of their age are not surprisingly strongly Byzantine in character. You will find them on the rear and right-hand walls of the presbytery. They describe *Scenes from the Creation* (Adam naming the animals, the birth of Eve, the Creation of Man, God banishing Adam), and the faded *Prophets* and *Patriarchs*.

Where to stay

Gattapone ★★★★

A perfect gem of a hotel overlooking the Ponte delle Torri and the Tessino gorge. Scenic, peaceful, and convenient location. Intimate, too, with eight small rooms (though they are sparsely furnished and rather thin-walled — those in the new extension are much better). Good restaurant and bar. Extremely popular, so booking in advance is strongly recommended. Via del Ponte 6. Tel. 36147. Rooms 11.

Dei Duchi ★★★

Very close to Piazza della Libertà, and the best-known of the central hotels. Old, reliable, and popular with festival performers. Garden, parking, and conference facilities. Viale Matteotti 4. Tel. 44541. Rooms 50. Bathrooms 11. Showers 39.

Clarici Commercio ★★★

Modern, moderate hotel just behind Porta Garibaldi on the edge of the old town. No restaurant. Piazza della Vittoria 32. Tel. 40735. Rooms 24. Bathrooms 9. Showers 16.

Motel Agrip ★★★

Out of town on the main road to Foligno; a motel in the truest sense of the word. Modern, high-rise, and cloned 'international hotel'. Popular for its straightforward convenience, efficiency, and size. An excellent restaurant (*closed Friday during the winter months*). Situated on the Via Flaminia, 2 kilometres north of the town. Rooms 57.

Nuovo Clitunno ★★★

Central but peaceful location. Reliable, small, and quietly well-known. Regulars return year after year. Piazza Sordini 6. Tel. 38240. Rooms 31. Bathrooms 2. Showers 30.

Lello Caro ★★

Large, convenient, and cheap hotel, but totally without frills. Piazza Garibaldi 40. Tel. 41979. Rooms 42. Bathrooms 6. Showers 10.

Dell'Angelo ★

Small *pensione* above the lovely *trattoria* of the same name. Very central. Via Arco di Druso 25. Tel. 32185. Rooms 6. Showers 5.

Camping

Il Girasole ★★

A peaceful location in the village of Petrognano (hourly buses from the station). Tel. 51335.

Monteluco

Small, convenient site behind the church of San Pietro. Ten minutes from Piazza della Libertà. Tel. 28158.

Where to eat

Il Tartufo ★★★

The restaurant in Spoleto since 1926, and still superlative, though there are those who criticize its pandering to the Festival's international public. Its menu, once a touchstone for typical Umbrian cuisine, has of late been watered down with frivolous novelties. Try, however, the various *bruschette*, the *penne* (pasta) with a variety of herbs and the *medaglioni* of meat with truffle or mustard sauces. Ask for a table downstairs, and you will be sitting on an original Roman pavement. It is also much cooler. Piazza Garibaldi 24. Tel. 40236. *Closed Wednesday and between 17 July and 5 August*. Expensive.

Sabatini

A restaurant of simple, wood-panelled elegance. The best in the old centre (Il Tartufo is down the hill towards the new town) with a wide range of Umbrian specialities. Large garden for summer *al fresco* eating. Corso Mazzini 52. Tel. 37233.

Trattoria Panciolle ★★

A romantic and peaceful hideaway. The perfect spot for *al fresco* eating, located in a lovely, lime-tree-filled piazza. Simple, straightforward food. Largo Muzio Clemente 4 (between Via Pianciani and Via del Duomo, off Via Fontesecche). Tel. 45598.

Trattoria del Festival

Usually full of locals — always a good sign — and a safe choice for a simple and medium-priced meal. Piazza della Fontana.

Ristorante Economico

Basic but extremely cheap meals provided by the local council. Scant choice, but food of good quality. Via San Carlo.

Piazza del Mercato

The piazza has several reasonably priced and fairly humble restaurants. Dell'Angelo, under the arch opposite San Ansano, is best, its pizzas cooked in a large wood-fired oven. Close by at No. 10 is an unnamed remnant from the ninteenth century, the favourite haunt of Spoleto's workmen and market-traders.

Note: **La Cantina** is the town's most appealing wine-bar, with light snacks and outside tables in the summer. Via Filetteria 10a. Tel. 44475. *Closed Tuesday*.

AROUND SPOLETO

Monteluco and east of Spoleto

Part of the reason for Spoleto's considerable popularity with visitors is its position relative to the rest of Umbria, one that makes it an ideal point from which to explore the surrounding countryside, and the mountainous region to the east in particular.

The city is effectively a watershed; to the east the new *autostrade* that have opened up the rest of Umbria give way to twisting country roads, prosperous towns are replaced by a patchwork of smaller villages, gentle hills become fully fledged mountains, and the landscape's tone of pastoral calm turns into one of rugged, even barren, grandeur. Five minutes the other way, to the west of the old Via Flaminia, however, and you are back in familiar territory; quiet and saintly Montefalco, 'the balcony of Umbria', with Gozzoli's frescoes of the *Life of St Francis*, and nearby Trevi, perched above the Clitunno valley on its pyramid-shaped hilltop; two of the most perfect Umbrian towns one could wish for (and the ideal day-trip from Spoleto, requiring a round journey of less than 50 kilometres).

Everything you will want to see, then, is close at hand, but what makes the town especially attractive is that her surroundings are accessible not only by car but also on foot. The area is a recognized centre for hiking and camping, and detailed summaries of local walks are available on request from the tourist office. For the less energetic, small roads reach high into many of the mountains, and from these well-worn tracks make even the highest peaks reasonably accessible.

The walk to the ancient woods on **Monteluco** is not what it would have been 20 years ago. Hotels and bars now cover the top of the sacred hillside, and it is probably better to drive or take a bus the 8 kilometres from Spoleto. Though it has been well and truly tamed for the tourist, the area is still very pretty, with superb views and miles of wooded footpaths. Its coolness in the summer can be a welcome relief, but you should be warned that it is a very popular place.

It takes its name from *lucus*, which means 'sacred wood', and has been a holy place since time immemorial. Early Christian refugees from Syria and the Middle East made it their home in the fifth century, and in 1218 St Francis chose it as the site for one of his first monasteries. Today, this once humble building has become the Franciscan Sanctuary of Monteluco, the goal of pilgrims, and is open to the public for most of the year.

The twisting drive here from Spoleto is straightforward (leave by the south on Viale Matteotti and follow the well-signposted road) and reaches a height of 804 metres, offering some marvellous views. There are also regular buses from Piazza della Libertà and the railway station.

Where to stay

There is little to choose between the new hotels and restaurants, most of which are full of longer-staying guests 'taking the air'.

Paradiso ★★★

Tel. 0743 37182.

Ferretti ★★

Tel. 0743 49849.

Michelangelo ★★

Tel. 0743 40289.

Montemaggiore, at 1428 metres, is the highest point of the spine of mountains that runs north and south of Spoleto, and which cuts the town off from the Nera valley to the east. In winter it becomes an attractive, if minor, ski resort. The summit is an hour and a half's walk from the hamlet of **Acera**, which is reached by taking the main road north from Spoleto for 5 kilometres and then turning right shortly after the small village of Eggi. Acera is 10 kilometres beyond.

Hotel Casaline ★

A little way off the main road (N3), close to the tiny village of Poreta. Tel. 0743 62213. Rooms 5.

Where to eat

Ristorante Casaline

Renowned not only for its excellent traditional cooking, but also for its rustic and beautiful setting. The homemade *dolci* in particular are very good. Details as for hotel. *Closed Monday.*

The slight detour required to reach **Eggi** is also worthwhile. It is a pretty village, with a castle built by the indefatigable Albornoz, and three churches, each with a sprinkling of frescoes by local artists (from the thirteenth to the sixteenth century).

The road to Acera is just one of several desolate and rough lanes that cross the mountains east of Spoleto and Trevi. All of them make striking journeys. That from **Bianca** over **Monte Serano** (1429 metres) is a little less rough than most.

Trattoria Pettino

In the hamlet of Pettino, in idyllic surroundings you will find this excellent small family-run restaurant that specializes in truffle cooking. Homemade cheeses, home-cured ham, and *salami* also figure in the menu, and the family's own olive groves produce all the oil used in the cooking. Tel. 0743 62124. *Closed Tuesday.*

The most important of these roads, and the one that really links Spoleto to the east is the No. 395. It leaves the main road north from the town after less than a kilometre and is signposted to Grotti and Cerreto di Spoleto. (After 2 kilometres there is a right turn to **Vallochia** (10 kilometres) from where it is an hour's walk to the top of Castelmonte (1038 metres). The road is no less winding than those to the north, but it is lower and in better condition and, as a bonus, has extraordinary views across lines of mountains stretching away from it in almost every direction.

The church at **Grotti** (13 kilometres) has frescoes by Umbrian painters of the fifteenth and sixteenth centuries, likewise the church of San Michele in Archangelo at **Meggiano**, a small village on the narrow and striking road that turns left from the No. 395 shortly after Grotti. This road hugs the slopes of Montemaggiore before dropping down to Cerreto on the more major No. 209 (for Triponzo and Norcia) but it is one for the adventurous only.

Where to stay

Dell'Hotel Panorama ★★

Colle San Sebastiano, near Cerreto. Tel. 0743 91223. Rooms 31.

Where to eat

Dell'Hotel Panorama

It specializes in fish dishes but also makes good use of the truffles found in abundance in the surrounding countryside. Details as for hotel.

If you ignore the minor road at Grotti and continue instead to **Piedipaterno**, you have an interesting and more relaxed drive towards Terni. This can be turned into a circular route, returning to Spoleto via L'Abbazia di San Pietro, Arrone, Montefranco, and the *superstrada* that links it to Terni, a round journey of about 70 kilometres.

Montefalco, Trevi, and west of Spoleto

Terzo San Severo (13 kilometres) just off the N48 road to Acquasparta is the starting-point for the hour's walk to **Cima Panco** (1012 metres). There is a good signposted track from the village to the summit. The local church has traces of fifteenth-century frescoes. Beyond San Severo is the village of **Montemontano**, built around a fourteenth-century castle. Here too the church has the faded remains of fourteenth–fifteenth century frescoes. The village is an hour and a half's walk from the top of Mount Montano (1094 metres) along a track-cum-road to the north-west. Massa Martana is a further hour from the summit down the long sloping ridge to the south-west.

This whole area is dotted with castles at **Morgnano** (in ruins), **Terzo La Pieve**, **Mercole**, **Busano**, **Perchia**, and **Firenzuola**, which also has a small and very pretty Romanesque church. There is a man-made lake at **Arezzo**, with fishing and (discreet) swimming, reached by turning off the road at **Crocemaggiore**, a kilometre past Baina.

Going north from Spoleto by road or rail towards Trevi and Foligno, the rather flat countryside has been a little spoilt by haphazard building. The first substantial village you reach is **San Giacomo** (8 kilometres). The parish church has two particularly good frescoes by Lo Spagna: *Coronation of the Virgin* and *St Giacomo* (1526).

Where to eat

Al Palazzaccio da Piero

Renowned for its excellent cellar and the range of its truffle dishes. Via Flaminia 134, San Giacomo. Tel. 0743 52168. *Closed Mondays.*

Fountain of Clitunno

12 kilometres from Spoleto, station 1 kilometre

Open 9–13, 14.30–dusk.
Admission charge.

This lovely spot has been famous since antiquity for its tranquillity and the purity of its spring waters. Writers of all ages, from Virgil to Byron, have celebrated it in verse; it has been painted by Corot and visited by any number of famous men, Caligula and Claudius amongst them. The Romans had a spa resort here (the waters used to be more plentiful before the underground springs were disturbed by earthquakes) and the site was also dedicated to the god Clitunnus, famous for his oracles. Nowadays the spot is very busy, even a little commercialized, with dozens of tourist buses visiting daily. However,

> But thou, Clitumnus! in they sweetest wave
> Of the most living crystal that was e'er
> The haunt of river nymph, to gaze and lave
> Her limbs where nothing hid them, thou dost rear
> Thy grassy banks whereon the milk-white steer
> Grazes; the purest god of gentle waters!
> And most serene of aspect, and most clear;
> Surely that stream was unprofaned by slaughters —
> A mirror and a bath for Beauty's youngest daughters!

And on thy happy shore a temple still,
Of small and delicate proportion, keeps,
Upon a mild declivity of hill,
Its memory of thee; beneath it sweeps
Thy current's calmness; oft from out it leaps
The finny darter with the glittering scales,
Who dwells and revels in thy glassy deeps;
While, chance, some scatter'd water-lily sails
Down where the shallower wave still tells its bubbling tales.

Byron, *Childe Harold's Pilgrimage* (Canto IV, 66–7)

fountain of Clitunno. (ISTO)

Nearby **Campello sul Clitunno** is another of those perfect little Umbrian villages, sitting on its olive-covered hill and protected from the outside world by still-substantial walls. It has only a few dozen houses, half of which seem to be hotels. Its only real claim to fame apart from its charm and tranquillity is a trout festival held in July.

Where to stay

Fontanelle ★★ Garden. Restaurant. Via dei Elci 1. Tel 0743 62191. Rooms 11. Bathrooms 8.

Ravale ★★ Restaurant. Ravalle Campello. Tel. 0743 62420. Rooms 20. Showers 20.

A little over a kilometre beyond the Fountain of Clitunno is the **Temple of Clitunno**. Although it looks for all the world like a Greek temple, it is in fact an early Christian church, built according to some authorities in the fourth

century and to others in the eighth. Fragments from earlier Roman buildings were almost certainly used in its construction. Inside the church (you will probably have to ring the bell on the small gate at the entrance) are what may be some of the oldest frescoes in Umbria, faint paintings of Christ, St Peter, and St Paul, dating from the eighth century.

Trevi

TOURIST INFORMATION: Piazza del Teatro
POPULATION: 7000
HEIGHT: 412 m

What to see

Trevi is one of the most striking small towns in the region, and a visit here is recommended. Few people bother to make the detour up its steep hillside, and the place has a pleasingly provincial and undiscovered air. Its art gallery (Palazzo Comunale, Piazza Mazzini) contains a mixture of paintings, Roman remains, sculptures, and ceramics, but its pride and joy is a large *tavola* by Lo Spagna, the *Coronation of the Virgin* (1522). (Like the similar work in Todi it was commissioned in imitation of Ghirlandaio's painting in Narni.) As in Spoleto, you are expected to negotiate several council departments before reaching the gallery itself. Look out also for a *Madonna* by Pintoricchio.

Trevi. (DL)

Unfortunately the Romanesque church of Sant'Emiliano (Via Placido Raccardi), while boasting a pleasing exterior, has all the usual eighteenth- and ninteenth-century alterations inside. However, it has managed to conserve a splendid *Altar of the Sacrament* (1521–4) by Mattia di Gaspare da Como, and a series of frescoes attributed to Francesco Melanzio (1510–12). The church is at the highest point of the town's sugarloaf-shaped hill and below it, as always, is a maze of twisting streets and blind alleys. (Notice their various and characteristic cobbled pavements,

laid out like giant mosaics, and the two sets of medieval walls, the inner one of which contains fragments from the original Roman colony.)

San Francesco (Via San Francesco), with its recently restored interior (the church has been refitted half a dozen times since its foundation in the thirteenth century), has several partially conserved Umbrian frescoes from the fourteenth century, but the best of Trevi's churches are a little way out of the town itself. **Madonna delle Lacrime**, on the steep, winding road from the station, has many paintings mainly from the sixteenth and seventeenth centuries, and a late *Epiphany* by Perugino (1521). (If you arrive by train — Trevi is a main stop on the Rome–Ancona line — catch a bus to the centre of the town, which is 4 kilometres from the station and much too far to walk, especially on a hot summer's day.)

The church of **San Martiro** (Via Augusto Ciufelli) has the best paintings of all, including works by Lo Spagna, Tiberio d'Assisi, and Pier Antonio Mezzastris. There are further excellent frescoes by the same artists in the small chapel to the left of the church, amongst them one of Lo Spagna's best paintings, the *Assumption with St Francis and St Antony* (1512).

Where to stay

Della Torre ★★★★

In the hamlet of Torre Mattige. A large hotel with all facilities, including swimming-pool and tennis-courts. Tel. 0742 670644. Rooms 140. Bathrooms 80. Showers 60.

Cochetto ★★

Restaurant. Via Dogali 13. Tel. 0742 78229. Rooms 22. Bathrooms 4. Showers 12.

Del Pescatore ★★

In the hamlet of Pigge 4 kilometres south of Trevi looking down on the Temple of Clitunno. Restaurant and garden. Via Comporeale. Tel. 0742 78366. Rooms 9. Bathrooms 9.

Where to eat

Il Cochetto

Lively restaurant, popular with locals, especially on Sundays. Garden terrace with superb view. Truffle dishes a speciality. Details as for hotel.

If you have taken the main road to Trevi and Montefalco and are returning to Spoleto, it is as well to be aware of the minor road that links the towns and makes an attractive alternative route. Starting from Spoleto itself, the village of **Maiano** has a good thirteenth-century castle; **San Brizio** is surrounded by walls and its church has a Roman sarcophagus as well as the inevitable frescoes. **Bruna** is little more than the strangely oriental sanctuary of Santa Maria della Bruna, built in 1510, but looking, it has to be said, rather like a medieval grain silo. **Castel San Giorgio**, not surprisingly, has a castle, built, like the Rocca in Spoleto, by Cardinal Albornoz. **Castel Ritaldi** is a good centre for local crafts and is surrounded by numerous tiny hamlets all with ruined castles and small, unspoilt churches. **La Pieve**, with its Romanesque church, is probably the best.

Montefalco

TOURIST INFORMATION: Corso G. Mameli 68. Tel. 79122
POPULATION: 6000
HEIGHT: 473 m
STD CODE: 0742

Of all the silent Umbrian hill-towns, Montefalco is one of the quietest, and, in view of the fact that eight saints were born here, perhaps one of the holiest as well. Tranquil and tiny cobbled streets, most of them too narrow for even the smallest of cars (and Italian cars can be very small indeed) wind gently to the Piazza del Comune, its unfinished and slightly forlorn square usually deserted except for an occasional cat stretching in the sun.

Square and town are dominated by one building, the Palazzo del Comune, from whose clock-tower you can enjoy the views that have earned Montefalco the title 'ringhiera dell'Umbria' — the balcony of Umbria — and though there are more spectacular views in the region, there are probably none quite as extensive.

Not quite as idyllic as the day it was described as a 'little strip of Heaven fallen to earth', the town is still a gem, thanks to its sleepy medieval air and a collection of paintings remarkable in a place of this size. (Only the collections of Perugia and Assisi are better.)

It is also famous, and rightly so, for two of Umbria's most distinctive wines: Sangrantino and Sangrantino Passito, both strong, ruby-red wines, whose extraordinary bouquets leave a lingering aftertaste of blackberries. (The latter, more like port than a simple wine, is best taken after meals.) Those who have no time to visit the *cantinas* in the surrounding countryside, and who are content to buy without tasting, should make for the small shop in Piazza del Comune, which has a good selection of local vintages.

History

Little is known of Montefalco's history before the Roman period, when it was probably part of the territories ruled by the colony then called Mevania, present-day Bevagna. In the seventh century, the town found itself trapped in a sort of no-man's land between areas controlled by the Lombards and the

Byzantines, leading the inhabitants, attacked from both sides, to convert many of the old scattered Roman villas into fortified *castra*. In time these grew together to form a settlement, which became known as Corrorone.

In 1180, having been a free commune, the town was annexed by the Dukedom of Spoleto and began to expand beyond the confines of its first set of walls, changing its name in 1249 to Montefalco following widespread destruction at the hands of Tommaso d'Acera, an over-zealous captain of Frederick II. The real spur to its fame, and one of the reasons for its rich artistic heritage, dates from 1306 when the delicate position of the Papacy (this was the period of the 'Two Popes') meant that the Papal Rector, Jean d'Amiel, could no longer remain in Spoleto and be sure of staying alive. Moving to Montefalco, with its high and isolated location, however, offered him a far more stable and secure future.

Lorenzo Maitini (later to work on the Duomo in Orvieto) was duly commissioned by Pope John XXII to strengthen the town's walls and build a fortress to house the new Legate, whose home was to remain in the town until 1354, when the building of the Rocca enabled the Papal seat to be re-established in Spoleto.

In the last years of the fourteenth century and up to 1439, Montefalco was dominated by Foligno's Trinci family, thereafter passing to the Papacy (though Papal rule could do nothing to save it from the ravages of the plague in 1527, nor from the devastation wrought by Orazio Baglioni's infamous marauding mob, the Black Band). The last 500 years of its history have been quietly prosperous, the only recent outrageous act of destruction having been the building of a vast water-tower on the outskirts of the town — obviously necessary in the drought-ridden summer months, but an ugly eyesore nevertheless in a place all but untouched by the twentieth century.

What to see

San Francesco (Via Ringhiera Umbra)

Admission charge.

After the pleasures of wine and losing oneself in the quiet streets, a visit to Montefalco is mainly about churches, of which **San Francesco** (second only in artistic terms to the Basilica of St Francis in Assisi) is by far the most important. Almost nothing on the outside prepares you for the splendour of its interior, a large single nave, virtually bare but for bright splashes of colour provided by dozens of paintings and frescoes, some of which — there are clearly too many to have been painted for this one building — were removed from surrounding churches when the gallery was created in 1890. Those that do belong here are the result of donations to, or commissions from, the Franciscan friars who ran the church in the 200 years following its foundation in 1336.

Chief amongst these are the frescoes of a Florentine, Benozzo Gozzoli, but the church's main importance stems from its collection of Umbrian paintings, whose variety and original setting are unparalleled. Their range is enormous, and spans several hundred years from the anonymous fourteenth-century works of artists influenced by Ottaviano Nelli and the Gubbian school, to local painters such as Giovanni Corraduccio and through to the more sophisticated painters of the Renaissance such as Perugino, Tiberio d'Assisi, and Montefalco's own Francesco Melanzio.

Gozzoli, its star, has been called third-rate by Florentine standards, but his presence in Montefalco in 1452, at a crucial moment in the development of Umbrian art, was extremely important. He was the means by which a great deal of its thought and energy were released, being responsible not only for introducing many of the innovations pioneered by the Florentines (in particular those of his teacher, Fra Angelico) but also for turning San Francesco into a place of pilgrimage for the up and coming artists who wished to learn the new techniques. Amongst the numerous painters who must have seen his frescoes were Fiorenzo di Lorenzo, Nicolò Alunno, Benedetto Bonfigli, and any number of the lesser anonymous artists whose work can be found in palaces and churches dotted around the region.

His paintings in the apse, a cycle depicting the **Life of St Francis**, though lacking the originality of his later work in Pisa and the Riccardi chapel, are anything but third-rate. Gozzoli had almost certainly seen Giotto's paintings in Assisi, and chose to portray similar episodes from the saint's life. Though he had neither his predecessor's genius, nor his innovation, he had the considerable advantage of being able to draw on almost two centuries of artistic development. It is hardly surprising, therefore, that at first glance his appear the more sophisticated of the two cycles. His portrait of the saint, however, lacks much of Giotto's spiritual depth. (Though, to be fair, Giotto had left little to be added to the Franciscan story by way of dignity and austerity.) Gozzoli picks instead on a different aspect of the saint, that happier and more lighthearted side of the man to which the painter's own temperament was more suited. (Bernard Berenson, in *The Italian Painters of the Renaissance*, hit the mark when he called Gozzoli a 'Fra Angelico who had forgotten Heaven and become enamoured of the earth'.) The result is a series of paintings that are neither profound nor innovative but rather radiant with a simple, sunny joy, which — and this is to Gozzoli's credit — St Francis himself would probably have rather liked.

The gallery is fairly well laid out, though not all the paintings are labelled. Starting from the main entrance and working anticlockwise, six distinct chapels, separated from the main nave by arches, precede the central apse containing Gozzoli's frescoes.

1 The first side-chapel is one of the best. Everything here is by Gozzoli and was painted between 1450 and 1452.

2 All the frescoes here are by the Folignese artist Pier Antonio Mezzastris (1461).

3 Two lovely paintings by Melanzio, both taken from the church of Sant'Agostino.

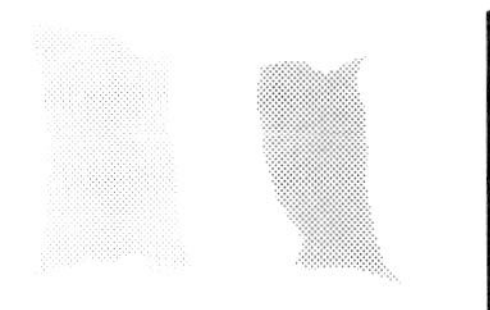

One, a *Mother and Child with Four Saints*, is his first dated work (1487).

4 The ceiling vaults, painted by Giovanni di Corraduccio in 1440, are rather crude but the *Madonna and Child with Six Saints* (1498) is one of Melanzio's best works, its style moving away from the influence of Alunno towards that of Pintoricchio.

5 The ceiling is again by Corraduccio, likewise the *Crucifixion with Saints* on the wall. The two lovely small panels in the glass cabinet, in the manner of Raphael, are attributed to Melanzio. Next to the cabinet is a framed *gonfalone* in poor condition, the so-called *Madonna del Soccorso* (1498–1500). Several versions of the same subject exist in neighbouring churches (in fact there is another, better, example in the next chapel). The patrimony of the story associated with the painting was widespread in Umbria and Marche, particularly in the Augustinian tradition from about 1480 to 1520, and concerns a young mother who, tired of her child's antics, cried in exasperation: 'Che il diavolo ti porti via' — 'Would that the devil might take you away'. The devil duly appeared, prompting the mother to invoke the assistance of the Virgin to save her child.

6 The last chapel has a rather confused collection of oddments and frescoes detached from other churches. The ceiling is by an unknown collaborator of Corraduccio. The right-hand wall has a good painting by Alunno, and to its right another fresco by Melanzio. Easily the best thing here is a *Madonna del Soccorso* (1510), probably by Tiberio d'Assisi.

Moving around the church, there is a small apse, which contains fragments of frescoes of the Umbrian school (fourteenth century), and a single small *tavola*, *Madonna della Selvetta* (1532), by an Umbrian painter who also appears to have worked in Santa Chiara. In the central apse, Gozzoli's frescoes of the life of St Francis begin in the lower left-hand corner and read left to right, moving upwards towards the arched ceiling vaults. Some panels contain more than one episode.

1 Birth of the saint.
2 A simple man holds his cloak before the saint.
3 St Francis gives his coat to a poor soldier.
4 The vision of the Church triumphant. (The narrative moves to the right of the central window.)
5 St Francis renounces his father's inheritance and is covered by the Bishop of Assisi.
6 The meeting of St Francis and St Dominic. Above, Mary placates Jesus, with St Peter's, Rome, in the background.
7 (Back to the left-hand side of the frescoes, above the first panel) St Francis supports the Church and Pope Onorio III approves his Rule.
8 St Francis chases the devils from Arezzo.
9 (To the right of the window) The saint preaches to the birds, blesses Montefalco, and refuses the offer of a bishopric.

10 The saint predicts his death at dinner with Orlanda da Celano.
11 (In the first arched section on the left, above the first panel) St Francis institutes the first Christmas Crib at Greccio.
12 The saint preaches before the Sultan and undergoes a trial by fire.
13 (To the right of the window) The stigmata.
14 The saint's death and the patrician Girolamo confirming the truth of the stigmata.

The 20 small medallions that surround the frescoes depict Franciscans who achieved fame. Petrarch, Dante, and Giotto are portrayed under the window. The arch around the window itself contains portraits of St Clare of Montefalco, Agnes of Assisi, St Fortunato, St Severus, St Elzear, and St Louis. The small apse to the left, like the one on the right, contains very early fragments of fresco, most damaged and faded. The small painting behind the metal grill is a fourteenth-century Umbrian piece, clearly influenced by Giotto.

Facing away from the apse towards the rear wall of the church, the wall on the right contains the following sequence of paintings:

1 A good work, *Three Saints* by Antonio Aquilio (1460–1508), framed by an arch that is also frescoed (with *St Sebastian* and a *Madonna and Child*) by Melanzio (1506).
2 The next wooden arch contains a large *Crucifixion* in poor condition, followed by a much better one set away from the wall by a local artist painting in the middle of the fourteenth century. Notice the fragments behind it.
3 The over-decorated baroque chapel that follows is rather out of character in an otherwise decidedly medieval church, but the altar painting by Fantino da Bevagna, is almost reasonable.
4 A niche containing frescoes by Mezzastris, a *Crucifixion* and *St Antony of Padua with two stories of the Saint.*
5 Another niche with an outstanding painting by Tiberio d'Assisi (1510), *Madonna and Child with Saints*, well up to the standard of the Perugino next to it.
6 This work was executed by Perugino, probably with the help of assistants, in 1515. The other faded works with it on the rear wall are by local followers of Gozzoli. The beautifully painted balcony is sixteenth century.

Sant'Agostino

San Francesco is in one of Montefalco's two main streets, **Sant'Agostino**, just a couple of hundred metres away, is in the other (Corso G. Mameli). Built in 1279 to a simple Gothic design, its rather grave facade is relieved by an elegant doorway and the soft gloom of its interior offset by several important frescoes.

The aim of simple mendicant Orders, such as the Augustinians, was primarily to preach, and so this church, like many others belonging to the Order, was designed to be large and relatively unadorned so as to reach as many people as possible without distracting them with unnecessary detail

and complicated architectural frills. Also common was the habit of building such churches outside town walls, and close to a main gateway, as was the case here (though in this instance, the church was swallowed up by the town's subsequent medieval expansion).

Some of the frescoes have been damaged by damp and none have been attributed to specific artists with any degree of certainty. On the left-hand wall starting from the front of the church are fragments (*Adoration of the Shepherds*) which recall Ottaviano Nelli, and then a large painting, *Coronation of the Virgin*, which is close to the work of the Sienese painter Ambrogio Lorenzetti. More fragments follow, before a damaged, though striking, *Madonna with St Augustine and St Nicholas of Tolentino*, attributed to a fifteenth-century Folignan artist, Ugolino di Gisberto. Above this is a much earlier work, which, like those in the sacristy (reached via a doorway on the left of the choir), still harks back to Giotto and the early Sienese, though their author was probably an Umbrian, painting at the turn of the fourteenth century. On the other side of the church, the penultimate chapel on the right contains frescoes from the school of Gozzoli, all dating from the end of the fifteenth century.

Santa Chiara

Leaving the confines of the town's walls, but staying with the Augustinians, a two-minute walk brings you to the church and convent of Santa Chiara (Via Verdi). Santa Chiara, or St Clare (1268–1308), who became a nun at the precocious age of 6, is the most revered of the town's saints, not to be confused with the more famous St Clare of Assisi, one-time companion to St Francis.

The baroque church itself is dull, but the convent behind it has several valuable and beautiful works of art. To see them you will need to summon one of the nuns by ringing the bell to the right of Santa Chiara's mummified body. Starting in the convent's small private chapel you will be shown a variety of relics associated with the saint's life: the crumbling remains of her heart and the knife and scissors used to remove it from her body (they both seem far too small for even such rudimentary surgery), a crucifix set with three of her liver stones (symbolizing the Holy Trinity), and a tiny cross-shaped piece of tissue from her heart. The nuns tell how Christ appeared to Chiara in a vision, lamenting the burden of the Cross and how the saint replied she would help Him by carrying it in her heart. When she died, her heart was examined and, sure enough, there was the 'cross' (just as she had prophesied). In another vision, your guiding nun informs you, Christ appeared to Chiara and planted his staff in the ground next to her. In time this grew into a tree whose gnarled remains are visible in the convent's lovely cloister. Cuttings from the miraculous original then produced all the healthier-looking trees you now see dotted around the garden. (They yield berries used by the nuns to make rosaries, and which, ground and treated in the correct way, are also supposed to have strange medicinal properties.) Botanical authorities claim that this type of tree does not grow naturally anywhere else in Europe.

The cloisters contain several very old wooden chests, one of which, in Lebanese cedar, was used as Chiara's coffin. Of the paintings the most impressive is a large *Crucifixion* on wood from the fourteenth century. The heart of the convent, the Cappella di Santa Croce, is covered in early and important frescoes on the *Life of St Clare*, painted in 1333 and well restored in 1932. Notice the small Fascist memorial, which the nuns, hampered by red tape, are having difficulty in removing.

Sant'Illuminato

Fifty metres from the convent, in Via Verdi, is the tiny church of **Sant'Illuminato**, preceded by a graceful, three-arched Renaissance portico. Inside, the walls are completely covered in frescoes attributed, with varying degrees of uncertainty, to Francesco Melanzio. Impressive for the quantity rather than their quality, most were painted in the first 10 years of the sixteenth century. The best, an *Epiphany*, and *Flight into Egypt*, are in the second niche of the small nave. Opposite Sant'Illuminato, the baroque church of **San Leonardo** is worth a quick look for an excellent altarpiece by Melanzio, painted in 1515.

San Fortunato

A 15-minute walk, with nothing to recommend it but a closer view of the water-tower, takes you to **San Fortunato**, situated on a very pretty wooded hillside of evergreen oaks, just outside the town. (To reach it, continue down Via Verdi from San Leonardo as far as you can go and then turn left at the first T-junction. The church is a few hundred metres beyond.) In front of it is a large courtyard, to the left of which is the small Cappella delle Rose, whose frescoes by Tiberio d'Assisi (1512) make the dull walk more than worthwhile. Above the main door of the church itself are the faded remains of the first frescoes painted in Montefalco by Gozzoli. Inside, on the right of the nave, is a more substantial work by the same artist of another of the town's saints, St Fortunato, who died in 390. Below the painting (which has darkened with age) is a macabre and gloomy collections of bones, those of the saint himself.

Where to stay

Nuovo Mondo ★
A small *pensione*, with restaurant, garden, and swimming-pool. Via Mameli 67. Tel. 79243. Rooms 5. Bathrooms 5.

Ringhiera Umbra ★
Restaurant. Via Umberto 1. Tel. 79166. Rooms 12. Bathrooms 2. Showers 3.

Santa Chiara ★
Via de Cuppis 18. Tel. 79144. Rooms 20. Bathrooms 9. Showers 11.

Where to eat

Ringhiera Umbra Corso G. Mameli. Tel 79166.

La Grotta Rossa In the nearby hamlet of Turrita (4 kilometres). Tel. 79373.

Where to buy wine

Antonelli F.lli, Azienda Agraria, San Marco. Tel. 79152.

Bea Paolo Azienda Agraria, Cerrete. Tel. 79688.

Borghesi Marcello Azienda Agraria Il Girasole, Cerrete. Tel. 79280.

Caprai Cantina Val di Maggio, Torre. Tel. 62433.

Pambuffetti F.lli, Azienda Agricola, Scacciadiavoli. Tel. 99126/53903.

Ruggeri Giovanni Montepennino. Tel. 79294.

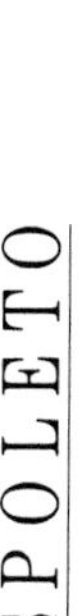

ORVIETO

General Information

TOURIST INFORMATION: Piazza del Duomo 24. Tel, 41772
Open 9–13, 15–19
On the rear right-hand side of the piazza as you face the cathedral. Good room-finding service and copious amounts of information

POPULATION: 25,000

HEIGHT: 325 m

POST OFFICE: Via Cesare Nebbia
Open Monday–Friday 8.30–19
Saturday 8.30–13

STD CODE: 0763

DISTANCE TO:
Florence 150 km Perugia 69 km
Rome 97 km Spoleto 77 km
Assisi 87 km Todi 34 km

Getting Around

The railway station is in the new, lower town, Orvieto Scalo. Regular buses (usually the No. 1) run from the station forecourt to Piazza Cahen and Piazza XXIV Marzo in the old town (10 minutes). Return buses depart from the same points. Tickets are available from the station bar. Buy one for the return journey to save time later.

Trains

Espressi and *diretti* to Rome and Florence. Slow, stopping *locali* to Chiusi (connections to Siena and Castiglione del Lago) and Orte (connections to Terni, Spoleto, and Foligno/Perugia).

Buses

ACT's longer-haul buses, with a wide range of services leave from Piazza Cahen (Tel. 53636 for information). There is one daily bus to Todi at 13.30. Buses for Viterbo (7 daily) leave from Piazza XXIV Marzo. Local buses depart from Piazza della Repubblica.

Road

Orvieto is on the A1 motorway, the *Autostrada del Sole*. The nearest junction is 3 kilometres south of the town. There is an excellent dual-carriageway to Todi (and hence to Spoleto and Perugia/Assisi). The N71 north to Città della Pieve is circuitous, busy, and slow. Roads west to Bolsena are minor, scenic, and slow.

Parking

Highly advisable to park in Orvieto Scalo and take a bus to the old town (see above). There is a medium-sized car-park behind the Duomo in Piazza Marconi, but you will need to arrive early to be sure of a place. If you must park in the centre, Via Postierla, Via Roma and Piazza Cahen are your best bets. The main Corso Cavour is pedestrianized.

One of Umbria's two big Etruscan cities (Perugia is the other), Orvieto's rather uncompromising bleakness is a permanent memorial to its dark and mysterious founders. For many, the town's leaden, brooding atmosphere comes as a disappointment. However, you would need to be world-weary indeed to be disappointed by the glittering cathedral, perhaps Italy's finest Gothic building. It was described by Burckhart as the 'Greatest polychrome monument in the world', and by Pope John XXIII as the 'Golden Lily of cathedrals'. (He added that on the Day of Judgement it would float towards Heaven carried by its own beauty.) Otherwise there's little to see, despite the good press given the town by many guides (though the cathedral alone is enough to merit a visit). Certain quarters have a dour medieval air, and one or two churches deserve a special look, but general wandering possibilities are more limited than elsewhere.

Orvieto's position, however, is unforgettable. The town stands on what is left of a huge table-top plug of lava (or *tufo*), the remnant of four volcanoes once active in the area. Way off to the north and west there are further outcrops from the same ancient craters. (The rich soils they laid down are responsible for Orvieto's famous white wine, the town's other claim to glory.) Precipitous (and crumbling) walls of rock climb sheer and majestic from the vine-covered valley floor. Reserve judgement on the overall effect, though, until you start the five kilometre drive up from Orvieto Scalo. From directly below the site looks less spectacular, less extraordinary, than from a distance or from the ramparts themselves. Then the valley, half-lost in haze, seems a world away, a tiny model of rivers, roads, and vineyards.

History

When Orvieto was first inhabited is not certain, but to judge by its extraordinary position and what has been found there, it must have been home to any number of Iron and Bronze Age tribes, making it, with nearby Cortona, one of the oldest towns in Italy. By 700 BC it had been discovered by Etruscan settlers moving inland from Tarquinia and Caere, and within 200 years had become a leading member of the Etruscan Confederation. In 264 BC the Romans entered the city following a request from leading citizens to put down an uprising of slaves and never got round to leaving. They removed in the process (according to Pliny's *Natural History*), 2000 sacred statues, suggesting that the city had assumed considerable importance as a religious centre.

Etruscan resistance to the Romans had virtually come to an end at Volterra five years earlier, so Orvieto's 'voluntary submission' was more or less bowing to the inevitable, though not all her inhabitants welcomed their new rulers with open arms. In the wake of 'defeat' some moved south to form a settlement on the site of present-day Bolsena, calling it Volsinii Novi, the new town, to distinguish it from the old town, Volsinii Veteres, they had relinquished. When the Romans came to name their new colony they followed suit, calling Orvieto by its earlier name, but translating 'old town' as 'Urbs Vetus', from which the present name derives.

After passing through the hands of Goths, Byzantines, and Lombards, the city became a free commune in 1137, evolving a civic administration as advanced and sophisticated as any in Umbria. In the second half of the twelfth century it started a policy of expansion aimed primarily at obtaining an outlet to the sea, and to this end concluded a treaty with Florence directed against the Sienese, whose territories, with those of the Aldobrandeschi, lay between the city and the coast. Within a few decades it had realized its ambition, and obtained the submission of a vast area stretching from Montalto on the Tuscan coast to the River Albegna in the north.

The next few years saw Orvieto at the height of its powers. A spate of civic and religious building accompanied its new prosperity, giving the city more or less the appearance it has today.

Religious architecture in particular, even excluding the Duomo, left a marked impression, thanks largely to the arrival of Dominican, Franciscan, and Augustinian monks, who, between 1233 and 1266, all built churches to

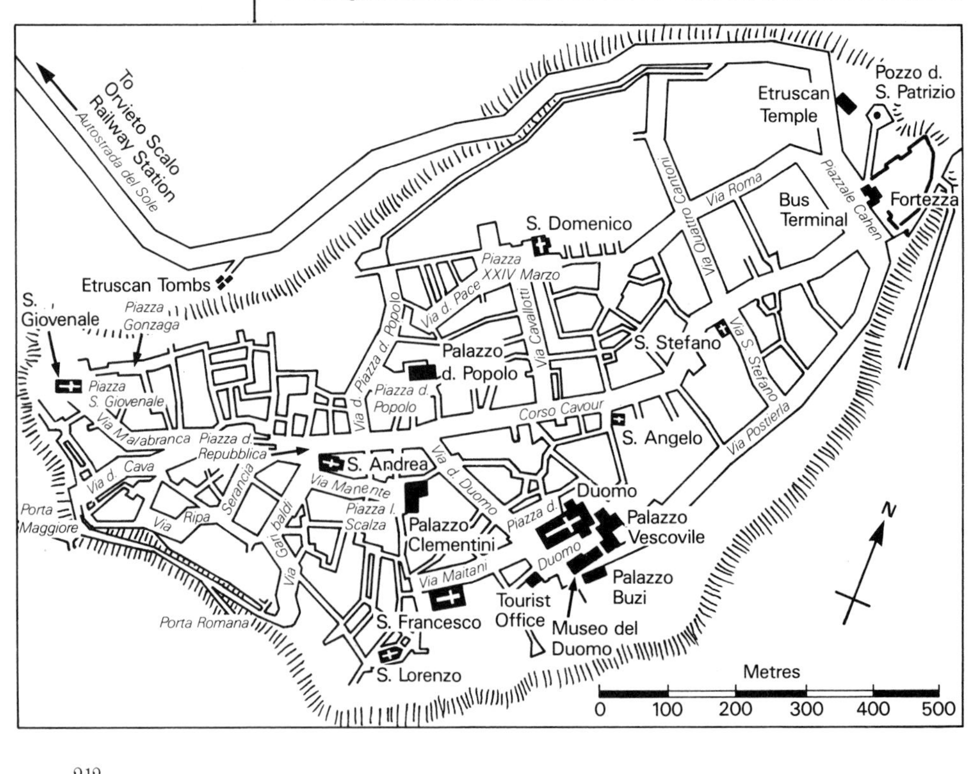

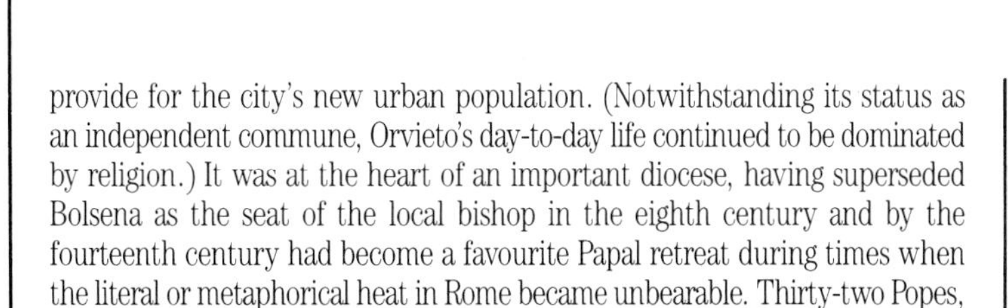

provide for the city's new urban population. (Notwithstanding its status as an independent commune, Orvieto's day-to-day life continued to be dominated by religion.) It was at the heart of an important diocese, having superseded Bolsena as the seat of the local bishop in the eighth century and by the fourteenth century had become a favourite Papal retreat during times when the literal or metaphorical heat in Rome became unbearable. Thirty-two Popes, in all, have stayed in the city, though not always with the warmest of welcomes.

During the first years of the fourteenth century, just as the building of the Duomo got under way, Orvieto was convulsed by that favourite of medieval pastimes, the public and cold-blooded murder of political opponents. Gualterio, an historian of the time, observed that: 'Perhaps the character of [Orvieto's] citizens provided more pretexts for hatred than anywhere else in the world; certainly in no other part of Italy was that hatred more barbarous in its expression, more insatiable in its appetite for blood.' This taste for blood was nowhere more marked than in the rivalry between the noble families of the Monaldeschi and the Filippeschi, a feud achieving such notoriety that Dante compared it in *Purgatorio* (VI, 107) to the quarrel in Verona between Romeo and Juliet's Montagues and Capulets. The dispute ended (not without considerable bloodshed and the destruction of half the city) in 1313, when the Filippeschi were defeated and driven into permanent exile, though if at this point Orvieto's hapless citizens thought their problems were over they were mistaken. The Monaldeschi, either bored with the prospect of time on their hands, or with an unquenchable thirst for battle, divided into rival factions, adopted suitably aggressive pseudonyms — the Dog, the Viper, the Eagle — and began to fight each other for control of the city. The arrival of the Black Death in 1348, an earthquake the following year, and an outbreak of disease in 1358 in which 5000 people died, did not make matters any better. It was to be another 100 years (when Orvieto became part of the Papal domain) before peace and a tranquillity of sorts came to its streets.

In our own century the arrival of the railway and more recently the opening of the *Autostrada del Sole* have brought Orvieto a new lease of life. However, the city is now faced with a danger that quite literally threatens to undermine its current prosperity, namely the gradual but apparently unstoppable collapse of the rock on which it is built.

The *rupe* has been protected since medieval time by laws to control illegal building on or near its edge, but these outdated injunctions are no longer up to dealing with the more insidious problems of our own age, amongst the most damaging of which have been the changes in the water-table brought about by the increased needs of a larger population, the weight and volume of traffic in the town centre, and the crumbling away of the rock face as a result of root action by vegetation that is no longer scrupulously cleared as it was in the past. All these factors have led in the last few years to a dramatic and dangerous increase in the number of landslips and rockfalls.

Millions of pounds have been spent since 1978 when the problem was first taken in hand, but millions more are still needed. In 1982 *Progetto Orvieto* was set up by the Ministry of Culture and the Umbrian regional authorities to put through a series of radical proposals designed to transform and thereby save the city. The scheme has the backing of no less a body than the European Parliament, who see it as a model for similar projects elsewhere, though the support of even so august an institution is no guarantee of success.

Amongst the measures put forward are the total pedestrianization of the centre, the building of large car-parks at the foot of the cliff, the reopening of the funicular (a wonderful water-operated contraption) to ferry visitors from Orvieto Scalo, and the creation of an 'archaeological park' based around the Etruscan tombs. A few of the more minor proposals, such as the virtual rebuilding of the Palazzo del Popolo and the restoration of Signorelli's frescoes, have already been implemented, but for the others the talking is still going on, and, several years after the project was set up, the funicular building in Piazza Cahen is still in ruins and finding a parking space in the summer months still à virtual impossibility.

Background

Festa del Corpus Domini

The festival dates back to 1264 and is traditionally held to commemorate the Miracle of Bolsena; that the miracle did not take place in the city at all is a fact long since forgotten (though Bolsena's aggrieved citizens hold a ceremony on the same day to rival Orvieto's). It revolves around the sacred *corporale*, which, along with its priceless silver reliquary, is brought out from the cathedral and put on display in the Piazza del Duomo (leaving the Bolsenans to worship a piece of the church floor where the miracle took place).

At eight o'clock on the evening preceding the festival, representatives from the four medieval quarters of the city — known respectively as the Serancia, Olmo, Corsica, and Santa Maria della Stalla — walk in torchlit procession from Bolsena to Orvieto in a reconstruction of the relic's original journey to the city. Next morning at around ten o'clock, a vast crowd gathers to watch 350 people, all in medieval dress, who accompany the reliquary on its journey through the streets. The process, preparations for which go on for three months, is headed by the Bishop of Orvieto, and follows a route through the streets that has remained unchanged since 1264.

Festa della Palombella

Orvieto's other marvellous, if curious, festival *La Festa della Palombella*, tailor-made to satisfy the Italian love of noisy and extravagant drama, takes place on Whit Sunday. It dates from the days of the Monaldeschi.

A large tableau, containing the figures of Mary and the Disciples (intended to represent the Last Supper), is built on the steps of the Duomo and set against

a temple-like construction of wood and plaster, whose Gothic design reflects that of the cathedral itself. From this small but lovingly made work of art a long wire is stretched to the spire of San Francesco some 100 metres away in Via Maitini. Here the *palombella*, a mechanical dove intended to symbolize the Holy Spirit and its descent from Heaven, is perched, awaiting the moment of its release.

This arrives, in a shower of sparks and in front of an excited and expectant crowd, on the stroke of midday. The bird careers at ever-increasing speed towards the Virgin and the Disciples, prompting on impact (to the great joy of all present) a large and violent explosion. (The harmless-looking tableau has been packed with every form of incendiary device the Latin imagination is capable of producing).

Much can, and usually does, go wrong with the ceremony, but according to popular superstition the fortunes of the city over the forthcoming year are dependent on the degree of success that attends it. There are those who suggest that the whole thing may be some kind of watered-down fertility rite, for when the flames have died down, the burnt and tattered remains of the *palombella* are retrieved and offered to Orvieto's most recently married couple.

Miracle of Bolsena

The Miracle of Bolsena, without doubt the single most important event in Orvieto's long and frequently troubled history, took place in 1263 and concerned a young Bohemian priest, Pietro di Prago, travelling to Rome in the hope of being absolved of a rather unhealthy, not to say heretical, inner scepticism. For some time he had been troubled by doubts concerning the dogma of transubstantiation — whether, in fact, the body and blood of Christ were truly present in the Eucharist — and it was while entertaining such doubts that he prepared to celebrate Mass at the chapel of Santa Cristina on the shores of Lake Bolsena.

Everything in the service proceeded as normal until the moment of consecration, at which point the Host literally became flesh and bright spots of blood began to fall onto the white linen cloth, or *corporale*, covering the altar. ('Each stain severally assuming the form of a human head with features like the Volto Santo, the face of the saviour.')

News of the miracle quickly reached Pope Urban IV, then in residence in Orvieto, who ordered the city's bishop, Bishop Giacomo, to verify the events and bring the Host and blood-stained *corporale* from Santa Cristina. Giacomo duly collected the two items, which, no sooner had they left Bolsena, began performing all the customary miracles required of such objects. By the time they arrived at the Ponte Sole, there to be met by the Pope in person, they had already assumed the stature of sacred relics, and soon became the objects of worship and veneration.

The Feast of Corpus Domini was instigated a year later on 11 August with the issue of a Papal Bull, 'Transiturus de mundo', drawn up by Thomas

Aquinas no less, who was teaching in Orvieto at the Convent of San Domenico. It provided for a solemn festival to be held every year on the first Thursday after Pentecost in honour of the Body of Christ. The tradition that both the annual *festa* and the building of the Duomo were instigated specifically to commemorate the miracle seems to be an invention, for Aquinas's text makes no specific mention of the event. The fact that the legend has grown up at all is probably the result of a piece of shrewd political opportunism on the part of the Papacy, who saw in the religious fervour inspired by the miracle a chance to recover some of the ground lost to the forces of secularism. This is not as cynical as it may sound: the events at Bolsena took place at a highly opportune moment for the Church, occurring during a period of general religious scepticism, and just a few years after the death of Frederick Barbarossa, a time when Italy was distracted by more than usually unpleasant disputes between the Papacy and the Empire. There was a great deal of political capital to be made out of the building of an awe-inspiring cathedral, whose grandeur, it was hoped, would underline the temporal wealth and authority of the Church, and whose mysterious *raison d'être* would serve as a reaffirmation of the central tenets of the Faith.

It was doubly fortunate for the Papacy that the miracle occurred near Orvieto, for the city at the time was one of the most prosperous in central Italy, and therefore a potentially powerful ally. If the tide of errant and free-thinking citizens could be turned in Orvieto, and their loyalty encouraged, if not guaranteed, then the same could probably be done in the rest of Umbria, perhaps even further afield.

What to see

Duomo (Piazza del Duomo)

Building

If ever there was a case of building by committee it was in the Duomo in Orvieto. The 300 years separating the bottom of the cathedral's facade from the angular cusp at the top are a catalogue of false starts, disagreements, alterations, inspiration, pauses, and piecemeal additions. In fact it is a wonder that the thing was built at all — work took place against a background of civic disorder so extreme that Orvieto's citizens at the time considered abandoning the city altogether. Progress was further hampered by constant changes in artistic and architectural taste, with the result that the initial plans for the building (designs which had taken a leisurely 30 years to draw up) were forever being modified to accommodate new ideas and changes of fashion.

The site initially chosen for the Duomo was at the highest point of the city, a position that had already been the site of an Etruscan temple, a Christian church, and Orvieto's original cathedral, Santa Maria Prisca. Although the idea for the cathedral had been conceived as early as 1264, the first stone was not laid until 1290.

When work started in earnest it was under the supervision of a Franciscan friar, Fra Bevignate, who, though he had designed the Fontana Maggiore in Perugia, in Orvieto was given the role of glorified foreman, leaving responsibility for the design to Arnolfo di Cambio (though there are those who dispute the claim), one of the leading architects of his day, whose work to that point had already included the Duomo and Palazzo Vecchio in Florence.

His plan for the cathedral was for a simple and orthodox Romanesque church with three naves and a semicircular apse, but although work started along these lines and progressed well in the early stages, disaster struck when Bevignate's successor, a local architect, attempted to introduce Gothic elements, which the Romanesque plan quite literally could not support. His heavy ribbed vaults and intersecting arches, though perfectly in line with the architectural thinking of the day, threatened to bring the project to a premature and permanent conclusion. At which point the Orvietans, faced with the total collapse of their cathedral, called in desperation upon the services of the Sienese sculptor and architect, Lorenzo Maitini. Although little more is known of the man than the date of his marriage, it is to his work over the next 30 years, that the Duomo owes its final form.

He strengthened the walls with four arches, retained the simple Romanesque nave, but removed the apse, so that the building began to assume a generally more Gothic appearance. At this point work also started on the facade, and here Maitini was largely responsible for the four enormous pillars with their bas-reliefs of scenes from the Old and New Testaments, the bronze canopy above the central door (known as the *baldacchino*), and the four figures of the Evangelists.

In 1350 work began on the Cappella del Corporale, which was designed to house the sacred *corporale* itself. The twin chapel, the Cappella Nuova (or the Cappella Signorelli, as it became known), was started in 1408, and both were housed under Maitini's strengthening arches.

Meanwhile, the building of the facade had run into difficulties. Seven different architects were consulted in the 20 years after Maitini's death, and only under Antonio Federighi (1452–6) did the work regain impetus and direction. He revised earlier designs and was largely responsible for introducing the niches and figures of the Apostles (finished in 1556) into the rose window's central pediment. (Marble for this section was removed from the ancient Temple to Jove on Rome's Capitoline Hill.) Fifty years later, the central triangular cusp above the window was finished, and in 1619 the smaller cusps on either side crowned a facade that had taken three hundred years to complete.

Subsequent problems were small by comparison. Two pillars in the nave required strengthening, and during a storm in 1795 the right spire was struck by lightning and had to be rebuilt, a mere 10 years of restoration. The facade's showiest features, the mosaics, have been added over the last 200–300 years to replace the originals, the majority of which were sent to Rome in 1785 on the orders of Pope Pius IV.

Facade

The 52-metre high facade, recently cleaned and restored, is so dazzling and well-proportioned seen from the stone seats of the Piazza del Duomo that it is easy to overlook its tremendous detail close-up. The four pillars at the base (now partly behind Perspex after vandalism), and the remarkable central door are well worth careful scrutiny. Their perfectly preserved and intricately worked marble reliefs, a sort of *Paradise Lost* in stone, describe episodes from the Old and New Testaments. Maitini is accredited with the finest, but an estimated 152 other sculptors were involved on the facade at one time or another. From left to right, and from the bottom of each pillar where the narrative begins, the stories (admittedly somewhat confused) are as follows:

First Pillar

1 Creation of the fishes, birds, plants and mammals, creation of man. **2** God gives life to Adam and creates Eve from one of his ribs. **3** Adam and Eve in the Garden of Eden. The Original Sin. **4** Cast out of Eden, Adam hoes and Eve plants seed. **5** The offerings of Cain and Abel. Cain kills Abel. **6** Naomi teaches a child to read; Jubal invents sounds and one of Adam's children uses a compass.

Second Pillar

(Here there are two vertical series)
1 Adam or Abraham sleeping. **2** Kings David, Solomon, Rehoboam, Abijah, Jehosophat with Christ and the Virgin, and the Prophets to either side. The Children of Israel in Egypt.

Third Pillar

(Also in vertical columns)
The Evangelists, Adam sleeping surrounded by Angels with the Prophets in the central column. The scenes from the bottom left are: the Annunciation, the Visitation, the Nativity and Epiphany, Flight into Egypt, the Massacre of the Innocents and the argument in the temple, baptism and a miracle of Jesus, His entry into Jerusalem and the kiss of Judas, flagellation and crucifixion, Mary at the sepulchre.

Fourth Pillar

(The Last Judgement in five vertical columns)
1 Christ the Judge with Angels, Prophets, Apostles, Mary, the instruments of the Passion and the Angels calling the dead to Judgement. **2** The Elected led to Heaven. **3** The Elected led to Heaven. **4** Separation of the saved from the damned. **5** The damned are banished to Hell.

The mosaics are colourful (especially on evenings when the facade is floodlit), but less arresting. The largest, in the top triangular cusp, represents the *Coronation of the Virgin* (1842–7); to its left is the *Marriage of the Virgin* (1612) and to its right the *Presentation of Mary* (1760–3). Nine separate mosaics occupy the triangular spaces below these and above the doors. From left to right they are:

1 *Gabriel* (1659). **2** *Baptism of Jesus* (1584). **3** *Annunciation* (1649). **4–6** *Apostles and the Assumption* (1388 but restored). **7** *St Joachim* (1713). **8** *Birth of Mary* (1364, restored 1713). **9** *St Anne* (1713).

The four mosaics in the corners of the square occupied by the rose window are the only early ones still reasonably intact. They date from 1388 (but have been restored) and represent the *Four Doctors of the Church* (St Agostino, St Gregory, St Giralmo, and St Ambrogio). The niches above the window contain the statues of the 12 Apostles (1556). Those to the side contain the prophets (fourteenth–fifteenth century). The carved head at the centre of the rose window itself is Christ. (Look out for the bronze figures above the bas-reliefs, especially the one that appears to be a large winged cow.) The central bronze doors, surprisingly, are very recent. They are by Emilio Greco and were made between 1964 and 1970, though in the best tradition of the Duomo were only installed after much discussion. They represent the 'Works of Mercy'. The left panel, from top to bottom, represents: Refreshing the starving; Clothing the naked; Sheltering the pilgrims. The right panel, from top to bottom represents: Visiting the sick; Visiting the prisoners; Burying the dead.

Interior

It would be difficult for the interior of any building to live up to such an extraordinary facade and at first sight the inside of the church appears a trifle bare. There is calm, peace, a warm light, and the beauty of the rose window to savour, but little more (though this in itself is plenty). It is comparatively small by Italian standards (90 metres long, 34 metres high, and 32 metres wide), but has been artfully designed to make it seem larger than it is. Rather as a theatre stage rises and narrows, so the floor of the Duomo inclines gently from the doors to the vast arches of the presbytery. Check the beautifully carved main pillars separating the naves to confirm this: their capitals become progressively lower as one moves towards the chancel (almost as if to focus attention on the gradual change of tone that takes place in the interior, from the austerity of the nave's striped marble walls to the sudden rich colour of the apse and two frescoed side-chapels).

Cappella del Corporale (1350–61)

The left of the two chapels, warm, intimate, and muted, and probably the one with fewer people in it. This is where the sacred *corporale* is housed, kept firmly locked up in the *Reliquario del Corporale*, a gaudy 75-kilogramme casket of precious metals and jewels, whose design, possibly by Martini, reflects that of the facade. Without very special permission, you will be lucky to get more than a glimpse of its splendours, as it only leaves its marble resting-place twice a year: on Easter Sunday and during the Feast of Corpus Domini. There is a single, freestanding painting on the right of the chapel: the *Madonna dei Raccommandati* (1320), an important and beautiful work by the Sienese artist Lippo Memmi, executed under the influence of Simone Martini. What really commands one's attention, however, are the frescoes (1357–64) that cover every wall of the high chapel. These are by the Orvietan artist Ugolino di Prete and several assistants, and though they have been heavy-handedly restored in places, are still very lovely. Along with the carving on the reliquary and the four marble reliefs in the chapel they tell

Interior of the Duomo. (ISTO)

the story of the Miracle of Bolsena and describe scenes associated with the Eucharist. The frescoes on the rear wall, by the same artist, are of the *Crucifixion* (1364).

Left-hand wall

Miracles of the Sacrament (main details). **1** St Gregory shows the Host made flesh. **2** The Host changes into a boy before an Anchorite. **3** A fish restores the Host to a priest three years after it had been fed to it by a fisherman. **4** St Hugo rejects the unconsecrated Host. **5** A Jewish child is found alive after his father had thrown him into a furnace. **6** Christ appears as a child in the Host before Christians and Saracens.

Right-hand wall

Miracle of Bolsena. **1** The miracle. **2** The Bohemian priest informs the Pope of the miracle. **3** The Bishop of Orvieto is sent to confirm the miracle.

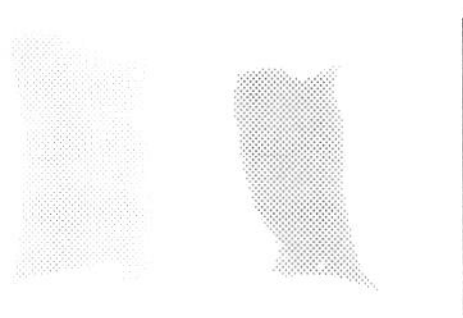

4 The Bishop looks at the blood-stained *corporale*. **5** The Pope outside the city. **6** The Pope shows the *corporale* to the people. **7** The Pope orders Thomas Aquinas to write the Office and Mass of the Holy Sacrament.

Cappella Nuova, or Cappella Signorelli

Signorelli's breathtaking paintings are the artistic centrepiece of the Duomo and one of the most outstanding fresco cycles in Italy, but it is only by a happy accident that they come to be here at all.

Fra Angelico, helped by Benozzo Gozzoli, started work on the chapel as early as 1447, and, but for the fact that he was called to Rome by Pope Nicholas V, would have completed his commission and painted the whole thing. As it was, he managed only to complete two panels, *Christ in Judgement* and the *Assembly of the Prophets*. Although Gozzoli then returned to Orvieto intending to finish the frescoes himself, he had scarcely got as far as painting the ribs on the vaulted ceiling before Arigio Monaldeschi, one of the city grandees, was murdered, and work on the cathedral came to one of its periodic halts.

Thirty years elapsed before another painter, Pier Matteo d'Amelia, was invited to submit sketches for the decoration of the vaults, a delay quite possibly caused by the reluctance of the church authorities to commit themselves to a course of action at a time when the figurative arts were in a state of almost constant flux. As it turned out, his ideas were deemed unacceptable and it was left to Perugino, 10 years later, to come up with something better. However, for reasons unknown, Umbria's leading painter managed only four or five days in the Duomo before leaving the city never to return. Another 10 years passed before Signorelli signed a contract to complete the work still outstanding on the vaults. Once started, he quickly restored Fra Angelico's frescoes (by then over 50 years old) and within six months had completed half of the remaining ceiling space to Angelico's original drawings. Convinced of his ability, the church authorities then agreed to his painting the whole chapel, which remarkable feat he finished with the help of his son Polidoro and several assistants, in the spring of 1504. The domed ceiling is divided into eight sections:

1 *Christ amongst the angels* (Fra Angelico). **2** *Choir of Prophets* (Fra Angelico). **3** *The Apostles*. **4** *Signs predicting the Last Judgement*. **5** *The Martyrs*. **6** *The Patriarchs*. **7** *The Doctors of the Church*. **8** *The Virgin*.

The main fresco cycle runs anticlockwise, so the narrative starts at the first panel on the left of the entrance to the chapel, the second is above the entrance arch, and so on. There are seven main sections, with one on each side of the altar.

1 *The Antichrist*. The figure with the blond beard in the second row of the left-hand group is thought to be either Cesare Borgia or Gian Paolo Baglioni, two veritable antichrists of the period. In the right-hand group, again in the second row, is the head of Dante in profile. Standing alone in the bottom left-hand corner are Signorelli himself and Fra Angelico (in the robes of a Dominican friar). **2** *The End of the World* (with Signorelli's signature). **3** *The Resurrection* *of the Flesh.* **4** *The Damned in Hell.* **5** *The Angels chase the Damned to Hell.* **6** *The Angels guide the Chosen to Heaven.* **7** *The Chosen in Heaven.*

Rest of the Duomo

The Duomo, like any building of its size, is full of tiny details that are easily overshadowed by more grandiose or more famous works of art. The three-tiered Gothic choir (1331–40 but since restored) while hardly small, is a case in point. Its stalls each have an inlaid letter which taken together make up the *Ave Maria*. The bishop's throne in the centre is decorated with 40 wooden panels, each depicting an individual saint. The impressive frescoes above the choir, like those in the Cappella di Corporale, are by Ugolino di Prete Ilario and assistants (1370–84). Clockwise from the bottom left-hand corner they tell the story of the Virgin. In places, high up the walls by the two strange side-windows, restoration was undertaken by Pintoricchio between 1492 and 1497. The 48 sections of the great arched window (1334 but since restored) describe the same story.

The large font in an otherwise bare nave was started in 1390 by Luca di Giovanni, a Sienese artist, and finished by two German sculptors in 1403. The small *acquasantiera* to its right, with a beautifully delicate base, is by Antonio Federighi (1485). A faint *Madonna and Child* (1425) by Gentile da Fabriano, one of Umbria's, or more properly one of the Marche's, rarer painters, is easily missed. It is in the first small niche on the left after entering the cathedral. Many other smaller treasures from or donated to the Duomo, along with items given to the city, are no longer housed in the cathedral itself, but are kept instead in the nearby Museo dell'Opera del Duomo.

Museo dell'Opera del Duomo

Open 9–13, 14.30–17.
Closed Monday.
Admission charge.

The museum is in the Palazzo Soligno (or Palazzo dei Papi) to the right of the Piazza del Duomo as one faces the facade of the cathedral. Leaving the Duomo by the door on the right-hand side, the Porta di Postierla, the entrance to the museum is directly ahead at the top of the external staircase.

Inside the large, slightly damp single hall (once used for Papal receptions) is a strange, poorly arranged collection of exhibits that range from meaningless stone fragments and rusty keys to beautiful and priceless paintings. In the centre of the room are several very old, woodwormy but extremely valuable sculptures: a *Madonna and Child* by Andrea Pisano (1347), and a figure of Christ by Nicola Nuti and Simone Martini are the best. Beyond these are five parts of a *polittico* also by Martini (1321), taken from the church of San Domenico when it was partly demolished in the thirties to make way for Orvieto's barracks (far and away the ugliest building in the city). San Domenico, incidentally, was the first Dominican church ever built (1233). On the right-hand wall is a *Madonna, Child, Christ and Angels* (1320) partly by Martini, and one of the most appealing things in the building. Its excellent condition is in marked contrast to some of the other paintings in the museum, which are decidedly the worse for wear. Still on the right-hand side, look for a small self-portrait by Signorelli. The man with him is Nicolo de Angelo, the accountant who oversaw the building of the Duomo at the end of the fifteenth century. Dotted around the hall are several striking works by Antonio Pastura (1450–1516), an artist from Viterbo and a follower of Perugino.

The higher paintings and fresco fragments around the walls are taken mostly from local churches; the ceramics in the dusty cases by the door look like dirty versions of what is for sale in Via del Duomo, but in fact are fourteenth-century works from Orvieto, Deruta, and Gualdo Tadino. The museum also contains the original bishop's throne from the Duomo (in terrible condition) and in the back left-hand corner a vast section of the old cathedral roof. Otherwise, it is a matter of looking carefully to find the gems (such as the tiny font full of carved fishes on the left-hand wall) amongst the coins, keys, medals, and beautifully embroidered vestments that make up the rest of this odd museum.

National Etruscan Archaeological Museum

This newly and well-restored part of the Palazzo Soliano is directly ahead of the steps that come down from the Museo dell'Opera del Duomo. At the moment it holds one-off exhibitions, but at some unspecified date it will house works at present scattered amongst Orvieto's other museums.

Etruscan Museum, or Museo Claudio Faino
(Piazza del Duomo)

Open 9–13, 15–18. Winter hours restricted.
Closed Monday.
Admission charge.

Check opening times at the tourist office. Orvieto's Etruscan Museum is rather lacklustre (a coat of paint would work wonders), but still of interest. On the left of the ground floor are exhibits unearthed during the last major excavations in the Etruscan tombs between 1960 and 1967, and opposite them a temporary collection of objects soon to be moved to the Palazzo Soliano (though no one knows when). Notice especially a bust known as *Larth Cupures Aranthia*, various decorations taken from the old Temple of Belvedere (420 BC) — which used to be on the site of the Duomo — and a fourth-century BC sarcophagus found in 1912 near the Torre San Severo — the best thing in the museum. Bas-reliefs around its base describe episodes from the stories of Ulysses and Achilles. On the upper floor is the Claudio Faino collection proper (Faino was a Perugian Count who bequeathed his collection to posterity in 1865); it is made up almost entirely of vases, some Greek, others Etruscan copies of Greek originals.

Palazzo del Popolo

The Piazza del Popolo is home to Orvieto's colourful and lively **market** (mornings only) and to the Palazzo del Popolo, which after years of restoration is at last approaching its original form. The palace was started in 1157 by Pope Adrian IV and then given to the city commune, who made it the seat of the *Capitano del Popolo*. Architecturally it has a Gothic plan overlaid with Romanesque detail, and in its earliest form at least conformed to the pattern of similar communal palaces in central Italy in that it was formed around a single large hall supported by four arched pillars (to allow maximum use of ground-space), straddled two piazzas and was reached by a wide external staircase. (Todi's Palazzo del Capitano is an almost perfect example of this same form.)

The Palazzo's simple roof-support, its barrel vaulting and evenly spaced windows are typical of Umbria, and similar features are repeated in several local buildings, notably the church of San Andrea and the Abbey of St Severo and St Martirio just outside the city.

In 1280 a series of alterations was started, which made the palace a complete hotch-potch of architectural styles. Some of the lower arches were closed, another room — the Caminata — was added, the size of the staircase was reduced, and a redundant bell-tower tacked onto the rear, but these have now largely been removed. At the time of writing, however, the building, still sadly dilapidated, remains closed.

Churches

San Giovenale (Via Malabranca/Piazza San Giovenale)

If you have not had enough of churches by now and have time for one more, it should be this one. Although it seems dull and unpromising from the outside, inside it is an interesting and ancient church, though quite how ancient no one is really sure. It was Orvieto's first cathedral, built according to one medieval historian, in 1004, though recent excavations have suggested that this was simply the date of its first restoration. The same excavations uncovered the original floor-level so that the rear of the church is almost a metre lower than the Gothic transept added in the second half of the thirteenth century. The division between the two parts is very clear and surprisingly effective, with the large Gothic arches of the presbytery meeting the much older Romanesque columns of the nave. Simple, almost crude, patches of fresco cover nearly every surface of the walls, all painted by local artists between the thirteenth and sixteenth centuries. These are mainly on familiar themes and tend to be in better condition in the higher parts of the church. The most interesting are

n Giovenale. (ISTO)

a *Tree of Life* to the right of the main door and a strange *Calendar of Funeral Anniversaries* to the left of the small side-door by which one enters. Sadly this door has covered half of this rather macabre but curious fresco. The lovely altar (1170) with its tiny columns fits perfectly into the church's musty, medieval atmosphere.

San Andrea
(Piazza della Repubblica)

With the bustle of the town's cental piazza just outside, the large unexceptional interior of this church is intimate and peaceful. It was built between the twelfth and fourteenth centuries, but traces of a sixth-century church as well as Etruscan remains have been uncovered in its foundations. They are reached from the entrance at the front of the church on the right. The key is kept in a nearby house, signposted from the church. Once downstairs the floor of the old church contains a hole that was once a tomb and three large stones from the sixth-century altar. The two panels of mosaics are later (ninth–eleventh century). Here too are the bases of the eight granite columns that form the nave of the church above. Though one would hardly think it to look at them, they are believed to date from the second century. Above the old floor are Etruscan and Roman fragments: the foundations of houses, part of a pavement, a conduit, and the remains of part of a piazza or a road. It is, however, hard to make out what is what. In the main church there are just a few patches of fresco and a lovely pulpit, perhaps the one from which Pope Innocent the Third proclaimed the Fourth Crusade in 1216. Cardinals have also been crowned here, amongst them the infamous future Pope Boniface the Eighth (the one who nailed heretics' tongues to doors).

San Lorenzo di Arari
(Via Ippolito Scalza/Piazza di Santa Chiara)

This is a tiny, simple, and lovely fourteenth-century church, built on the site of an earlier church rather uncharitably destroyed in 1291 because the sound of its bells disturbed the monks in the nearby abbey of San Francesco. Now silence, along with the austere graciousness of the Romanesque, is one of its charms. The newly restored frescoes high up on the left are *Four Scenes from the Life of St Laurence* (1330), and describe him drawing people from a cave, his burning and chastisement, an audience before the king, and his healing.

The altar table contains an Etruscan sacrificial slab to which the church's name refers (*arari* means 'altar').

Pozzo di San Patrizio (St Patrick's Well)

Open daily. Summer: 10–19; winter: 9–12, 14–16.
Admission charge.

This is one of Orvieto's more unusual sights, and for many visitors the only thing they see apart from the Duomo. It is found off Piazza Cahen at the extreme eastern end of the city close to where the No. 71 road leaves for the station. While here have a look at the nearby public gardens (one of the few patches of green in the town) and the remains of the half-hearted Albornoz Rocca (1364).

St Patrick's Well (Pozzo di San Patrizio). (ISTO)

The well was commissioned by Pope Clement VII in 1528 following his stay in the town. Rome, sacked by the imperial army the previous year, was becoming unsafe, to say the least, and for a while Orvieto looked destined to become a place of regular Papal refuge. If this was to be the case then at some point it was likely to be besieged and so there was a pressing need for a reliable water supply. A local architect, Antonio Sangallo, was commissioned to build a well designed to tap the veins of water thought to be trapped in the rocks below the city. He started to dig above the springs of St Zero, which emerge from the foot of the cliff, but after 30 metres found not water, but an Etruscan tomb, now tastefully preserved in the well's structure. (You can still see it, a little under halfway down.) Eventually he struck water, work being completed in 1537. The well owes its strange name to a supposed resemblance to St Patrick's Cavern in Ireland.

This is no ordinary well, with a winch and small bucket, but a vast cylinder

62 metres deep and 13 metres wide. (Spendthrifts in Italy are said to have pockets as bottomless as 'il pozzo di San Patrizio'.) Within its walls (initially cut out of the rock but lined with bricks lower down) are two spiral staircases, one for descending the other for ascending, each totally independent of the other, and each with 240 steps large enough to accommodate the donkeys once used to carry water to the surface. Seventy-two windows cut into the walls light the stairs from the central shaft, but the well is nevertheless gloomy and dank, even in midsummer, so dress to avoid chills. Also bear in mind that medieval engineering did not stretch to lifts — it is quite a climb from the bottom.

Where to stay

La Badia
★★★★

The most attractive hotel in the area, and one that is becoming increasingly well known. Situated in a converted thirteenth-century monastery 2.5 kilometres south of Orvieto, amidst glorious countryside and with good views of the town. Distinguished by the rustic elegance of its original surroundings, though some touches may veer too much towards Hollywood for some tastes. Air-conditioning, swimming-pool, tennis-courts, parkland, restaurant, and parking. Booking in season essential. La Badia 8. Tel. 90539. Rooms 22. Bathrooms 18. Showers 4. *Closed 1 January–28 February.*

Maitini
★★★★

The best hotel in the town itself, and but a stone's throw from the Duomo. Under the same management as Ristorante Il Molino (see below). Located in the sixteenth-century baroque palazzo that was once home to Duomo architect Lorenzo Maitini. Boasts an internal garden and moderately panoramic terraces. Air-conditioning. No restaurant. Via Maitini 5. Tel. 42001. Rooms 43.

Virgilio
★★★

The main selling point of this otherwise average hotel are the rooms facing directly on to the piazza and their full-frontal view of the cathedral's facade. Make it clear that these are the rooms you want. Restaurant. Piazza del Duomo 5–6. Tel. 41882. Rooms 13. Bathrooms 2. Showers 11.

Grande Hotel Reale
★★★

Traditional, venerable, and practical hotel — one of the town's oldest — and centrally situated in the large, if somewhat forlorn, Piazza del Popolo. Restaurant. Piazza del Popolo 25. Tel. 41247. Rooms 32. Bathrooms 25. Showers 5.

Antico Zoppo
★★

An attractive, but slightly self-conscious medieval setting in a quiet, off-centre location. Clean and recently given a new coat of paint. Downstairs there is a bustling and picturesque restaurant. Via Marrabottini 2. Tel. 40370. Rooms 9. Bathrooms 4.

Corso
★

At the lower end of the town towards Piazza Cahen. Corso Cavour 343. Tel. 42020. Rooms 9. Showers 9.

Note: The majority of cheaper *pensione* and rooms are either at the Piazza Cahen end of Corso Cavour or in Orvieto Scalo. The latter are really only acceptable as a last resort, though prices overall are lower. If you are room-hunting through the tourist office make your preferences for new or old town clear.

Camping

Camping Orvieto ★★★

On the southern shore of Lago di Corbara near Civitella (10 kilometres from Orvieto). Rooms available to rent. Claims an excellent swimming-pool. Tel. 950240 or 957351 (off-season). Places 65. *Open 1 April–1 October.*

Scacco Matto ★

Lago di Corbara. Tel. 950163. Places 20. *Open all year.*

Where to eat

Il Molino ★★★

In the same family since 1946, and host to the likes of Richard Burton, Elizabeth Taylor, Walt Disney, and Marlon Brando, Orvieto's most famous restaurant these days is living a little on its reputation but still offers a reliable (if expensive) selection of Umbrian specialities. Some, like *crostini* with thrush pâté, however, are for adventurous palates. An excellent cellar (the house wines — specially made for the restaurant — are outstanding) and elegant (veering to 'over the top') service. Via Garibaldi 41. Tel. 41952. *Closed Wednesday, and from 6 to 31 January.* All major credit cards. Expensive.

Le Grotte del Funaro ★★

Located in a series of tufa caves reached via a dizzying set of steps, but more than a mere novelty. Umbrian cooking (again) with the emphasis on roast meats (again). The evening piano bar and *pizzeria* are a little less enticing. Via Ripa Serancia 41. Tel. 43276. *Closed Monday.*

Del Pino del Cecco ★/★★

One of the best of the cheaper restaurants; large (180 places), but with the intimacy of a private house. An ex-President of Italy made hostess Isolina a Knight of the Republic for services to cooking! Via di Piazza del Popolo 15–21. Tel. 42661. *Closed Tuesday (except during the summer) and for all of January.*

Dell'Ancora ★

A big neighbouring stand-by if the above is full. Via di Piazza del Popolo 7. Tel. 42766. *Closed Thursday.*

Da Pepe ★

A straightforward restaurant in one of the town's quieter and prettier corners. Ideal for a cheap and unpretentious meal in clean and pleasant surroundings. Just 70 settings. The summer garden is particularly recommended. Via Beato Angelico 4. Tel. 41688. *Closed Wednesday.*

CRAMST

Far and away the town's cheapest food. Run as a co-operative, it is an enormous bustling place (seats for 450), extremely popular with locals, and surprisingly central. There are restaurant, *pizzeria*, and self-service options, with some outside tables in good weather. Via Maitini 15. Tel. 43302. *Closed Sunday.*

Note: Most of the town's cheap, lively and late-night *pizzerias* are grouped together at the lower end of Corso Cavour, next to Piazza Cahen.

AROUND ORVIETO

Orvieto to Tuscany

Orvieto is very close to some of the prettiest towns in southern Tuscany — Volterra, Sorano, and Pitiliano (which could almost be its twin), and, thanks to the *Autostrada del Sole*, within easy reach of several others, such as Pienza and Montepulciano further north. Roads in what is the ancient heart of Etruria, however, are as scarce and as winding as they are in Umbria. If you have no time to make the longer trips into Tuscany, there are two pretty pockets of countryside just west and north of Orvieto that can be seen comfortably in a morning.

Start any tour of Orvieto's environs, however, with a visit to the sixth-century BC Etruscan tombs, the **Crocifisso del Tufo**, a mere 200 metres from the city walls on the N71 road, which twists down to Orvieto Scalo. (*Open daily 9–dark. Admission free.*)

Wanton and disorganized excavations in 1830 damaged the graves in the then-common eagerness to get at the valuables buried in these so-called 'monumental tombs', which were the reserve of only the richest or most important Etruscan citizens (in contrast to the tombs at Cerveteri (Caere), which also made provisions for slaves, well-treated, it seems, by the Etruscans, even in death). The dead, laid out in all their finery, were provided with all they would need in the afterlife, rather in the manner of the Pharaohs, but in Orvieto, as elsewhere, most of this buried wealth has found its way not to the next world, but more prosaically to either the Louvre or the British Museum.

Above the entrance to each tomb is an inscription that reads from right to left, and probably means simply 'here is . . .' or 'here lies . . .', but none of the graves contain any of the vigorous and often lewd painted decorations that make Tarquinia's tombs so interesting. The stones that originally stood above the graves to denote the sex of those buried, now stand by the entrances, toppled by nineteenth-century carelessness. Here these markers are not as clear as at Cerveteri, where there are large phallic stones for the men, and smaller carved containers, or 'arks', for the women. Inside the simply arched tombs themselves there are usually two stone slabs at right-angles to each other on which the bodies of husband and wife were laid. In one grave, leaning against a small wall, is a large stone, which was used to seal the tomb before the entrance was covered in soil. Towards the rear-left-hand corner of the site is an interesting tomb, a metre square, which contained adult bones on tiny stone beds. These bones were thought to have come from a very old tomb that was disturbed during the digging of the 'newer' tombs in the sixth century. Out of respect for the dead, the bones were then reburied in this miniature grave.

Continue on the N71 to the base of the rock and turn right, away from the station. A little less than 2 kilometres down the main road is a small left

turn to the **L'Abbazia di SS. Severo e Martirio**, a lovely group of twelfth-century Romanesque buildings, of which the campanile, visible from some distance, and the small frescoed church on the left of the courtyard, are most interesting. For the adventurous Etruscan fantatic there are more small tombs, the **Poggio dei Sette Camini**, 3 kilometres further along the tortuous road beyond the abbey.

Back on the road to Viterbo after 10 kilometres of sharp bends and a superb retrospective panorama of Orvieto, there is a right fork signposted to San Lorenzo (quite possibly where Turner painted his view of the town, which is now in London's Clore Gallery). This road, and the minor one to **Castel Viscardo**, 7 kilometres later, makes a pretty drive through the wooded heart of Monte Rubiaglio country, famous for its wine and Vin Santo. Alternatively the main road continues towards Viterbo before turning right to Bolsena (21 kilometres) (which is worth a visit, if only for the lake. There is swimming south of the town). From here it is 28 kilometres to Orvieto by the shortest route and only a little further via the minor road to **Bagnoregio**, which has a pretty church. Close by is the abandoned **Civita**, 'la città che muore' — the town which is dying — because of the erosion of the rock below it. Connected by an isthmus to Bagnoregio, it is an eerie, almost deserted, ghost-town. The population has been declining since 1695. There were 600 inhabitants in 1925; today there are just 8. The whole place is becoming something of an attraction by virtue of its strangeness. Recommended.

Orvieto to Todi

This alternative route to Todi takes the old road on the northern side of the Tiber valley. It twists and turns through high and remote countryside, so those in a hurry should take the quicker road from Baschi (see 'Todi'). From Orvieto station turn left away from the town, pass under the railway and the motorway, and then take the N79 signposted to Prodo and Todi. The road climbs steeply, with good views of Orvieto through the trees gradually giving way to some even better ones of the Tiber valley, Lake Corbara, and Perugia to the north. Otherwise there is next to nothing: expansive countryside, the odd car, fresh air, a few sleepy bars, and the village of **Prodo**, with its inevitable but picturesque castle. Just outside the village, off the curving road, is the small farm, **Casale Sosselva**, which produces and sells homemade cheeses and a selection of excellent jams.

North of here there stretches a large area of tranquil countryside dotted with tiny hilltop hamlets, and miles of deserted roads and tracks. Its woods, fields, and rivers are renowned for the richness and variety of their wildlife (it is about the only place in Umbria where you can see otters, for example), and especially for its birds, who owe their survival to an ancient tract of land protected by a *bandita demeniale di caccia* — a place in which hunting is outlawed. (In most other parts of Umbria you are awakened every Sunday morning by the popping of shotguns.)

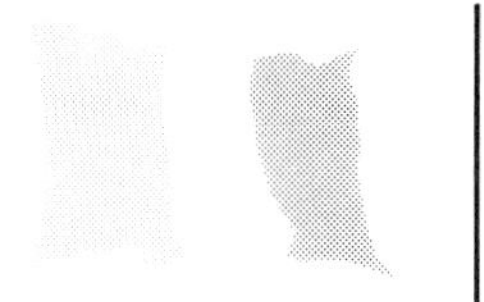

Turn off the Todi road at **Colonnetta** for **Monte Peglia** (known locally as *la Montagna degli Animali*); on the map it seems full of promise, but all that is there is a bar and a radio-mast. **San Venanzo** is the largest of the many picturesque villages. **San Vito in Monte** has spring waters and the usual castle (there are so many in Umbria you do become blasé). The Gormenghast-like **Castel di Fiori** is the best. **Pornello**, be warned, like many of the so-called villages, exists only as several scattered farms. **Montegiove** is an exception, tiny, castled, and fast asleep on its hilltop. **Parrano**, too, with its walls and turrets, is more substantial and still faintly medieval despite some clumsy restoration. One kilometre away from the village is the very well-known **Podere Lalla** (Tel. 0763 88154), producer of the very best, first-pressed olive oil, fruit, and vegetables (in season), as well as its own lightly sparkling wine. Montegabbione to the north, despite its medieval centre, has been a little spoilt by the new holiday homes spilling down its hillside.

Where to stay

Le Casette ★★
Garden and restaurant. Via G. Amendola 50, Montegabbione. Tel. 0763 87541. Rooms 13. Showers 13.

L'Incontro ★
A small, very peaceful *pensione* in the hamlet of Ospedaletto. Restaurant. Tel. 075 870911. Rooms 6. Bathrooms 6.

Tulliola ★
In the village of San Venanzo. Garden and restaurant. Tel. 075 8709147. Rooms 15. Bathrooms 5.

Italia ★
Small, simple and cheap. Via della Vaschetto 5, Montegabbione. Tel. 0763 87495. Rooms 5. Bathrooms 2. Showers 1.

Youth hostel

Centro Turistico Giovanile
Monte Peglia, San Venanzo.

Città della Pieve

TOURIST INFORMATION: Piazza Matteoti 4. Tel. 28031
POPULATION: 6500
HEIGHT: 509 m
STD CODE: 0578

Città della Pieve is just one junction away from Orvieto on the motorway, a little before the Fabro service station.

Where to eat

La Bettola del Buttero

Right on the motorway exit from Orvieto to Città della Pieve. Most of the food is cooked on a large wood-fired oven in the centre of this very good, medium-priced *trattoria*. Tel. 0763 82466. *Closed Saturday evening and Sunday.*

From the junction Città della Pieve is another 20 kilometres on the N71 road via Monteleone. This same road has come up alongside the motorway from Orvieto, and though intermittently pretty, can also be a long and laborious drive. **Ficulle** is a centre for local crafts, and noted wines, available from the famous **Cantina Antinori**, Castello della Sala, Sala. Take time to look around the *cantina*, which is located in a fourteenth-century castle, built, like many in the area, by one of Orvieto's infamous Monaldeschi family. Visits should be arranged beforehand.

History

The town itself, close to the Tuscan border and dominating the Valdichiana, is just about worth a visit in its own right, but, as most of the small town can be seen in an hour or so, it is advisable to make the trip part of a longer visit to Perugia, Cortona, or Lake Trasimeno (even if the roads out of the town to these places are a little dull).

It is famous primarily as the birthplace of Perugino — several local churches contain paintings by him — but has a sleepy, if slightly forlorn, charm of its own over and above that of the works of art. The first thing that strikes you about its houses, huddled together and surrounded by heavily wooded hills, is that they are made from tiny and ancient red bricks, the result of a shortage of locally suitable building stone — and a not unpleasant surprise after the tufa and rock of Umbria's other towns. Amongst its narrow geranium-hung streets is one that claims to be the narrowest in Italy — the Via Baciadonna — the width, or so its name suggests, of a woman's kiss. Equally charming, thanks to miraculous Italian plumbing, is the tradition whereby the town's main fountain runs with wine for the duration of the annual *festa*, held every April. (The same thing happens in nearby Panicale.)

The town's history is vague, so vague that a local historian writing in the 1920s suspected some sort of cover-up, speaking of the 'pertinace silenzio', or determined silence, with which his enquiries were met. It was probably a small Etruscan settlement before becoming a very minor staging-post on the old Via Cassia, but, hampered by a poor and isolated position, never achieved the importance optimistically suggested by its title *città*. Fame of a sort, apart from that gained by being the birthplace of Perugino, arrived in 1601 when it was made a bishopric.

'à della Pieve. (JD)

What to see

The **Duomo**, in Piazza di Plebiscito (or Piazza Gramsci depending on your politics) has been much altered and added to since its twelfth-century foundation, and only the stone tower is original. Inside, the walls are covered in an overwhelming amount of fake marble (whose combination of colours is seldom, if ever, found in nature), making for a rather gloomy interior. Perugino is given credit for the *Baptism of Jesus* (1514) in the first chapel on the left and for the *Madonna and Saints* (1514) behind the main altar, but the more sombre painting to the right of the altar, though also attributed to the painter, is more likely to have been the work of one of his pupils. Outside the Duomo, if the tourist office is shut, is a useful map showing the whereabouts of the town's other important paintings and landmarks.

Santa Maria di Bianchi (close by in Via Pietro Vannucci, opposite the Duomo) contains Perugino's *Adoration of the Magi*, painted when the artist was 58 and claimed by many to be the best and most characteristic of his works still in Italy. If you look carefully you can see Lake Trasimeno in the background as well as the figures of Raphael (left of the porch close to a pillar) and Perugino himself, holding a bird. There are also copies of Perugino's contract to undertake the painting on the opposite wall. (If the church is closed, ask for the key at the tourist office or at Corso Vannucci 29.) Towards the end of Via Garibaldi is the drab church of **San Antonio Abate**, its dullness not helped by bleak surroundings, though it does have another painting by Perugino, *St Antony with St Marcellus and Paul the Hermit* (1517). Two hundred metres further down Via Garibaldi and outside the town walls, the baroque church of Santa Maria dei Servi has part of a *Deposition* (1517), another late work by Perugino.

Where to stay

Barzanti ★★ — Efficient, modern hotel with air-conditioning, garden, tennis-courts, and a swimming-pool. Via Santa Lucia 23. Tel. 298010. Rooms 33. Bathrooms 33.

Vannucci ★ — Restaurant, garden, and parking. Via I. Vanni 1. Tel. 298063. Rooms 11. Showers 11.

Baglioni ★ — A *pensione* in the nearby village of Ponticelli. Tel. 248078. Restaurant. Rooms 3. Bathrooms 2.

Where to buy wine

Vinicola Umbra — Five kilometres from Città della Pieve on the road to Chiusi, in the village of San Litardo. Tel. 0578 298064.

Narni

TOURIST INFORMATION: Piazza dei Priori 12
POPULATION: 21,000
HEIGHT: 240 m
STD CODE: 0744

Trains — Connections to Orte, Terni (for Todi), Spoleto, and stations beyond.

Narni is easily reached from Orvieto, either by motorway (via Orte — 56 kilometres) or more slowly through the splendid winding country roads between Lugnano and Amelia. **Lugnano in Teverina**, 11 kilometres from the Attigliano motorway junction, 30 kilometres south of Orvieto, has one of the most characteristic churches in Umbria, Santa Maria Assunta, a target for lovers of the Romanesque, which is not to be missed. As a bonus it contains a fine triptych by Nicolò Alunno and a crypt with a wonderfully sculptured screen and Cosmatic mosaic work. At **Giove**, close to the motorway exit, **Costa del Gallo** (Piazza del Convento 2) sells a wide range of organically grown fruit and vegetables, and local honey.

Narni, confined to a long narrow hill jutting out in a sharp bend of the River Nera and dominated from above by one of Albornoz's bleak and imposing Papal fortresses, is the first major town in Umbria coming north from Rome. Its majestic position, a little reminiscent of Orvieto's, has left virtually no room for expansion and the present-day town is probably no bigger now than it was in Roman times. What has changed are the surroundings, and though at heart Narni is still the medieval hill-town so familiar in Umbria, the views for which it was once famous have been spoilt by the arrival of the twentieth century in the shape of a steel mill, chemical works, and the haphazard town (Narni Scalo) that has grown up around them. The area is far from ruined however, the worst of Terni's industrial overspill having been artfully concealed behind conveniently sited hills, and there is plenty in the town to justify a short morning's visit, perhaps on the way to Todi or Spoleto, both within easy reach on fast modern roads.

History

Nothing is known of Narni before 300 BC, when it first appears in Roman records as the colony of Narnia (one of the earliest in Umbria), though Livy talks about the existence of an earlier walled village on the same site. It begins to figure more prominently in Umbrian affairs in 220 BC, when the Via Flaminia was driven through the town (following the present-day course of Via XX Settembre and Via Mazzini) making Narni the last substantial hill-town before the Tiber valley, and the literal gateway to Rome and routes to the Adriatic. This position, of course, gave it great strategic importance, and in time its large military garrison became one of the key links in Rome's outer defences.

By the twelfth century, having regained the power and independence lost during the Barbarian invasions, it was able to rebel against Papal rule in 1112, and to withstand the attacks of Frederick Barbarossa, Frederick II, and a certain Rinaldo, pretender to the Dukedom of Spoleto. In 1242 it made common cause with Perugia against the Empire, but by 1373 had fallen into the hands of the Dukes of Orsini.

The 300 years of comparatively peaceful prosperity that followed were shattered almost overnight in 1525 when the town was attacked and partly destroyed by German mercenaries (the *Landsknechten*, or country serfs) intent on getting in a little practice for their subsequent sack of Rome.

Narni never really got over the shock, and for four centuries slumbered on as little more than a village (D'Annunzio included it in his *Cities of Silence*) and only became officially recognized as a town (*una città*) in 1950. Since then the industries mentioned earlier and the improvement of communications have brought Narni a degree of prosperity unusual by Umbrian standards.

What to see

The Romanesque **Duomo** (Piazza Garibaldi), consecrated in 1145, greatly altered in the sixteenth century but well restored in 1967, has many minor works of art and one or two major ones, notably a ninth-century mosaic of Christ on the right of the nave (only discovered in 1955) and a wooden sculpture by Lorenzo Vecciatta on the left (1474). The ruins of the **Rocca** are easily reached from Piazza Garibaldi by taking Via del Monte, a street that threads its way through the *terziere di Mezule*, one of the three areas into which the medieval town was divided. Beyond the piazza two lovely buildings rise on either side of the narrow Piazza dei Priori, Narni's Roman and medieval heart: first, on the right as you enter from Via Garibaldi, the fourteenth-century (though much added to) **Palazzo dei Priori**, with its tower and graceful **Loggia** designed by Gubbian architect Gattapone (today it houses the town's fruit and vegetable market) and then on the left the **Palazzo del Podestà**, an eccentric building originally created by joining three houses-cum-towers together. Its gauntness is only partly relieved by six mullioned windows added by an unknown Renaissance builder, and by the much-photographed bas-reliefs to the right of the central door (reminiscent, if you have seen them, of those on the facade of San Pietro in Spoleto). Here the far more modest sculptures represent a duel between knights, a lion and a griffin, and a hunting scene. On the first floor of this palace, in the Sala del Consiglio, are an important painting by the Florentine artist Domenico Ghirlandaio, the *Coronation of the Virgin* (1486) and a fresco by Lo Spagna, *St Francis receiving the Stigmata*. (Lo Spagna was commissioned to make two copies of Ghirlandaio's painting, which are now in Todi and Spoleto.) Back in the piazza itself there is a large fountain built in 1303 which bears a striking resemblance to the Fonte Maggiore in Perugia. Notice, too, the carved pulpit beside the tower to the right of the Palazzo dei Priori. It dates from the time of the commune and was used by the *banditore*, or town-crier, to issue civic proclamations.

Just beyond the piazza, a little further down Via Garibaldi, is the tiny church of **Santa Maria in Pensole**, unaltered since it was built in 1175 (the

alazzo del Podestà: detail. (ISTO)

date is inscribed above the door) which boasts a beautiful stone frieze running across the width of its facade, one of Umbria's small treasures and one that is often overlooked. Also worth a look is the church's crypt, a strange and primitive affair (only discovered in 1974) that bears traces of a Roman tomb. The town's art gallery and museum are housed in the ex-church and one-time cathedral of **San Domenico**, halfway down Via Mazzini in Piazza XII Guigno. Amongst its many paintings and sculptures are two outstanding pictures: an *Annunciation* by Benozzo Gozzoli and *Bernadino da Feltre* by Fiorenzo di Lorenzo, the latter artist one of the rarest of painters. The nearby gardens of **San Bernado** offer good views of the Nera valley and the recently restored church of San Cassiano in the woods below the town.

Via Garibaldi ends in Piazza Galeotto Marzio, from where several short walks taking in the town's ancient fortifications are possible. North of the town is one of the sights that is not as impressive as some guides would have you believe. Goethe was told to see it, but arriving in Narni in the middle of the night, missed it completely. It is the **Ponte d'Augusto**, or what remains of it — a single arch near the road to the station (the railway passes almost right under it). In Roman times it formed part of a massive bridge, 130 metres long and 30 metres high, that carried the Via Flaminia over the River Nera.

Where to stay

Note: The same applies to Narni as applies to Orvieto: avoid the new town around the station.

Dei Priori ★★★★ Vicolo del Comune 4. Tel. 726843. Rooms 19. Bathrooms 2. Showers 17.

Da Carlo ★★ Via Ortana Vecchia. Tel. 742215. Rooms 22. Showers 22.

La Rocca ★★ Restaurant. Parking. Via Cavour 60, Lugnano. Tel. 0744 902129. Rooms 10. Bathrooms 2. Showers 8.

Giardino ★★ Via dei Gelsi 23, Penna in Teverina (near Giove). Tel. 0744 993178. Rooms 10. Showers 9.

Where to eat

La Loggia An excellent restaurant, and remarkably cheap in view of the quality of the cooking. Many Umbrian specialities (try the *ciriole*) and startling inventions, which vary according to season and the mood of the chef, Gastone Canton. Vicolo del Comune. Tel. 0744 722744. *Closed Monday and the second half of July*.

Where to buy wine

Azienda Montoro In the village of Montoro Umbro. Tel. 0744 747128.

Azienda Tiberi In the village of Castelchiaro. Tel. 0744 744106.

Immobiliare Umbra Viale Regina Margherita 7, Lugnano. Tel. 0744 902105.

Amelia

TOURIST INFORMATION: Via della Repubblica 2
POPULATION: 11,000
HEIGHT: 370 m
STD CODE: 0744

History

Amelia, a delightful town of grace and modest splendour, famous for its white figs (eaten with a mixture of nuts and chocolate), and for its

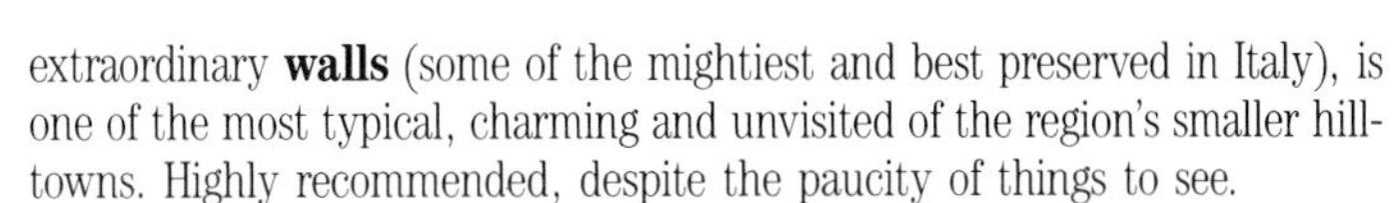

extraordinary **walls** (some of the mightiest and best preserved in Italy), is one of the most typical, charming and unvisited of the region's smaller hill-towns. Highly recommended, despite the paucity of things to see.

If you believe Cato and Cicero, who both give the date of its foundation as 1164 BC, then it is also one of the oldest. The walls, at least, made from vast polygonal blocks of stone resting on each other without the aid of cement, are Umbrian, though their precise age, and that of the city, are unknown. The fifth century BC is the best guess.

The Romans built a colony here as a staging-post on the Via Amerina, one of nine military roads that linked Etruria to the Via Flaminia, but during the Barbarian invasions it was almost completely destroyed by Totila. After its recovery it became part of the Lombards' Roman dukedom. In the Middle Ages, though a free commune, the town suffered all the familiar internal disputes between rival factions of Guelph and Ghibelline and was fought over by most of the neighbouring towns, as well as by powerful Roman-based families. The earthquake of 1812, which badly damaged a large part of the town, came as something of a *coup de grâce*.

What to see

Santi Filippo e Giacomo (Piazza Augustus Vera) is a thirteenth-century church (1287) with a baroque interior (1767) and a beautiful fifteenth-century double cloister. The first chapel on the right of the three naves contains six tombs carved by the leading Florentine sculptor, Agostino di Duccio, for the local Geraldini family; the upper two, those belonging to Matteo and Elisabetta, command most attention (1477). Close by, in Via Farattini, the **Palazzo Farattini**, designed by Antonio di Sangallo (also responsible for the Pozzo di San Patrizio in Orvieto) contains the restored remains of a Roman mosaic. The **Duomo**, which dominates the top of Amelia's pyramid-shaped hill, was virtually destroyed by fire in 1640, and has since been the victim of bad restoration and nineteenth-century frescoes. The column you see on the right immediately after entering the church is the one to which St Fermina, Amelia's patron saint, is said to have been tied and then martyred. In the second chapel on the same side are two Turkish flags captured during the Crusades at the Battle of Lepanto. Left of the altar (whose painting has rather dubiously been credited to the Sienese master Duccio) is the tomb of Bishop Geraldini, with further bas-reliefs by Agostino di Duccio (of the Virgin and Child, with figures of Faith, Hope, Charity, and Fortitude). Here too, in the left transept is an altarpeice of the *Madonna and Child*, an Umbrian work of the fifteenth century. In the **Palazzo Comunale**, and more particularly in its courtyard, are miscellaneous Roman and medieval remains waiting to be transferred to the 'proper' museum they deserve. The many Roman fragments incorporated in the town's buildings will have to stay where they are.

Where to stay

Scoglio dell'Aquione ★★★
Garden, restaurant, and conference facilities. Via Orvieto 23. Tel. 0744 983005. Rooms 38. Bathrooms 4. Showers 34.

Le Colonne ★★
Small and intimate, and the best restaurant in Amelia (open to non-residents). Via Roma 191. Tel. 0744 982268. Rooms 8. Bathrooms 2. Showers 6.

Anita ★
Moderate hotel, but an excellent restaurant (open to non-residents). Via Roma 31. Tel. 0744 982146. Rooms 22. Bathrooms 5. Showers 6.

Where to buy wine

Cantina Sociale dei Colli Amerini
In the village of Fornole. Tel. 0744 989203.

Nottala Canzio Fattoria Le Rille
Tel. 0744 97151.

Zanchi Licurgo Azienda Agraria
Via Ortana. In the village of Trivoli. Tel. 97627.

Otricoli

Otricoli, 15 kilometres from Narni, is almost the southernmost point in Umbria and as characteristic a first or last taste of the region as one could wish for, being small, surrounded by walls and towers, and full of medieval houses perched above steep cliffs. Originally an Umbrian town (*ocre* meant 'hill' in Umbrian) it was taken over by the Romans in about the third century BC, who subsequently abandoned its hilltop site in favour of one nearer the Tiber (which was then still navigable). Over the centuries, as times became more troubled, the new settlement was abandoned in turn and people moved back to the greater security of the original town. Nowadays it is the Roman **Otriculum**, just over a kilometre from the modern town, that is the main reason for a visit.

In 1586 Montaigne described the place as 'infiniment plaisant' and spoke of the ruins (later painted by Turner — the picture is in the British Museum) as 'grandes et importantes', yet today, half-lost amongst trees and vegetation, the spot is almost unknown, visited, if at all, only by local people and archaeologists. This looks set to change, however, when the site, now 'officially' recognized as part of Umbria's heritage, becomes the centre of a 190-hectare 'archaeological park' — though quite when this will happen no one is yet sure. In the meantime, most of the ruins remain evocatively half-buried.

The only previous excavations, those that brought the site its modest degree of fame, took place in 1776 on the order of Pope Pius VI, when numerous

statues (including a famous head of Jove), mosaics, and sarcophagi were removed to the Vatican Museum.

Since then almost nothing has been touched. Unlike most outlying Roman colonies, Otriculum has no walls, because the town was a sort of holiday resort for rich Romans rather than a military outpost, and consisted of small villas, baths, cisterns, and temples rather than elaborate fortifications. Some distance away from what was the forum are the most impressive of the remains, a partly buried tufa amphitheatre and a succession of arches on two levels, which must have once supported a temple or other important public building.

While in the vicinity it is worth visiting **San Vito** (some 6 kilometres off the main road back towards Narni), for its marvellous views and a splendid set of walls.

Where to stay

Villa Carla ★★

In the nearby hamlet of Pareti. Restaurant and garden. Tel. 0744 719297. Rooms 10. Bathrooms 10.

Umbria ★

Restaurant and garden. Via Roma 18, Otricoli. Tel. 0744 719122. Rooms 9. Bathrooms 6.

TODI

General Information

TOURIST INFORMATION: Piazza del Popolo 38. Tel. 883062 Located underneath the barrel vaulting of the Palazzo del Capitano. Information and free guide published by Retro clothes shop in Via del Duomo 16

POPULATION: 18,000

HEIGHT: 410 m

POST OFFICE: Piazza Garibaldi

TELEPHONES: Tourist Information Office

STD CODE: 075

POLICE: Via Borgo Ulpiana Tel. 882323

DISTANCE TO:
Perugia 42 km Narni 30 km
Spoleto 46 km Orvieto 34 km

Trains

Todi is on the privately owned, single-track *Ferrovia Centrale Umbra* (FCU) that links Terni with Città di Castello via Perugia. Its trains — charming, frequent, but slow — are occasionally replaced by a bus service. There are two stations serving the town, each 4 kilometres distant. Buses link both to the centre, but not always connecting well with incoming trains.

Buses

There are buses to many local villages. Most leave at 13.30 in the guise of school buses from Piazza Jacopone. Tickets from the fruit shop next to the Jacopone Restaurant. Eight daily buses from Perugia but only one to Orvieto. Additional services to Terni and Rome.

Road

Todi is connected by excellent new dual-carriageways to Terni (Narni and the A1), Orvieto (the N448 — a scenic and recommended route), and Perugia.

Parking

The town centre has a baffling one-way system, and streets that are so narrow as to be virtually impassable to cars. Only Porta Perugina is open to incoming traffic, so try to park around the walls (near Porta Romana, for example) or in the small car-parks near Santa Maria della Consolazione and Piazza Oberdan.

Curiously named Todi is often cited (wrongly) as one of Umbria's least-known smaller towns, and (rightly) as one of its most characteristic leftovers. Its fairy-tale position atop a lofty hill, drifting dream-like into the Umbrian haze, is

amongst the region's most memorable. Within its three concentric rings of walls is a town in a world of its own, once untroubled by the twentieth century, but now accommodating Rome's arts and media types, and the first flush of tourists. (Not to mention foreign property owners.) The sleepy charm that first attracted gentrification appears fairly resilient. Already, however, the antiques shops are opening and the first ramshackle estate agents springing up.

It is still, though, an enchanting place; mellow and unmistakably Umbrian in foundation, and with a **medieval piazza** considered by many to be amongst Italy's finest. Other sights are few, but quiet charm — and a superb restaurant — are more than compensation.

History

Todi is one of the oldest of the Umbrian cities. It was founded, according to legend, on the spot where an eagle dropped a cloth taken from the table of an Umbrian family; an eagle with a cloth in its claws has long been

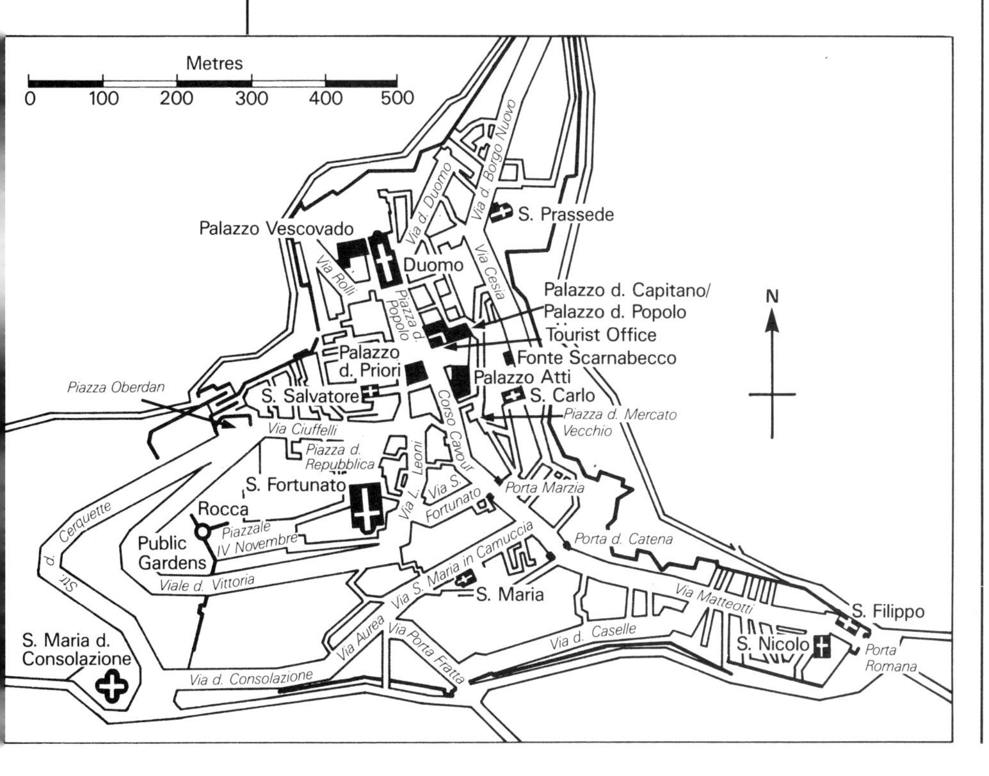

TODI

the town's insignia. A superb defensive position, commanding the valleys of the Tiber and the Naia, made it inevitable that some kind of settlement would develop on the site. The earliest town was founded by the Umbrians between the third and fifth centuries and was later annexed peacefully (or so it is assumed) by the Etruscans.

Coins found bearing the town's Etruscan name, Tutare, suggest that Todi enjoyed considerable independence during the period of Etruscan rule. *Tutare* means 'border', and the town was probably one of several outposts used by the Etruscans to defend their eastern frontier along the Tiber.

The Romans turned Todi into a military camp under the name Colonia Julia fida Tuder, and added a second set of walls to those already built by the Etruscans. An amphitheatre, baths, and temples to Jupiter, Minerva, Juno, and Mars were also built, but almost nothing of them now remains. Todi gained a reputation for ferocious fighting in the wars against Hannibal, and subsequently stood up to Totila and other Barbarian attempts to dominate her.

Despite internal and external quarrels, especially between rival factions of Guelphs and Ghibellines, Todi prospered, and became a free town in the twelfth century. Its colonial ambitions, however, were modest, and it reached the limit of its territorial expansion by overcoming Amelia in 1208 and Terni in 1217. During the next 30 years the main civic palaces were built, along with a third set of walls, which almost completely enclosed the town until the 1970s.

After losing its civic independence in 1368, Todi entered a period of decline and was ruled by a series of powerful noblemen with the aid of mercenary armies. Its decline continued into the fifteenth century despite a spate of building, which included the church of San Fortunato. The lowest point in its fortunes occurred in 1523, when half its population was wiped out by the plague. After this setback, only the single-mindedness of Angelo Cesi, the town's bishop, succeeded in restoring life to the town.

He instigated a programme of public and private works that saw the building of the Palazzo Cesi and Palazzo Viviano degli Atti (1552) (the Atti were leading members of the Ghibelline faction and ruled Todi for many years during the sixteenth century). The church of Santa Maria della Consolazione, having been consecrated in 1508, was opened for worship by the bishop in 1606.

Eventually the town became part of the Papal States (Albornoz, inevitably, had already paved the way years earlier with the building of a Rocca), and was ruled by a pontifical governor until Italy's unification in 1860. It escaped damage in the Second World War, but, like Orvieto, has recently been subject to several serious landslips. A tragic fire in 1982 at one of the summer antiques fairs, claimed the lives of 35 people.

What to see

Etruscan, Roman, and medieval walls

Todi has three sets of walls, which mark the Etruscan, Roman, and medieval limits of the city. Between and among these are small, winding streets hanging with geraniums and rhododendrons — Via San Fortunato is particularly picturesque. Occasionally, you will come across old wells and signs — *prima cerchia* and *seconda cerchia* — which mark the first and second sets of walls.

Street in Todi. (JD)

The best-preserved parts of the Umbro-Etruscan wall can be seen near Porta Libera, along the Via Paolo Rolli, Via della Mura Antiche, and Via del Montarone, whilst the Porta Marzia, between Corso Cavour and the Via Roma, is the sole remaining gateway from the period. (An Etruscan city was obliged to have at least three gates, one for each of the three main Etruscan gods.) The remains of the Roman wall are best seen at the Porta della Catena, just below the Porta Marzia, and again at Porta Libera near Santa Prassede.

Piazza del Popolo

The best way to enter the piazza is from one of the narrow streets at either end — the Corso Cavour or the Via del Duomo — rather than the Via Mazzini, so as to get the full effect of its sudden and rather austere grandeur. It has been the centre of the town since Roman times, and traces of pavement and cisterns from this period still exist near the Palazzo dei Priori. (They were rediscovered in 1262 during the paving of the piazza and continued to be used for the piping of water until 1572.) In the Middle Ages the entire square could be sealed off by four enormous gates, but these were removed in the sixteenth century.

Palazzo dei Priori

This is the single, southernmost building in the piazza, and has just been extensively restored (1987). The seat of the town's successive administrations — from priors to pontifical governors — it was started in 1293 to a Gothic plan, subsequently enlarged, and finally completed in 1337. The tower was added in 1369. Despite renovation by Pope Leone X in 1513, the building retained its medieval character. A bronze eagle *Aquila Tuderie*, the town's symbol cast in 1339, can be seen high up on the outside wall.

Palazzo del Capitano/Palazzo del Popolo

The two buildings are today linked by an impressive flight of stone steps, but originally were separated by a small street. With the Duomo on your left, the right of the two Palazzi is the Palazzo del Popolo. It was started in 1213, and is one of the oldest civic palaces in Italy. Both it and the neighbouring Palazzo del Capitano house council offices and occasionally host concerts and small exhibitions. The Palazzo del Capitano (1292) contains the town's art gallery (climb the second flight of steps) which inexplicably (it is only a tiny collection) has been closed for 'reordering' for an incredible 10 years. Should it ever reopen, its most important piece is a large *tavola*, the *Coronation of the Virgin* (1507) by Lo Spagna, commissioned, like a similar work in Spoleto, to be a copy of Ghirlandaio's Florentine version of the same subject in Narni's Palazzo del Podestà. The 25 figures below the Virgin are saints, but additional

Palazzo del Capitano. (ISTO)

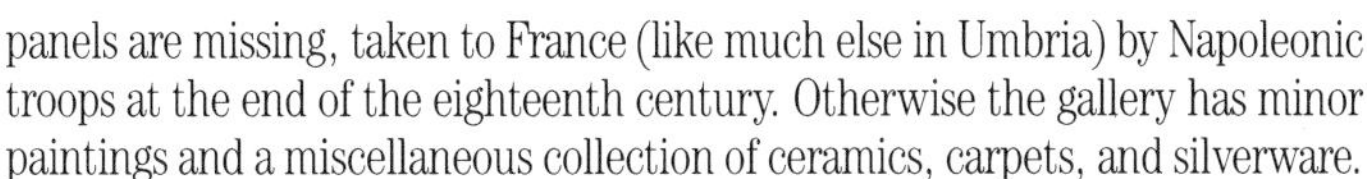

panels are missing, taken to France (like much else in Umbria) by Napoleonic troops at the end of the eighteenth century. Otherwise the gallery has minor paintings and a miscellaneous collection of ceramics, carpets, and silverware.

The **Etruscan and Roman collection** in a neighbouring room, also closed to the public at the moment, is small but interesting. The Etruscan articles run the gamut of Etruscan daily life and death, and include examples of the three-legged oil-lamps common to the tombs around Todi, and four *bucceri*, types of pot, which owe their grey–black colour to the mixing of charcoal with the clay before firing. The perfectly preserved 20-kilogram bronze pig is unmissable (an Etruscan door-stop?), while amongst the vast variety of smaller objects look out for the sets of small stones that were probably used in an Etruscan version of 'knucklestones'. The bronze statue of Mars is a copy of a famous statue found just outside Todi in 1837 (like many Umbrian treasures, it is now in the Vatican Museum). The museum also has one of the three existing Etruscan statues of Celtic soldiers in Italy. They were known to the Romans as Gauls, and their tall, blond appearance and fearsome reputation rather worried both them and the Etruscans, though they eventually settled peaceably in northern Italy and founded the city that was to become Milan.

Most of the Roman items were found near the old Via Flaminia, which more or less follows the course of the present day E45 road. Amongst the miscellaneous articles are a first-century BC altar fragment carved with olive trees, and a sarcophagus with part of a carving of Romulus and Remus under the wolf of Rome.

Duomo

Each of the Umbrian cities has a cathedral as individual as the city itself. Todi's is earlier and simpler than most, but, thanks to an elegant facade and medieval setting, lacks nothing by way of beauty. It was started at the beginning of the twelfth century, the site chosen being that of an earlier temple to Apollo, and added to sporadically until the end of the seventeenth century.

The facade, finished in a weathered pink and white marble that makes the best of any light, is dominated by a marvellous rose window (1520) and by an equally impressive Gothic doorway framed with swirls of carved acanthus leaves. (Square facades of this kind — with three doors, three rose windows, and wide flight of steps — are a common feature of churches in the neighbouring region of the Abruzzi.) The ornately carved doors were made in the seventeenth century. The Gothic campanile is thirteenth century, but the dull spire was unnecessarily added in 1839 (and is in the process of being removed). The otherwise late-Romanesque exterior is far more complicated than the simple facade might suggest, and walks down either Via del Duomo or Via del Seminario offer interesting views of the church which are not normally seen.

The interior's most striking feature is a beautiful carved wooden **choir** (1530) by Antonio and Sebastiano Bencivenni from Pesaro, one of the best works of its kind in Italy. Each of the stalls has a picture in inlaid wood with the Annunciation reserved for the central throne. Notice the panels right at the front, low down near the floor, in which are described the various woodworking tools used during the carving of the piece. The crucifix above the choir, a particularly good example of the genre, is from the thirteenth century.

The naves are separated by columns whose capitals are interesting because they represent the meeting between the last of the Romanesque forms and the first of the Gothic ideas that were beginning to filter through from France. The right-hand nave has fragments of fresco by Lo Spagna and, more notably, an altarpiece by Giannicola di Paolo, usually dappled with light from the delicately coloured nineteenth-century stained-glass windows beside it.

The painting that fills the back (west) wall is the *Last Judgement* by Ferrau da Faenza (1562–1645), a not terribly good imitation of Michelangelo's work in the Sistine Chapel. It is worth going down into the crypt where there are Roman, perhaps Etruscan, fragments from the original pagan temple.

San Fortunato

This church is the most interesting thing in the town after the Piazza del Popolo, and is set amongst gardens just a minute's walk from the piazza, off Via Ciufelli. It is at the highest point of a high city (and its tower dominates Todi's skyline for miles around), but close up and at first glance it is anything but impressive. The facade is as squat as the day it was left unfinished (despite having been recently cleaned and restored), redeemed solely by a superb Gothic doorway (1420–36), which stands comparison with that of the Duomo in Orvieto, and only inside do you appreciate the church's true grandeur.

Some idea of its scope can be gained from the fact that building went on almost continuously between 1292 and 1460 (which is also why it is a mixture of Romanesque and Gothic styles). Its size (far larger than you would expect from the exterior) has recently been highlighted by the reopening of windows in the side-chapels, and by the repainting of the ceilings and pillars in their original white.

There was a strong Umbrian Romanesque tradition for a vaulted hall church, and San Fortunato's single low-pitched roof is similar to smaller, wooden-roofed 'barn' churches common throughout Umbria and Tuscany, which were distinguished, as here, by the equal height of their naves and aisles. Building to such a large, open scale, however, was more a feature of late Gothic architecture, and again Umbria has several examples of the form, most notably in the Duomo and church of San Domenico in Perugia.

San Fortunato also shows the increasing use made of side-chapels (there are 13), brought about by the need to accommodate the rising demand for daily masses as the Franciscan Order became more clerical. The use of such chapels had already become much more common in Catalonia and southern France during the thirteenth century. (Notice the small interconnecting arches

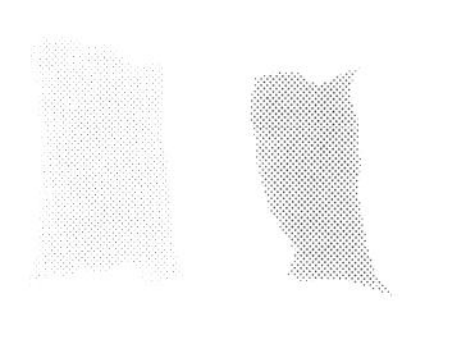

he choir, San Fortunato. (JD)

between the chapels: an unusual feature.)

The fourth of these chapels on the right contains a late work by Masolino da Panicale (1348–1447), a *Madonna and Child* (1432), which, though the town's most famous painting, is badly damaged. The fragments in the sixth chapel, scenes from the life of St Francis, are far more arresting. The chancel has another beautiful choir (by Maffei da Gubbio, 1590), later and more baroque than that in the Duomo. The first three stalls on either side are especially good. The crypt contains only the rather gaudy marble sepulchre of Jacopone, medieval poet and mystic.

Public gardens

Turn left out of San Fortunato and follow the small lane along the side of the building and you come to the Liceo-Ginnasio, which has a lovely set of cloisters. Continue up the stony track to the right and you find yourself in Todi's public gardens, a shady, peaceful oasis, with some wonderful views. They contain the squat, circular remains of Albornoz's Rocca, built in 1373 and destroyed by Ludovico degli Atti. From one of the many winding paths choose one that bears right (known as 'La Serpentina') and follow it down to Via Ciufelli, just below San Fortunato. Turn left at the bottom into Viale della Consolazione and a 10-minute walk brings you to Todi's other important church, Santa Maria della Consolazione.

Santa Maria della Consolazione

This late-Renaissance church was started in 1508, two years after the first stone of St Peter's in Rome had been laid, and is often regarded as a simplified

Santa Maria della Consolazione. (ISTO)

version of Bramante's plan for St Peter's itself. It contains one of his trademarks, the so-called 'rhythmic bay', an exterior of alternating windows, arches, and pilasters, but he was not the only architect to have a hand in its design. Scalza, responsible for many of the buildings in Orvieto was also involved, along with a whole host of others, but the net result of their labour is a cold and unappealing church. It is often considered to be Todi's pride and joy, which is strange because its ordered austerity is quite out of keeping with the rest of the town's sunny medievalism. To many it seems appropriate that it is outside the confines of the town proper, though Edward Hutton, writing at the end of the last century, considered it 'one of the most lovely, if not the loveliest of Renaissance churches in Italy — that is to say, in the world.'

It is built in the form of a Greek cross (like the almost identical churches in Cortona and Montepulciano), and its most notable features are its carved pillars, ornate ceiling, and the custodian who looks after the place. The statues in the niches are the figures of the Apostles.

Other sights

Todi's other sights can be covered quite quickly. There are four small churches worth seeing if you have time. **Santa Maria in Camuccia** (Via Santa Maria in Camuccia off Corso Cavour), pretty from the outside, baroque on the inside, has an ancient wooden statue of the Virgin and a large collection of miscellaneous Roman objects that have been turned up in the numerous restorations since the church was built in the thirteenth century. In the other direction, below the Piazza del Popolo, is the tiny Romanesque church of **San Carlo** or **Sant'Ilario** (Via Cesia) built in the year 1000 and often locked to protect its Lo Spagna frescoes. At the bottom of Via Matteotti, on either side of the Porta Roman, are **San Filippo**, dull except for some frescoed panels on the right-hand wall, and the more interesting **San Nicolo**, a Gothic church built on the site of the older **San Nicolo de Crintis** (1093), part of whose facade remains intact. Inside are a striking wooden ceiling, three large Gothic arches, and two small Umbrian frescoes on the left-hand wall.

Between the Piazza del Popolo and Sant'Ilario you will have passed the so-called **Roman niches** (Piazza del Mercato Vecchio), four large arches that formed part of a large Roman building whose precise function is unknown. Below the niches, partly obscured by weeds, are the remains of a Doric frieze and mosaic pavement. Carrying on beyond Sant'Ilario down Via Cesia you reach the **Fonte Scarnabecco**, built on the orders of a Podestà from Bologna of the same name in the middle of the thirteenth century. Today its scarce waters are collected by townspeople for drinking in preference to tap-water, but in the Middle Ages it was primarily for horses. (At a time when owning a horse was a mark of aristocracy, there were estimated to be over 1000 in Todi, which gives some idea of the town's medieval importance.)

Where to stay

Bramante
★★★★

Not central, but long-established and the best of the town's up-market hotels. Preferable to the overpriced and gaudily modern San Valentino nearby. Tennis-courts, air-conditioning, gardens, and a good restaurant with views and an outside terrace. Via Orvietana. Tel. 8848381. Rooms 43. Bathrooms 14. Showers 29.

Villa Luisa
★★★

A large, standard hotel with full facilities, central location, and garden. Via A. Cortesi 147. Tel. 8848571. Rooms 41. Bathrooms 24. Showers 17.

Cavour
★★

Cheap hotels are scarce in Todi, though likely to become more common as the town's popularity increases. This one is small but very convenient, and overlooks the Piazza del Popolo. Corso Cavour 12. Tel. 882147. Rooms 19. Bathrooms 2. Showers 12.

Youth hostel

Ostello per la Gioventù

Eccentric opening times so check with the tourist office for latest details. Via Maestà dei Lombardi. Tel. 882686.

Where to eat

Umbria
★★★

Straightforward and appealing restaurant made exceptional by its terrace, which mut have one of the finest views in central Italy. (The restaurant is tucked away under the arches of the Palazzo del Capitano.) The day's food is laid out, open to inspection, in the adjoining kitchen. The cooking is traditional Umbrian, but in season try the house speciality — *boscaiolo* — a pasta sauce made with wild asparagus tips. Via Bonaventura 13. Tel. 882390. *Closed Tuesday.*

Degli Angeli
★★★

This restaurant is in a small hamlet 11 kilometres south-east of Todi and is open only to those who make a prior telephone booking. It has a considerable reputation based on a wide and inventive menu that ventures beyond Umbria's usual culinary borders. Good cellar. Prices on the high side. Colevalenza di Todi. Tel. 887283. *Closed Tuesday and all of July.*

Jacopone
★

Only if the above is full. Acceptable food but sham 'olde worlde' setting with irritating piped music. Piazza Jacopone. Tel. 882366.

Ristorante Cavour

A busy, central *pizzeria*. Via Cavour 21. Tel. 882491. *Closed Wednesday.*

Where to buy wine

Cantina Sociale

Ponte Rio. Tel. 882082.

Todini Franco Azienda Agraria

Colevalenza. Tel. 887222/887107.

Vailuca Ugo Azienda Agraria

Fontignano. Tel. 882082.

AROUND TODI

Deruta and north to Perugia

Todi is fortunate in being linked to all the surrounding major towns by modern and fast roads so that you can be in Orvieto or Perugia in less than 40 minutes. But there are slower ways of getting about. New roads have

superseded older ones, which have now reverted to being under-used and tranquil country lanes, and it is to these you should turn if you have time. Note that the Tiber valley to the north is not picture-postcard pretty. It is littered with unsightly light-industrial plants, but if you head for the hills then the area is not beyond redemption.

Going north from Todi on the main E45, turn left at the first major junction after Ponte Rio and follow the signs for the spectacularly sited **Monte Castello di Vibio**. This eagle's nest of a village dominates the countryside almost more than Todi, and was once one of a reputed 365 castles that formed a defensive barrier around the medieval town. There is a splendid view from its breezy central piazza and the adjacent church is worth a look for its grey *trompe-l'oeil* ceiling. Take a walk around its tiny streets, kept beautifully clean by some unseen hand, and look out for the tiny nineteenth-century theatre, which, having escaped reincarnation as a cinema, is now in the process of being restored. An unmade but passable road (via Canonica), makes a pleasant return drive to Todi.

Below Monte Castello is the less-spectacularly sited **Fratta Todina**, a walled village with a castle strengthened in 1416 by the infamous Braccio Fortebraccio as a winter billet for himself and his troops. Near the centre of the village is a charming Franciscan monastery, which features in several stories and legends of the Order. **Marsciano**, to the north, is a new town spoilt by light industry. The less said about it the better. **Cerqueto**'s parish church beyond it contains the first confidently dated frescoes attributed to Perugino (*San Sebastian*, 1478). Other paintings at the edge of the village in Maestà di Santa Lucia are also attributed to him, but are in poor condition. **Sant'Elena**, just a kilometre away, has the remains of a fifteenth-century castle. Returning to the E45, **Casalina** also has the vast and crumbling remnants of one of the area's most important castles.

Follow the main road north towards Deruta and be sure to stop at the small church of **Madonna dei Bagni** on the right about 2 kilometres south of the town. It was 16 July 1657 when 'Christoforo, a merchant of Casalina, placed a holy image [actually a picture of the Madonna on a broken piece of tile], praying for the recovery of his wife from an agonizing illness. Returning home he found her cheerfully sweeping the house.' Amongst the multitude of Umbrian churches, few have a background story quite as explicit and as disarmingly simple as this one. Madonna dei Bagni was built 30 years later, close to the oak tree on which Christoforo had fixed his small fragment of tile. Since that date the walls of the church have accumulated almost 600 votive tiles, providing a unique and eccentric record not only of popular religious practice, but also of Deruta's social and ceramic tradition over three centuries.

Day-to-day life in the fields, the insides of houses, means of transport (from horse to carriage to car), and the mode of dressing are represented in the lively and untarnished colours of Deruta's medieval craftsmen. Alongside them are tiles offered as thanks for 'miraculous' escapes from a host of dangerous (and not so dangerous) situations: a fall from a horse or a tree, fire, flood, famine, an accident at work, a kick or bite from an animal. But make your visit soon; over 100 tiles were quietly removed in 1980 and disappeared into the unscrupulous depths of the antiques market, with the result that opening times in the church are now severely restricted. Weekday mornings, Saturdays (when coach parties arrive in some force) or the six o'clock Mass are the best times to find the doors unlocked. Otherwise make enquiries at the tourist office in Deruta.

Alternatively, before turning towards Deruta from Casalina, turn south, and after some 4 kilometres take the lovely road that winds through olive groves, pine, and oak forest to **Collazzone** (470 metres), with its narrow streets, medieval air, and extensive views, one of the nicest villages in the area. Jacopone, Todi's great mystical poet, died here (surrounded by like-minded eccentrics) in the convent of San Lorenzo, on Christmas Eve 1306. The ancient abbey, once owned by the Benedictines, has now been taken over by the Poor Clares. Another road, unmade this time, leads from Casalina to **Castelleone**, little more than a high-walled and towered fifteenth-century castle in the pretty hills behind Deruta. Within its walls the church of San Dorato has some good frescoes by the Umbrian painter Matteo da Gualdo (1453–1507).

Deruta

TOURIST INFORMATION: Piazza dei Consoli. Tel. 075 971159

History

You hardly need to be told Deruta is famous for its ceramics; the verges of the road miles to either side of the town are packed with stalls selling everything from egg-cups to what look like pottery dustbins. The best pieces are to be found in the workshops of the ugly new part of the town, located just off the main road and below the new town on the hill. It is *the* place (closely followed by Gubbio) to shop for some of the most beautiful pottery in Italy.

The old town, worth visiting for its own sake, has old but obscure origins. It was linked to Perugia for most of its early medieval history, fortified in the thirteenth century, destroyed twice (once by Braccio Fortebraccio in 1408 and then by Cesare Borgia in 1500), and finally passed to the Papacy in 1540.

Ceramics are first mentioned in the town's records in 1387 (but the tradition probably goes back 100 years earlier) and developed here because of the suitability of local clay and silicates (the latter being an important element in the glazing process). The clay was mined from the surrounding hills, broken down, washed and then filtered through silk before being laid out on earthenware tiles to dry to the right consistency for working. After the first firing (known as the *biscotto*,), objects (initially fairly everyday items such as bowls or wine jugs) were dipped in glaze composed of two parts sand to one part lead and tin, to which was added *la feccia di vino*, the dregs left over after the making of wine. They were then hand-decorated (still Deruta's forte), usually in the early days, in brown or a distinctive green known as *ramina*. In the fifteenth century, craftsmen discovered how to synthesize a sunflower yellow and a peacock blue, and began to work on a more monumental scale, using the vast and complicated range of colouring techniques that brought Derutan ware international renown. By the sixteenth century, the craft had reached its height, with some 50 workshops operating in the area. Amongst the town's numerous *maestri* the most important were Giacomo Mancini and Francesco Urbino, whose work has found its way into many of the world's major museums, including the Louvre, the Hermitage, and the Victoria and Albert in London. Since the nineteenth century there has been little in the way of innovation either in design or production, and the town has survived largely by making copies of older work, which, their lack of originality notwithstanding, are still both varied and beautiful.

What to see

Museo Regionale della Ceramica
(Piazza dei Consoli, next to the tourist office)

Open Monday–Saturday, 9–13.
Closed Sunday.
Admission charge.

The museum contains a varied collection of ceramics, including works by contemporary craftsmen. Its most interesting exhibit is an entire floor removed from the church of San Francesco, dated 1524. Resembling a large quilted patchwork of tiles, it is the best and most original work of its kind in Italy. The town's small Pinacoteca is in the same building and is noted for a collection of seventeeth-century classical paintings left to Deruta by the biographer Leone Pascoli. It also has a painting of *St Rocco and St Romano* (1478) by Fiorenzo di Lorenzo (the town in the background is Deruta) plus an early but lovely work by Nicolò Alunno, *St Antonio Abate* (1457), and a double-sided *gonfalone* by the same.

San Francesco

The church was built in the second half of the twelfth century, rebuilt after an earthquake in 1303, and, despite restoration in the eighteenth century, has preserved its original Romanesque and Gothic elements. Amongst the fragments of fresco curiously fossilized in the new plaster are two complete paintings: *Madonna and Saints* by Domenico Alfani and G. B. Caporali (in a niche on the left-hand wall), and a depiction of the *Martyrdom of St Catherine*

(1389), by a member of the Sienese school. (St Catherine is the town's protectress and is commemorated with a *festa* every 25 November.)

Where to stay

Nel Castello ★★

In the village of Castelleone. Very small and peaceful. Situated in an old castle, and one of Umbria's most evocative hotels. Exceptional restaurant (open to non-residents), swimming-pool, and garden. Recommended. Tel. 075 9711302. Rooms 9. Bathrooms 2. Showers 5.

Del Billo ★

In the village of San Nicolo di Celle. Cheap hotel with small swimming-pool, garden, and tennis-courts. Tel. 075 944192. Rooms 8. Showers 8.

South of Todi

The E45 south of Todi, with the railway to Terni alongside, follows the route of the Roman Via Flaminia, and the whole area has many important Roman remains and connections. When the original road was being built (220 BC) the Romans constructed a *Statio ad Martis*, a resting-place for travellers and soldiers, at a point where a second road left the Via Flaminia for Bevagna to the north. Documentary evidence points to the existence here of temples to Apollo, Mercury, Ceres, and Mars. (Take the minor road from Todi, and at the point where it meets the E45 (11 kilometres south of the town on a sharp bend) there are the remains of the only Christian catacombs yet discovered in Umbria, still largely unexcavated, and an arch from an old Roman bridge, the Ponte Fonnaia.) Further south at **Carsulae** (near San Gemini) are some of the most extensive Roman remains in the region, still, like much else around Todi, virtually undiscovered. More than anything however, the area is renowned for its Romanesque churches, which were often built over the tombs of local saints and martyrs who lived here at a time when the region was the first Christian stronghold in Umbria.

One kilometre from the E45, on the turn-off to Massa Martana, is the **Villa San Faustino**, built on the site of an old Roman villa, the Villa Marciana. Much of the earlier building was used to construct the new one, which was the burial site of an anonymous Christian martyr, and later a Benedictine abbey. Continue down the same road for another 2 kilometres until you reach the Romanesque church of Santa Maria in Pantano. (*Pantano* incongruously for a church, means 'bog', which is what the area was until it was drained by the Benedictines.) Parts of the church date back to the seventh century, but the majority is thirteenth. The campanile to its right was added in the sixteenth century. Inside, there are many traces of fresco and several Roman inscriptions. Turn off the road just before Massa Martana, as if returning to Todi, and follow the steeply descending lane (past the church of **Santa Maria**

della Grazie, with its fourteenth-century frescoes) until you reach the twelfth-century **Abbazia di Santi Fidenzio e Terenzio**, 3 kilometres and a right turn further on. The interior, supported by tenth-century pillars, has an ancient altar, a rare thirteenth-century pulpit, and traces of very old frescoes in the crypt. A kilometre to the west is an even older, eleventh-century, church, the elegant **Sant'Illuminata** (now abandoned), which incorporates the remnants of a building more ancient still.

Massa Martana itself is a dull village with just a few, poor medieval towers (the best one is on the Palazzo Comunale), but the Renaissance church of Santa Maria della Pace incorporates a small museum of local archaeological finds. The road continues north to the interestingly named but charmless **Bastardo**, after which it is a lovely drive right through to Montefalco. Also pretty are the tiny and twisting lanes to Giano dell'Umbria, and those that climb to Monte Martano beyond. Some are unmetalled, but most are in good condition. The whole area is dotted with churches, which in any country but Italy, which has so many, would be outstanding. **Santa Maria di Viepri** (near Viepri) and **San Felice** (near Castagnola), are the highlights.

Back on the E45, 21 kilometres south of Todi, you reach **Acquasparta**, which as its name suggests is a spa town. A kilometre north of the town centre is **L'Acqua dell'Amerino** (Via San Francesco. Tel. 0744 93921) open to visitors between May and October. Its spring waters, which run at a constant temperature of 14°C, are slightly radioactive, but have a wide range of therapeutic properties (all taken very seriously by the Italians). Just to the south of the town, off the minor road that runs alongside the E45, are more springs, the **Terme di Furapane** (Tel. 0744 930103), renowned since Roman times, whose waters are recommended for stomach and liver disorders. (Also open between May and October.) Slightly further away, midway between Acquasparta and Massa Martana, are the area's most famous springs, the Terme di San Faustino, whose waters are sold all over Italy (Tel. 075 8856109). In Acquasparta itself the Palazzo Cesi is worth seeing. For many years it was in a poor state of repair, but since becoming part of the University of Perugia, a great deal of restoration has taken place. The carved wooden ceilings in many of the rooms are outstanding. In 1624 Galileo and other scientists sheltered here from Vatican disapproval of their *outré* ideas.

From Acquasparta you could branch off into the hills behind the village, taking the road signposted to **Montecastrilli** (10 kilometres). Alternatively Montecastrilli can be reached from Todi on a very pretty road via **Fiore** (whose single restaurant is excellent) and Avigliano. The countryside is likewise excellent and the initial views back to Todi quite magical. Montecastrilli, with a good fifteenth-century castle, is at the heart of an area with yet more small churches, of which the best are: **San Martino**, 2 kilometres away on the road to Amelia, **Santa Maria**, at **Quadrelli**, and **Santa Vittoriana**, in the small hamlet of **Dunrobba**. **Montenero**, 8 kilometres away, has the best of the many castles in the area.

The road west from the village passes through the high and wooded hills of Monte Cimamonte and Monte Croce di Serra, a beautiful but wild region with very little in the way of habitation or relief. A far quicker and equally scenic way of reaching Orvieto, is to take the excellent No. 448 road directly from Todi. It follows the Tiber (perfect fishing and picnic country) before climbing into a sudden and quite spectacular gorge that eventually opens out into the manmade Lake Corbara. A village not to be missed before hurrying on to Orvieto, is **Baschi**, which, despite its proximity to the *autostrada*, has maintained a completely medieval aspect.

The ruins at Carsulae. (ISTO)

If you decide not to go west, but continue driving south from Acquasparta towards Narni, then the most interesting thing to see (virtually the only thing if you are in a hurry) is the old Roman colony of **Carsulae**. The town was once known as the Pompeii of central Italy, and probably first rose to prominence around 220 BC, when the building of the Via Flaminia attracted a new influx of people into what had previously been an area of scattered settlements. It was not a town blessed with good fortune (though it was reputed to be very beautiful — Tacitus and Pliny the Younger both spoke of it in glowing terms), and after several centuries of civil war and earthquakes, it was abandoned for good. Its pink marble was plundered by local aristocrats for their palaces, weeds covered the once-fine pavements, and with the passing of time it was soon forgotten completely. It was saved from total ruin by the taste for archaeology acquired in the sixteenth century by men of fashion. Two such, Federico Cesi and Sebastiano Graziani of Todi, initiated a series of excavations at the site which have since continued more or less to the present day.

To reach the ruins, take the first junction for San Gemini Fonte (that is, the one *before* the long tunnel going south on the N3). Just prior to the village of San Gemini Fonte (*not* San Gemini itself) there is a sign that leads you along a dusty track to the midst of the remains. It is best to start a visit on the left of the road (which actually bisects the old colony) at the church of San Damiano, a medieval building made from materials taken from the old Roman forum. Behind the church are the original cobbles of the Via Flaminia itself, which you should follow northward towards the northern gate of the

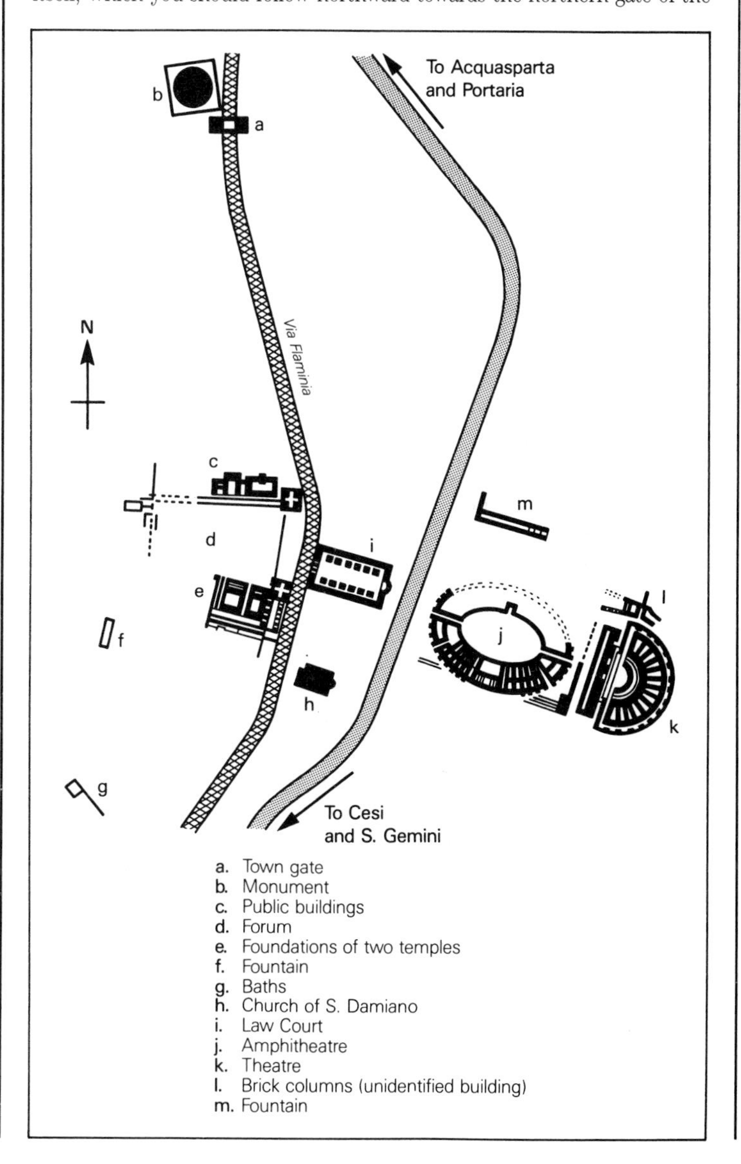

town, still marked by one of its original three arches. Outside the gate there were several monumental sepulchres, of which the square base of one is still visible beyond the arch to the left. 'Gazing at the moon has taken three months of my life' laments the inscription on another, dedicated to one Senzio, who died at the tender age of 18.

Walk back towards the church and notice the grooves in the road made by Roman carts and carriages. Before the church on the left are the remains of the *basilica forense*, the old law courts, and on the other side of the Flaminia opposite, the site of the forum. Here, facing away from the church, are the remains of two identical temples and the foundations of a public building whose precise nature is unknown. Away behind them to the left is a fountain, and further left still the baths, of which there were many on this stretch of the Flaminia, thanks to the extensive system of underground springs.

Cross the modern lane and you find the amphitheatre, 86 metres by 22 metres, built in the hollow of a natural depression, and beyond it an impressive theatre with its 'orchestra' still intact. Behind it are further remains (two small temples and three cisterns), still awaiting excavation.

While in the area there are two small villages that are worth seeing if you have time. The first, **Portaria**, is clearly visible from the N3, as a long, rather mysterious-looking collection of houses and towers straggling along the foot of the cliffs on the eastern side of the valley. It is reached by continuing along the road beyond Carsulae for 3 kilometres, and going straight on at the crossroads shortly after the ruins. There are good views of the valley below from its tangle of extremely narrow, but very tidy streets, and a small *trattoria* in its main piazza which serves humble but honest food.

The other village, **Cesi**, is more substantial, and is reached by taking the road through San Gemini Fonte instead of turning left for Carsulae. It was an Umbrian city (there are some remains of their distinctive polygonal walls below the church of Santa Maria), but today has the picturesque medieval aspect that is so common in Umbria. There are a handful of small churches, each interesting in its own way; San Angelo, built in the eleventh century with materials filched from Carsulae, San Andrea (1160), with fragments of Roman sarcophagi cemented into its walls, and San Antonio with a large but rough *Crucifixion* (1425) by a local artist from Narni. Best of all is the parish church of Santa Maria, which has several valuable works of art, notably a *Madonna and Child with Saints* (1308) by the gifted but unknown Maestro di Cesi, a wooden statue of the Madonna (1100), and fragments of fresco from various epochs. There are also the ruins of an imposing Rocca, where in 1323 a certain Guitto Farnese whiled away the hours printing vast amounts of counterfeit money. Beneath the village is a large cave rich in stalactites and stalagmites, occasionally open to members of the public willing to brave a donkey ride. A 10-minute walk from the top of the village brings you to the small church of Sant'Onfrio, situated in a lovely and isolated position, from where you can enjoy the views that led Cesi to be called 'la ringhiera della valle ternana', the balcony of the Terni valley. Beyond this, a recently constructed

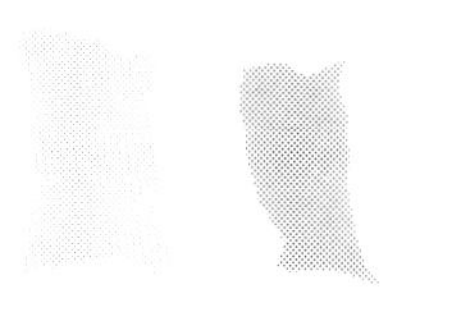

road passes the twelfth-century church of Sant'Erasmo, enabling you to drive right to the summit of nearby Monte Torre Maggiore (1120 metres).

Where to stay (west and south of Todi)

Castello di Monte Schignano ★★

Garden and restaurant. Viepri. Tel. 075 880165. Rooms 10. Showers 9.

Gallo Antico ★★

Via XXV Aprile 8, Massa Martana. Tel. 075 889145.

Martini ★

Via G. Marconi, Acquasparta. Tel. 074 93638.

Where to eat

Vissani

Just off Lake Corbara, close to Civitella del Lago, this is one of Umbria's most famous restaurants. It is run by Gianfranco Vissani, amongst Italy's leading proponents of the *nouvelle cuisine*. Success — and it has been considerable — has gone to his head. Recently cooking and style have teetered on the edge of burlesque (waiters in white gloves?) but the food is still exceptional. Tel. 0744 950206. *Closed Wednesday*. Expensive.

Il Padrino

Vissani's father runs this restaurant situated in a nasty building on the lake shore, where standards are still high, but prices are lower. Decor and ambience, however, are tacky.

Terni

TOURIST INFORMATION: Viale C. Battista 5. Tel. 0744 409201

Terni, being Umbria's biggest town, with a population of over 100,000, should really merit more than the brief mention that it receives here, but following its almost complete destruction in the last war (101 air-raids between 1943 and 1944 destroyed 80 per cent of the buildings), there is very little of its Roman or medieval heritage still standing. Its aspect is fifties modern and bears no relation (being situated anyway on a large plain) to the hill-towns of the rest of the region. In fact, it resembles nothing so much as a post-war, Eastern European city, and unless you are determined to make an obsessively comprehensive tour of Umbria, it is not a place in which you will want to linger. Its chief importance is as a communications centre. There are train connections to Todi (FCU line), Spoleto, Orte, and the Abruzzi.

Even before the war it was an industrial town, thanks to the cheap electricity from the Marmore hydroelectric scheme, and as early as the nineteenth century it was known as 'the Manchester of Italy'. Now, even though most of the factories (steel, arms, and chemicals) are outside the town proper, and there are few points in its regimented streets from which you cannot see the countryside, it is difficult to be kind about the place. One Italian guide stuck for material has tried to put together a tour of its industrial archaeology, but unless you are a real fan, it is not really one to be considered. (The town has two claims to fame: the gun that shot Kennedy was made here, and it was the birthplace of **St Valentine**, patron saint of lovers and friend to the greeting card manufacturers. The saint's body — minus his head, stolen in 1986 — can be seen in the Basilica of San Valentino, 2 kilometres south-west of the city centre.)

Where to stay

Note: Being a large modern town, Terni has hotels and restaurants to match. These could provide a base for exploring the southern part of the region, but remember there are always more rural alternatives close at hand (Piediluco, for example, see below).

Valentino ★★★★

Large, modern, and air-conditioned. Full facilities. Via Plinio il Giovane 3. Tel. 0744 55246. Rooms 60. Bathrooms 54. Showers 9.

Garden Hotel ★★★

Similar facilities to the Valentino, but about half the price. Pretty terraces and a swimming-pool. Via Bramante 6. Tel. 0744 43846. Rooms 58. Bathrooms 28. Showers 30.

Brin ★★★

Viale Brin 148. Tel. 0744 454141. Rooms 8. Bathrooms 8.

Where to eat

Da Carlino

On the edge of the town with a large and beautiful garden full of ancient gnarled trees. Best bet for a simple, standard meal. Via Piemonte 1. Tel. 0744 420163. *Closed Monday.*

La Fontanella

Smart restaurant and a rendezvous for the town's businessmen. 'International' and local cuisine. Excellent food and high prices. Details as for Hotel Valentino. *Closed Sundays and all of August.*

Ludovico Tre Colonnne

Elegant and newly popular. Noted for its trout (from the nearby River Nera), *fettucine alla boscaiola*, and selection of local cheeses; try in particular the spicy *caciotta* from Norcia. Via Plebiscito 13. Tel. 0744 54511. *Closed Monday.*

The only things that are likely to lure you to Terni are the **Marmore** waterfalls and **Lake Piediluco**, both within easy reach of the town. (Take the road east for Rieti for 7 kilometres, turn left after the village of Marmore and then follow the queues. Regular buses make the trip.) The 160-metre falls mark the dramatic confluence of the rivers Nera and Velino, but, splendid as they are, can be turned on and off (which takes away some of their wonder). They are a manmade creation that came into being first when the Romans drained marshland to the south, and in a second incarnation with the damming of Lake Piediluco in 1938. During the week when their waters are used to drive hydroelectric turbines, there is little more than a trickle left over for public edification, but on Sundays and holidays, when they are left to run at full tilt, they make a marvellous sight. The falls are open at the following times: *weekdays 15 July–11 August, 17–18.30; Saturday March–April, 18–21, May–August 17–21; Sunday May–August 10–13, 15–23, September–October 10–12, 15–21, November–15 March 15–18*. The lush green of the surroundings, the play of light and the gleaming marble polished by years of cascading water are all impressive (the more so if you see them at night when they are floodlit),

he Marmore waterfalls. (ISTO)

but it is impossible not to feel that it would all be a little more beautiful if the factories were not so close by. (You can see the falls from a belvedere in Marmore itself, or from below on the SS209 road. A (muddy) track connects the two points.)

If you drive a further 3 kilometres twentieth-century intrusions, however, are left behind and you reach the very beautiful **Lake Piediluco** (a sort of reproduction in miniature of one of Italy's northern lakes). At its head the road divides; you should take the right fork (that is, the one that follows the railway) and after a little under a kilometre turn left along a rough road that hugs the southern, less-visited, side of the lake (for being so close to Terni it is obviously a popular destination). At the end of this road you come to Monte Caperno (which can also be reached by boat from the village of **Piediluco** on the northern shore), where you will find a lot of people screaming at the tops of their voices, all trying out the area's famous four-second echo. Piediluco itself is picturesque, with a particularly good Rocca (Cardinal Albornoz even got down here) and facilities for fishing, bathing and watersports. (Be warned — the water is *very* cold.) If it is too busy try **Cornello** or **Capolozza**, further round the shore, which tend to be quieter.

Where to stay

Casalago ★★★ Piediluco. Restaurant, garden, parking, and conference facilites. Tel. 0744 68421. Rooms 47. Showers 49.

Lido ★★ Piediluco. Tel. 0744 68354. Rooms 22. Bathrooms 1. Showers 16.

La Brace ★ Via R. Salvati 3. Tel. 0744 68142. Rooms 4.

Where to eat

Lido On the lakeshore, and naturally a menu consisting mainly of freshly caught fish. Details as for hotel. *Closed November to March.*

Grottino del Nera On the Terni–Ferentillo road near Arrone (14 km north of Piediluco). A simple, rustic *trattoria* that is a stone's throw from the River Nera, noted for its fresh crayfish and its truffle sauces. (The Urbani family, top 'producers' of the region's famous black truffle, live just 15 kilometres away in Scheggino.) *Closed Wednesday and January.*

NORCIA

General Information

TOURIST INFORMATION: Piazza San Benedetto. Tel. 816165

POPULATION: 6000

HEIGHT: 604 m

STD CODE: 0743

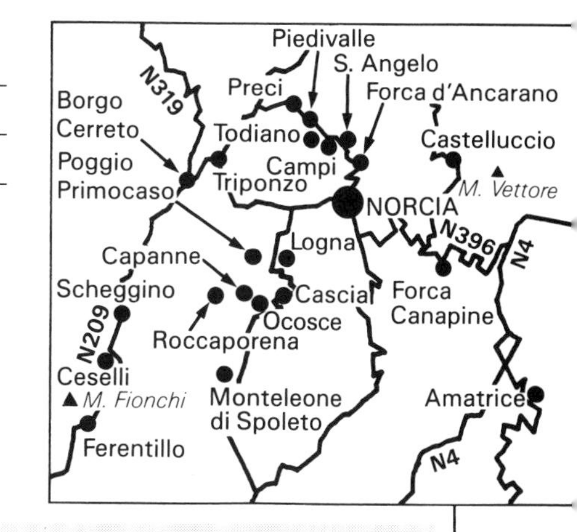

Earthquake-ravaged Norcia lies at the heart of the remote Valnerina, a mountain retreat, bleak, stolid, and a world away from the pastoral citadels to the west. Of largely modern appearance, it is not, however, without charm and things to see. Your main reason for coming here, though, will probably be the marvellous scenery of the high country close by.

Nowhere can you get away from the ubiquitous *salami* — either in guide-books or in the town itself — they have been a selling-point and staple export for centuries. Pork butchers in parts of Italy are still called *norcini* (after the town) because it was principally expatriate Norcians who spread the art of *salami*-making to the rest of Italy.

Norcia, however, did not only give the world the sausage. It was the birthplace of St Benedict, founder of Western monasticism — yet another of Umbria's extraordinary catalogue of premier saints — and of his twin sister, St Scholastica. The town has also been noted for its doctors and surgeons. Norcia's ancient (pre-Roman) name was Nursia, and as *norcino* became synonymous with 'butcher', so *nursino* came to mean 'one who cares for other people'. The medieval practitioners, were believed to be the only ones properly capable of castrating a boy unfortunate enough to show operatic potential. Whether the butchering and surgical skills were connected is not recorded.

History

In the fifth century BC, Norcia was the northernmost town of the Sabines, descendants of the tribe believed to have entered Italy with the Latins and the Umbrians. In the centuries before that, it was an important Neolithic site, one of the region's oldest. Under the Romans it was a *prefettura* and later a minor *municipio*. Foligno's bishop, San Feliciano, brought it round to Christianity in 250.

A remote easterly position was not enough to put it beyond the reach of the Barbarians. Isolation only meant that the town took longer to recover from its various batterings, though it later had the effect of encouraging the growth of independent fortress villages.

The town has constantly been subject to earthquakes, which have periodically laid it low and discouraged any lasting development. The last tremor, a particularly violent and damaging one, was in 1979. This is one of the reasons for the thick walls and heavy reinforcements of many of the town's houses — protection against collapse — and perhaps why you have to forgive Norcia its occasionally squat, leaden atmosphere. (A law of 1859 actually forbade the building of houses over 12.5 metres.)

For five centuries, up to the unification of Italy, the town was effectively a frontier-post between the Kingdom of Naples (the *Regno*) and the Papal States. Because bandits could escape justice by slipping over the border, it became a prime target for attacks. Papal reaction was to build the Castellina (1554), a gaunt fortress that still dominates the town centre. Safe behind its walls Norcia became a judicial centre, the *Prefettura della Montagna*, responsible for a swathe of territory that extended almost to Spoleto.

This was the town's heyday. Thereafter, with the combined effects of

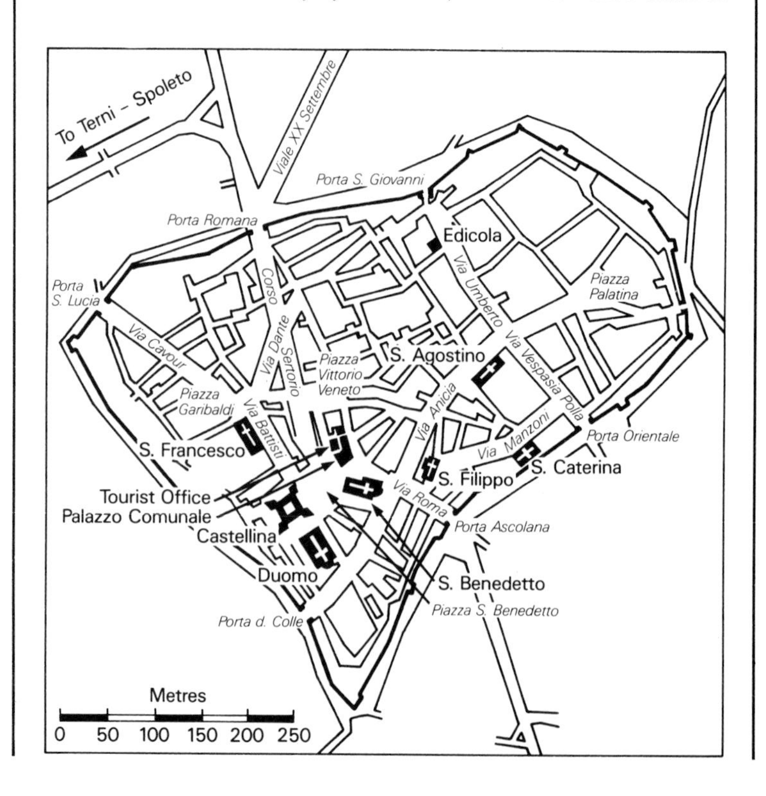

earthquakes and emigration, it faded gently into somnolence. This trend has only recently been reversed (or at least tempered) by the development of nearby Castellucio and Forca Canapine as minor winter resorts.

The Valnerina

The Valnerina refers literally to the valley of the River Nera, which rises just north of Norcia and flows through Terni to join the Tiber at Orte. The appellation has, however, come to mean most of the upland region around Norcia and Cascia, the area where Italy's central ridge of limestone mountains, the Apennines, cuts through Umbria. The landscape is one of great natural beauty, rich in flora and wildlife, dotted with wooded mountain slopes, tumbling streams and almost Alpine peaks (many snow-covered for much of the year). The upland areas are interspersed with plains of wheat and wild flowers, isolated hamlets, and scattered farms, where families till land and live lives unchanged for centuries. It all makes for scenery not found elsewhere in Umbria, and a way of life that owes more to the Abruzzi, or the south, than the traditionally more prosperous and cosmopolitan *Italia meridionale*. It is one of Italy's forgotten and unknown corners, a delight for the visitor in search of something a little different.

(Charming as it may be to outsiders, however, the way of life is one that many people wish to escape; the countryside has emptied quickly since the 1950s, and continues to do so.)

The porous limestone of the region has produced a complicated pattern of underground drainage, giving rise to cave systems and rivers that suddenly disappear, to re-emerge as springs some miles away. Sixth-century Benedictine monks made use of the phenomenon to create the so-called *marcite* — strips of cultivated land (anything up to 100 hectares in area) irrigated by a maze of interconnected canals. The thing that makes them different (Italy's only other examples are in Lombardy) is the fact that the underground water used for the irrigation runs at a constant temperature of 10–11°C. This artificially mild 'climate' allows several crops of hay every year (even in winter), bringing innumerable benefits to farms whose livelihoods depend mainly on grazing sheep and cattle. The best examples are to be found on the Piano di Santa Scholastica, south of Norcia (see below).

What to see

San Benedetto (Piazza San Benedetto)

According to tradition, San Benedetto was built over the house owned by the saint's parents. Like most important churches, however, it was probably more the spiritual kudos generated by an earlier pagan temple that attracted Christian builders to the site. (This is borne out by the remains of a semicircular apse close to the entrance, and parts of a wall in the crypt, both thought to be parts of a temple from the old Roman forum). The present facade is the sole remnant of a 1389 version of the church, and even that, like the rest of the building, has been restored many times: the top of the facade was added after the 1859 earthquake; the good Gothic door was added in 1578.

Set next to Assisi's Basilica the church is paltry indeed. The big monuments to Benedict are all elsewhere — no Giotto or architectural miracles here. The best work of art is the altarpiece by Filippo Napoletano, *St Benedict and Totila* (1621). Norcia's citizens were so pleased with the painting that they made Filippo an honorary member of the town. It is worth popping down for a look at the crypt, mainly for the small chapel at the end of the left-hand nave, claimed to have been the spot where Benedict and his sister were born.

Next to the church on the left is the Bishop's Palace, now the town's library, and on its right the Loggia dei Mercanti, once the merchants' exchange, and now used as a market place.

Duomo

Most of the buildings you might want to see in Norcia are conveniently grouped around Piazza San Benedetto. The cathedral, to the right of San Benedetto,

Piazza San Benedetto. (ISTO)

is the least interesting of all of them. Its less-than-dominating position is a result of its comparative modernity — it was built in 1560, reconstructed after the earthquakes of 1703 and 1730, and yet again in 1859.

Castellina

This big quadratic fortress, with towers at every corner, makes no concessions to architectural subtlety. It is bleak and solid in the extreme — but impressive too, in a grim sort of way. A Papal stronghold for something like 300 years, since 1967 it has been the seat of the town's Civic and Diocesan Museum (top floor *10–12.30, 2–5. Closed Monday. Admission charge*). The chief highlights of its five small rooms are sculptures. In the entrance hall look out for the *Deposition*, an extremely rare group of thirteenth-century wooden figures: very few Umbrian works of this kind exist with all the figures present and intact.

Other sights

Sant'Agostino (Via Anicia)

One of several religious houses built in Norcia during the fourteenth century, Sant'Agostino was restored with a baroque gloss in the seventeenth century. A few fifteenth and sixteenth-century frescoes survive and there is a good choir, one of several fine examples in the town. At the end of the street, beyond Piazza Palatina, and to the right, stands Sant'Agostino Minore, lurking behind what looks like a simple housefront at No. 12. Inside are some sixteenth-century choir stalls and an extremely rich baroque altar.

Edicola (Via Umberto I)

One of Norcia's more noted and unusual sights, the Edicola is a small, eccentric building from the mid-fourteenth century. A pair of large arches, decorated with bas-reliefs, open to the street on two sides, explain perhaps why the building is nicknamed the *Tempietta*, or 'little temple'.

Finally, you should walk up to the highest part of the town, the north-eastern section known as the *Quartiere Capolaterra*. It fell into disrepair during the Middle Ages and was taken over by shepherds from Castellucio (see below). They made it their own, as you can see from the small houses (with stalls for the sheep) and a jumble of streets which contrast with the centre's more organized plan. Notice the church of San Antonio Abate — St Antonio was the shepherd's saint, invoked to watch over and protect their flocks.

Where to stay

Grotta Azzurra ★★★

Distinguished by an above-average restaurant. In Norcia, of course, it is essential to start with lashings of *antipasti* (*salami*, sausage, and *prosciutto*). Its prized black truffle (in season) should also be eaten at least once, just to say that you have tried it. Via Alfieri 12. Tel. 816513. Rooms 36. *Restaurant closed to non-residents Tuesday.*

Posta
★★★

Distinguished by its sixteenth-century setting, but the restaurant, while acceptable, is inferior to that of the Grotta Azzura. Via C. Battisti 10. Tel. 816274. Rooms 30.

Monastero S. Antonio
★

Restaurant and garden. Via dei Virgini 13. Tel. 816657. Rooms 35.

Da Benito
★

Restaurant. Via Marconi 5. Tel. 816670. Rooms 9.

AROUND NORCIA

North of Norcia

A quartet of roads connects Norcia to the outside world, radiating from the town to the four points of the compass. They branch off into a network of narrow but exhilarating country lanes, any of which you could pick and not be disappointed. This is an area for a car, perhaps combined with some walking, but most of all it is one for those who enjoy random exploration, or better still, getting lost and seeing what happens. 'Touring' country, perhaps; grand scenery to take your time over, and dozens of isolated hamlets to string together on a half-planned itinerary. What follows are just the bare bones of trips you could make on return journeys to either Terni or Spoleto. Bear in mind that distances on these roads are greater than they appear on the map.

The road north from Norcia to **Preci** and **Triponzo** is one of the steepest you are likely to encounter in Umbria. It reaches its highest point 6 kilometres from the town at **Forca d'Ancarano**, an ancient sacred site near the summit of Mount Patino. The twists and turns continue for several kilometres to **Sant'Angelo**, whose church is comprehensively frescoed by Domenico da Leonessa (1476). **Campi Vecchio** has kept its medieval appearance (like Abeto and Piedivalle nearby). If you make the effort to climb to the top of its hill, don't leave without seeing San Salvatore, the outstanding white-stone church a little out of the hamlet itself. Both it and the house alongside — partly constructed of Roman fragments — contain paintings by a variety of Umbrian artists. The best, a *Crucifixion*, is at the end of the left-hand nave.

Four kilometres beyond, back on the 'main' road, a track leads off to **Todiano**, whose church contains several paintings, amongst them a *Madonna and Saints*, remarkably attributed to Filippino Lippi. Shortly before Preci is the **Abbey of San Eutizio** (678 metres), amongst the area's highlights. One of the cradles of the Benedictine movement, it started life as a cemetery for

JD

hermits in the surrounding hills, but quickly became a thriving community, at one time controlling more than 100 castles and local churches. The present Romanesque church was built in 1190; the apse and blind arches are part of additions made in the fourteenth century. Nicola da Siena painted a *Crucifixion* (?1461) for the (restored) interior (and left other paintings in churches dotted about Norcia's desolate hills). Behind it is the sepulchre of San Eutizio (1514), and a simple wooden choir.

Preci, very near by, is the only place of any real size before Triponzo, and has the characteristic appearance of the area's mountain villages, that of being squeezed between its central castle and surrounding walls. In the sixteenth century it was renowned throughout Europe for a school of surgeons, who (for some peculiar reason) made a speciality of removing kidney and liver stones. Thirty families in the town devoted themselves to the art. While here it is worth looking at the churches of Santa Maria and Santa Caterina. A valuable painting was stolen from the former in 1970; what is surprising is that more haven't disappeared — all the remote churches in the area are ridiculously easy targets.

At this point you could pop into the Marche and visit the interesting town of Visso, following the extremely picturesque road beyond it that threads along the Nera valley. The mountains hereabouts reach heights of over 2000 metres. Make for Castelsantangelo, and then if you want to head back for Norcia, take the stunning road over the Gualdo Pass (1496 metres) via Castellucio (see below) through wild, solitary country.

Otherwise take the road south-west from Pontechiusita (below Preci) and follow the steep wooded valley of the Nera to **Triponzo** (8 kilometres). Shortly before the town are the ruins of a medieval bath-house, started, but never finished, by a bishop of Norcia. They are near a sulphurous spring, whose therapeutic fame goes back to Roman times. Triponzo gets its name from the three bridges that cross the Nera, Corno, and their confluence — a strategic (notice the big tower) and, needless to say, beautiful spot, with soaring peaks and V-shaped valleys disappearing in three directions. The village, however, received a hammering during the 1974 earth tremor. A lovely drive follows the second valley (the Corno) back to Norcia (18 kilometres). (The road is the N396). Until 1968, when it was abandoned, what was apparently one of Italy's most scenic railways ran alongside on its way from Spoleto. A castle tower (Torre Argentigli) heralds Biselli (9 kilometres), which is quickly followed by Serravalle, where you can buy fresh river trout (or stay in its outstanding hotel — see below).

Where to stay

Hotel Italia ★★★

Small, comfortable hotel in the hamlet of Serravalle. Restaurant and garden. Tel. 0743 818120. Rooms 19. Showers 19.

Biancoforte ★

This tiny *pensione* is in the village of Piedivalle, immediately below the Abbey of San Eutizio. Restaurant. Tel. 0743 99185. Rooms 5. Bathrooms 5.

Agli Scacchi ★★

Restaurant and swimming-pool. Quartiere Scacchi, Preci. Tel. 0743 99224. Rooms 12. Showers 12.

Del Cacciatore ★★

Located in Biselli. Restaurant and garden. Tel. 0743 81826. Rooms 14. Showers 14.

Camping

Il Collaccio ★★★

The campsite is at Castelvecchio, close to Preci. Swimming-pool and tennis-courts. Tel. 0743 99430. Off-season 0743 99138. *Open 1 April–31 October.*

East of Norcia

The vast landscape east of Norcia is one of central Italy's strangest. Faintly reminiscent of the Scottish Highlands, with its barren, treeless wastes and broad whaleback mountains, its most extraordinary aspect consists of the famous *piani*, or plains — prairies almost — enormous, rather eerie stretches of land without trees, hedges, or buildings of any kind. The film director Franco Zeffirelli used the largest, Il Piano Grande (8 kilometres long and 1250 metres high) as a setting for his Franciscan film, *Brother Sun, Sister Moon*. In spring they are a blaze of wild flowers and meadow grasses, but at any time they are strange and compelling. Try to see them if at all possible. **Castelluccio**, which overlooks the plain, is the village to aim for; at 1452 metres it is one of Umbria's highest. The road to it from Norcia skirts the plain's western edge. Until recently, when winter skiers and summer hang-gliders appeared, it was

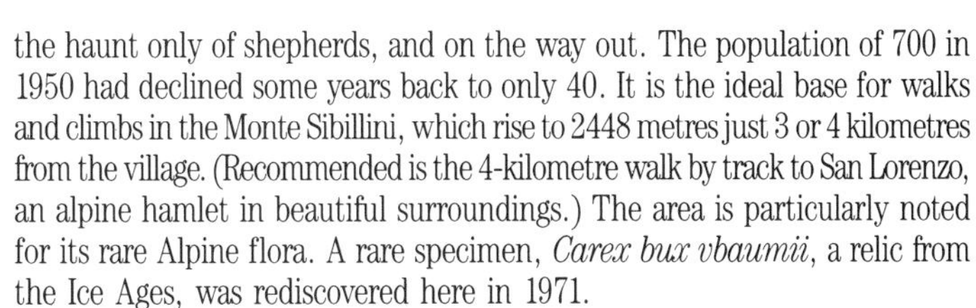

the haunt only of shepherds, and on the way out. The population of 700 in 1950 had declined some years back to only 40. It is the ideal base for walks and climbs in the Monte Sibillini, which rise to 2448 metres just 3 or 4 kilometres from the village. (Recommended is the 4-kilometre walk by track to San Lorenzo, an alpine hamlet in beautiful surroundings.) The area is particularly noted for its rare Alpine flora. A rare specimen, *Carex bux vbaumii*, a relic from the Ice Ages, was rediscovered here in 1971.

It is easy to imagine how difficult and dangerous it must be at times to cross the plain. In the past, the region's Papal rulers forbade the crossing completely from November to March. On dark and murky days the bells of Castelluccio are rung continuously to help shepherds, who might lose their way in its featureless landscape.

The road east to Arquata del Tronto in the Marche is a stupendous drive — twisting and turning all the way (a new, fast trans-Apennine road, however, is likely to be built in the near future). The views are wonderful, as they are throughout the region. The road touches on two of the most developed winter resorts, Forca Canapine and Tartufoli.

Where to stay

Sibilla ★ — A small, simple *pensione* in Castelluccio itself. Restaurant. Tel. 0743 870113. Rooms 13. Showers 8.

Canapine ★ — In the village of Forca Canapine. Restaurant. Tel. 0743 816508. Rooms 41. Bathrooms 11. Showers 22.

South to Cascia

For its first 8 kilometres the road south from Norcia crosses an old lake-bed, the broad Piano di Santa Scholastica. After the village of Savelli, however, it starts to climb, with marvellous views of a mountain-ringed Norcia in the distance. Until 1979, several minutes' drive beyond the village, along a winding road, would have led you to an elegant Renaissance church at La Madonna della Neve (1077 metres). The earthquake of that year put paid to its elegance, however. Bramante was responsible for the design (1565), which was (and should be again if the rebuilding happens) in the form of an octagonal Greek cross. Its name — Madonna of the Snow — comes from the fact that a man buried here for three days in driving snow survived by invoking divine assistance. Several kilometres further on, and a couple of hundred metres higher (1227 metres), take the unmetalled road to Cascia (via Maltignano) but turn right *before* Cascia on the minor lane for Cani and Serravalle. After 4 kilometres of winding valley, a very convoluted track bears off to the right for **Logna**, in whose church there are numerous tiny treasures, including votive frescoes from the Umbrian school, carvings, and a fifteenth-century Gothic reliquary. Further down the valley road another rough lane strikes off to **Piandoli** (931 metres), an attractive hamlet, with more sweeping views (no shortage of these in this region) and the odd piece of sixteenth-century *bric-à-brac* in its church. Retracing your steps and picking up the Serravalle road brings you to Cerasola, which has a modest ruined tower, and an even more modest eleventh-century church.

Cascia

TOURIST INFORMATION: Piazza Garibaldi 1
POPULATION: 4000
HEIGHT: 653 m
STD CODE: 0743

Cascia's name is firmly linked with that of St Rita, who was born near Spoleto in 1381 and died here in 1457. In Italy (less so abroad) she has achieved considerable popular status, especially amongst women (she is almost their uncrowned patron saint), mainly because of the 'Everywoman' nature of her troubled life. She was a battered and abandoned wife, a widow, a mother (who lost her two sons), and a powerful peace-maker in local feuds. Finally, late in life and against considerable odds, she became a nun. Sanctification, however, did not come until 1900. Her feast day is 22 May.

As Assisi is to Francis, Cascia is to Rita; the town is more or less given over to her. Many of the monuments, however, are modern, and unless you are a pilgrim there is not much here to tarry for. This said, it is the focus of local communications (such as they are) and thus a launching-pad for trips into the empty (but always beautiful) tract of land along the Lazian border.

History

Cascia's history is as troubled as Rita's life. It was initially a Roman *municipio*, Cursula, which was destroyed by an earthquake at the beginning of the first millennium. Surviving inhabitants, wise after the event, built what they thought was a safer settlement on Mount Ocosce. From this developed present-day Cascia, first mentioned by name in 553. This too was destroyed; first by the Lombards, then by the Saracens, and then again by another earthquake. From 1300, the town took to fighting with a vengeance, and amassed an impressive collection of opponents — Norcia, Leonessa, the King of Naples, Spoleto, the Church, L'Aquilia, the Orsini, Montereale, Cittareale, Monteleone — all for nothing; in 1599 it was ravaged by another

ascia. (ISTO)

earthquake. Finally the tremor of 1730 destroyed it completely. At this point the richest families gave Cascia up as a bad job, and left the hilltop for what they hoped was a safer town in the valley. Today, the division is still there: not between rich and poor, but between new and (faintly) medieval Cascia.

Naturally the earthquakes have done nothing for the town's monuments; most have lost something in the course of their many rebuildings.

What to see

Basilica di Santa Rita

The Basilica is a new building (1937–47) (on an old site), that does its best to imitate early Romanesque and Byzantine styles. The design (adopted in preference to a baroque monstrosity) was the work of the Vatican engineer,

Spirito Maria Chiapetta. The facade, framed by twin towers, has a richly finished doorway surrounded by episodes from the life of St Rita. The most interesting thing about the interior is a story, the one behind the reliquary on the main altar. It concerns the feast of Corpus Christi, and has parallels with Corpus Domini, which came out of Orvieto's Miracle of Bolsena. It also revolves around a miracle. In 1330 a priest, called to the house of a dying man, found that the Host he had been carrying between the pages of his breviary had turned to blood. Awestruck, he gave the glued and bloodstained book to Simone di Cascia, an Augustinian preacher, who in turn took it to Perugia, where the two pages in contact with the Host were declared sacred relics. One page was returned to Cascia, and the other given to the church of Sant'Agostino, from where it mysteriously disappeared in the middle of the last century. The cult and feast of Corpus Christi were recognized by Papal Bull in 1401.

The left arm of the church's Greek cross contains the over-ornate Cappella di Santa Rita, where the saint's mummified body reposes in some splendour. The more humble monastery where she died is outside, to the left of the Basilica. As well as some good views you can see her cell, her sarcophagus, a vine she apparently planted, and a variety of minor paintings and silverware.

San Francesco (Piazza Garibaldi)

San Francesco is about the first thing you encounter in the upper town. It was built in 1424, restored in the seventeenth century and again in 1925, when the Gothic vaults destroyed by earthquakes were removed. There are a few works of art. In a small niche to the left of the main door is a *Madonna, Child and Saints* by Nicola da Siena. To the rear, close to the left-hand pulpit, are three frescoes by Bartolomeo di Tommaso of Foligno, active 1525–55. The very best thing is the fourteenth-century Gothic choir in the apse.

San Antonio Abate

From San Francesco take the street downhill to the right, pass through Porta Orientale, and then turn left for San Antonio Abate, a fifteenth-century church transformed two centuries later. (You might have to ask at the tourist office for admittance.) The apse contains 16 frescoes on the *Life of San Antonio* by an unknown Umbrian artist from the first half of the fifteenth century. With luck a door from the apse will be open and let you see further paintings by Nicola da Siena — the *Story of the Passion* (1461).

Santa Maria (Porta Santa Maria)

This is Cascia's oldest church — St Rita was baptized here in 1381 — but it too has been badly damaged by earthquakes over the years. The three-naved basilica has a few fifteenth–sixteenth century frescoes, most little more than fragments. In the nearby oratory (the entrance is in Via del Pago) is

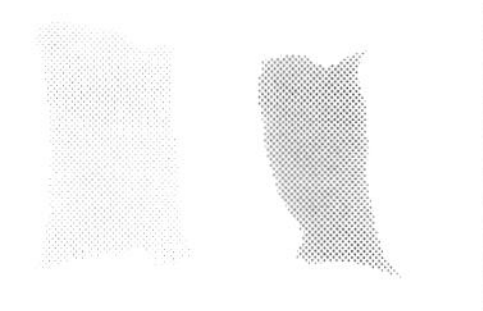

a good sixteenth-century *Madonna and Saints* from the school of Perugino.

The rest of the town is soon seen. Santa Chiara (Via Santa Chiara) has a sixteenth-century *Crucifixion*, and Sant'Agostino (next to the Rocca) several Umbrian frescoes and the remains of an older (eleventh-century) church.

Where to stay

Delle Rose ★★★

A big hotel resolutely aimed at the pilgrim market. Via del Santuario. Tel. 76241. Rooms 160. Bathrooms 13. Showers 160. *Closed 15 October–15 March.*

Cursula ★★★

A more intimate alternative, with garden and good restaurant (see below). Via Cavour 3. Tel. 76206/7. Rooms 30. Bathrooms 4. Showers 30.

Mini Hotel ★★

Via G. Palombi 1. Tel. 71387. Rooms 8. Bathrooms 8.

Where to eat

Cursula

A rustic and homely restaurant with an extremely high reputation, so booking is advisable during potentially busy periods. Traditional cooking. Try the lamb, lentils, and the home-cured hams. Details as for hotel. Claims not to close.

Around Cascia

There is plenty to see within 5 kilometres or so of Cascia, especially if you fancy some easy walking. **Roccaporena** (707 metres), the birthplace of St Rita, lies at the end of a scenic road that runs along the Corno valley to the west of the town. It is a pretty village, dominated by a sugarloaf-shaped hill, and much visited by pilgrims. Most make for Rita's house or thirteenth-century San Martano (fifteenth-century frescoes) where she was married. Whether paying homage or not it is worth a quick look before you turn round (the road is a dead-end), return along the valley and branch off into the hills for **Capanne di Collegiacone**. The church in the hamlet is decorated inside and out with fifteenth-century frescoes, though you could as easily enjoy the views and the countryside. A hour's walk north-west across upland meadows brings you to the Santuario della Madonna della Stella, situated in lonely country on the slopes of Mount Maggio (1416 metres). (It is actually more easily accessible by car from the Borgo Cerreto to Monteleone road.) Abandoned in 1630, the monastery was restored in 1833; the most evocative bits are some 20 rude cells, little more than caves cut out of the hillside, that were 'homes' for what must have been very resilient monks.

Poggio Primocaso (831 metres), like Roccaporena, is within walking distance of Cascia (it is 7 kilometres from the town), and is similarly isolated at the end of a poor but scenic road. With a tower and ruined castle it is a small summer bolt-hole for those with second homes (like many an Umbrian hamlet these days). The new parish church has a noteworthy and valuable twelfth-century sculpture (a *Madonna and Child*) removed from nearby San Francesco. **Ocosce** (911 metres), 4 kilometres to the south-west (off the Monteleone road) is another of Cascia's attractive 'resorts'.

Cascia to Leonessa

There are two routes south to Leonessa (and thence to Terni, Rieti, and Piediluco), with little to choose between them. Both pass through high, wild country, and both are very scenic (notwithstanding some old lignite mines on the Lazian border). The first and shorter (23 kilometres) is via the Rua La Cama pass (938 metres), touching **Monteleone di Spoleto** (978 metres), the only place of any size for miles. It is an attractive and popular tourist spot, noted for its wood-crafts and many a local delicacy (truffles, wine, oil, olives). The church of San Francesco (distinguished by an exceptional Gothic doorway) contains artistic and archaeological fragments collected from the surrounding countryside. (An Iron Age sepulchre and later sixteenth-century tomb were discovered intact outside the town; unfortunately their best objects have wound up in the Metropolitan Museum in New York.) There are also odd Umbrian frescoes, the remains of a subterranean church, and — if the right doors are open — a cloister and some fine views.

The second route (32 kilometres) takes the lane east out towards Maltignano for a kilometre, and then veers off right towards Castel San Giovanni and the Forca di Chiavano (a 1140-metre pass). There is precious little to see apart from the scenery, though there are the remains of a Graeco-Roman temple at Villa San Silvestro (just off the road to the right about a kilometre after Chiavano).

Lower Nera valley

If you have not time to spend in aimless exploration, then the most appealing part of the Nera valley is the stretch from Borgo Cerreto to Arrone. You could take it in either on the way from Norcia, or as a straightforward excursion from Terni and Lake Piediluco. Whichever route you decide on, any itinerary — any Umbrian itinerary almost — should include the **Abbazia di San Pietro in Valle**, one of the most important monasteries in central Italy.

It is located 5 kilometres north of Ferentillo on the N209 road (which traces the route of the river up from Terni), and at the end of a rough lane that strikes off up the western side of the valley from Sambucheto.

Much about the monastery and its history is still shrouded in uncertainty. It was probably built on the site of a sixth-century hermitage by Faroaldo II, a Duke of Spoleto, in about 720. (He turned to the monastic life after being

Abbazia di San Pietro in Valle. (STO)

deposed by his son Trasamondo II.) In time, its sphere of influence extended over much of Umbria, Lazio, and the Abruzzi. All down the Nera valley you will see countless castles, towers, and fortified villages — testaments to the time it was a bone of contention between the Dukedom of Spoleto and the Kingdom of Naples. The monastery, naturally, occupied a pivotal point in the area's strategic balance.

Its basic interest stems from the fact that it is one of Umbria's few direct memorials to the Lombards and the Dukedom of Spoleto. Over and above that, the frescoes in the church are some of the first expressions, prior to Pietro Cavallini (and Cimabue), of an attempt to create 'Italian art', to move away, that is, from the prevailing forms and themes of Byzantine painting. The pictures are found mainly on the walls of the nave and in the apse. They date, in all probability, from the last decade of the twelfth century. Those on the left wall are stories from the Old Testament — mainly the *Creation* and *Adam in Paradise*. Those on the right wall deal with the *Nativity* and the *Crucifixion*. Other Giottesque frescoes from the thirteenth to the sixteenth century are slipped in alongside. The apse is dominated by a large depiction of Christ and a *Madonna and Child with Saints and Angels*.

Architecturally, too, the main church is distinguished, being unusual, first, for the vaulted space behind the apse, and second, for the fact that the basilica's single nave tapers towards the transepts. Such features are found elsewhere only in French and German churches from the tenth century, certainly nowhere else in Italy during this period.

Dotted around the building are various objects of artistic interest. Most notable are the five third-century Roman sarcophagi (how they got there no one is sure) and the main altar, a striking and rare example of Lombard art. A door at the beginning of the right-hand nave leads out to some superb twelfth-century cloisters and offers a view of the campanile. The latter is of a type common in Lazio and around Rome, but is distinguished here by the use it makes of numerous fragments from the earliest eighth-century building. Finally, and rather incongruously, you might want to have a meal in the restaurant, evocatively situated in the church's crypt. (Note that parts of the abbey are in private hands.)

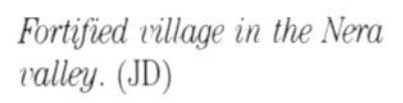
Fortified village in the Nera valley. (JD)

Elsewhere up and down the valley there are numerous fortified villages, each of them worth a glance (except for the somewhat modern Cerreto di Spoleto). If you want to start with the best, make for **Vallo di Nera**, 16 kilometres north of the abbey. Two gates and a ponderous tower allow admittance to what is more a castle than a village. It is all very evocative, with a churchful of thirteenth–fifteenth-century frescoes in Santa Maria to give some focus to your wanderings.

Moving south from here (that is, back towards the abbey) you arrive at the village of **Sant'Anatolia di Arco**, another of Umbria's small gems. Based (again) around a castle and reasonably preserved walls, it has been inhabited continuously since the eighth century BC (finds from the era are in Florence's Archaeological Museum). Just north of the village is a tiny, but outstanding, twelfth-century Romanesque church, San Felice del Narco. The facade is utterly plain — pared down to the essentials — arched doorway, rose windows, and two pairs of narrow windows (a familiar Umbrian motif). (Note the road from here to Monteleone, an extremely picturesque route through high country.) **Scheggino**, 3 kilometres beyond, is another hamlet centred

on the inevitable castle. Tradition has it that the bronze doors of the Pantheon in Rome, melted down to be used in St Peter's, were worked in a Vatican foundry outside the walls. The real reason for stopping here, however, is for a fine restaurant (see below) or to sample the area's noted truffle — this is home to the famous Urbani family, the biggest 'producers' of the precious fungus.

At **Ceselli**, notice the interesting 'short-cut' to Spoleto via Cese and Mount Fionchi (1337 metres) — an arduous, but scenically rewarding, trip (on a largely unmetalled road). **Ferentillo**, guarded by twin towers, is an attractive, though somewhat scattered village, distinguished by the unexpected presence of mummified corpses. The village is really two villages, one on each side of the valley; you will find the bodies in Precetto (the other half is called Mattarello) in the crypt of Santa Stefano. They are a fairly motley crew — strange, not to say much-decayed, companions in death. There are two French soldiers who were hanged in the Napoleonic wars, and a nineteenth-century Chinese couple who somehow wound up in Umbria on their honeymoon, caught cholera, and died. They have been preserved by the dry, sandy soil in which they were buried, and by the desiccating effects of the wind roaring through the open window of their tomb. More enticing roads lead off into the mountains from the village — you might try the climb eastwards up to Castellonalto.

Finally, a little way south, both Arrone and Montefranco are worth a visit — Montefranco perhaps more so for its superbly wooded and panoramic position.

Where to stay

Fontegaia ★★★

Close to Montefranco in the hamlet of Ragognano. Most facilities, including restaurant, garden, and parking. Tel. 0744 78241. Rooms 19. Bathrooms 12. Showers 8.

Del Ponte ★★

Restaurant. Via di Borgo 17, Scheggino. Tel. 075 61131. Rooms 12. Showers 12.

Ninfa del Nera ★

Well-placed for the Abbey of San Pietro in Valle. Restaurant, garden, and air-conditioning. In the hamlet of Sambuchetto. Tel. 0744 780172. Rooms 9. Bathrooms 5.

Where to eat

Trattoria del Ponte ★★

Crayfish, truffle, and freshwater specialities in well-above-average restaurant. The *fettucine con gamberi e tartufi* has achieved wide renown, but truffles in any form — with lamb, trout, or rabbit — are a delight. Details as for hotel. *Closed Monday and 1–15 September.*

Grottino del Nera

More truffle and crayfish dishes in a nicely situated restaurant. The risotto, lamb, kid, and pigeon are all good. Via Valnerina 20, Arrone. Tel. 0744 78104. *Closed Wednesday and 1–15 January.*

INDEX

Artists, architects, painters, and sculptors are indexed separately. Route planners will find cities, towns, and villages in **bold type**; the lists of hotels etc. and eating places which follow each sub-section in the text, have been grouped in this index under 'Accommodation and eating places'.

Artists, Architects, Painters, and Sculptors

te: Early artists are often known only from their place of work, e.g. Andrea d'Assisi (Andrea from Assisi).
iese artists are listed under their first names.